To my parents, who always believed in me

TCP/IP Analysis and Troubleshooting Toolkit

Kevin Burns

Wiley Publishing, Inc.

Executive Publisher: Robert Ipsen
Vice President and Publisher: Joe Wikert
Editor: Carol A. Long
Developmental Editor: Kevin Kent
Editorial Manager: Kathryn Malm
Production Editor: Pamela M. Hanley
Text Design & Composition: Wiley Composition Services

This book is printed on acid-free paper. ♾

Library of Congress Cataloging-in-Publication Data: is available from the publisher

ISBN: 0-471-42975-9

10 9 8 7 6 5 4 3 2 1

Contents

Acknowledgments

This book never would have been a reality without the following people: Emily Roche, who helped me open the door to writing and took me to my first book proposal seminar; Toni Lopopolo, who taught the seminar and put me in contact with my great agent Jawahara Saidullah. I want to thank Tony Fortunato for patiently reviewing my book for technical accuracy. Thanks also goes out to everyone at Wiley Publishing who worked so hard on this book, including my great development editor Kevin Kent, who held me to task on making sure readers would be able to easily understand the complex case studies and examples in the book. Last but not least, I want to thank my parents, who have given me everything and asked for nothing in return. This book is for you.

About the Author

Kevin Burns is the founder of Tracemasters, Inc., of Philadelphia, Pennsylvania, a consulting organization specializing in network analysis and training. Kevin's 10 years of experience consist of the design, implementation, and analysis of various multiprotocol, multivendor networks. This book comprises the techniques he has used in diagnosing complex network and application problems, which he also teaches to students at various seminars and corporate settings. Kevin can be reached at kburns@tracemasters.com.

Introduction

Why I Wrote This Book

Network engineers face difficult challenges on a daily basis. Servers can crash, WAN links can become saturated, and for unknown reasons, an application's performance can come to a crawl, pitting network engineers against application developers in a complicated blame game, usually without facts. Without the proper tools and training, when something breaks, network engineers often have to ask why: Why can't users obtain DHCP addresses, why can't users log into the server, and—the ever so bothersome question—why is the network slow? During all of this commotion, upper management is usually also asking why—Why haven't these problems been resolved? Most large network infrastructures have a mix of troubleshooting tools at their disposal, but more often than not the wrong tools are selected for the wrong job. How can you best use the tools at your disposal and the knowledge of your networks to assist you in quickly and decisively solving problems on your network infrastructures? The answer to that question is the subject of this book.

I wrote this book for the people on the front lines, the network field engineers. I have a great respect for field engineers. They are the doers, the people that make things work; they are also the first people whose pagers start beeping when things don't work. In my over 10 years of experience supporting desktops, servers, and large complex network infrastructures, I've come to the conclusion that the best field engineers are the ones who can solve the really tough problems.

People who are good problem solvers are usually tenacious and curious. These two qualities drive these people to stay up all night to try to solve a problem. They know the answer is there somewhere, waiting to be uncovered, and they are tenacious enough to dig until they find it. The truly curious will most likely have read many good books on the TCP/IP protocol, including W. Richard Stevens' *TCP/IP Illustrated* (Addison-Wesley January 1994) and Douglas Comer's *Internetworking with TCP/IP (Prentice Hall January 2000)*. To date these books are the flagship manuscripts on understanding TCP/IP, but they focus intensely on theory and lack in practical examples. (That said, I still recommend every analyst have a copy of them on their bookshelves.) I have attempted to bridge the gap left by these two books by taking the most important concepts on the protocols and applying them to the most common problems a network analyst sees on TCP/IP networks. For the more curious, interested in the intricate details and inner workings of the protocol, I have provided an appendix further detailing the website.

The goal behind the *TCP/IP Analysis and Troubleshooting Toolkit* is to give the reader the information needed to successfully maintain the protocol in real-world networks. Since TCP/IP is the most common protocol in use today, this made the decision to concentrate an entire book on the subject of its analysis and troubleshooting methods easy. Rather than write a book about the many intricate and often-mundane details of the protocol, I attempt to empower you with the knowledge to understand and diagnose problems related to the TCP/IP protocol.

You will quickly notice that many of the examples in the book are either Cisco or Microsoft specific. Since those are the two most prevalent vendors in use today, I have chosen to use examples pertaining to their systems. The examples are by no means exclusive to either Cisco or Microsoft. In almost all cases, you can take the examples and apply them to any vendor's hardware or software. Specific examples that apply to a certain vendor are noted. Along this line, you might also notice several analysis tools mentioned or used in the examples. The type of tool is not typically important, just as long as it provides the functionality needed or described.

An understanding of the technology is what's important and that is what this book concentrates on.

Who Should Read This Book

Although this book does provide an introduction to network analysis techniques and the TCP/IP protocol, it is not for beginners. A basic understanding of the OSI model is important, as well as a decent level of experience managing server operating systems running TCP/IP.

More advanced readers already familiar with the protocol will benefit greatly from the case studies presented in each chapter. This book will help you become a better network analyst. If you are a network administrator eager to learn more about understanding communications between clients and servers, this is a good place to start. If you are already familiar with configuring routers and switches, this book will teach you the technology behind the configuration commands; it will help you learn to think "outside the box."

This book is about technology and how to best use tools at your disposal to keep your networks running smoothly.

How This Book Is Organized

The book is organized into three parts:

- **Part I: Foundations of Network Analysis** answers such questions as "Why protocol analysis?" and "What tools do I use?" It explains the process of capturing and manipulating trace files. It also provides a refresher of the OSI model and the basic concepts of network communication that are needed to benefit from the material presented in the later chapters.

- **Part II: The Core Protocols** builds the foundation for understanding the protocols that TCP/IP is built upon. It is these protocols that provide the support for all other application-layer protocols.

- **Part III: Related TCP/IP Protocols** extends the search for understanding by revealing the inner workings of standard and vendor-independent protocol implementations. Applications such as DNS (Domain Name System), HTTP (Hypertext Transport Protocol), and FTP (File Transport Protocol) are thoroughly analyzed, and a deep investigation is conducted into Microsoft's TCP/IP implementation, including the ever-so-mysterious Server Message Block protocol.

In each chapter, the material is complemented with numerous case studies and examples from real, live networks. These examples and case studies are given to illustrate how the knowledge and techniques discussed can be put to use.

Tools

This book uses several different analysis tools to illustrate the troubleshooting examples. While the tools are not necessary to understand the examples, you do need them to view the trace files included on the companion Web site. The Web site includes instructions for downloading the freeware version of the Ethereal protocol analyzer, which can be used to view the traces.

The Companion Web Site

The companion Web site to this book (which can be found by pointing your browser to www.wiley.com/compbooks/burns) contains protocol standards such as RFCs (Requests for Comment), IETF (Internet Engineering Task Force) standards, and other resources concerning the protocols discussed in the book. It also contains online videos of most of the books example materials and trace files from the actually case studies, which you can load and examine for yourself. Finally, it includes several freeware and shareware utilities that are a must in the network analyst's toolkit. For more specific information as to what is on the Web site, see Appendix A.

PART

One

Foundations of
Network Analysis

Introduction to Protocol Analysis

What is protocol analysis? A *protocol* is defined as a standard procedure for regulating data transmission between computers. Protocol analysis is the process of examining those procedures. The way we go about this analysis is with special tools called *protocol analyzers*. Protocol analyzers decode the stream of bits flowing across a network and show you those bits in the structured format of the protocol. Using protocol analysis techniques to understand the procedures occurring on your network is the focus of this book. In my 10 years of analyzing and implementing networks, I have learned that in order to understand how a vendor's hardware platform, such as a router or switch, functions you need to understand how the protocols that the hardware implements operate. Routers, switches, hubs, gateways, and so on are simply nothing without the protocols. Protocols make networks happen. Routers and other devices implement those protocols. Understand the protocol, and you can largely understand what happens inside the box.

A Brief History of Network Communications

For years, complex processing needs have been the driving factors behind the development of computer systems. Early on, these needs were met by the development of supercomputers. Supercomputers were designed to service a single application at a very high speed, thus saving valuable time in performing manual calculations.

Supercomputers, with their focus on servicing a single application, couldn't fully meet the business need for a computing system supporting multiple users. Applications designed for use by many people required multiple input/output systems for which supercomputers were not designed. These systems were known as time-sharing systems because each user was given a small slice of time from the overall processing system. The earliest of these systems were known as mainframes. Although not as fast as supercomputers, mainframes could service the business needs of many users running multiple applications simultaneously. This feature made them far more effective at servicing multiple business needs.

The advent of mainframes thus led to the birth of centralized computing. With its debute, centralized computing could provide all aspects of a networked communications system within a tightly controlled cohesive system. Such systems as IBM's S/390 provided the communication paths, applications, and storage systems within a large centralized processing system. Client workstations were nothing more than text screens that let users interact with the applications running on the centralized processing units.

Distributed computing followed on the heels of centralized computing. Distributed computing is characterized by the division of business processes on separate computer systems. In the late 80's and early 90's the dumb terminal screens used in centralized computing architectures started to be replaced by computer workstations that had their own processing power and memory and, more importantly, the ability to run applications separate from the mainframe. Early distributed systems were nothing more than extensions of a single-vendor solution (bought from a single vendor) over modem or dedicated leased lines. Because the vendor controlled all aspects of the system, it was easy for that vendor to develop the communication functions that were needed to make their centralized systems distributed. These types of systems are known as "closed" systems because they only interoperate with other systems from the same manufacturer. Apple Computer and Novell were among the first companies to deliver distributed (although still proprietary) networking systems.

Distributed processing was complicated. It required addressing, error control, and synchronized coordination between systems. Unfortunately, the communication architectures designed to meet those requirements were not compatible across vendors' boundaries. Many closed proprietary systems were developed, most notably IBM's System Network Architecture (SNA) and Digital Equipment Corporation's DECNet. Down the road, other companies such as Novell and Apple followed suit. In order to open up these "closed systems," a framework was needed which would allow interoperability between various vendors' systems.

OSI to the Rescue

OSI (Open System Interconnection), developed by the International Organization for Standardization (ISO), was the solution designed to promote interoperability between vendors. It defines an architecture for communications that support distributed processing. The OSI model describes the functions that allow systems to communicate successfully over a network. Using what is called a layered approach, communications functions are broken down into seven distinct layers. The seven layers, beginning with the bottom layer of the OSI model, are as follows:

- Layer 1: Physical layer
- Layer 2: Data link layer
- Layer 3: Network layer
- Layer 4: Transport layer
- Layer 5: Session layer
- Layer 6: Presentation layer
- Layer 7: Application layer

Each layer provides a service to the layers above it, but also depends on services from the layers below it. The model also provides a layer of abstraction because upper layers do not need to know the details of how the lower layers operate; they simply must possess the ability to use the lower layers' services. The model was created so that in a perfect world any network layer protocol, such as IP (Internet Protocol), IPX (Internet Packet Exchange), or X.25, could operate regardless of the physical media it runs over. This concept applies to all of the layers, and in later chapters you can see how some application protocols function identically over different network protocols (and sometimes even different vendors—Server Message Block (SMB) is a perfect example of this as it is used by Microsoft, IBM, and Banyan's server operating systems). Most communication protocols map very nicely to the OSI model.

NOTE OSI actually consists of not only the model but also a suite of complex protocols. Although the protocols are rarely used today, their original purpose was to provide a single protocol suite that all vendors could adopt into their systems, allowing for interoperability. The model survived, but unfortunately, the protocols did not.

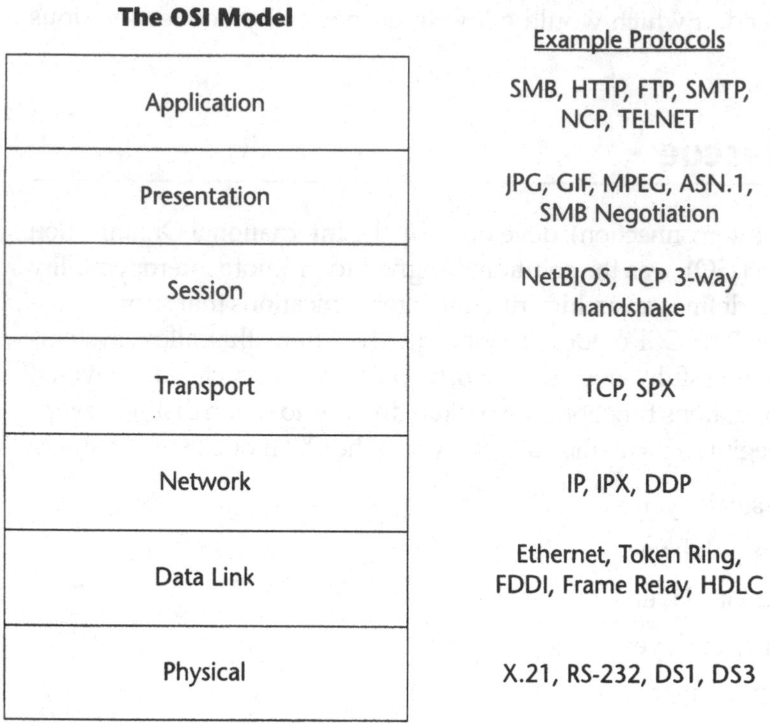

The OSI Model

Example Protocols

The OSI Model	Example Protocols
Application	SMB, HTTP, FTP, SMTP, NCP, TELNET
Presentation	JPG, GIF, MPEG, ASN.1, SMB Negotiation
Session	NetBIOS, TCP 3-way handshake
Transport	TCP, SPX
Network	IP, IPX, DDP
Data Link	Ethernet, Token Ring, FDDI, Frame Relay, HDLC
Physical	X.21, RS-232, DS1, DS3

Figure 1-1   The OSI model.

Defining the Layers

Because almost all protocols are based on the OSI model, it is important to completely understand how the model operates, and to understand the protocols, you must first understand the framework. The following sections explain the seven layers in more detail, and Figure 1-1 gives examples of protocols that reside at each layer.

Layer 1: Physical Layer

The simplest definition of the physical layer is that it deals with how binary data is translated into signals and transmitted across the communications medium. (I talk more about media in the "Detailed Layer Analysis" section later in this chapter.) The physical layer also comprises the functions and procedures that are responsible for the transmission of bits. Examples would be procedures such as RS-232 handshaking or zero substitution functions on B8ZS T1 circuits. The physical layer concerns itself only with sending a stream of bits between two devices over a network.

Layer 2: Data Link Layer

Layer 2, the data link layer, handles the functions and procedures necessary for coordinating frames between devices. At the data link layer, zeros and ones are logically grouped into frames with a defined beginning and end. Unlike the physical layer, the data link layer contains a measure of intelligence. Ethernet, a common Layer 2 protocol, contains detection algorithms for controlling collision detection, corrupted frames, and address recognition. Higher layers depend on the data link layer not only to provide an error-free path but also to detect errors that may occur. Corrupted data should never be passed to upper layers.

Layer 3: Network Layer

Layer 3 is the end-to-end communications provider. Whereas the data link layer's responsibility ends at the next Layer 2 device, the network layer is responsible for routing data from the source to the destination over multiple Layer 2 paths. Applications utilizing a Layer 3 protocol do not need to know the details of the underlying Layer 2 network. Layer 3 networks, such as those using the Internet Protocol, will span many different Layer 2 technologies such as Ethernet, Token Ring, Frame Relay, and Asynchronous Transfer Mode (ATM). Some examples of Layer 3 protocols are IP, IPX, and AppleTalk Datagram Delivery Protocol (DDP). Although the network layer is responsible for the addressing and routing of data from source to destination, it is not responsible for guaranteeing its delivery.

Layer 4: Transport Layer

Networks are not reliable. On Ethernet networks, collisions can occur resulting in data loss, switches can drop packets due to congestion, and networks themselves can lose data due to overloaded links (the Internet itself experiences anomalies such as these on a daily basis). Protocols that operate in the transport layer may retransmit lost data, perform flow control between end systems, and many times add an extra layer of error protection to application data. While the network layer delivers data between two endpoints, the transport layer can guarantee that it gets to its destination.

Layer 5: Session Layer

The session layer provides the ability to further control communications between end systems by providing another layer of abstraction between transport protocols and the application. If an application layer protocol possesses this functionality, a session layer protocol may not be needed. NetBIOS, as you will see later in this chapter, is a perfect example of a session layer protocol. Sometimes the session layer does not reveal itself as a protocol, but rather as a procedure performed to allow a protocol to continue its functions. Even though a protocol will exist at a certain layer, a procedure of that protocol can sometimes perform functions that normally reside in another layer. I will note instances in later chapters where this anomaly takes place.

Layer 6: Presentation Layer

The presentation layer is another layer that sometimes does not manifest itself in obvious ways. The presentation layer handles making sure that data formats used by application layer protocols are compatible between end systems. Some examples of Layer 6 would be ASCII, JPG, and ASN.1. Just as I indicated was the case with Layer 5, some protocol functions performed in other layers fit nicely into the description of the presentation layer.

Layer 7: Application Layer

Many people confuse Layer 7 with the applications used on servers or workstations. Application layer protocols are not user applications but instead the protocols that allow those applications to operate over a network. A user browsing the Internet with Internet Explorer utilizes an application layer protocol called HTTP. Microsoft Word users saving files to a network server make use of the Server Message Block (SMB) protocol. To a user, a network drive simply appears as G:\, but in the background there are powerful application layer protocols that allow G:\ to represent a location on a remote server. Other examples of application layer protocols are FTP and Telnet.

Protocol Analysis of the Layers

The following sections comprise a protocol analysis approach to the OSI model. They explain what each layer does and, more importantly, why. How each layer performs its function is left up to the protocol designers. I discuss how TCP/IP performs its functions in Chapters 3 through 6. More advanced readers may notice some vague or overly generic descriptions of packet descriptions in the following sections. I have written the descriptions this way to provide a generic blueprint for describing the layer's functionality; the details follow later in the book.

Layer 1: The Physical Layer

As I indicated earlier in the chapter, the physical layer concerns itself with how communications signals are transmitted across a medium. Appropriately, a medium is defined as a path where communication signals can be carried. A path is anything from copper, water, or air to even barbed wire if you can get the signals to successfully transmit over it. Media carry communication signals. In wireless networks, signals travel over air as RF (radio frequency) radio waves. On 10BaseT Ethernet networks, they are carried as electrical voltage. In Fiber Distributed Data Interface (FDDI) networks, glass is used as the medium; the signals travel as pulses of light over glass fiber-optic cables. Many reasons exist as to why specific types of media are used in different technologies. Theoretically, you should be able to use whatever medium you want to carry the signals; unfortunately, the way those signals are represented places limitations on the types of media you can use.

Analog Signaling

Communications signals are transmitted in two ways. The first method, analog, is used to transmit signals that have values that vary over time. Sound is a perfect example of an analog signal. Sound is measured as an analog signal in cycles per second or hertz. The range of the human voice varies from about 100 Hz to 1,500 Hz. When early telephone networks were developed, it was difficult to create good-quality long-distance communications using analog signals because when these analog signals were amplified there was no way to distinguish the noise from the voice signal. As the analog voice signal was amplified, so was the noise. Converting analog voice signals to digital signals was one way to solve this problem.

Digital Signaling

Unlike analog signals, digital signals have only discrete values, either a one or a zero. Early digital telephone engineers figured out a way to modulate an analog signal onto a digital carrier using something called pulse code modulation, or PCM. PCM lets the instantaneous frequency of an analog signal be represented by a binary number. Instead of an amplifier having to guess at which signal to amplify, now it just had to repeat either a zero or a one. Using this method greatly improved the quality of long-distance communications. When computer data needed to be transmitted across network links, the decision to use digital signaling was easy. Since computers already represented data using zeros and ones, these zeros and ones could very easily be transmitted across networks digitally.

How these ones and zeros are represented is what digital signaling is all about. On 10BaseT Ethernet networks, data is represented by electrical voltage; a one is represented by a transition from –2.05 V to 0 V and a zero is represented by a transition from 0 V to –2.05 V. Over fiber-optic networks, a one might be represented by a pulse of light and a zero by the absence of light. The process isn't quite that simple, but the concept is basically the same. Different digital-signaling methods create ones and zeros on the media. Now, with the ability to have only two kinds of signals to recognize, it is much easier for amplifiers to pick out the digital ones and zeros from the background noise. With this ability to tell signals apart from noise, it became much easier to build networks capable of carrying computerized binary data over long distances.

NOTE There are many types of digital signaling. One of the factors that drives the type of digital signaling used in a specific technology is its efficiency and method of bit representation. For example 10-Mb Ethernet uses what is called Manchester encoding (a type of digital signaling), but for 100-Mb Fast Ethernet, Manchester was inefficient if not impossible to use because the cabling available at the time (the late 1980s) couldn't support its high bandwidth. Instead, Fast Ethernet uses what is called Non Return to Zero Inverted (NRZI) encoding and in certain configurations Multi-Level Three (MLT-3). Other data link technologies use different digital signaling methods. Token Ring uses Differential Manchester and T1 circuits use AMI or B8ZS encoding.

Layer 2: The Data Link Layer

So how do a bunch of ones and zeros become IP packets that traverse the network? For the network interface card (NIC) to put bits on the wire, it first must have a method of accessing the media. This method is called the media access method. All data link protocols designed for use in shared networks have one. One function of the media access method is letting the destination station recognize which bit is the first bit of the Media Access Control (MAC) frame. Once the first bit of the frame is found, the NIC can start grouping the ones and zeros into a Data Link Control (DLC) frame. Just as there are different methods of digital signaling, there are different types of DLC frames. In Ethernet, the IP protocol is carried by Ethernet II frames. On Token Ring, IP is carried by Token_Ring_SNAP frames.

NOTE Since the objective of this book is to learn how best to analyze TCP/IP networks, I won't detail the many frame types that exist. For more information on the various frame types, refer to *Data Link Protocols* by Ulysses Black (Prentice Hall Professional 1993).

It is important, however, to understand the basic details of Layer 2 framing. Each DLC frame has five basic parts:

- Media access portion
- Addressing
- Service access points
- Upper layer data
- Frame protection

These five basic parts are illustrated in Figure 1-2 and discussed in detail in the sections that follow.

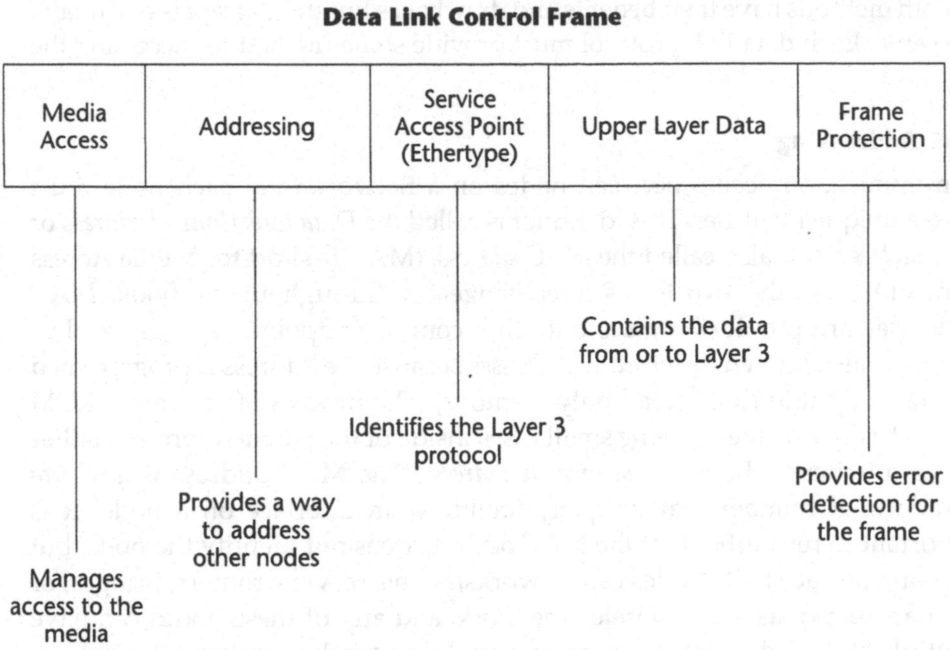

Data Link Control Frame

Media Access	Addressing	Service Access Point (Ethertype)	Upper Layer Data	Frame Protection

Contains the data
from or to Layer 3

Identifies the Layer 3
protocol

Provides a way
to address
other nodes

Provides error
detection for
the frame

Manages
access to the
media

Figure 1-2   Data Link Control frame.

Media Access Portion

The media access portion of the frame consists of certain bit patterns and reserved bits for use by the NIC driver software. Media access means just what it says; the NIC must access the media. A NIC cannot always transmit at will; sometimes the media is being used by another node on the network. This scenario is where the term *shared networks* comes from. In a shared network only one node at a time can be transmitting bits out onto the wire. A shared network may physically consist of many wires and hubs, but logically it acts as one piece of wire. Only one station at a time may transmit on that wire. Consider the following examples:

- Ethernet uses a collision back-off algorithm called CMSA/CD. Using this algorithm, a station listens to see if the media is free and then transmits if it is. If it hears another station transmitting (this is called a collision) both stations back off for a certain time and try again until one station successfully obtains access to the media.

- Token Ring and FDDI use what is called a token-based access scheme whereby a small token frame circulates around the logical ring. When the token arrives at the appropriate station, that station marks the token as busy and attaches data to it for transmission around the ring.

Both methods have their benefits and drawbacks but the concept is essentially the same. Each data link protocol must provide some method for accessing the media.

MAC Addressing

Communication occurs between nodes on a network, and each node must have a unique identifier. This identifier is called the *Data Link Control address* or *DLC address*. It is also called the *MAC address*. (MAC is short for Media Access Control.) I use the two terms interchangeably throughout the book. MAC addresses are provided by the data link control endpoint, typically a NIC. (They are also known as *burned-in addresses* because the address is programmed permanently into ROM [read-only memory]. The process of creating a ROM chip actually involves *burning* small fuses inside of the chip to represent either a 1 or a 0, hence the name *burned-in-address*.) The MAC address is a 6-byte hexadecimal number that uniquely identifies an interface on a node. It is important to remember that the MAC address does not identify the node, but only an interface to it. Nodes can be workstations, servers, routers, bridges, or even access points into a wireless network, and any of these nodes can have multiple NIC cards (that is, endpoints) on the network. A router, for example, may have many interfaces. On the other hand, a server may have just two connections, one to the production LAN and one to a backup LAN.

There are three types of MAC addressing, and Table 1-1 illustrates the three types.

- **Unicast.** Processed by a single endpoint
- **Multicast.** Processed by multiple endpoints
- **Broadcast.** Processed by all endpoints

The first one, a unicast address contains 6 bytes (in hexidecimal) that make up the entire address. The second, a multicast address, also contains 6 bytes. The third address, the broadcast address, has the same 6 bytes but each byte is the same value "FF." Why is this?

Table 1-1   Three Types of MAC Addresses

TYPE	EXAMPLE
Unicast	00-00-0C-45-A9-D5
Multicast	01-23-7D-34-1E-9A
Broadcast	FF-FF-FF-FF-FF-FF

Half-duplex NIC cards, when not transmitting data, listen on the wire for a MAC frame containing their own address. For example, on Ethernet, a node hears another station's transmission and synchronizes on its bit pattern. When it recognizes the first bit of the frame, it looks at the first 48 bits to determine if the frame should be copied off the wire and sent to the upper layers. Why 48 bits? Because there are 8 bits in a byte; therefore, 48 bits equals exactly 6 bytes, the length of the MAC address.

NOTE Ethernet is by its nature a half-duplex protocol. At the time of its creation, only shared hubs existed; there was no switching. When an Ethernet card is connected directly to a switch port, there are only two stations on the segment, the Ethernet card on the computer and the switch port. By turning off collision detection and allowing both the NIC and the switch to transmit at will, the connection becomes full-duplex. Full-duplex is really just the disabling of collision detection on both ends of a point-to-point Ethernet segment.

Nodes on a network need to be able to transmit data frames to a single station, multiple select stations, or all stations. A frame transmitted to a single station is known as a unicast frame, one transmitted to multiple stations is a multicast frame, and one transmitted to all stations is a broadcast frame. When a NIC card sees its own address in the destination portion of a MAC frame, it copies the frame off of the wire and determines to what upper-layer protocol it should be passed. The multicast address operates the same way, except that nodes must be told to listen for a specific multicast address. Video multicasting applications use this technique to stream a single video stream to multiple clients on the same Layer 2 network. The broadcast address (FF-FF-FF-FF-FF-FF) is the one MAC address that all stations must listen to. When a station sees a destination address of all Fs, it must copy the frame from the wire and look at it, even if the data in the frame is destined for an upper-layer protocol that the station doesn't support. In that case, the NIC simply discards the frame.

MAC addresses also have a unique way of identifying the hardware to which they belong. The first 3 bytes of each MAC address are known as the *Organizationally Unique Identifier (OUI)*. Each vendor who manufacturers NIC cards requests an OUI from the Institute of Electrical and Electronics Engineers (IEEE). The vendor uses this 3-byte value as the first 3 bytes in the NIC cards it manufacturers and then assigns the remaining 3 bytes. Because the first 3 bytes are static and cannot change, the vendor can manufacturer around 1.5 million NIC cards using the remaining 3 bytes. Table 1-2 contains a list of common vendors' OUIs.

Table 1-2 Sample OUIs

OUI	COMPANY ASSIGNMENT
000102	3Com
00508B	Compaq
000142	Cisco
0002B3	Intel
0004AC	IBM
0020D8	Nortel
00007D	Sun Microsystems

Figure 1-3 illustrates a breakdown of different reserved bits in the MAC address format.

The first bit (broadcast bit) is always set to 1 in multicast and broadcast frames. The second bit (universal/local bit) is reserved for organizations that use nonpublic NIC cards. This bit lets organizations choose their own OUI without being concerned with which ones have already been reserved by other vendors. If the local bit is set to 1, you know you are seeing a NIC card that is not in public use. Non public NIC cards are used for specific purposes and are not often mixed with NIC cards publicly sold by NIC manufacturers.

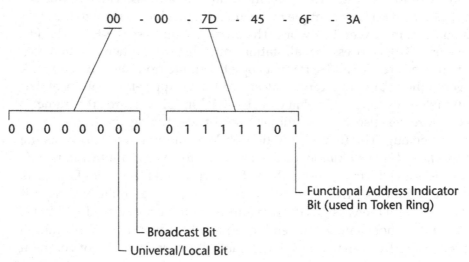

Figure 1-3 MAC address bit definitions.

MAINTAINING AN OUI LIST

Maintaining a handy reference of current OUI registrations can be very helpful in troubleshooting situations. Although most protocol analyzers have many OUIs already programmed into them, there are always new products on the market with OUIs your analyzer might not know about yet. When you are analyzing transactions at the data link layer, a handy OUI list makes it easier to spot which MAC addresses in the protocol trace belong to what hardware.

Several years ago I was analyzing broadcast traffic on a client's network and was seeing many strange IPX broadcasts on our IP-only segments. Comparing the MAC addresses from which the broadcasts were originating revealed that they all contained the same the 3 bytes (the OUI). After looking up the OUI, I realized that the broadcasts were coming from our print servers, which were incorrectly configured with IPX. Disabling IPX stopped the unnecessary broadcasts. The current list of OUIs registered with the IEEE can be found at `http://standards.ieee.org/regauth/oui/oui.txt`.

Ethertypes

At any given moment, a data link layer protocol is performing one of two tasks. It is either receiving a data link frame from the network and passing it to the network layer or it is receiving data from the network layer that needs to be transmitted out onto the network. The next couple paragraphs investigate this process further.

After the data link layer fully receives the frame, its next job is to determine the identity of the Layer 3 protocol to which the frame's data should be delivered. However, a workstation might be running multiple Layer 3 protocols besides IP; in mixed vendor environments, a workstation may have Novell IPX or AppleTalk running. How then does the data link layer determine which Layer 3 protocol should receive the data?

Inside the MAC frame there is a 2-byte field called an *Ethertype*. The value of this field determines what Layer 3 protocol should receive the data. Table 1-3 shows a partial listing of Ethertypes and their values.

Table 1-3 Sample Ethertypes

VALUE	DESCRIPTION
0000-05DC	IEEE 802.3 Length fields
0101-01FF	Experimental (For development)
0200	Xerox PUP—Conflicts with 802.3 Length field
0201	PUP Address Translation—Conflicts with 802.3
0600	Xerox XNS IDP

(continued)

Table 1-3   *(continued)*

VALUE	DESCRIPTION
0800	DOD IP
0806	ARP (For IP and CHAOS)
0BAD	Banyan Systems, Inc.
8137-8138	Novell IPX

In the reverse situation, when the data link layer is transmitting data passed down to it from a Layer 3 protocol, the data link layer simply places the correct Ethertype value inside the Ethertype field that corresponds to the Layer 3 protocol from which it received the data.

SERVICE ACCESS POINTS

Another method of upper-layer protocol identification is what are called service access points. Service access points are used with a frame type called the Logical Link Control, or LLC. LLC is more than just a frame format, it is an entire protocol used extensively in IBM Source Route bridge networks. Instead of Ethernet_II frames, LLC uses Ethernet_802.3 frames. It is also used by the NetBEUI protocol, which I will discuss in Chapter 3. Instead of an Ethertype, the LLC frame format uses a source service access point and a destination service access point, called SSAP and DSAP, respectively. The SSAP and DSAP values like Ethertypes tell the data link layer what upper-layer protocol should receive the data in the Layer 2 frame. Below is a decoding of an LLC frame. Instead of an Ethertype field, the 802.3 frame has a 2-byte length field. We can see that the SSAP and DSAP values are 0xF0, which tells the data link layer that the upper-layer protocol is NetBIOS.

```
802.3 Header
  Destination:           00:10:A4:AD:1E:75
  Source:                00:04:5A:76:F3:29
  LLC Length:            47
802.2 Logical Link Control (LLC) Header
  Dest. SAP:             0xF0  NetBEUI/NetBIOS
  Source SAP:            0xF0  NetBEUI/NetBIOS
  Command:               0x03  Unnumbered Information
NetBEUI/NetBIOS - Network Basic Input/Output System
  Length:                44
  NetBIOS Delimiter:     0xEFFF
  Command:               0x0E  Name Recognized(Wait)
  Option Data 1:         0x00  Reserved
  Session Number:        4
  Name Type:             0  Unique Name
  Xmit/Resp Correlator:  0x00000060
  Destination Name:      KEVIN_98        <0x00>
  Source Name:           SERVER          <0x20>
```

Upper-Layer Data

The purpose of MAC frames is to carry upper-layer data from one Layer 2 interface to another. Figure 1-4 shows two different examples of Layer 2 communications carrying upper-layer data.

NOTE Data link protocols can carry multiple types of upper-layer protocols. Note that Figure 1-4 shows Ethernet encapsulating both IP and IPX.

Frame Protection

After receiving all data from the network layer and before transmitting that data out to the network, the data link layer performs one more task to help protect the integrity of the data as it travels along the network path. At the end of each MAC frame it appends a 4-byte value called a CRC. This *CRC*, or *cyclical redundancy check*, is a value that is calculated by a complex formula based on the data inside the MAC frame. When the destination NIC receives the frame, it performs the same calculation on the data to see if the value is the same. If it is, the frame's data is passed on to the network layer. If not, the data link layer discards the frame since its integrity cannot be guaranteed. These types of errors, where a frame's contents are corrupted during the transmission over the local media, are called CRC errors. Figure 1-5 illustrates the CRC operation.

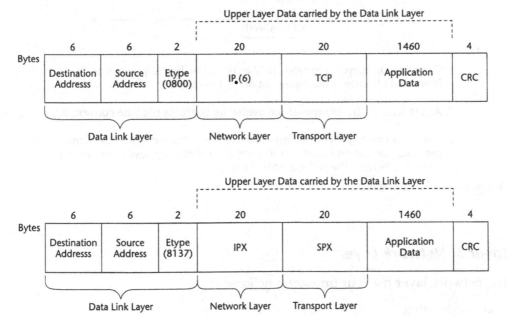

Figure 1-4   Layer 2 encapsulation examples.

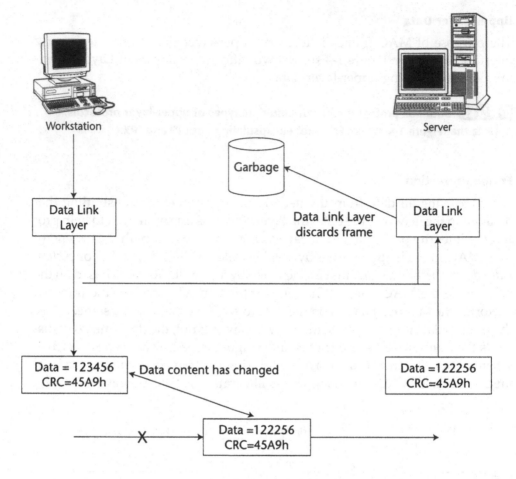

Figure 1-5   CRC operation.

1. The Data Link Layer calculates the 2-byte CRC value, appends it to the frame, and transmits the frame out on to the media.

2. As the frame is traveling over the media, its contents become corrupted.

3. The Data Link Layer on the destination receives the frame and performs the CRC calculation based on the frames contents. Because the resulting value is different, the NIC discards the frame.

Layer 3: Network Layer

The network layer has four primary functions:

- Addressing
- Routing
- Path management
- Multiplexing

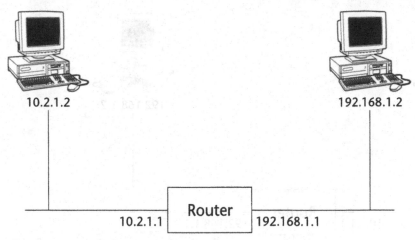

Figure 1-6   Routed IP network example.

The addressing function provides a Layer 2 independent address. Unlike a Layer 2 MAC address that can change as data is routed through an internetwork, the Layer 3 network address of an endpoint remains the same throughout the entire path.

Layer 3 addressing also provides the means for creating subnetworks for the purpose of logically partitioning a large Layer 2 LAN. Figure 1-6 illustrates two IP networks connected by a router. Notice how each subnetwork contains its own addressing scheme.

CROSS-REFERENCE I discuss network addressing in more detail in Chapter 3.

The network layer also provides for the end-to-end routing and delivery of datagrams through multiple networks. To accomplish this, protocols known as routing protocols distribute address reachability information throughout the entire network. Figure 1-7 shows a simple version of how the RIP (Routing Information Protocol) advertises information between routers. (Again, this material is discussed further in Chapter 3.)

The network layer must also handle path management issues such as rerouting around failed links, MTU (maximum transmission unit) discovery, and processing control information messages received from routers. ICMP (Internet Control Message Protocol) works in tandem with IP to provide critical information on the state of the network.

Also, because other upper-layer protocols use the services of the network layer, it must provide multiplexing and demultiplexing functions in order to pass data back and forth between layers. IP uses a very similar concept to Ethertypes, except that in the network layer they are called *protocol identifiers*. Table 1-4 shows a partial list of common protocols and their IP protocol IDs.

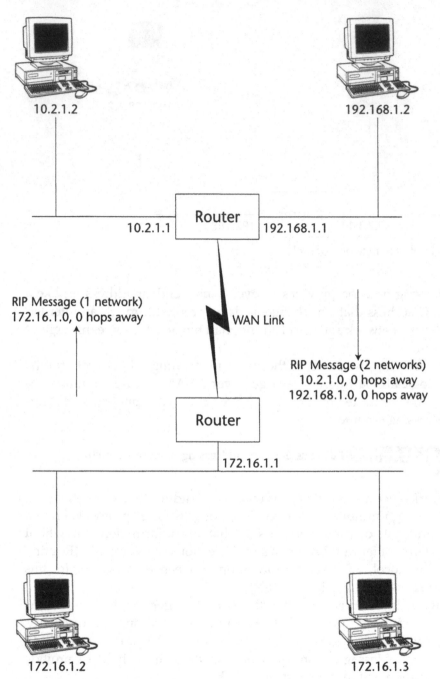

Figure 1-7 RIP operation.

Table 1-4 Example IP Protocol IDs

DECIMAL	KEYWORD	PROTOCOL
1	ICMP	Internet Control Message Protocol
2	IGMP	Internet Group Management Protocol
6	TCP	Transmission Control Protocol
17	UDP	User Datagram Protocol
37	DDP	Datagram Delivery Protocol
41	IPv6	Ipv6
50	ESP	Encapsulating Security Payload
51	AH	Authentication Header
83	VINES	Vines

Layer 4: Transport Layer

The transport layer can provide reliable or unreliable service. Why would any application developer want to use unreliable services when reliable services are available? The choice depends on the nature of the application. In the context of the transport layer, it makes sense to define what is meant by reliable and unreliable:

- Reliability in the transport layer refers to the ability of a transport protocol to provide some guarantee of the delivery of data over a network. By providing a guarantee, the data delivery becomes reliable.

- Unreliability in the transport layer refers to the lack of a transport protocol's ability to guarantee data delivery over a network.

As I stated earlier in the chapter, networks are unreliable. A number of events can occur in the lower three layers that may need to be handled by the transport layer. The transport layer needs to provide a method of detecting packet loss so that it can retransmit the lost data. Sometimes the network layer may route multiple packets over separate links, causing them to arrive at the destination in the wrong order. The transport layer must have a means of reassembling them into the correct order so that the data can be passed to the application. Since most applications exchange data in a structured format, the data needs to be reassembled into the proper order in which it was sent. Figure 1-8 illustrates an example of data being lost during its transmission over a network and the subsequent retransmission of the data by the transport layer protocol (in this case TCP).

TCP Retransmissions and Reassembly

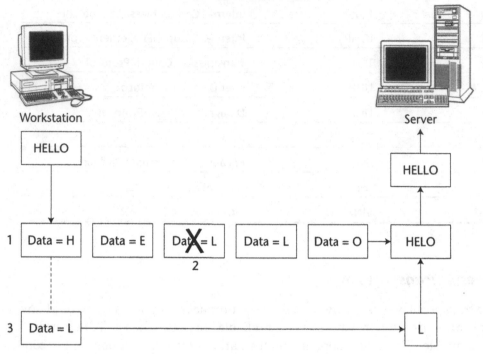

1. Data handed down to the transport layer is broken up into multiple data segments and transmitted across the media.

2. One of the data frames is dropped by the network during transmission and the receiving station receives only four of the five segments.

3. After a time period, the transport layer retransmits the lost segment of data.

Figure 1-8 Reliable transport protocol example.

The transport layer must accommodate both of these situations. The answer to the question of why you might not want a reliable transport layer is that the choice of reliable versus unreliable services depends on the type of information being exchanged by the application. Obviously, a user saving a critical finance spreadsheet to a network server wants reliability in case a packet or two is lost during the file transfer. In that case, the transport layer simply retransmits the data and all is well, because this is how the transport layer provides reliability. However, consider the example of a phone call being routed through an IP network. Would it make sense to retransmit all data that might be lost during the conversation? Every time a packet containing voice was lost, the transport layer would have to retransmit it behind voice data already received by the user. That retransmission would obviously lead to very garbled reception on the receiving end of the call. Could the transport layer wait and hold transmitted data in a buffer until the lost packets are retransmitted? It certainly could, but with the added delay for retransmission and reassembly, the quality of the voice call would be severely degraded. Thus, it would be preferable to use an unreliable protocol for transmitting voice data over an IP network.

CROSS-REFERENCE In Chapters 5 and 6, I discuss two types of transport layer protocols, UDP (User Datagram Protocol) and TCP, and the purposes for their use.

Layer 5: Session Layer

The session layer is the layer about which people most commonly ask, "Why do we need this layer? Don't other layers already possess the same functionality?" The answer is yes, other layers do possess this functionality, but the concept of a session layer still exists whether it exists in the form of a protocol or not. Further, many times an application layer protocol needs the services of the session layer to take on extra functions such as connection establishment and maintenance or data segmentation and reassembly. Figure 1-9, which appears later in the chapter, shows two types of session layer activities.

The first is a name resolution function that allows a host to determine the IP address of another host, given its name. The second, in this example, is the session layer setup performed by NetBIOS. It can only be performed once the IP address of the destination host is known. The degree that an application understands the heuristics of the transport layer determines its dependence on transport layer protocols. In pre-Windows 2000 environments, Microsoft's Server Message Block (SMB) protocol needed session layer services of NetBIOS since it could not natively communicate with transport layer protocols like TCP. In the discussion of the SMB protocol in Chapter 8, I show how SMB relies on the session layer to segment blocks of data for delivery to the transport layer.

Layer 6: Presentation Layer

The presentation layer is the most difficult to analyze simply because it sometimes does not exist in the sense of being a working protocol format. The presentation layer deals with how information is represented, how it is exchanged, and what structure it is stored in. The best example of the presentation layer is the method of data exchange between applications. For example, ASN.1 is a data format used in the SNMP protocol for querying the Management Information Databases (MIBS) on network devices. ASN.1 is the format used to make the request. Application layer protocols utilize the services of the presentation layer, and in the case of ASN.1, SNMP utilizes its format (that is, its presentation). In the case of ASN.1, not only is it used as a representation of data, but it also specifies the methods for exchanging the data. For example, an SNMP MIB file will define the types of information a device supports. It will also specify the types of methods the device supports for obtaining that information. SNMP traps are a fine example of how the ASN.1 format is used in MIB files to define a method of information exchange. An SNMP trap is when, based on certain conditions, a device will send out (trap) information to a centralized management system.

Layer 7: Application Layer

The application layer handles the exchange of information. All software, such as word processors, browsers, and email clients, in some way exchange information. A user opening up a Web page is viewing information; a user saving a document is storing information. Application layer protocols contain the functionality to perform these tasks. Application layer protocols must handle situations that arise in data storage such as what happens when two users attempt to open a file simultaneously or how many attempts should be made at saving a file before notifying the user of an error. The application layer is the last line of responsibility in interpreting events in all lower layers.

Putting It All Together

Figure 1-9 shows (and this section explains) what goes on behind the scenes inside the OSI model when a user opens a file on a network server.

1. The open file request is passed from the client software to the application layer protocol, in this case, the Server Message Block (SMB) protocol. SMB cannot act on its own; it must pass the request down to the awaiting Session layer protocol, NetBIOS.

2. Upon receiving the SMB open file request, NetBIOS must perform two functions of its own. First, it must resolve the destination host name\\Server to an IP address. Second, it must open up a NetBIOS session with the destination host using this IP address.

NOTE Take a look at the processes that have taken place so far—File Save Request, Name Resolution, Session Setup, and Transport Layer Connection. It's easy to see how many things have to happen even before the file can be transmitted across the network.

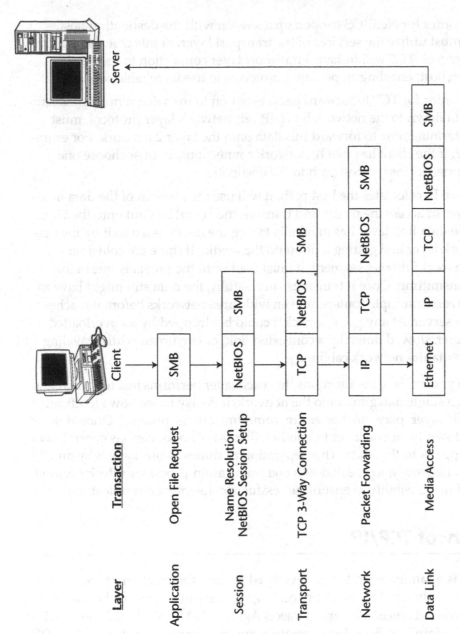

Figure 1-9   Layer-by-layer operation.

3. In order for NetBIOS to open up a session with the destination host, it must utilize the services of the transport layer, in this case the TCP protocol. TCP will initiate a transport layer connection to the destination host, enabling upper layer protocols to use its reliable services.

4. In order for TCP to forward packets out on to the wire, it must pass its data down to the network layer. IP, our network layer protocol, must determine how to forward this data onto the layer 2 network. For example, if the client has two IP network connections, it must choose one connection as the best path to the destination.

5. Once IP calculates the best path, it will use the services of the data link layer to access the media and transmit the actual bits out onto the wire. The data link layer has to handle taking the data passed to it by the network layer and getting it out onto the media. If there are collisions on the local Ethernet segment, it must wait until the media is free before transmitting. Once it transmits successfully, the data still might have to traverse multiple routers or even wide area networks before it reaches the server. At any point, a packet could be dropped by an overloaded router, slowed down by a congested link, or corrupted while traveling over faulty network cabling.

When you analyze the functions that each layer performs just to format and transmit a single datagram onto the network, it is easy to see how significant a part each layer plays in the entire communications process. Once data is passed down from one layer to another, that layer no longer has control over what happens to that data. This separation of duties is precisely why an OSI model is necessary, to break down communication processes into individual layers of responsibility to ensure successful end-to-end communication.

History of TCP/IP

TCP/IP is a family of protocols developed around the creation of the original ARPANet (Advanced Research Projects Agency network). During the late 1970s, the Defense Advanced Research Projects Agency (DARPA) funded the University of California at Berkeley to create a low-cost implementation of TCP/IP. Since the Unix operating system was widely used at universities across the country, it was the first operating system to run the TCP/IP protocol. Finally, over many years, TCP/IP was adopted as the official ARPANet communications protocol. The collective networks using the TCP/IP protocol were referred to as the Internet. The pioneering engineers of TCP/IP, Vinton Cerf and Bob Kahn, couldn't have known the meaning that term would come to mean 10 years later as the Internet exploded into a worldwide communications phenomenon.

The original Internet suite of protocols was not actually based on the OSI model but a similar model from the Department of Defense (DoD), called the DoD model. The DoD model is actually a condensed version of the OSI model. Figure 1-10 shows how the four-layer DoD model maps to the OSI model. The model consists of four layers: network access, Internet, host to host, and process/application. For beginners trying to learn network communications, it is sometimes easier to think of communications in terms of this four-layer model.

- Network access refers to how you get data onto the local media.

- The Internet layer represents the end-to-end connectivity between two hosts over a network.

- The host-to-host layer performs the same job as the transport layer, doing its best to guarantee that your data makes it to the destination host despite any degraded network conditions.

- Finally, the process/application layer is the actual process, such as a file transfer or email protocol, that handles the processing of your data from the user application.

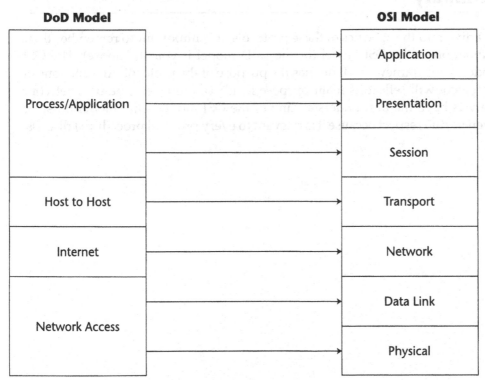

Figure 1-10 Mapping the DoD model to the OSI model.

A communications model such as the DoD or OSI model is just that, a model. It doesn't matter which model you refer to as long as you understand the function of each layer. The DoD model handles the categorization of the protocols that I discuss in Chapters 3 through 6 quite nicely, but as I start talking about the upper layers, only the OSI model will do the protocols justice. The majority of the TCP/IP protocols I talk about are the "core" protocols—IP, ICMP, UDP, and TCP. These exist at Layers 3 and 4. For Layers 5 through 7, I discuss protocols that are not necessarily bound to the core TCP/IP protocols, but due to the timeline of their development, they typically run only over TCP/IP, although there is no reason they could not run on other network and transport layer protocols. In fact, several popular application layer protocols have been ported to Novell NetWare and other non-TCP/IP platforms. I cover protocols such as NetBIOS, HyperText Transport Protocol (HTTP), File Transfer Protocol (FTP), Domain Name System (DNS), Dynamic Host Configuration Protocol (DHCP), and SMB in respect to Layers 5 through 7. TCP/IP does not specifically have any protocols at Layer 2 but does utilize the services of one Layer 2 protocol called ARP. ARP is considered a helper protocol to TCP/IP and is discussed in Chapter 3.

Summary

As I dive into the specifics of these protocols, it is important to remember their foundation in the OSI model (or the DoD model if you so choose). The OSI model is our framework. It defines the purpose of the protocol. All functions of a protocol will reflect its main purpose inside of the layer. The best network analysts have the best understanding of the OSI model. That model must be given its due respect because it is relevant to every protocol procedure I discuss.

Analysis Tools and Techniques

Knowledge of communications protocols is useless unless it can be applied. Network analysis tools allow you to apply that knowledge using a variety of techniques. In this chapter, I discuss these tools and how they can best be applied to assist in proactively and reactively managing your networks. Because the objective is to apply these techniques and tools to analyzing TCP/IP, I concentrate heavily on the use of protocol analyzers, because these are the tools that allow us to understand a protocol as it operates over a network.

I use several tools to illustrate the protocols and techniques throughout the book. My goal is not to promote any single product but to explain the techniques that can be applied to a variety of analyzers. Each problem requires certain troubleshooting techniques to solve it, and these in some part dictate what analyzer features you need to troubleshoot it successfully. I start by reviewing the different types of network management tools that are available. I then shift the focus to utilizing protocol analyzer tools, explaining their use and benefits, and giving an overview of their functions. The last section of this chapter concentrates on analysis techniques that are applied in the upcoming chapters on the specifics of each protocol.

I have selected three products to use in illustrating the protocols and techniques presented in this book:

- *WildPackets EtherPeek NX* is used as our heavy-hitter analyzer. Its rich selection of functionality and features provides us with an excellent ability to attack problems in the TCP/IP protocol suite.

- *Microsoft NetMon*, a part of the Microsoft Systems Management Server (SMS), is a low-cost protocol analysis option for Microsoft environments. Its remote agent option provides users with a distributed analysis system without their having to deploy costly remote analyzers or probes around the network.

- *Ethereal* is selected because of its excellent decodes and its unbeatable price—it's freeware. A user wishing to get started in protocol analysis need only be armed with Ethereal and several books on communication protocols.

> **NOTE** There are a variety of protocol analysis products on the market, their prices ranging from free (Ethereal) to over $20,000 and up. The case studies presented in this book were all analyzed and solved using analysis software costing under $5,000. Price does not equate to success in troubleshooting problems; knowledge and techniques do.

Reviewing Network Management Tools

The network management section of any networking trade magazine presents you with an array of tools to help you manage your networks and avoid downtime. One would think that with an unlimited budget and all the tools money could buy, a network would be without any problems. Fortunately for network analysts, this is far from the truth.

Categorizing Network Management Tools by Function

The types of tools available for network management can be grouped into four general categories by the functions they perform:

- Fault management systems
- Performance management and simulation
- Protocol analyzers
- Application-specific tools

The next four sections discuss each of these categories in turn.

Fault Management Systems

Fault management systems are the staple of any corporate network management center. They usually consist of a large centrally located computer or computers that actively poll devices on the network to confirm that the devices are still functioning. A standard database called a *Management Information Base (MIB)* allows a management station to query network devices and obtain statistics, such as uptime, utilization, or error information, from this database. A management station using a protocol called SNMP (Simple Network Management Protocol) can retrieve virtually any piece of information that you can configure the device to store in the MIB.

NOTE SNMP stands for Simple Network Management Protocol, an active application-layer protocol that management stations use to proactively monitor network devices and gather statistics.

Management stations typically contain large maps of the network infrastructure that are color-coded to provide instant feedback as to the state of the network. A device that is up and functioning is usually colored green, a device whose MIB agent is failing but is still responding may be colored yellow, and a device that does not respond at all is colored red. The fewer red icons on a management station, the healthier a network is, or at least appears to be.

Some of the more common fault management systems include the following:

- HP OpenView
- Aprisma Spectrum
- IPSwitch WhatsUp Gold

Performance Management and Simulation

Performance management has come a long way in the last several years. Many tools are available today that are able to proactively monitor the thousands of intricate transactions that occur on high-speed networks. The advent of client/server computing has driven the need for application response time statistics in order to provide service level agreements (SLAs) to end users. There are two basic types of proactive performance management.

- One is *active management* whereby traffic simulating the type of application you are managing is constantly transmitted back and forth across the network. These active management systems use predefined scripts of hundreds of applications on the market. The scripts simulate the types of traffic over the live network and monitor the results.

- The other type of performance management is *passive*, where a management station or probe in promiscuous mode watches all traffic over a network and gathers response time information on transactions seen over the wire.

Active management is best suited to situations where you have a good understanding of the types of application transactions you want to manage. For example, you could create a script that emulates a Web server or database transaction over the network. The script would be essentially the same as a real transaction with the exception that a computer instead of a real user is performing it. These types of transactions are called *synthetic transactions* for exactly that reason. As the transactions are performed, the system logs and monitors the trends of the response times to create an application baseline. If, in the future, the synthetic transaction yields a poorer than normal response time, then there is a good chance that users are experiencing the same degraded response time. The shortcoming of active management is that you can only track a finite amount of transactions.

Passive management will look at all transactions and come up with an average transaction response time. The average response time represents an average of all transactions performed on the network. This method allows you a much greater view of how an application is performing on a whole than just relying on several synthetic transactions performed at various points.

Common tools for performance management and simulation include:

- CompuWare Vantage (formally Ecoscope)
- NetIQ Chariot (formally Ganymede)
- OpNet IT Guru
- Shunra Cloud

Protocol Analyzers

Protocol analyzers are tools that capture raw bits seen on the network and reassemble them into the communication protocols at different layers of the OSI model. Protocol analyzers operate just like a workstation on the network, except that they operate in promiscuous mode, copying all frames off the wire and storing them in a buffer for later analysis by the user. They enable us to watch the communications and transactions between networked systems in real time, which allows us to observe time-outs, delays, and specific protocol interactions, which may indicate problems.

Specific protocol analyzers include:

- Network Associates Sniffer
- WildPackets EtherPeek
- Microsoft NetMon

NOTE I use the term protocol analyzer and network analyzer interchangeably throughout the book.

Application-Specific Tools

Application-specific tools focus on understanding and analyzing an application in action. These tools typically have the ability to decode the specifics of exactly what tasks an application is performing over a network, allowing the analyst to use the metrics it creates for simulation or troubleshooting purposes. Some of the more common application-specific network management tools include:

- NetIQ Chariot
- Compuware Application Expert
- OpNet IT Guru

Classifying Tools by How They Perform Functions

Just as there are types of network management tools based on what functions they perform, there are classifications you can give those tools based on how (or when) they perform those functions. Network management tools can generally be grouped into one of four classifications based on how or when they do what they do. Two of these classifications, active and passive, I already touched on in my discussion of active and passive performance management in the previous section. The other two classifications are proactive and reactive. It is important to understand how a tool goes about doing its job. Many vendors would have you believe that their product is the be all and end all in network and application management when the product is really suited only for a single purpose. I have attempted to categorize some of the more popular tools into the four categories I think they are best suited for. The four categories are as follows:

- **Proactive.** Proactive tools are used before a problem occurs. They are typically standalone systems such as SNMP network management stations, RMON (Remote Monitoring) probes, or application response time probes. Data collected from proactive systems informs you of problems before or as they occur. They are typically informational tools. When a router icon on an HP OpenView console goes from the color green to the color red, OpenView is telling you that it can no longer contact the device. This information allows you to make a judgment on how to handle the problem. If multiple routers at a single site are red, the problem could simply be a downed wide are network (WAN) circuit.

If several routers on a single part of the network are transiting between red and green, there may be a problem with the network backbone they are connected to or possibly even a LAN switch. Immediate proactive feedback from these types of systems is invaluable in determining if a problem exists and, if it does, what its nature is.

- **Reactive.** Reactive tools help you manage problems that you already know exist. When users complain about performance, you deploy network analyzers in a reactive nature, trying to resolve a problem.

- **Active.** Active tools perform an action to do their job. PING is an active tool because it is initiated by a user to measure latency. SNMP queries used by Network Management Stations are a perfect example of an active method of analysis.

- **Passive.** Passive methods use existing data on the network to provide analysis information. Tools that listen promiscuously on a network, gathering traffic data, are passive analysis tools.

NOTE Regardless of the tool, it is important to have an intricate understanding of how your network operates. I have seen countless instances of network administrators chasing down "phantom" problems reported by network management systems. There is no substitute for knowing how your network operates, from bandwidth and response time to realiability. Networks are living breathing entities and must be treated as such.

Table 2-1 lists some common tools and how they fit into these classifications.

Table 2-1   Classifying Tools by How They Operate

TOOL	PRIMARY FUNCTION (PROACTIVE/REACTIVE)	ACTIVE/PASSIVE
Fault Management Tools (HP OpenView, Aprisma Spectrum, IP Switch WhatsUp Gold)	Proactive	Active
Performance Management and Simulation (NetIQ Chariot, Shunra Cloud)	Proactive	Active/Passive (promiscuous)
Protocol Analyzers (Network Associates Sniffer, WildPackets EtherPeek, Microsoft NetMon)	Reactive	Passive
Application-specific Tools (NetIQ Chariot, Compuware Vantage)	Proactive/Reactive	Active/Passive

Protocol Analyzers—Problem-Solving Tools

Walk into any corporate network operations center and you'll most likely encounter large screens displaying multilayered maps of the corporation's network. The maps contain icons for routers, switches, and hubs that change colors depending on the state of the network. These management systems implement the concept of proactive network management—discover the problem before the users do. When something goes awry, you need to know about it immediately. I've seen operation centers crammed with many types of these systems, one for the local area network (LAN), one for the WAN, one to manage the servers, one for the server hardware, and others to properly manage the Frame Relay network, which uses a proprietary management protocol incompatible with SNMP. Network managers like these kinds of tools because they are doing something, such as pinging devices on the network or gathering the latest error counts from the MIB tables; as I discussed earlier in the chapter, they are being "proactive."

After these devices indicate a problem, what then? Sometimes the problem is a simple hardware failure, a downed T1 line, or bad code causing a router to reboot. The management stations let you know that something happened, and you fix it. However, often something happens that the management station never knows about. For example, a group of users is having performance problems, or the Accounting Department can't log into the NT Domain even though the management system shows all servers as being available. What then? What's your next step when the tools costing several thousands of dollars can't tell you what's wrong?

The one type of tool that few companies make substantial investments in is protocol analyzers. Why? The answer is simple. Protocol analyzers aren't flashy, they don't show a nice map with graphs of how things are performing, and they can't give a network manager the 99 percent uptime reports in a nice 3-D bar chart that they require weekly so that they can bill the lines of service for their provision of outstanding uptime. Nevertheless, protocol analyzers, which without the knowledge of the protocols are useless to most people, are the tools of trench warfare, the down-and-dirty troubleshooting tools. In the following sections, I talk about what a protocol analyzer is, explain how it operates, and cover some techniques that apply in the later chapters of this book that deal with the details of TCP/IP. In later chapters, I present some network problems and discuss in more detail how some of the problems presented could have been solved only by using protocol analysis tools and the knowledge of the protocols.

Why Protocol Analysis?

I have a personal story that clearly illustrates the need for these tools.

Several years ago I was involved in supporting a group of network engineers in a network migration project for a large financial corporation. The project took on many aspects. We were upgrading the legacy Token Ring user segments to Fast Ethernet, we were installing a new DNS/DHCP architecture, and we were implementing new core switches and routers. To avoid downtime, we spent most of the weekend performing the migration tasks, and by early Monday morning only a handful of issues remained to be resolved. Later that morning as users arrived at work, we were presented with our first problem of the day. Apparently users on certain segments were unable to access any network resources. With network analyzer in hand, we visited the local user segment and began to analyze the problem.

After querying the users as to the nature of their difficulties, I hooked up the analyzer and began to capture traffic from a user's workstation as he booted up and attempted to log onto the network. Very quickly it was evident that although the user had a connection to the network, he was not receiving an IP address from the DHCP server. DHCP is a protocol that allows a user to obtain an IP address from a centralized addresses server without the need to statically configure the workstation with an address. The client sends out a DHCP Discover packet and waits for the server to offer the client an address to use. During my analysis I could see the client send out a DHCP Discover broadcast, but never saw the DHCP server respond with an Offer packet. I phoned the DHCP administrator and had him check the DHCP server, which he notified me was up and running and leasing out addresses to clients. He verified that the specific user I was analyzing also showed up in the logs as receiving an address. If the DHCP server was correctly leasing out addresses, why wasn't the user receiving an Offer packet? Could the problem lie in the network? Only more analysis would reveal the answer.

Because the user segments and the DHCP servers were separated by a router and several switches, it was realistic that the problem could be the network. I've seen similar situations where a router or switch, even though properly configured, would discard certain types of packets for no reason. With this in mind, I picked up my protocol analyzer and traveled to the server segment where the DHCP server was located. Using the port-mirroring feature of the Ethernet switch, I mirrored the switch port the DHCP server was connected to. This operation allowed me to see all traffic going into and out of the server. If the DHCP server wasn't receiving the user's DHCP Discover packets, I would know instantly. When I had the user reboot and attempt to log in again, I saw the DHCP Discover packet from the user coming over the wire. Because I was seeing the same traffic that the DHCP server was, I knew that the DHCP did indeed see the DHCP Discover packet, but again, I never saw it send out a DHCP Offer packet in response. When I presented this information to the

DHCP administrator, he checked the DHCP logs. Even though I never saw the DHCP server transmit an Offer packet to the client, the server logs indicated that it had occurred. Regardless of what the log showed, the protocol analyzer had allowed me to ascertain without a doubt that the DHCP server was to blame. Fortunately, a quick reboot of the server fixed the problem. The DHCP server vendor supplied us with a software patch that prevented the problem from reoccurring.

The problem-solving scenario described in this story is a very common troubleshooting situation. Many times a device's configuration or a log file contradicts what you see on the protocol analyzer. Protocol analyzers are often a last resort in problem solving. Their use as well as knowledge of how the protocols operate can sometimes be the only thing between you and a downed network. The next section takes a look at some of the functions of protocol analyzers and how they can be used to troubleshoot problems.

Protocol Analyzer Functions

Protocol analyzers provide roughly five distinct functions, depending on the individual analyzer you are using. They are:

- Data capture
- Network monitoring
- Data display
- Notification
- Logging
- Packet generation

Data Capture

The first step in the protocol analyzer operation is capturing the data you need to analyze. The problem you are going to analyze determines the factors in how you go about capturing the data.

Local Analysis

In order to capture traffic locally you need two things: an interface to the local network (typically Ethernet or Token Ring) and a network card capable of capturing all the data it sees, not just data addressed to its MAC (Media Access Control) address. The capability of a NIC to capture all traffic is called *promiscuous mode*.

Several interfaces are available for local analysis, and it is important to be able to capture traffic from all local interfaces such as an Ethernet interface, a modem interface, or a VPN (virtual private network) interface. This flexibility gives you great latitude in troubleshooting problems a user may have using these same network access methods.

- **Local LAN.** Local LAN interfaces, such as Ethernet, allow packet capture from the local LAN.
- **RAS dial-up.** RAS (Remote Access Service) dial-up interfaces are especially useful when you are troubleshooting a problem dialing into the network or accessing resources once connected.
- **VPN.** The prevalence of VPN solutions necessitates the ability to capture data from these logical connections also.

NOTE Due to the secure nature of VPN connections, the analyzer may be able to capture only the unencrypted portions of the data packets it captures. This will prohibit you from analyzing any upper-layer protocols that may be experiencing problems.

Figure 2-1 shows a screenshot of an analyzer interface selection menu.

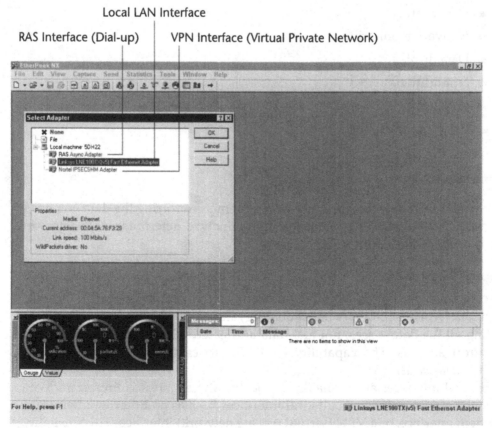

Figure 2-1   Analyzer interface selection menu.

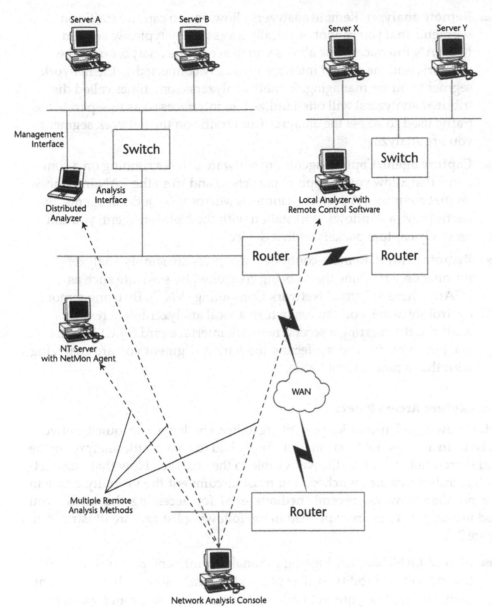

Figure 2-2   Remote analysis points.

Remote Analysis

A problem is not always going to reside on the same segment as your analyzer.
When a problem occurs across large geographical boundaries, the local analysis
features of your analyzer are useless. There are three types of remote analysis
options shown in Figure 2-2.

■ **Remote analyzer.** Remote analyzers allow you to capture traffic on segments that you cannot physically access. They typically contain two LAN interfaces. One allows you to access the analyzer over the network, and the second interface is usually connected to the network segment you are managing. Remote analyzers (sometimes called distributed analyzers) will often utilize two interfaces so as to separate the traffic used to access the analyzer from traffic on the network segment you are analyzing.

■ **Capture agent.** Capture agents are software drivers running on a computer that allow you to capture packets to and from the LAN interfaces on that computer. A perfect example is Microsoft's NetMon agents. By configuring a Windows workstation with the NetMon agent, you can remotely capture packets on that device.

■ **Remote control.** Remote-controlled analyzers are simply analyzers running on a machine that is being controlled by software such as PCAnywhere or Virtual Network Computing (VNC). By using remote control software, you can easily turn a local analyzer into a remote analyzer. By inserting a second network interface card (NIC) into the machine, you can avoid affecting the remote segment you are analyzing with the remote control traffic.

Data Capture Access Points

Today's switched networks present visibility challenges to quick network analysis. In a shared LAN, an analyst simply had to connect the analyzer to the local shared hub and all traffic was visible to the analyzer. Now that most network architectures are switched, you must circumvent the visibility problem in a number of ways. Several methods exist for accessing the media you need to analyze. They are explained in the following list and are illustrated in Figure 2-3.

■ **Shared LAN.** Simply plugging the analyzer into any port on a shared hub provides visibility to all traffic on the local segment. It is important to make sure that your network interface is set to the proper speed and duplex for a shared LAN. A NIC set for full duplex on a shared LAN could wreak havoc because it does not listen for collisions and transmits when it wants to.

■ **Port mirroring.** Most switches offer a configuration option whereby you may copy all frames that are received or transmitted from one port to another port, essentially mirroring that same data on the second port. This setup enables an analyzer in promiscuous mode to capture all traffic from, for example, a DHCP server.

> **WARNING** Caution is advised when turning on port mirroring because it could adversely affect a host on the network if configured incorrectly. Accidently mirroring an uplink port on a switch to a server port could easily oversubscribe the server's port and render it useless. If you are using Cisco switches and need IP communications on the same port you are mirroring, you can use the `inpkts` option. This allows the mirrored port to participate in the Virtual LAN (VLAN) and communicate on the IP network. I have found this option useful when using a network analyzer with remote control software.

- **In-line taps.** In-line taps sit between a device and the switch that the device is connected to. The traffic transmitted by the switch and by the device are both copied to ports on the analyzer and then interweaved into a valid conversation.

- **Capture agents:** Capture agents are configured by an analyzer to capture traffic on a remote device. The agents are typically drivers that copy all traffic to and from the NIC to a local buffer or file.

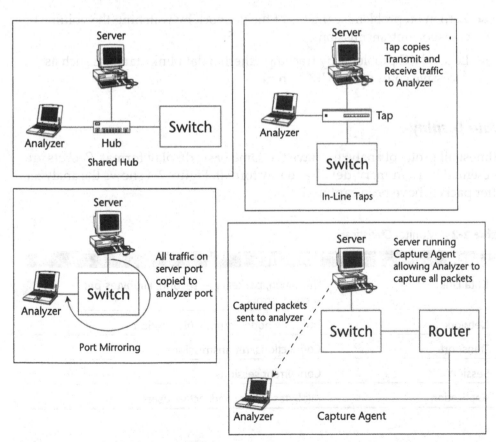

Figure 2-3 Analysis capture points.

Network Monitoring

Because analyzers operate in promiscuous mode, they are able to view all traffic on the local media. This characteristic allows them to provide a wide range of statistics about what is happening at each layer of the OSI model. A list of common statistics is included in Table 2-2.

NOTE Not all analzyers provide these statistics. For example, Ethereal and NetMon only provide statistics up to the network layer. EtherPeek NX and other high-end analyzers will allow you to see minute details of what's happening in the application layer.

The wealth of information provided by an analyzer's monitoring functionality can be used in a variety of ways:

- Combine data-logging statistics to give you the ability to look back into time at a snapshot of the conditions on a network.
- Pinpoint power users on the network by using kilobytes per second and total bytes.
- Zero in on problem segments of the network by watching the volume of transport retransmissions.
- Locate NIC problems by tracking Ethernet data link statistics such as excessive collisions or CRC errors.

Data Display

Almost all protocol analyzers have the same basic display format. Packets are presented in a summary, detail, and raw format. Figure 2-4 shows the analyzer after packets have been captured.

Table 2-2   Monitor Statistics

LAYER	STATISTICS
Data Link	Utilization, packets per second, kilobytes per second, errors
Network	Traffic by node, routing information
Transport	Connections, retransmissions
Session	Concurrent sessions
Application	Kilobytes per second, active users

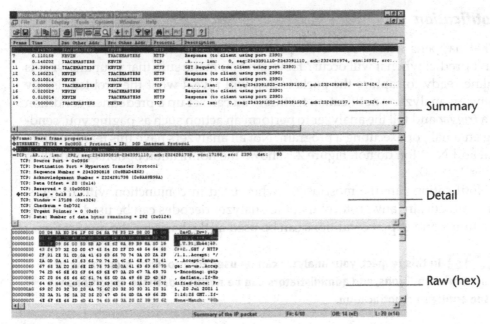

Figure 2-4   Captured packets.

The *summary pane* gives a top-level view of the packets captured. Most analyzers contain features that enable the user to select the layer of the OSI model that he or she wishes to display. For example, when you are troubleshooting a routing problem, it is advantageous to see the IP layer. When you are analyzing an FTP failure, it is helpful to see the summary of FTP protocol operations. The summary pane makes such observation possible.

The *detail pane* shows the protocol decoding of the currently selected packet. Each layer of the packet is decoded in a top-down fashion, starting with the data link layer at the top and the application layer at the bottom.

The third window you see in Figure 2-4 is the "raw," or hex, decoding of the packet. This window shows you the raw hexadecimal values of the frame's contents. You might ask yourself what good seeing the raw data is to an analyst. Sometimes frames are not fully decoded, and patterns that exist in the hex, indicating the type of packet or ASCII data, may give you a further indication of what's happening on the wire. Sometimes an analyzer may not fully decode a protocol's application layer. If you have a decent understanding of what is happening in the packet trace, you might be able to find clues in the hex portion of the packet. For example, the hex decode below represents an Enter User Name prompt from a PCAnywhere session. This information can be used to match up user activity to packets on the wire.

```
Data Area:
    00 26 08 20 0D 0A 45 6E 74 65 72 20 75 73 65 72    .&. ..Enter.....
    20 6E 61 6D 65 3A 20                                user.name:.....
```

Notification

What happens when you have a problem that you need to analyze but you can't predict when it will occur? How can you make sure that your analyzer is online ready to capture the packets that will reveal what the problem is? By using an analyzer's notification feature, you can set up a predefined condition in a *trigger* and tell the analyzer to perform an action such as paging you, sending an email, or executing a program. Not all analyzers have this feature; Ethereal and NetMon do not. Figure 2-5 shows the notification options window in EtherPeek NX.

Notifications are the most useful when used in conjunction with triggers. Since practically any protocol that the analyzer decodes can be used as a trigger, filters and expert conditions can be used as the basis for the notification.

NOTE In this respect, your analyzer can be used for proactive monitoring of network conditions, and administrators can be notified of those conditions via the configured notification.

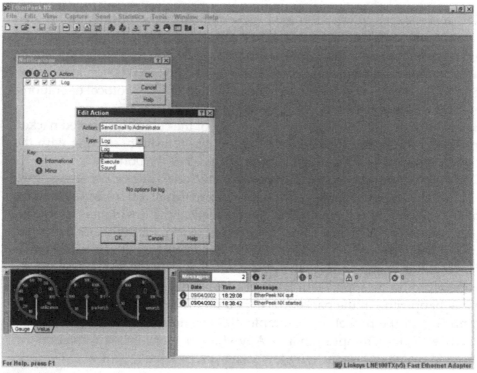

Figure 2-5   Configuring analyzer notifications.

Logging

Logging features allow you to gather information from the analyzer without user intervention. Statistics such as utilization, errors, and packet counts are viable options for data logging. The nature of the problem you are analyzing will largely determine what data logging will be of use. When troubleshooting performance problems, I typically look at the volume of retransmissions and packets sent. This gives me an idea of how much traffic is being retransmitted. I also look at the utilization of a segment to make sure that it's not saturated and that users aren't being starved of bandwidth.

Packet Generator

Packet generators are excellent tools for testing the ability of the network to pass specific packets or data. They allow you to replay saved protocol traces over a live network. Some analyzers allow you to edit the contents of a frame and then transmit the edited frame on to the media.

At one client's network, I was troubleshooting connection problems across a wide area network (WAN). I noticed that for some reason a connection request packet wouldn't make it across a certain WAN link. Looking into the data of this particular packet, I noticed that it contained almost all zeros. Zeros can sometimes be troublesome on WAN links because many WAN links don't code zeros with a positive voltage transition, causing the WAN equipment to lose timing. By editing this packet and changing the zeros to ones and using the packet generator, I verified this was the problem when I was able to transmit the packet with the new data pattern across the network. The local WAN carrier also notified me they had discovered an equipment problem, which they later fixed.

Configuring and Using Your Analyzer

Now that you have had a chance to look at the basic functions of a protocol analyzer, I want to turn to talking about the different configuration options available on the three selected analyzer platforms. Please note that not all three platforms contain all the options I talk about in this section. I largely use the EtherPeek NX platform in describing these features because it contains all of them. For example, all three platforms have the ability to perform filtering, but only EtherPeek can perform filtering at the bit level. The same goes for the write to disk and trigger features.

Capture Configuration

Before you do anything with your protocol analyzer, you want to make sure it's configured to capture data properly. There are three settings you need to be concerned about before starting to capture data.

- The network speed varies depending on the local network you are analyzing.
- The buffer settings vary depending on how much data you need to capture.
- Depending on the protocols you need to analyze, you may be able to trim the amount of data you capture by using packet slicing.

Finally, if you are limited in the amount of buffer space, you can use the write-to-disk feature to copy packets to disk.

Network Speed

Although most analyzers will autodetect the speed of your network connection, it is beneficial to hard-set this setting to the appropriate speed. When a situation arises and you need to start the analyzer in a hurry to begin capturing packets, you don't want autodetect to be taking precious seconds when hundreds of packets can go by without being captured. You also may run into NIC and switch autodetect compatibility problems that may cause your analyzer to autodetect at the wrong speed, for example, 10MB instead of 100MB.

Buffer Settings

When an analyzer captures packets, it stores these packets in a predefined data buffer until you stop the capture. The size of this buffer depends on how much data you need to capture and also the amount of memory in your computer. A computer with only 64MB of memory is going to have serious problems if you start using more than half of its memory for your buffer. The amount of buffer you use is relative to the amount of data you are capturing. I typically start with a 16MB buffer and increase it if necessary. I rarely need a buffer larger than 16MB because I use capture filters to granularly choose what data I want captured off the wire.

NOTE There are ways to trim down the amount of data you capture by using what is called packet slicing (discussed in the next section).

Packet Slicing

Packet slicing does what it says, it slices packets, meaning that it reduces the size of the data packets. The slicing, though, is done during the packet capture process. On Ethernet networks, data packets are a maximum of 1,514 bytes; on Token Ring, they are usually a maximum of 4,096 bytes. Unless you are troubleshooting data deep into the application layer, you usually don't require the entire frame to be captured. Some typical packet slices are as follows:

- **Ethernet header.** 64 bytes
- **IP header.** 84 bytes

- **TCP header.** 104 bytes
- **Common application headers.** 140 bytes

NOTE If you have the memory and buffer space available, try to avoid packet slicing. I generally use packet slicing only when I need to capture more data than my buffers will provide and when I need to increase the performance of my captures. There may always be some piece of information in the application data portion that you might need to solve a problem.

Suppose that you are troubleshooting the IP layer for fragmentation problems (something I talk more about in Chapter 3). Do you need to capture entire 1,514-byte packets? No. You can slice the packets down to the appropriate number of bytes that you need to capture (note the slicing option on Ether-Peek's capture window). Slicing packets is useful when you need to capture a large amount of data in your buffers, and the layer you need to analyze is at the lower end of the OSI model (Layers 3–5).

Write to Disk

What happens when you can't packet slice your data and you need to capture data that is larger than the size of your capture buffers. In this case, you can enable the write-to-disk feature of the analyzer. Not all analyzers have this feature, but the ones that do enable you to troubleshoot problems that need a large amount of data captured over a long period of time. Figure 2-6 illustrates the write-to-disk feature in EtherPeek NX. The analyzer continuously writes your capture buffer data to individual files on your hard disk, stopping only when you reach the maximum allotted disk space.

Triggers

As I indicated earlier in the chapter when I discussed notification, triggers are used when you can't be next to the analyzer to push the start capture button. Triggers let you set up a predefined set of parameters to tell the analyzer when to start capturing data and when to stop. If you are troubleshooting a specific transaction between an application server and a database server that occurs every night at 3:00 A.M. and ends at 3:30 A.M., you could set the trigger condition to start capturing at 2:45 A.M. and end at 3:30 A. M., adding an extra 15 minutes at the beginning and end to guarantee that all data is captured. You could also add a filter condition into the capture to permit only packets between the two servers to be captured. Figure 2-7 illustrates EtherPeek NX's ability to configure triggers for time and specific filters.

Packet Slicing

Write to Disk   Buffer Size

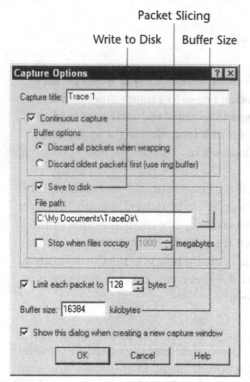

Figure 2-6   EtherPeek NX capture options.

Depending on the analyzer you use, triggers can be configured to start and stop on a number of conditions including events, time, and expert analysis conditions.

NOTE Expert analysis conditions, discussed later in the chapter, are analyzers' built-in artificial intelligence. Essentially, an analyzer with this capability can tell you when it sees conditions it is preconfigured to recognize occurring on the network.

Filtering

Most of the time you are going to be analyzing communications between two or more hosts. Depending on your capture access point, your analyzer may be seeing more traffic than you actually need to capture. By using your analyzer's filtering features you can program the analyzer to only capture the packets that you need to see. This also cuts down on the need to reduce your buffers and employ packet slicing. Filtering is also useful after you've captured a buffer full of packets and want to zoom in on a specific conversation.

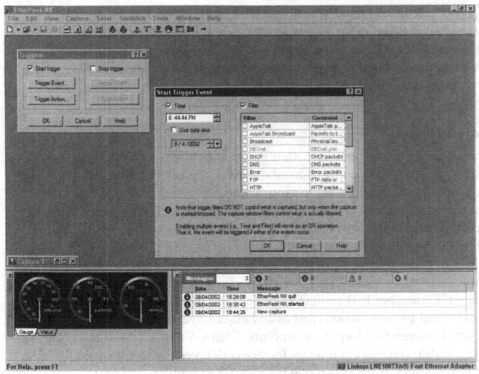

Figure 2-7   Trigger event configuration in EtherPeek NX.

TIP If you have the buffer space available for packet capture, it is always good to keep your filters wide open instead of narrow and specific. This way you have a better chance of capturing packets that might be related to the problem you are analyzing. For example, a filter between a workstation and file server won't reveal a failed DNS lookup because the lookup packets will be between the workstation and the DNS server, not the file server.

There are three types of packet filtering you can use for capturing and displaying packets—protocol, address, and pattern match; they are detailed in the next three sections.

Protocol Filters

Protocol filters allow you to zero in on a specific protocol, capturing just packets containing that protocol. Most analyzers already contain a list of protocols that may be easily selected for capture or display filtering (see Figure 2-8).

> **NOTE** Not all vendors refer to the same protocols by the same name. For example, EtherPeek refers to SMB as CIFS. They are essentially the same protocol. Some vendors also call DHCP BOOTP, or vice versa. It is extremely important to be familiar with the protocols on your network so you will recognize them quickly on your analyzer.

Address Filters

When analyzing data between two network devices (workstations, servers, routers), *address filters* come in handy to help you filter out unwanted traffic. For example, you might want to capture traffic between only two hosts or even two routers. Address filters help you accomplish this. Figure 2-9 illustrates two kinds of address filters: MAC address and network address.

For example, a filter that would capture all traffic between Router A and Router B (and not Router C) would have to be a MAC address filter. Since the routers are on the same Layer 2 network, they communicate using the MAC address. Remember that routers listen for their own Layer 2 MAC address on the wire and process packets just as any other Layer 2 device does. To capture packets between two Layer 3 endpoints (Client A and Client B in Figure 2-9, for example), you need to filter on the network layer address because the MAC address changes as packets move from router to router.

Figure 2-8   Protocol filters on EtherPeek NX.

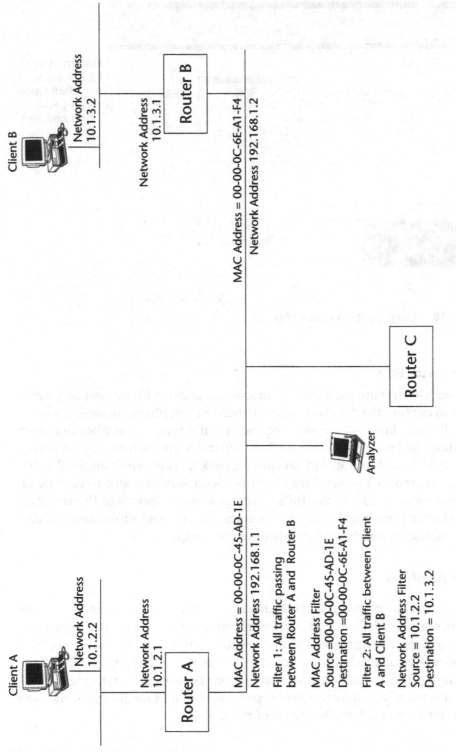

Figure 2-9   Configuring address filters.

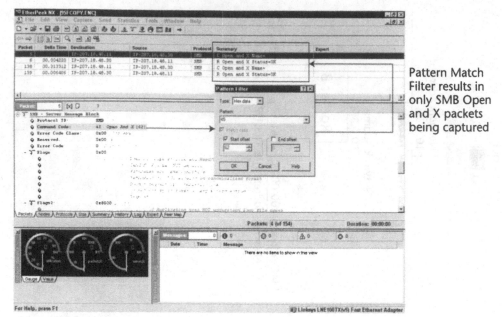

Pattern Match
Filter results in
only SMB Open
and X packets
being captured

Figure 2-10   Using a pattern match filter.

Pattern Match Filters

Pattern match filters are used when protocol and address filters are not specific enough to capture the data you desire. Pattern match filters are most useful in the application layer where you require specific types of application layer transactions to be captured. Figure 2-10 illustrates an analyzer set up with a pattern match capture filter to capture all packets containing an SMB Open and X command to a server. This filter allows an administrator to capture all File Open requests to a server for security purposes. Packets in the resulting capture buffer contain only File Open requests, and the administrator can easily see what source addresses are opening files on the server.

Expert Analysis

Expert analysis refers to the artificial intelligence that some analyzers possess, enabling them to tell you what's wrong on your network. Expert analysis systems operate by providing you with a "virtual network analyst" that watches over the many packets being captured by the analyzer and determines where problems lie. The "virtual analyst" watches protocols in each individual transaction and gives you information on performance and connection time-outs and responses indicating other types of problems.

WARNING Contrary to popular belief, expert analysis systems tend to do more harm than good to beginner analysts. It is important to understand the logic behind how expert analysis systems work. I've seen many a beginner analyst chasing down resolutions for a symptom given by the expert system that was actually completely normal activity. If you don't have an understanding of the intelligence behind an expert analysis system, that system will provide little or no benefit to you.

Table 2-3 lists some TCP/IP (and related protocols) expert symptoms found by EtherPeek NX.

Table 2-3 Expert Symptoms

EXPERT SYMPTOM	DESCRIPTION
IP Zero Address in Broadcast	A UDP packet is being broadcast using the old IP broadcast address of 0.0.0.0.
CRC Error	The CRC recomputed by the analyzer when the frame was received did not match the CRC at the end of the frame, indicating one or more corrupt bits in the frame.
IP Local Routing	Two IP packets that are identical except for the TTL (time to live) field have been detected.
IP ICMP Error	ICMP messages will indicate the cause, such as network, host, protocol, or port unreachable, datagram redirect from a router, TTL expired, and so on.
IP Header Checksum Error	The header portion of the IP datagram is in error. One or more bits have erroneously changed since the IP datagram was transmitted by the source IP host.
IP Missing Fragment	An IP datagram has been fragmented by the host application or a router, and one of the fragments is missing.
UDP Invalid Checksum	The UDP header and/or data is in error. One or more bits have erroneously changed since the UDP datagram was transmitted by the source IP host.
TCP Zero Window	The recipients TCP receive buffer is filling up (low window) or full (zero window).
TCP Too Many Retransmissions	The source IP node is sending another TCP packet with a sequence number that matches a previously sent TCP packet to the same destination IP address and TCP port numbers. "Too many" is when the percentage threshold exceeds that of total transmitted packets.

(continued)

Table 2-3 *(continued)*

EXPERT SYMPTOM	DESCRIPTION
TCP Stuck Window	The TCP window size has not changed for three or more consecutive packets and has dropped below a percentage of the maximum window.
TCP Slow First Retransmission	The first retransmission is taking longer than the threshold, which may indicate slow recovery time and throughput.
TCP Slow Acknowledgement	The recipient appears to be slow in acknowledging TCP data segments.
TCP Retransmission	The source IP node is sending another TCP packet with a sequence number that matches a previously sent TCP packet to the same destination IP address and TCP port numbers.
TCP Reset Inactive Connection	The sender has set the Reset (RST) flag in a TCP packet.
TCP Reset Connection	One end of a TCP connection has set the RST flag in a TCP packet, which sometimes indicates an abrupt disconnection.
TCP Repeated Connection Attempt	A client is attempting multiple times to establish a TCP connection.
TCP Low Window	The application is not keeping up with the incoming TCP segments.
TCP Low Starting MSS	The TCP maximum segment size (MSS) is at or below the threshold setting.
TCP Lost Connection	TCP data is repeatedly being sent with no acknowledgement until the sender gives up and resets the connection.
TCP Invalid Checksum	The TCP header and/or data is in error. One or more bits have erroneously changed since the TCP segment was transmitted by the source IP host.
TCP Idle Too Long	The TCP connection hasn't been used since the threshold setting in seconds.
TCP Fast Retransmission	The source IP node is retransmitting a TCP data segment before the TCP fast retransmission threshold.
TCP Connection Refused	The host is rejecting a client's initial TCP connection attempt.
SMB Repeated or Loop on Transaction	An SMB application or operating system (OS) has sent the same (back to back) transaction command within the threshold time setting.
SMB Command Rejected	An SMB command has been rejected.

Table 2-3 *(continued)*

EXPERT SYMPTOM	DESCRIPTION
HTTP Slow Response Time	The average response time from the HTTP server is equal to or higher than the threshold.
FTP Slow Response Time	The average response time from the FTP server is equal to or higher than the threshold.
DNS Slow Response Time	The average response time from the DNS server is equal to or higher than the threshold.
DHCP Low Lease Time	A client has been offered an IP address lease in which the lease time is at or below the threshold.
Client/Server Slow Server Response Time	The average response time from the server is equal to or higher than the threshold.
Client/Server Slow Client to Server Throughput	The throughput from the client to the server is at or lower than the threshold.
Client/Server Slow Server to Client Throughput	The throughput from the server to the client is at or lower than the threshold.
Client/Server Inefficient Client	"Chatty" conversations in which data packets from a server have small average packet sizes. The higher the sensitivity, the higher the likelihood that this problem will be flagged.
Client/Server Busy Network or Server	There is a moderate to high fluctuation in response time. The higher the sensitivity, the higher the likelihood that this problem will be flagged.

Notice in Table 2-3 that most of the Expert Symptom descriptions seem to depend on threshold values. This detail is very important to know when evaluating the output from an analyzer's expert analysis system. Many times an analyzer's expert system will show multiple active symptoms from the network traffic it analyzes. The analyzer is making these assumptions based on predefined threshold settings (notice in Figure 2-11 the sensitivity and threshold setting options on EtherPeek NX). For an analyzer's expert analysis mode to provide useful information, the user must first understand the normal baseline operation of network traffic. For example, if the expert system is reporting DHCP Low Lease Time symptoms, the cause may be from dial-in users being allocated an IP address. Dial-in users are typically allocated a very low lease time in comparison to LAN users, but if you yourself don't know this fact, you may act on the symptom given you by the expert system even when there is no problem. Expert modes are valuable tools to have in your toolkit, but you must understand the logic behind the assumptions they make when providing you with symptoms on your networks. I make note of specific expert symptoms in case studies in the upcoming chapters.

Expert Threshold Setting

Expert Symptom Sensitivity

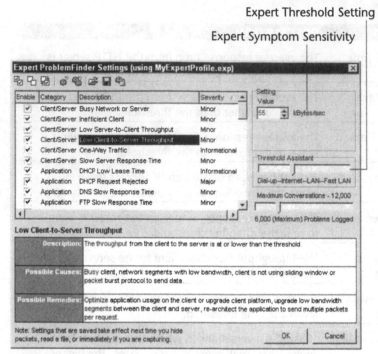

Figure 2-11   Expert threshold settings in EtherPeek NX.

Measuring Performance

There are two important things you can measure with your analyzer:

- Throughput
- Latency

Before I get into these two things, however, I want to briefly discuss how your analyzer timestamps data. All analyzers have three measures of time:

- *Relative time* is time relative to a fixed, or marked packet.
- *Delta time* is the time that has elapsed between the transmission or reception of one packet and the next packet in the trace.
- *Absolute time* is the time of day.

Absolute time is good for matching a problem up to a certain packet in a trace file. Relative and delta time are used to measure latency and throughput.

Latency

Latency is the amount of time that elapses between the beginning of a transaction and the first response to that transaction. PING is a great way to measure latency on a network because it uses a simple command-response protocol. PING uses the Echo command of the ICMP protocol (more about ICMP in Chapter 4). It sends out a data pattern to a network node and requests the node to respond with the same pattern. This process allows the PING program to measure the elapsed time from its request to the received response. This is called the network round-trip latency or RTL. Figure 2-12 shows how an analyzer is used to measure the round-trip latency.

NOTE Round-trip latency measured with PING responses should just be used as a generic baseline. There are many factors that affect latency of different protocols and applications. For example, a 40-millisecond RTT using PING might be slightly lower than the time it takes an application to receive a response. You need to take into consideration overhead such as application processing when comparing latency to that found when you use PING.

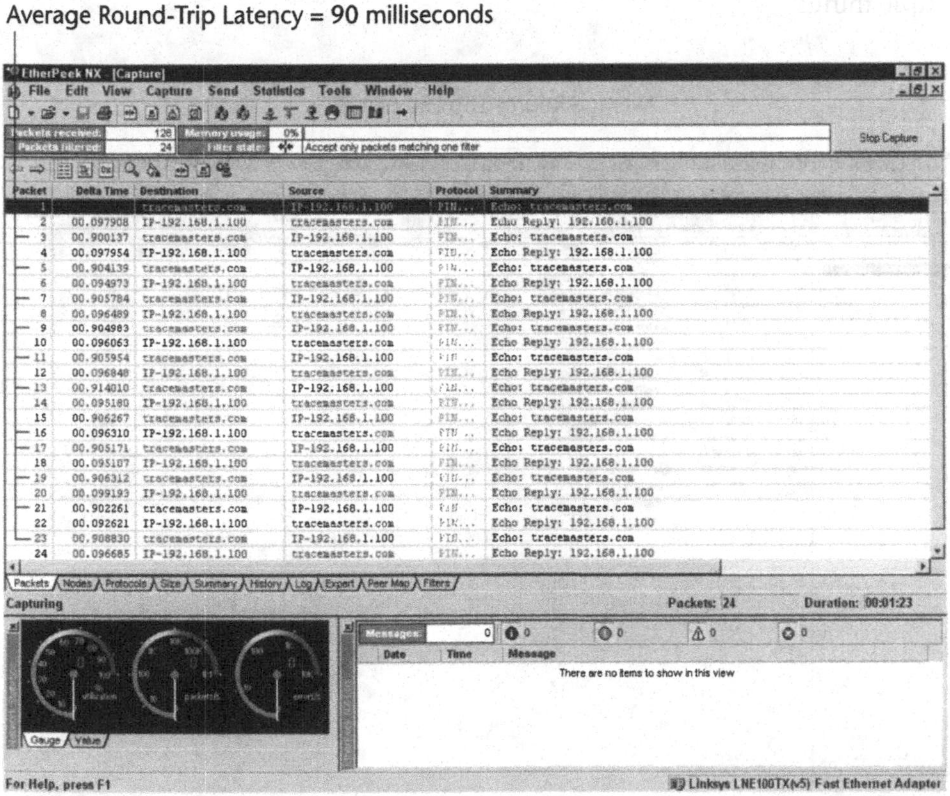

Average Round-Trip Latency = 90 milliseconds

Figure 2-12   Measuring latency.

Another fine tool available for measuring latency is called Ping Plotter. Ping Plotter is a visual Traceroute program that plots latency across each link of the network. The Ping Plotter program breaks down the round-trip latency and illustrates where the latency is occurring over each router hop over the entire path. Figure 2-13 shows the Ping Plotter program giving the same round-trip latency measurement as the analyzer, but now you can see that most of the latency is between routers trb1-p013201.wswdc.ip.att.net and trb1-po12401 .sl9mo.ip.att.net.

CROSS-REFERENCE I discuss in detail how tools like Ping Plotter and Traceroute use ICMP to measure latency in Chapter 4.

Throughput

Throughput is defined as the amount of data transferred from one device to another over time. Throughput is typically measured in kilobytes per second (KB/sec). In order to measure throughput with a protocol analyzer, you need a couple things.

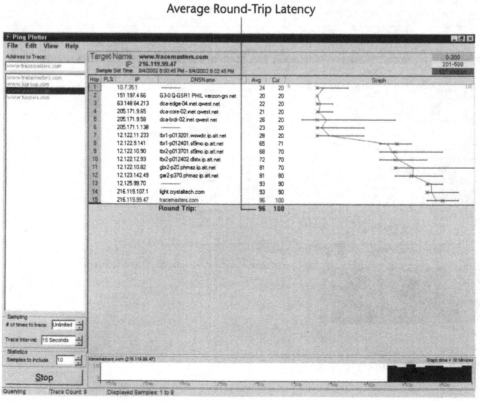

Figure 2-13 Measuring latency with Ping Plotter.

- One is the ability to zero out the relative timestamps for a specific packet, allowing you to start counting time from a specific packet reference.

- The next thing you need is a cumulative bytes column that also can be set to zero, which allows you to start counting the amount of bytes transferred over the exact time period from which you set your zero (relative) time reference.

Notice in Figure 2-14 how both the Relative Time and Cumulative Bytes columns are set to zero and how they start incrementing as you move down through the packet trace.

Figure 2-15 is the end of the transaction you want to measure. If you take the total cumulative bytes and divide them by the total relative time (bytes/sec), you have your measured throughput over the entire transaction. You can use this technique to measure the throughput of just about any transaction. I talk more about how to determine whether the throughput is within acceptable boundaries in Chapter 3.

Relative Time and Cumulative Bytes Zeroed Out at Frame 53

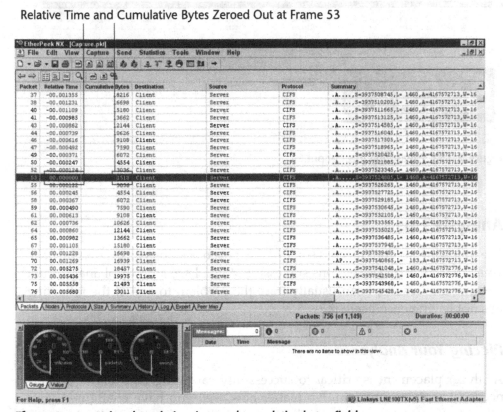

Figure 2-14   Using the relative time and cumulative bytes field.

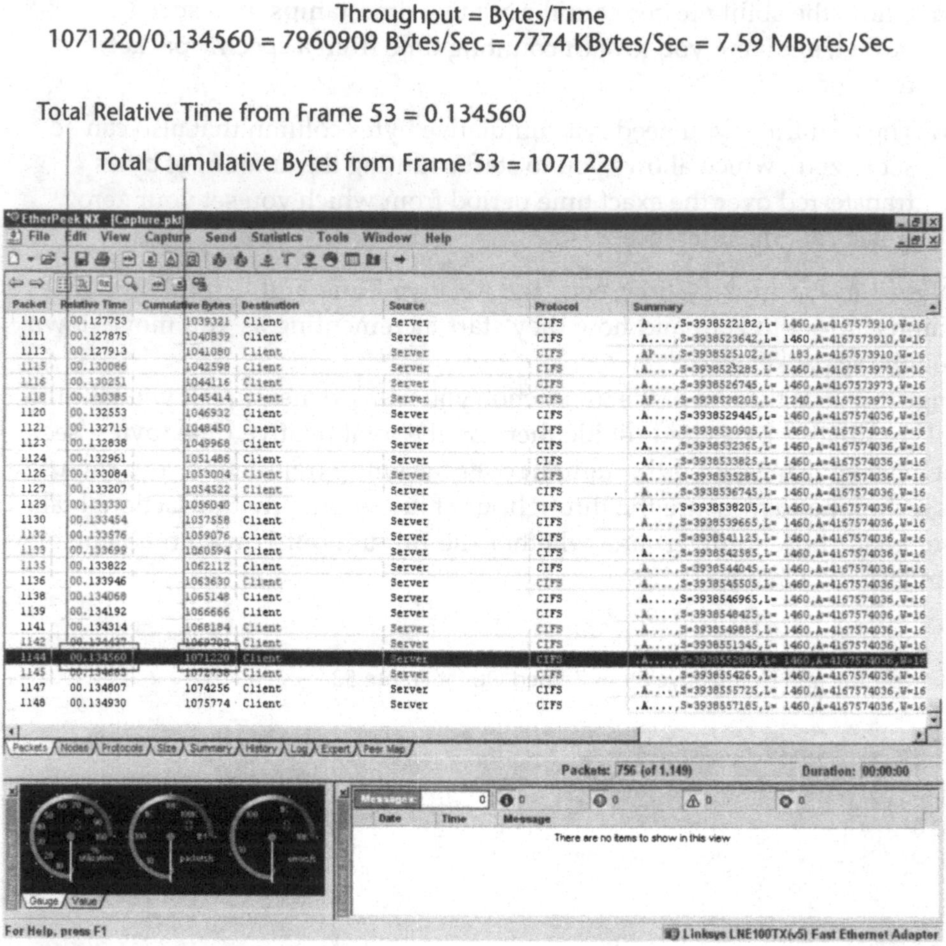

$$\text{Throughput} = \text{Bytes/Time}$$
$$1071220/0.134560 = 7960909 \text{ Bytes/Sec} = 7774 \text{ KBytes/Sec} = 7.59 \text{ MBytes/Sec}$$

Total Relative Time from Frame 53 = 0.134560

Total Cumulative Bytes from Frame 53 = 1071220

Figure 2-15 Measuring throughput.

Analysis Tips

The following sections discuss some of the most basic tips you can use to make your protocol analysis sessions successful. When I see a protocol analysis not yielding any results, I can usually trace the problem to one of the following tips not having been heeded.

Placing Your Analyzers

Analyzer placement is critical to successfully capturing the flow of packets needed to solve a problem. No matter how well you have configured your filters, buffers, or triggers, you will not capture the traffic you need if your analyzer is on the wrong segment. Assume that Figure 2-16 shows a network with three possible capture points.

- Analyzer 1 will be able to capture traffic between Client A and Client B at the data link layer using port-mirroring or shared hub.

- Analyzer 1 will be able to capture traffic between Client A and Server X at the network layer.

- Analyzer 1 will not be able to capture traffic between Client C and Server X because it is not on either segment or in between the path of traffic.

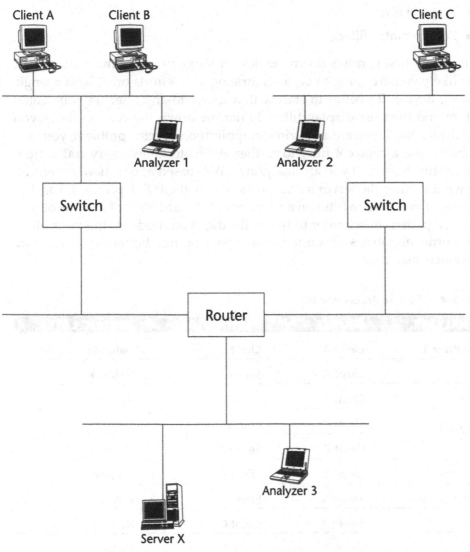

Figure 2-16   Analyzer capture points.

Table 2-4 illustrates some of the conversation layers that can be captured by the different analyzer placements shown in Figure 2-16.

Using Proper Filters

Once the analyzer is in place, you may want to set capture filters to further narrow down the traffic you are capturing. Filters should be configured in the following order:

- Address filters
- Protocol filters
- Pattern match filters

This order first narrows down the flow of traffic to one or more endpoints. Most likely you are going to be concentrating your efforts on at least a single network device. It's better to start with a source-to-any filter on your initial capture and then use display filters to narrow down the conversations you need to analyze. If you are analyzing an application-specific problem, you may be able to use a protocol filter to further eliminate unnecessary traffic from your capture buffers. If you are analyzing a Web-based application server, you will want to filter the server's address as well as the HTTP protocol. Last but not least, if you need to filter on a range or byte value inside of a protocol, you can use a pattern match filter to isolate the data you need. Setting your filters in this order eliminates unwanted data in your capture buffers and saves you time when analyzing.

Table 2-4   Capture Access Points

ANALYZER	SOURCE	DESTINATION	TRAFFIC LAYER
Analyzer 1	Client A	Client B	Data link
	Client A	Server X	Network
	Client A	Client C	Network
Analyzer 2	Client C	Router	Data link
	Client C	Server X	Network
	Client C	Client B	Network
Analyzer 3	Server X	Router	Data link
	Server X	Client C	Network
	Client B	Client C	Network

Troubleshooting from the Bottom Up

The biggest mistake that beginning analysts make is that they do not troubleshoot from the bottom up. Each layer of the OSI model is dependent on the layer below it. If there is a problem in the data link layer, then analyzing the interactions of the TCP protocol (transport layer) isn't going to help you solve the problem. Problems often show up in multiple layers. For example, packet corruption in the data link layer will cause retransmissions in the transport layer and also possibly application time-outs. It is critical to verify the proper operation of each layer before analyzing the next-higher layer.

Knowing Your Protocols

As data moves down through the OSI model and packets are formed for transmission on to the network, the responsibility for data integrity and transmission changes hands. After an application passes data down to the transport layer, it's the responsibility of protocols like TCP to retransmit the data during packet loss. After the IP protocol passes data down to the data link layer, it is the responsibility of protocols like Ethernet or Token Ring to transmit that data across the local link. If you can verify that one layer is performing its job correctly, more often than not the problem lies in the operation of the lower layers. This is not to say that you should troubleshoot from the top down. You need to understand a protocol well enough to know when it is doing its job correctly. The dependencies between the protocols allow you to eliminate those layers that contain the protocols that are doing their job. When you know who is doing their job, it's easy to find out who isn't and why.

Comparing Working Traces

When there are no problems to troubleshoot, you have a great opportunity to analyze how the network behaves normally. Building a database of trace files allows you to have a reference point for when things go wrong. You can then go back and compare normal SQL database transactions to the traces captured when a performance issue occurs. Most of the time the differences in the two traces will reveal the problem.

TIP I typically try to obtain captures of all custom or nonstandard applications running on the network. Oftentimes an application will perform functions over the network that are not apparent without actually seeing the traffic passing on the wire. This is especially true with firewalls. Many times users find out about an application's behavior only after a firewall is installed, blocking the traffic that the application uses and that the administrator never knew about beforehand.

When analyzing an application, note the following:

- **Dependent systems.** Which end systems are involved in the application's processes; what nodes do you see in the trace files? For example, a Web server may "talk" to two or more database servers to retrieve the information it needs for building a response to a user query. Any end systems used by an application are called dependent systems because the application as a whole relies on them to complete its tasks.

- **Transaction time.** As you capture traces of different application transactions, note the total time it takes to complete the transaction. If your analyzer does not decode the application information, you can simply write down the beginning and ending frame numbers from the analyzer's capture window. Also be on the lookout for data in the hex decode pane that you can use to identify a transaction.

- **Throughput.** At transaction time, make sure to note how much data the application is transferring. You can use the cumulative bytes and relative column to record both the total bytes and the throughput of the transaction. Throughput and total time will provide an excellent baseline for comparison when a performance problem arises.

- **Packets per transaction and packet size.** By noting the total packets and packet size, you can easily see if a performance problem has resulted from reduced packet sizes. A transaction that is using smaller packets will most likely need to transmit more packets in order to complete the transaction. More packets means more round-trip latency and lower throughput.

- **Ports and protocols.** Always pay attention to what transport layer ports (such as UDP and TCP) an application is using. Also note higher layer protocols such as SMB, FTP, Telnet, or HTTP. I have seen instances where applications actually use the Telnet protocol to transfer HTML-type data and instances where HTTP is used as a terminal protocol. Never assume the method that an application or system uses to perform its job. By noting the protocols and ports an application uses, you can create a nice matrix that can be used in the future to plan for firewall rulesets.

- **Files/directories.** By recording the directories that an application uses, you will be able to make sure that changes to those directories and files are carefully controlled by the server administrators. If you do not already know which files and directories an application uses, you can filter on SMB CreateAndX or OpenAndX packets because they contain the destination filename that the application is opening.

Analyzing after Each Change

When attempting to reconfigure a router or server to solve a problem, always make one change, and then reanalyze. I have seen many instances where the urge to solve a problem takes precedence over proper analysis techniques. Changes to configurations of routers, switches, or registry entries should be made based on intelligent analysis results. When you make a change, make one change at a time and perform a postchange analysis before making another change. If the change did not make a difference, back it out and attempt your second change. Always reanalyze the information between changes. Too many consecutive changes give you nothing but confusion as you work to sort out which of your changes is causing new additional problems.

Summary

The techniques and analyzer operations discussed in this chapter are by no means the only ones you will ever need to use. Other analysis platforms may provide the same or different toolsets at your disposal. And the techniques you develop to troubleshoot problems will often be ones you have crafted from your own experience. The ones I have discussed in this chapter are here to get you started. In the next part of this book, I examine the core TCP protocols and sample case studies taken from real networks. I will demonstrate how to apply the techniques from this chapter along with a knowledge of the protocols to begin creating a strong foundation for analyzing and problem solving in the TCP protocol suite.

The Core Protocols

Inside the Internet Protocol

Now that Part I of the book has discussed the building blocks of communication (the OSI model) and some techniques on how to analyze those communications, it's time to start discussing what makes communications happen—the protocols. This next part of the book discusses the core TCP/IP protocols that allow all other upper-layer protocols to operate. The approach is once again layer by layer, starting with Internet Protocol (IP) in this chapter and moving on to the most complex core protocol, Transmission Control Protocol (TCP). It is important to understand how the bottom layered protocols such as IP work before you begin trying to understand the higher-layer protocols. Since each of the higher-layer protocols (such as UDP and TCP) use the services of the lower-layer protocols (such as IP), it's important to understand the impact of each layer's responsibility to the entire communications process. Such understanding is critical in troubleshooting situations. I begin this chapter with a review of Layer 2 communications and how the limitations of Layer 2 create a need for Layer 3 protocols. Then, instead of generic layer descriptions, I begin the discussion of the actual functions of the protocols at each layer, starting in this chapter with IP and other supporting protocols at the network layer.

Reviewing Layer 2 Communications

The next sections provide a quick review of what Part I revealed about the functions of Layer 2.

Multiplexing

Layer 2 packets encapsulate the data of all other upper-layer protocols. As is discussed in Chapter 1, Ethertypes are used by Layer 2 to determine the destination Layer 3 protocol of the data.

For example, Figure 3-1 shows a decoded IP packet. Notice how even though you tend to think of Ethernet as a bottom-layer protocol (it resides at Layer 2), the analyzer shows it listed under the Ethernet Header section of the decode panel. Analyzers decode the packet detail in reverse, showing you first the lower layers and then, as you scroll down, the upper layers, listed in the decode panel as IP, UDP, and NetBIOS Name Service. In the decode panel, you can see that the packet has several protocols inside of it. Starting with Ethernet at the data link layer, then the Internet Protocol, on top of that you have the User Datagram Protocol, and then finally NetBIOS.

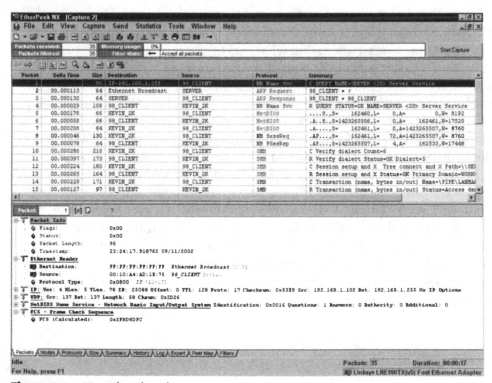

Figure 3-1   IP packet decode.

Looking at the Ethernet Header section of the decode panel, you can see that the Ethertype value is 0800, which indicates to the data link layer that the next upper-layer protocol is IP. When the data link layer receives the frame off the wire and sees the Ethertype value of 0800, it knows to start decoding the next portion of the packet as IP. Your protocol analyzers use the same method to figure out what the next layer is that needs to be decoded, by looking at the Ethertype.

Error Control

In Chapter 1 I discussed the Ethernet CRC and how it's used to protect data being transferred across the local media. In Figure 3-1 you can see that the analyzer also performs the same CRC calculation that our NIC cards do to confirm that the frame was received without error. (This is shown at the bottom of the decode panel under the FCS—Frame Check Sequence section.) This kind of confirmation is important in troubleshooting because you want to be able to guarantee the integrity of the data you are seeing in your analyzer at each layer. Because the CRC is calculated over the entire contents of the frame, you have a pretty good guarantee that what you have received is exactly what the source station sent.

NOTE Although this book is primarily concerned with Layers 3 and up, it is still important to understand how errors are detected at Layer 2 since reliable protocols such as TCP attempt to mitigate those errors in order to guarantee data delivery. In the Chapter 6 discussion of TCP, you can see how that happens.

Addressing

At Layer 2, nodes on the network are addressed by the burned-in addresses on their network interface cards (NICs), called MAC addresses. Each NIC listens for its own MAC address over the wire, and upon "hearing" it, copies the frame off the wire, parses it, and forwards it along to the proper network layer protocol indicated by the Ethertype value. The NIC also listens for the broadcast address, and when configured to, the specific multicast addresses.

CROSS-REFERENCE You will see how multicast addresses are used in the next case study on NetBEUI, as well as learn the drawbacks of broadcast packets.

In Figure 3-1, you can see in the decode panel under the Ethernet Header section that a source station with MAC address 0C-10-A4-AD-1E-75 has transmitted an IP packet to the destination station with MAC address FF-FF-FF-FF-FF-FF. If you recall from Chapter 1, this destination address is the broadcast address. It will become clearer later in this chapter why the broadcast address is used in certain situations. For now, understand that it is used to address "all stations" on the local media.

Case Study: NetBEUI Communications

The three functions of data link protocols I have just reviewed—multiplexing, error control, and addressing—are also apparent in functions of the higher-layer protocols. However, before jumping immediately into IP, I want to take a look at how a simple protocol called NetBIOS actually uses the services of the data link layer. The same processes and functions performed by NetBIOS are also performed by IP. Those same functions exist in almost any protocol suite. Once you are familiar with them in NetBIOS, or even IP, you can map them to another protocol very easily.

NetBIOS is an application program interface (API) developed by Sytec, Inc., for IBM. It originally operated on proprietary Sytec data link protocols until IBM migrated the use to its Token Ring networking architecture. To allow older Net-BIOS based applications to continue working on its platforms, IBM also implemented a NetBIOS driver on its PC LAN Support Program. At around the same time, Microsoft developed its LAN Manager system, which used NetBIOS. In the strictest sense, NetBIOS is not a protocol but an API. NetBIOS stands for Networked Basic Input/Output System, and early on was an extension of a computer BIOS. The NetBIOS API provided a rich set of functions for which application developers could write applications that would communicate over a network. By itself NetBIOS has no communication functionality unless combined with something called the *NetBIOS Extended User Interface*, or simply *Net-BEUI*. The combination of the two is what is referred to as the *NetBEUI protocol*, or simply the *NetBIOS Frames Protocol*. NetBIOS is a very simple protocol that I can use to illustrate some of the functions that occur on networks.

Computers on a NetBEUI (or NetBIOS) network each have a unique 16-character NetBIOS name. For a node to communicate via NetBEUI it needs to first obtain the NetBIOS name of the destination node. Each node uses this name to establish a NetBIOS session with the destination computer. For example, assume that you have two stations, Node1 and Node2. Assume that Node1 wants to transfer a file to Node2; there are certain processes that Node1 must complete in order to do this. Table 3-1 shows these processes and the layer of the OSI model they belong to, and the next few sections of this chapter discuss each process.

Table 3-1   NetBIOS Communications by Layer

PROCESS	OSI LAYER
Name resolution	Session layer
Reliable connection setup	Transport layer
NetBIOS session setup	Session layer
Application processes	Application layer

Wait! Where is the network layer? There is none with NetBIOS. Not all protocols religiously follow the OSI model in a strict sense. In the case of a NetBIOS network, there is no network layer. All communication is done at Layer 2, the MAC layer. Because of this, NetBIOS isn't routable, because it has no network layer addressing. I will talk more about the limitations at the MAC Layer later in the chapter, but first I want to get into more detail on the process a NetBIOS node uses to communicate.

Name Resolution

The first frame in Figure 3-2 is a perfect example of how multicast packets are used.

The frame's MAC layer address, shown in the decode pane, is 03-00-00-00-00-01 (dashes used to separate octets). This destination address is a reserved multicast address and is used by the NetBEUI protocol. Any station configured with the NetBEUI protocol listens for this multicast MAC address. Further, Figure 3-3 breaks down the first octet of the NetBIOS multicast address down into binary; in this figure, you can see how the multicast/broadcast bit is actually set to one.

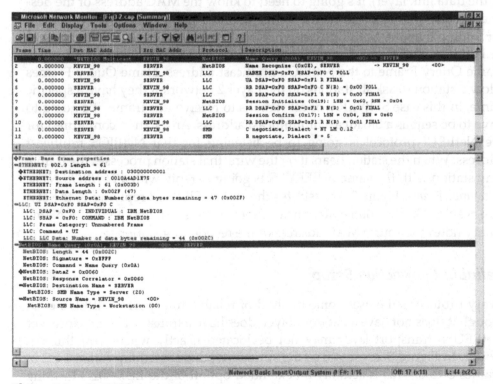

Figure 3-2   NetBIOS name query.

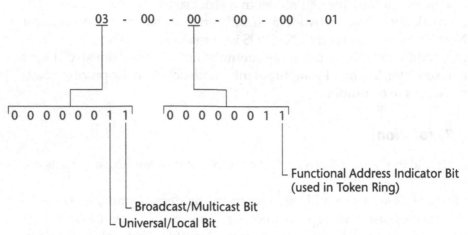

Figure 3-3   NetBIOS multicast address.

Why is this packet's destination a multicast address? To answer that you must first step back and think about the order of communications. In order for one station to transfer data to or from another station over the local media (that is, the data link layer), it's going to need to know the MAC address of the destination station. Furthermore, the source station is going to need a mechanism for finding that out. NetBIOS uses what is called a *NetBIOS Name Query Frame*. In Frame 1 of Figure 3-2, you see the source station (Kevin_98) send out a Name Query Frame to the NetBIOS multicast address. Name Query Frames allow a station to ask all stations on the Layer 2 network if they have a specific name, in this case SERVER. For all stations to receive this frame, it's going to have to be sent as a broadcast or multicast address. Any station configured for the NetBEUI protocol is going to be listening for that NetBIOS multicast address. When the station hears it on the wire, that station processes the frame. Any station with the name of SERVER is going to reply with a *NetBIOS Name Recognize Frame*. Figure 3-4 illustrates the station SERVER replying to the station Kevin_98. The source station that sent out the original NetBIOS Name Query notes the source MAC address of the responding station.

Reliable Connection Setup

Every protocol suite uses some method of reliable transport. NetBEUI, even though it does not have a network layer, does have a transport layer. However NetBEUIs' transport layer may not be located exactly where you think it would. In Figure 3-2, you see in the summary pane something called LLC in Frames 3 to 6. This is actually an extended option of the LLC 802.3 framing method that allows reliable communications. It is called *Logical Link Control Type 2*. Even though the transport layer functionality is technically located in the data link layer, it's still a transport function.

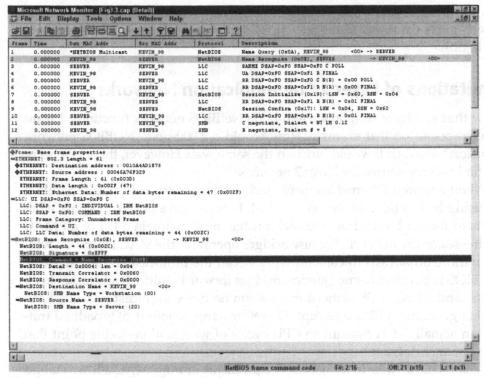

Figure 3-4 NetBIOS name recognized.

> **TIP** Such arrangements are not uncommon in protocol suites. Just remember that the OSI model is not a hard-and-fast rule on where a layer's functionality is located.

NetBIOS Session Setup

After the reliable connection setup is done via LLC Type 2, NetBIOS needs to create its own session setup. This setup creates a logical NetBIOS session layer connection between the two stations. Then and only then can the application layer start to do its job. Referring back to Figure 3-2 again, Frame 7 is the NetBIOS Session Request, and Frame 9 is the NetBIOS Session Response, confirming that the session has been set up.

Application Process

After our session layer and transport layer protocols have finished their respective setup functions, the application layer is allowed to do its job. The application layer could be anything from an FTP session to an SMB server logon or SQL database transaction. Regardless of the application layer in use, it's important to know that the application layer cannot begin its job unless the lower layers (in this case the session and transport layers) are finished with their jobs.

Limitations of Layer 2 Communication Networks

Now that you have seen how a two-node NetBIOS network functions, I want to extrapolate on that example. How would a 2,000-node NetBIOS network function? Answer: It would function the same way. However, there is a point of diminishing returns for Layer 2 networks.

When a shared Ethernet segment starts hitting its capacity, you separate it by using *bridges* (also known as *switches*). In order for a bridge to know what ports to forward, each frame to each bridge must maintain a list of all MAC addresses on the network. Because bridges operate at the MAC layer, you will-have more broadcasts to contend with. Recall the multicast address used by NetBIOS to perform Name Queries. Bridges forward multicast addresses to all ports, and all NetBIOS stations must examine those multicast packets. Each packet generates a CPU interrupt. Therefore, large amounts of broadcast traffic can actually start consuming CPU cycles of workstations to the point that performance degrades.

What is the answer to mitigating the problems of huge MAC address tables and broadcasts on Layer 2 networks? The answer is *routing*. "But," you may say, "I thought you said NetBIOS isn't routable." It isn't. But it can be routed when used in conjunction with a network layer protocol such as IP. I show how this works in Chapter 8. By separating the network segments with routers you create what are called broadcast domains. A *broadcast domain* is a defined area over which broadcast traffic propagates. Layer 2 networks separated by bridges (or switches) forward broadcasts; routers, though, do not forward broadcast traffic. In a Layer 2 network of 5,000 nodes, each bridge has to store all 5,000 MAC addresses in its bridge tables to know where it needs to forward frames. By implementing routing, however, you can separate the network into 10 subnets of 500 nodes. This separation reduces the size of the MAC address tables, and more importantly, reduces the level of broadcast traffic each node sees. Now, each subnet has only 500 nodes worth of broadcast traffic to handle, not 5,000.

Broadcast domains have another name you may have heard of, VLANs. A Virtual LAN *(VLAN)* is simply a broadcast domain that can be configured "virtually" inside of a switch. In the past when networks were separated by routers, each router had a separate physical connection to each subnet. With VLANs, the separation of networks is done with the software inside of a switch by grouping certain ports together into a VLAN. Routers don't have to be physical anymore either. The Cisco Catalyst Series of switches has a router blade called a Route-Switch-Module that can have virtual interface connections to any VLAN. Placing all routing and bridging into a single device is known as *collapsed backbone networking*. The backbone of the network is now literally the backplane of the switch.

Network Layer Protocols

Unlike data link protocols, network layer protocols do not rely on the data link layer addresses for end-to-end communication between nodes, although they do rely on MAC addresses for transmission on the local media. Network layer protocols add another layer of addressing for communications between nodes. Very similar to how NetBIOS uses computer names, network layer protocols (IP is one such protocol) have their own naming method, called network layer addresses. Network layer protocols are routed protocols. Bridges forward packets by examining the destination MAC addresses; routers forward packets by examining the network layer address. Each network layer protocol uses its own type of addressing. When you design a network with more than one broadcast domain you are in essence creating a routed network. Since broadcasts are terminated at the router boundary, you can no longer use Layer 2 communications to reach other broadcast domains. Instead you communicate via Layer 2 to a router that can reach other broadcast domains. This router then makes a forwarding decision based on the address in the network layer protocol. The router then uses Layer 2 communications to reach the destination host. Figure 3-5 shows what happens when a packet is sent through a router versus when it is sent through a bridge.

When a packet is forwarded by a bridge, the MAC addresses stay the same since the destination MAC address is truly the address of the interface in the destination host. When a packet is forwarded by a router, the MAC addresses change. The destination MAC address is replaced with the MAC address of the next Layer 2 device in the path, whether it is another router or the destination node. The source address is replaced by the router's own MAC address on that network. The router will also modify other fields in the IP (Layer 3) section of the packet. Because of this, it will need to recalculate the Ethernet CRC before transmitting the packet out onto the local media.

In the next section of this chapter, you will see how packets are sent to and forwarded by routers. In a routed network the network, layer address is what is used to make forwarding decisions, not the MAC address. The MAC source and destination change as packets pass through routers, but the IP source and destination addresses remain the same.

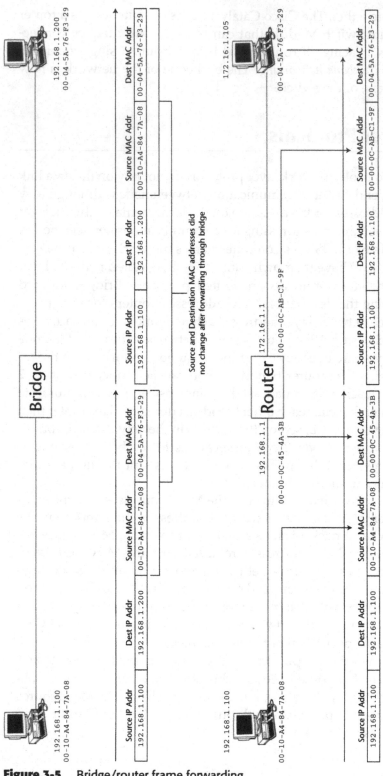

Figure 3-5   Bridge/router frame forwarding.

ROUTING VERSUS BRIDGING

There has been a lot of confusion over which is better, routing or bridging. The reasons that most people went to routing was to build more scalable networks that at the time couldn't be handled simply by bridging. When routing became the "thing to do," a lot of the vendors who made only bridges had a big problem on their hands because they didn't have routers to sell in the new "router-centric" marketplace. Their answer was to invent a new technology called a switch. By reinforcing the advantages of switching over routing, they convinced the industry that routing was slow, complicated, and unnecessary. After all, why route when you can switch? Switching was nothing other than a new term for bridging. The only difference was that switching was done in hardware instead of software. Switches also had a newer method of forwarding called *cut-through*, which would forward packets immediately after receiving the first 6 bytes of the destination MAC address. When the industry was done buying into the switching trend, something interesting happened; their networks suddenly became more complicated. No longer could they determine the location of a node simply by looking at the IP address and associating it with a subnet. Now, a node's MAC address could be found anywhere on the network. Many people unaware of broadcast problems on small networks suddenly became aware of them as they started affecting the entire network. What was the industry's answer to this? Simple, move back to routing. Except that this time they didn't call it routing; they called it *Layer 3 switching*. What did everyone do? Of course, they followed the industry trend and moved to Layer 3 switching, completely unaware that they were using the same routing technology that had existed years ago.

Regardless of the marketing terms, the processes of packet forwarding have gone largely unchanged. Whether people call a product a switch, bridge, or router, it still has to handle the same layers of the OSI model that were around before the product.

Internet Protocol Addressing

The Internet Protocol (IP) provides another interface, this time an interface to an IP network. Using just the data link layer interface, as seen in the previous NetBEUI example, limits scalability because of large MAC address tables and broadcast traffic. However, the IP interface is a logical one, not physical, though it still uses the physical connection to the media in order to communicate. In the NetBEUI example, you saw how all end-to-end communication was done at the data link layer using MAC addresses. In contrast, IP network communications use IP addresses for end-to-end communication. Layer 2 still provides access to the physical media, but now terminates at the IP network boundaries.

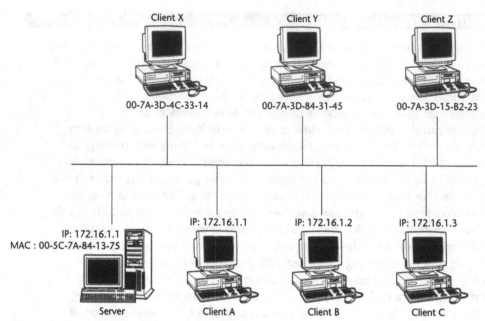

Figure 3-6   IP and NetBEUI network.

A node using the IP protocol has one or more IP addresses, depending on how many adapters are configured for use with IP. Consider an example. Figure 3-6 shows a small network with several clients and a server. Clients A, B, and C communicate with the server by using IP. Clients X, Y, and Z communicate with the server using NetBEUI. Even though all clients are on the same local network, they cannot communicate with each other because they are not all configured with the same protocol. When a protocol is configured to operate on a NIC, this is called *binding* the protocol to the NIC card. In large multivendor networks, it is not uncommon to have multiple protocols "bound" to the NICs of servers or clients. In the example in Figure 3-6, all the clients communicate with the server at Layer 2, but only the IP clients communicate at Layer 3 using IP addresses.

TIP   When a client has the ability to communicate using multiple protocols, it is critical to know which protocol the client is using in order to communicate with a specific resource on the network. I have seen many instances of network administrators who had no idea which protocols were being used on their network. When someone inadvertently turned off bridging on a network segment, users who were using NetBEUI to access servers would start experiencing problems. In fact, in the early deployments of Microsoft Windows NT networks, many network administrators actually thought you needed NetBEUI configured on clients in order to access NT servers. Their claim was that whenever you removed NetBEUI, the clients were unable to access certain servers on the network. The reason they were having problems had less to do with NetBEUI and more to do with how their networks were set up with a combination of bridging and routing.

NetBEUI clients could access servers only through a bridged path, thus it was believed it was a required protocol.

IP Addressing

Before I discuss IP addressing, I want to clarify a couple of things about how numbers are represented in binary. A computer only understands two numbers, zero and one. Any numbers created in binary must be in a series of ones and zeros. Binary numbering is called the Base-2 system because it's based on two digits, one and zero. When you write a binary number, each of the digits has a place value just as a regular decimal number does. For example, the number 1,000 in decimal has a zero in the one's place, zero in the ten's place, zero in the hundred's place, and a one in the thousands place. That is where the number 1,000 comes from. Each placeholder is based on the number 10 so it's not a coincidence the decimal numbering system is called Base 10. Binary digits are based on twos. The same number, 1,000, in binary is equivalent to the number 8 in decimal. The one's place contains a zero, the two's place a zero, the four's place a zero, and the eight's place a one. The following shows some examples of decimal and binary numbers.

```
15425 decimal = 10,000 + 5000 + 400 + 20 + 5
10101 binary = 16 + 0 + 4 + 0 + 1
234 decimal = 200 + 30 + 4
111 binary = 4 + 2 + 1
```

IP addresses are simply 32-bit numbers represented by dotted decimal notation. Each of the 4 bytes (32 bits) is separated at octet boundaries by a decimal. Each byte has 8 bits that represent a Base-2 number placeholder. The bit placeholders from the high order to low order (left to right) would represent the Base-2 places of 128, 64, 32, 16, 8, 4, 2, and 1.

```
Base-2 Placeholders: Value = 128 64 32 16  8  4  2  1
                     Bit     7  6  5  4  3  2  1  0
```

When you convert an IP address into binary, you must convert each octet separately. The IP address 172.16.15.2 is converted as follows.

Starting at bit 7 keep subtracting the largest value possible from the number. Any bit value that can be subtracted sets that value's bit to a 1. In the example that follows, only 128, 32, 8, and 4 can be subtracted, so only those binary bits are set to a one. So, to convert 172 (the first number of the example IP address):

```
172 decimal = 172 - 128 = 44      Bit 7 = 1
               44 - 32 = 12       Bit 5 = 1
               12 - 8 = 4         Bit 3 = 1
                4 - 4 = 0         Bit 2 = 1
```

So, 172 decimal equals 10101100 binary.

```
16 decimal = 16 - 16 = 0        Bit 4 = 1
```

And 16 decimal equals 00010000 binary.

```
15 decimal = 15 - 8  = 7        Bit 3 = 1
              7 - 4  = 3        Bit 2 = 1
              3 - 2  = 1        Bit 1 = 1
              1 - 1  = 0        Bit 0 = 1
```

And 15 decimal = 00001111 binary.

```
2 decimal = 2 - 2 = 0           Bit 1 = 1
```

And 2 decimal equals 00000010.

So, the IP address 172.16.15.2 equals the binary notation of 10101100. 00010000.00001111.00000010.

Every node on an IP network has its own unique IP address. An IP address actually has two parts:

- **The network portion.** Indicates to the host which IP subnet it is a part of.
- **The host portion.** Indicates to it what its own address is on that subnet.

It is impossible to tell what part of the address is used for the network or host without something called the *subnet mask*. A subnet mask is a 32-bit number that you use to apply a calculation to the IP address to obtain the host's network. This calculation is called a logical AND operation. A logical AND operation is a binary logic operation used by computers. Without getting into the details of binary math, the basics of the AND operation are that a 1 AND 0 = 0 and a 1 AND 1 = 1. The subnet mask is a pattern of ones and zeros you use to compare to the IP address, performing the AND operation on each bit of the IP address. This operation is illustrated in Figure 3-7. First, you must convert each octet of the IP address and subnet mask into binary. Once they are both in binary, you perform a logical AND on each bit of the IP address. The result of the operation is the network address of the IP subnet upon which the host sits.

Why is it important for the local host to know what IP subnet it is on? If you remember, with network layer protocols, not all end-to-end communication is done via the data link layer anymore. You now have routers that handle the processing of packets destined for other IP subnets. Once a host knows which local IP subnet it is on, it then knows to send any packets destined for subnets other than its own to the local router. This local router is known as the client's default gateway. In order for a node to communicate on an IP network it needs to know three things:

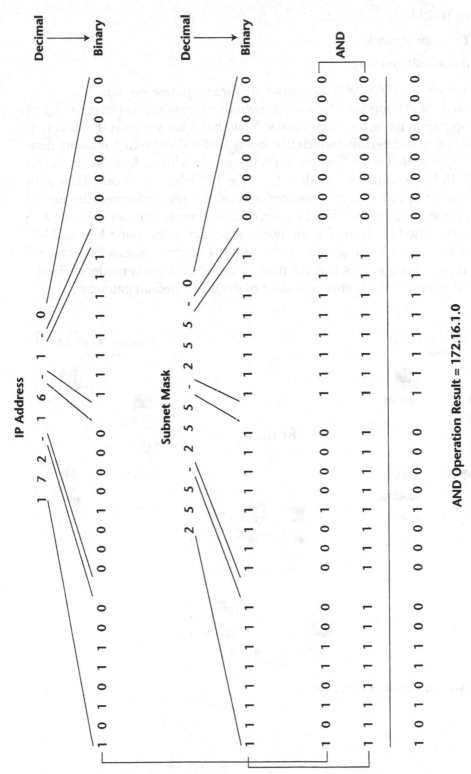

Figure 3-7   Subnet mask operation.

- Its IP address
- The subnet mask
- Its default gateway

Figure 3-8 illustrates an IP network with three separate subnets.

When a client boots up it looks at its own IP address and performs a logical AND operation using the subnet mask. Now that it knows what IP network it is on, it is able to determine which IP subnets are local and which ones are nonlocal. Suppose that node X wants to communicate with node Y. Node X is on the 172.16.1.0 network, and node Y is on the 192.168.5.0 network. They both know their respective local IP networks because they performed the logical AND operation using their IP address and subnet mask. In order for node X to determine if node Y is local or nonlocal, it performs the same logical AND operation on node Y's IP address. If the result is not the same as its own local network, the node knows that the destination IP address is nonlocal. Traffic destined to nonlocal IP networks is sent to the host's default gateway.

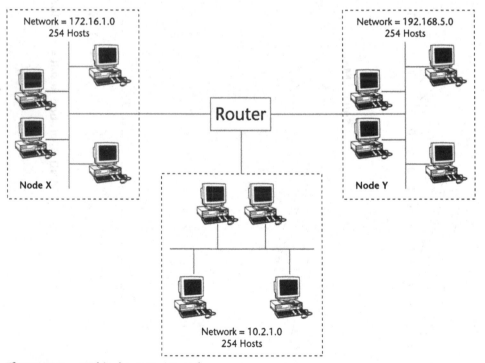

Figure 3-8 Multisubnet IP network.

TIP When you subnet a network, it is important to always use contiguous subnet masks. Contiguous means that the masks should contain either a portion of contiguous zeros or a portion of contiguous ones, but not a mixture of the two. The mask bits that determine the network portion of the address should start with the highest order bit (bit 128) and be contiguous all the way across the mask. 11100000 is an example of a contiguous mask because the entire network portion contains ones throughout. 11010000 is not a contiguous mask because a zero separates the ones in the network mask portion. It's not only a good idea to not use noncontinuous masks, but in most cases an IP stack won't even function if it contains a noncontiguous mask. I recently discovered this when troubleshooting a nonfunctioning Windows 2000 machine that had its mask incorrectly set to 255.255.255.244. 244 equals 11110100 in binary, which is noncontiguous. Due to the mask, the machine had no idea what network it was even on, and its IP stack was nonfunctioning.

Reserved Addressing

IP addresses are really just a series of 32 binary digits that make up the entire 4-byte IP address. Hosts and routers on an IP network each have their own unique IP address for packet-forwarding purposes. Within the address range of each IP network (as shown in Table 3-2), there are two 32-bit address formats that are reserved for special purposes. The first is called the "This" network address. It is a special IP address that is used to represent the network portion of the address. 172.16.1.0 is an example of a "This" address. "This" network addresses are unique in that the host portion of the address contains all zeros. An IP address of 172.16.1.0 with a subnet mask of 255.255.255.0 has all zeros in the host portion because the fourth octet has all zeros in it.

The exact opposite of an all zeros host portion would be the IP broadcast address. The IP broadcast address contains all ones in its host portion. The IP network 172.16.1.0 with a subnet mask of 255.255.255.0 would have a broadcast address of 172.16.1.255. Each IP subnet contains two reserved addresses for the "This" address and the broadcast address. Figure 3-9 shows an example of the "This" address and the broadcast address.

Due to the reservation of the "This" address and broadcast address, each IP network range loses two addresses. Table 3-2 shows some IP networks and the amount of hosts available on each subnet.

Classful Addressing

IP address ranges are categorized by class of address. The first 3 bits of the 32-bit address determine which class the address belongs to. Table 3-2 shows the bit settings and how IP addresses are classified. In the early days of the Internet,

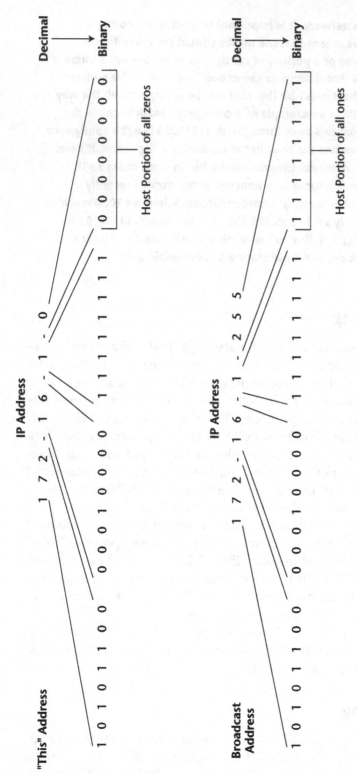

Figure 3-9 Network and broadcast address.

a company needing connectivity would request either a Class A, B, or C address, depending on the size of their network and number of connected hosts. The Internet Assigned Numbers Authority (IANA) would assign the network portion of the address, and the user would be responsible for assigning the host address within the network range.

Table 3-2   Address Classes

IP ADDRESS CLASS	FIRST OCTET	FIRST FOUR BITS OF FIRST^F OCTET	SUBNET MASK	NUMBER OF HOSTS
Class A	1–126	0000	255.0.0.0	16777214
Class B	128–191	1000	255.255.0.0	65534
Class C	192–223	1100	255.255.255.0	254
Class D	224–239	1110	Undefined	
Class E	240–254	1111	Undefined	

Address classes provide a simple method of subnet masking. Any addresses in the range of 1.0.0.0 to 126.255.255.254 have a 255.0.0.0 mask; 128.0.0.0 to 191.255.255.254, a 255.255.0.0 mask; and 192.0.0.0 to 223.255.255.254, a 255.255.255.0 mask. The predefined subnet masks are known as Class A, B, and C masks, respectively.

Sharp-eyed readers might have noticed that between the Class A and Class B ranges the 127.0.0.0 range is missing. This range is among one of the several ranges and addresses that are reserved for special purposes by the IANA. Other address ranges reserved are shown in Table 3-3.

Table 3-3   Reserved IP Address Ranges

ADDRESS	SUBNET MASK	DESCRIPTION
0.0.0.0	255.0.0.0	"This" network
10.0.0.0	255.0.0.0	Private-use networks
14.0.0.0	255.0.0.0	Public-data networks
24.0.0.0	255.0.0.0	Cable television networks
39.0.0.0	255.0.0.0	Reserved but subject to allocation
127.0.0.0	255.0.0.0	Loopback
128.0.0.0	255.255.0.0	Reserved but subject to allocation
169.254.0.0	255.255.0.0	Link local

(continued)

Table 3-3   *(continued)*

ADDRESS	SUBNET MASK	DESCRIPTION
172.16.0.0	255.255.0.0	Private-use networks
191.255.0.0	255.255.0.0	Reserved but subject to allocation
192.0.0.0	255.255.255.0	Reserved but subject to allocation
192.0.2.0	255.255.255.0	Test-Net
192.88.99.0	255.255.255.0	6 to 4 Relay Anycast
192.168.0.0	255.255.0.0	Private-use networks
198.18.0.0	255.252.0.0	Network interconnect device benchmark testing
223.255.255.0	255.255.255.0	Reserved but subject to allocation
224.0.0.0	240.0.0.0	Multicast
240.0.0.0	240.0.0.0	Reserved for future use

Of particular interest in Table 3-3 are the private address class ranges. When developing the address schemes for use on the Internet, the IANA reserved these ranges as ones that would never be routed over the public Internet. They are for use only inside of private networks. The private network addresses are useful only if you never need to connect to the Internet. Internet routers never contain routes for these addresses. If you happen to use a private address range and need Internet connectivity, you have to implement *Network Address Translation* or *NAT*. NAT is a configuration option on most routers and firewalls that allows a translation between the private address ranges and the public ranges on the Internet. A company with a 10.x.x.x internal network range configures their router or firewall to translate any internal 10.x.x.x addresses into a publicly addressable range on the Internet. With something called *PAT (Port Address Translation),* a company doesn't even require a public range near the size of their internal address range. The router or firewall uses specific source ports that are mapped to the addresses on the internal network for all traffic with destinations on the Internet. When the router receives a response, it performs a simple lookup on the port-to-address table and substitutes the correct internal address and forwards the packet.

CROSS-REFERENCE I talk more about ports in Chapters 5 and 6.

Classless Addressing

The original Internet was never architected for the size that it has grown to today. Consider the following:

- When the IANA originally assigned IP address ranges, the class ranges were not suitable for small networks. If you needed over 254 hosts, you were assigned a Class B network address that allowed for 65,534 hosts. Much of the address space allocated on the Internet was wasted.

- The second problem with the addressing was that it was not assigned in a hierarchical fashion. Class C networks such as 192.10.5.0 or 192.10.7.0 were often located on entire different backbones of the Internet, making their summarization impossible. So instead of advertising a route for 192.10.0.0 that would represent all subnets below it, separate Class C networks had to be advertised, which led to an explosion of the routing table size on the Internet.

- Then, to add to the already inefficient addressing design, Class B addresses were being depleted at an alarming rate.

Something had to be done to correct all this. The answer was *Classless Inter-Domain Routing (CIDR)*. The basis of CIDR is that instead of assigning an organization a Class B address, they are assigned a number of Class C addresses based on their needs. If the organization requires 1,000 host addresses, they are assigned four Class C networks of 254 hosts each. Routers no longer have to advertise multiple Class C networks because the multiple Class C networks are advertised using something called an aggregate prefix.

CIDR uses something called *variable length subnet masking*, or *VLSM*. VLSM gets rid of the concept of class in an IP address. No longer is an IP address defined by a class. Instead, its network and host portion are decided strictly by the subnet mask. This capability allows a Class B network to have more or less networks or hosts than the assigned Class B mask of 255.255.0.0.

For example, Figure 3-10 shows an organization with a need for five network segments, consisting of 150 to 200 hosts each. The IANA assigned this organization a Class B network of 130.10.0.0. The administrators subnetted the network into several separate Class C networks, each with 254 hosts. Because this Class B address was allocated solely to this one organization, the rest of the Class B subnet range is unusable by other organizations on the Internet.

A case like the one shown in Figure 3-10 is why classless addressing was introduced. With CIDR addressing, the same organization would be allocated five Class C addresses with a prefix range. The prefix acts like a subnet mask in defining the range of addresses within the CIDR block. The bits within the range of the prefix mask do not change, allowing the advertisement of the address range with a simple IP address and prefix. Figure 3-11 shows an example of how a summary prefix can be used to advertise a block of addresses. The prefix defines the range of common high-order bits in the CIDR block. Notice how the high-order bits 7 through 3 don't change throughout the range of addresses. This commonality of the bits can be advertised by the prefix mask.

Network Assigned a Class B Address of 130.10.0.0/255.255.0.0

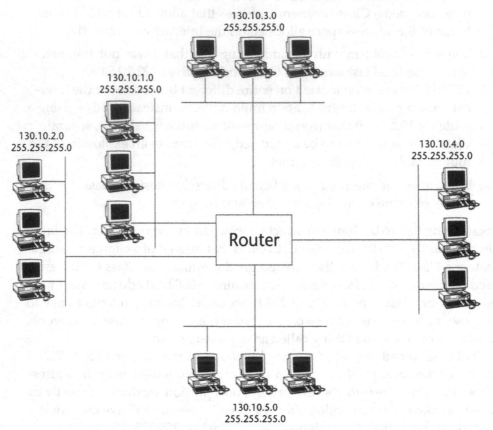

130.10.3.0
255.255.255.0

130.10.1.0
255.255.255.0

130.10.2.0
255.255.255.0

130.10.4.0
255.255.255.0

Router

130.10.5.0
255.255.255.0

Figure 3-10   Classful networks example.

Essentially, the prefix mask says that for a specific IP address, the bit range specified by the prefix mask does not change, which allows a range of addresses (that is, the CIDR block) to be advertised by one address and the prefix mask. The process of advertising ranges of subnets with a prefix mask is called *summary aggregation*. In order to advertise summary address spaces, you need a routing protocol that supports the ability to advertise summary prefixes. Once Internet service providers started moving to routing protocols supporting this feature, they began restructuring their address spaces. No longer were network subnets randomly distributed over different geographical areas without consideration for the ability to summarize them. The IANA is still, even today, in the process of fixing the addressing mess that was created before summary aggregation was available.

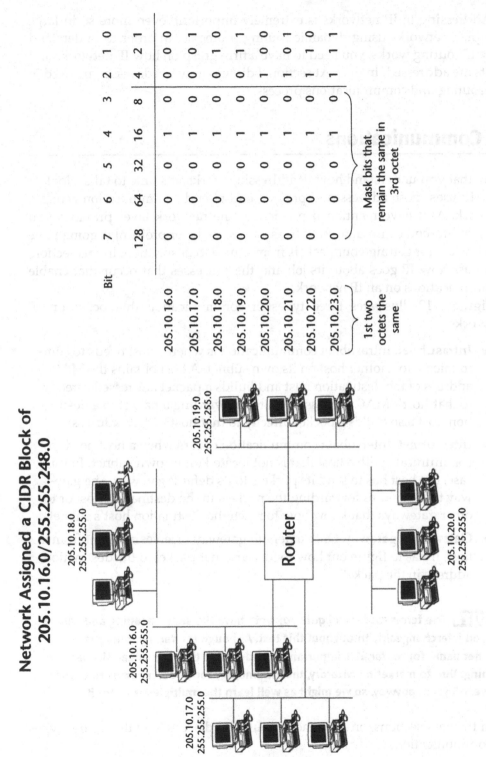

Figure 3-11   CIDR block example.

Addressing in IP networks is extremely important, even more so in large complex networks using dynamic routing protocols. In order to understand how IP routing works, you need to have a firm grasp on how IP networks and hosts are addressed. In the next section, I discuss how IP addresses are used in the routing and communications process.

IP Communications

Now that you understand how IP addressing works, it's time to take a look at how IP uses those addresses to provide end-to-end communication across a network. As I have mentioned previously, the network layer provides you with end-to-end communication. IP as a network layer protocol is going to be responsible for getting your packets from source to destination. In this section, I discuss how IP goes about its job and the processes that occur that enable communications on an IP network.

Figure 3-12 illustrates three types of communication that occur on IP networks.

- **Intrasubnet.** Intrasubnet communication is when a host needs to communicate to another host on its own subnet. A host obtains the MAC address of the destination host and builds a packet addressed directly to that host's MAC address. A router forwarding a packet to a destination host also builds a packet directly to that host's MAC address.

- **Intersubnet.** Intersubnet communication occurs when a host needs to communicate with a host that is not located on its own subnet. In this case, the host has to send its packets to its default gateway. The gateway then handles forwarding the packets to the destination host or to other gateways that know how to reach the destination host's subnet.

- **Gateway to gateway.** Once a default gateway receives a packet from a host, it has to figure out how to forward that packet to the destination address in the packet.

NOTE The terms *router* and *gateway* both have the same meaning and will be used interchangeably throughout this text. Although the term *gateway* is an older name for *router*, it is important to understand that they mean the same thing. Due to marketing wizardry, the terminology for a router seems to change every 5 years anyway, so we might as well learn the multiple terms for it.

In the next sections, on ARP and IP routing, I discuss how these three types of communications are handled.

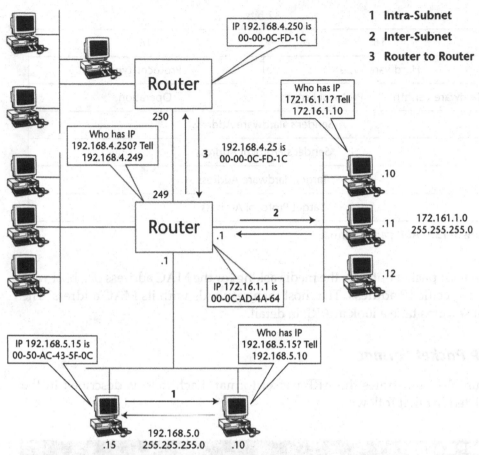

Figure 3-12   Three types of communication in IP networks.

Address Resolution Protocol (ARP)

When a host needs to communicate with another host within its own subnet (intrasubnet communication), that host needs to obtain the MAC address of the destination station. In the example earlier in the chapter explaining how NetBEUI uses the MAC address to communicate, you saw how NetBIOS utilizes a function called the NetBIOS Name Query. The NetBIOS Name Query is sent out on the local media to a multicast address that all hosts running NetBIOS listen for. When the host with the NetBIOS name in the query packet receives the frame, it responds with a NetBIOS Name Recognized packet to the host making the query. That host then caches the MAC address in a NetBIOS name table for further use. IP hosts use a similar protocol to obtain the destination MAC addresses of hosts on their own subnets. This protocol is called the *Address Resolution Protocol*, or *ARP*. ARP allows a host to send a single

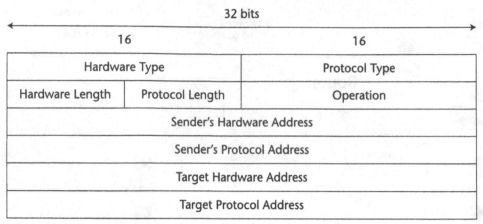

Figure 3-13   ARP packet format.

broadcast packet out onto the media asking for the MAC address of a host who has a specific IP address. That host then responds with its MAC address. The next sections take a look at ARP in detail.

ARP Packet Format

Figure 3-13 illustrates the ARP packet format. Each field is described in the bulleted list that follows.

ARP CACHES

All vendors have different ARP cache settings. For example, Windows 2000 and XP keep unused ARP cache entries for 2 minutes before timing them out and refreshing the entry. Windows 95/98 and NT keep entries in the cache for 10 minutes before they are automatically refreshed. ARP cache time-outs should be reasonably short, in the span of several minutes. For example, assume that a network administrator needs to replace a faulty NIC in a server. At minimum, the process of changing the NIC would take several minutes. Any devices that still have the ARP entry for the old NIC in their cache will have problems communicating with the device because the new NIC will have a new MAC address. Usually after several minutes the device's cache is refreshed, and it obtains the new MAC address. One particular router vendor I've come across kept its ARP cache for 3 hours. Every so often I would observe operations staff pulling their hair out as to why an icon wouldn't go green on the management station after they replaced the NIC in a device. As you might imagine, a simple NIC replacement could cause hours of downtime simply because those routers were using the old MAC address for up to 3 hours. Furthermore, this router vendor had no method of manually flushing the cache. Finally, after a lot of pressure, the vendor came up with a software patch allowing us to manually flush ARP cache entries.

- **Hardware Type.** Describes the type of hardware address.

- **Protocol Type.** Specifies the protocol address that is being resolved. For IP, the value will be 0x800.

- **Hardware Length.** Specifies the length of the hardware address. For IP, the hardware length will be the length of the MAC address, 6 bytes.

- **Protocol Length.** Specifies the length of the protocol address. For IP, it will be the length of the IP address, 4 bytes.

- **Operation.** The ARP protocol has several options, most of which are rarely used anymore. RARP stands for reverse ARP and is used by diskless workstations in order to obtain an IP address. Because the use of diskless workstations today is almost nonexistent, so is the use of RARP. InARP stands for Inverse ARP and is used to obtain an IP address given a MAC address. InARP is commonly used on Frame Relay networks. The values of these operations are as follows:

  1 ARP Request

  2 ARP Reponse

  3 RARP Request

  4 RARP Response

  5 Dynamic RARP Request

  6 Dynamic RARP Reply

  7 Dynamic RARP Error

  8 InARP Request

  9 InARP Reply

- **Sender's Hardware Address.** This is the ARP requester's hardware address in bytes.

- **Sender's Protocol Address.** This is the ARP requester's protocol address in bytes.

- **Target Hardware Address.** This is the ARP responder's protocol address in bytes. It is set to zero during an ARP request.

- **Target Protocol Address.** This is the ARP responder's protocol address in bytes. It is set to zero during an ARP request.

Figure 3-14 illustrates an example of how ARP works. The protocol trace is a simple capture of one host pinging another host on the same subnet. You can see the ARP Request in Frame 1 and the ARP Reply from the target host in Frame 2. Notice how the Target Hardware Address contains the MAC address of the responding host.

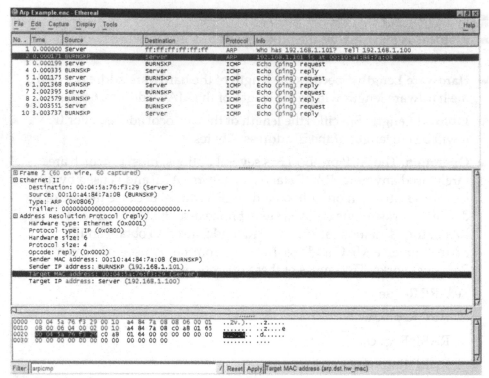

Figure 3-14   ARP trace.

After a host obtains the MAC address of another host, it saves this information in a special IP-to-MAC address mapping table. This table is called the ARP cache. The following output shows the command-line operations that generated the packets in Figure 3-14. First, you look at the ARP cache by using the command-line ARP utility with the -a option to display the cache. Notice that the ARP cache contains only a single entry for 192.168.1.1. This is the entry for our default gateway. When you ping the host at 192.168.1.101, you have to first use the ARP protocol to obtain its MAC address. When you do an `arp -a` to list the ARP cache, you can see how it has been saved. If you need to communicate with that station again, you can search your own ARP cache instead of sending an ARP Request out onto the local media.

```
C:\>arp -a

Interface: 192.168.1.100 on Interface 0x1000004
  Internet Address        Physical Address      Type
    192.168.1.1           00-04-5a-e0-d4-1f     dynamic

C:\>ping 192.168.1.101

Pinging 192.168.1.101 with 32 bytes of data:

Reply from 192.168.1.101: bytes=32 time<10ms TTL=128
```

```
Reply from 192.168.1.101: bytes=32 time<10ms TTL=128
Reply from 192.168.1.101: bytes=32 time<10ms TTL=128
Reply from 192.168.1.101: bytes=32 time<10ms TTL=128

Ping statistics for 192.168.1.101:
    Packets: Sent = 4, Received = 4, Lost = 0 (0% loss),
Approximate round-trip times in milliseconds:
    Minimum = 0ms, Maximum =  0ms, Average =  0ms

C:\>arp -a

Interface: 192.168.1.100 on Interface 0x1000004
  Internet Address      Physical Address     Type
  192.168.1.1           00-04-5a-e0-d4-1f    dynamic
  192.168.1.101         00-10-a4-84-7a-08    dynamic
```

Case Study: Troubleshooting IP Communications with ARP and PING

During the writing of this book, I was involved in several infrastructure projects where servers were being moved from one geographic location to another. Invariably, as everyone in this industry knows, very bizarre problems tend to rear their ugly heads during a move. For no apparent reason we had a server that could not communicate on the local network once it was booted up. However, by using two simple command-line tools we were able to isolate the problem to the IP stack running on the server. The detailed steps were as follows. The command-line output is in the code block following the steps.

1. **Ping the default gateway.** By pinging the default gateway we were able to ascertain whether we could in fact ping another host on the network. Because other stations were able to ping the default gateway, we knew already that the problem was most likely within the server itself, but how could we prove this?

2. **Ping our own IP address.** We should be able to ping our own IP address if our IP stack is functioning properly. In this case we couldn't, further leading us to believe the problem was within the server.

3. **Ping the loopback address.** The *loopback address* is an IP address that is internal to the IP stack of a host. Usually if the loopback address is unpingable, then there is a problem with the IP stack. Strangely enough, we could ping the loopback address, but not the host's own IP address. Something was very awry.

4. **Examine the ARP cache.** By examining the ARP cache with the arp -a command, we could see that there was an ARP entry for our default

gateway. The entry was listed as a dynamic entry, meaning that it was obtained by using the ARP protocol and an ARP response was received.

5. **Test ARP functionality.** If the ARP protocol were, in fact, obtaining the MAC address of the default gateway dynamically, then we knew without a doubt that the NIC was functioning properly, and traffic was being transmitted and received over the local network. Deleting our default gateway's MAC-to-IP mapping in the ARP table by using the arp −d option, we attempted to ping the destination address and force the ARP protocol to repopulate the cache. After deleting the entry, we pinged the default gateway. We still didn't receive a response, but the ARP cache was repopulated with the default gateway's MAC address.

```
C:\>ping 10.17.2.1

Pinging 10.17.2.1 with 32 bytes of data:

Request timed out.
Request timed out.
Request timed out.
Request timed out.

Ping statistics for 10.17.2.1:
    Packets: Sent = 4, Received = 0, Lost = 4 (100% loss),
Approximate round trip times in milli-seconds:
    Minimum = 0ms, Maximum =  0ms, Average =  0ms


-----------------------------------------------------------

C:\>ping 10.17.2.18

Pinging 10.17.2.18 with 32 bytes of data:

Request timed out.
Request timed out.
Request timed out.
Request timed out.

Ping statistics for 10.17.2.18:
    Packets: Sent = 4, Received = 0, Lost = 4 (100% loss),
Approximate round trip times in milli-seconds:
    Minimum = 0ms, Maximum =  0ms, Average =  0ms


-----------------------------------------------------------

C:\>ping 127.0.0.1

Pinging 127.0.0.1 with 32 bytes of data:

Reply from 127.0.0.1: bytes=32 time<10ms TTL=128
```

```
Reply from 127.0.0.1: bytes=32 time<10ms TTL=128
Reply from 127.0.0.1: bytes=32 time<10ms TTL=128
Reply from 127.0.0.1: bytes=32 time<10ms TTL=128

Ping statistics for 127.0.0.1:
    Packets: Sent = 4, Received = 4, Lost = 0 (0% loss),
Approximate round-trip times in milliseconds:
    Minimum = 0ms, Maximum =  0ms, Average =  0ms

------------------------------------------------------------

C:\>arp -a

Interface: 10.17.2.1 on Interface 0x1000004
  Internet Address        Physical Address        Type
  10.17.2.1               00-04-5a-e0-d4-1f       dynamic

------------------------------------------------------------

C:\>arp -d 10.17.2.1

C:\>arp -a
No ARP Entries Found

------------------------------------------------------------

C:\>ping 10.17.2.1

Pinging 10.17.2.1 with 32 bytes of data:

Request timed out.
Request timed out.
Request timed out.
Request timed out.

Ping statistics for 10.17.2.1:
    Packets: Sent = 4, Received = 0, Lost = 4 (100% loss),
Approximate round-trip times in milliseconds:
    Minimum = 0ms, Maximum =  0ms, Average =  0ms

------------------------------------------------------------

C:\>arp -a

Interface: 10.17.2.1 on Interface 0x1000004
  Internet Address        Physical Address        Type
  10.17.2.1               00-04-5a-e0-d4-1f       dynamic
```

The previous five steps provided us with enough evidence to convict the IP stack as the culprit in the problem. We determined that the ARP protocol was functioning normally, because it was sending out ARP resolution broadcasts and receiving responses. We also knew that the NIC was functioning properly because ARP was able to successfully resolve the default gateway's MAC address. For some reason though, the IP stack was not functioning. We could ping the loopback address, but not our own IP address. The IP protocol was not functioning. After reinstalling the networking drivers and stack, IP functioned normally. This incident shows a perfect example of bottom-up troubleshooting. Immediately after we realized that we couldn't ping our own IP address, we moved on down the stack to confirm that the operations there were working correctly. After we confirmed that the lower layers were functioning properly, the only layer left that the problem could be located in was the network layer.

This example illustrates how powerful a simple command-line utility can be in network troubleshooting. Whenever possible I try to utilize the most efficient tool for the job. The problem just discussed could have easily been solved by the use of a protocol analyzer, but was much better suited to quick command-line tools. As I discussed previously, you should always confirm the correct operation of all dependent layers. The network administrators in the example scenario were actually going to replace the NIC to "solve" the problem. By using quick efficient command-line tools, I was able to prove that the IP stack and not the NIC was the cause of the problem, saving valuable time that would have been wasted on a senseless hardware reconfiguration.

ARP Types

There are three types of ARP:

- The first is *regular ARP*, which is used when a station needs to simply obtain another host's MAC address.

- Another type of ARP is something called *Gratuitous ARP*. Gratuitous ARP allows a station to transmit an ARP request for its own IP address. Gratuitous ARP is used to check for duplicate IP addresses on an IP subnet. If a host, after ARPing for its own address, receives a reply from another station, it knows that another station already has been configured for the address it has. This situation is called an IP address conflict. Microsoft Windows hosts use this Gratuitous ARP technique when they boot up to check for conflicting IP address assignments.

- Another form of ARP is called *Proxy ARP*. Proxy ARP allows a host to answer an ARP request if it knows how to reach the subnet. Proxy ARP can be dangerous when implemented on routers. A host with an incorrect subnet mask could be able to communicate with hosts outside of its own subnet because a local router might be answering ARP requests for nonlocal subnets. Proxy ARP allows incorrect IP configurations to work when they normally shouldn't. Suppose that a host with an IP address of 172.16.1.10 and a subnet mask of 255.255.0.0 is on a local subnet of

172.16.1.0 with a mask of 255.255.255.0. The host thinks the network is 172.16.0.0 when it is actually 172.16.1.0. When it tries to access a host with an IP address of 172.16.2.0, it will broadcast an ARP packet to try and obtain the host's MAC address. It does this because it believes (based on the subnet mask) that the destination host is on its local subnet. If the router has Proxy ARP turned on, the router will respond to the ARP request with its MAC address. The host, thinking that the destination host has responded to its ARP request, will send packets to the router's MAC address. If the Proxy ARP configuration is ever removed from the router's subnet, clients that previously relied on it are not going to be able to access nonlocal networks anymore until their subnet mask is corrected. Cisco routers have Proxy ARP enabled by default. It is important to be aware of the situation that Proxy ARP can create in an IP network.

ARP in IP Communication

This section reviews how ARP functions in the three types of IP communications I discussed earlier in the chapter.

- In intrasubnet communication between two hosts on the same network, a host is able to build a packet addressed directly to the MAC address of that host. It compares the destination host's IP address to its own network address. If the network portion of both addresses is the same, the host sends an ARP request out onto the wire asking the host to respond with its MAC address.

- In intersubnet communication, a host compares the network portion of its own address to the destination IP address. If they are different, it knows that the subnet is not local, and it needs to forward all packets to the default gateway.

- Routers also use the ARP protocol. In router-to-router communication, a router needs to obtain the MAC address of the next-hop router in order to forward packets along in the internetwork. The router also needs to obtain the MAC address of the destination host when forwarding packets to a host. (Again, you can refer to Figure 3-12 for an illustration of the three types of communications used by ARP.)

Case Study: Incomplete ARP

Figure 3-15 presents a firewall segment consisting of a router and two Sun firewalls.

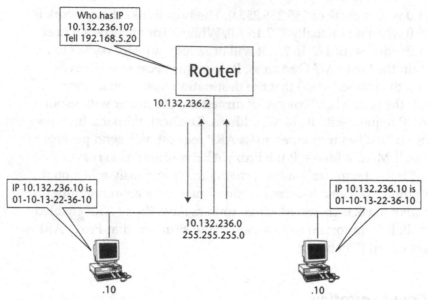

Figure 3-15   Incomplete ARP network.

Both firewalls are running what is called a *hot standby system*, allowing one firewall to assume the IP and MAC address of the other if it fails.

A team I worked with encountered a problem with this type of system once, though; we couldn't get any traffic to pass through either firewall. To troubleshoot this problem, we did the following:

1. Starting at the data link layer, we telneted into the local router console on the firewall subnet and attempted to ping the interface address of the firewall. There was no response.

2. Our next step was to move one layer lower and examine our data link connection. We did this by looking in our ARP cache to see if the router had resolved the MAC address of the firewalls IP address. What we saw was an entry for the IP address, but it was marked as incomplete.

3. This puzzled us, so we broke out our protocol analyzer and obtained the capture seen in Figure 3-16.

   Both firewalls responded to the ARP request, so we knew our Layer 2 communication was good. But once again, the ARP entry in the router stated it was incomplete. Doing our research, we found out that the incomplete entry was placed in the hardware address field of the table when the router sent out an ARP request and was still waiting for a reply. We saw on our analyzer that the reply was received, so why would the router not place the destination MAC address of the host in the table?

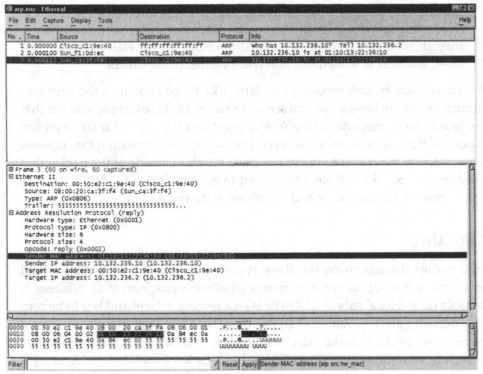

Figure 3-16   Incomplete ARP trace file.

4. Actually, after staring at the protocol decode for several minutes, we realized the answer was right in the detail of the packet. In Frames 2 and 3 we noticed that the MAC address of the firewalls was not the same MAC address being placed into the Sender MAC Address field of the ARP packet. What was being placed there was the MAC address of 01-10-13-22-36-10. Looking at the first octet, we realized why the router might have a problem with this address. If you recall back in Figure 3-3 earlier in the chapter, I showed what bits of an Ethernet address were reserved for indicating whether the MAC address is a multicast or broadcast. The first octet of this MAC address, 01, indicates that it is a multicast address. Doing a little more research, my team found something very interesting in *RFC 1812: Requirements for IP Version 4 Routers*. It states in Section 3.3.2, "A router MUST not believe any ARP reply that claims that the Link Layer address of another host or router is a broadcast or multicast address."

5. Seeing that the returned address was a multicast address, we now knew why our router was ignoring the ARP Reply. Looking further into the packet detail, we figured out why the firewalls were responding with this address. If you look at the IP address in the sender's protocol address and compare it to the Sender's MAC address, you see that the

firewall was simply copying the 32-bit IP address into the MAC address field and putting a 01 in the first octet. After we contacted the vendor, they showed us a method of manually setting the firewall's virtual MAC address to something that wasn't a multicast packet.

When you are troubleshooting problems like those shown in the previous example, always believe what you see on the wire. In this example you see that there was in fact a response to the ARP request, but the router for some reason did not use the response. When you see a router or a host ignoring the contents of a packet, you need to ask yourself: Is there anything inside of the packet that would cause a problem? Here, I found out that, based on RFC 1812, there was a valid reason why the router had a problem with the ARP reply.

IP Routing

In the earlier discussion on the three types of IP communications, I talked about how a host or router determines whether a destination IP address is reachable on the local subnet (ARP) or is on a remote subnet and has to be sent to the default gateway. Rather than perform the AND operation every time a host or router needs to make a decision about a route location, it creates a table in which to store this information. This table is called a *routing table*. *Routing* is defined as moving a packet from a source to a destination. How each host and router performs this function is the subject of this section.

The Routing Table

Every IP host or router has a routing table. When it needs to forward a packet to a destination, it consults the routing table to see if information already exists as to how the packet should be routed. By way of illustration, I want to take a look at a routing table from a very common source, the Windows 2000 operating system.

Figure 3-17 shows the results of the `route print` command on a Windows 2000 desktop.

Shown in the figure is the routing table kept in memory by the TCP/IP stack. Whenever it needs to forward a packet, it looks at this table. The table has several sections.

- The first section shows the *interface list* on the local computer. All interfaces, logical and physical, are listed.

- The second section contains the *active routes* list. The active routes section has six entries:

```
C:\>route print

=================================================================
Interface List
0x1 ..................................... MS TCP Loopback interface
0x2 ...44 45 53 54 42 00 ...... NOC Extranet Access Adapter
0x1000004 ...00  04  5a  76  f3  29 ...... Linksys LNE100TX(v5) Fast Ethernet Adapter
  NDIS5 Driver

=================================================================

=================================================================
Active Routes:
Network Destination        Netmask          Gateway        Interface    Metric
        0.0.0.0            0.0.0.0        192.168.1.1    192.168.1.100      1
      127.0.0.0          255.0.0.0          127.0.0.1      127.0.0.1        1
    192.168.1.0      255.255.255.0    192.168.1.100    192.168.1.100      1
    192.168.1.100  255.255.255.255        127.0.0.1      127.0.0.1        1
    192.168.1.255  255.255.255.255    192.168.1.100    192.168.1.100      1
      224.0.0.0          224.0.0.0      192.168.1.100    192.168.1.100      1
255.255.255.255  255.255.255.255    192.168.1.100              2          1
Default Gateway:           192.168.1.1

=================================================================

Persistent Routes:
None
C:\>
```

Figure 3-17   Windows 2000 routing table.

- **Network Destination.** This is the destination IP address or network that packets need to be sent to. It can contain two types of routes, host routes or network routes. A host route has a mask of 255.255.255.255. A network route has a mask with some portion of the host bits set to zero. The destination can also be a default destination where packets are sent when the routing table does not contain any more information as to where they should be sent. A default route has a network destination address of 0.0.0.0 and a network mask of 0.0.0.0.

- **Network Mask.** The network mask performs the function of identifying what portion of the address is the network portion and what portion is the host portion.

- **Gateway.** The gateway is the actual destination of where the packets are forwarded to reach the network destination.

- **Interface.** The interface is the local interface on the host's computer that is be used to forward the packet out to the gateway address.

- **Metric.** The metric is used for setting prioritizing routes. A routing table may consist of two gateways for a single network destination. The metric is used to indicate a preference of which gateway address is used. A higher metric number indicates a lower preference for the gateway.

- **Default Gateway.** The default gateway is the address of the destination where all packets are forwarded when there is no other information contained in the route table to indicate how to forward them.

- The third section shows something called *persistent routes*. These are manual route entries added by a user. They are called *persistent* because they are saved in the registry so that they are available in the future even if the computer is rebooted.

I want to take a look at seven route entries individually.

NETWORK DESTINATION	NETMASK	GATEWAY	INTERFACE	METRIC
0.0.0.0	0.0.0.0	192.168.1.1	192.168.1.100	1

This first entry is the default route entry. All default route entries have a network destination and subnet mask of all zeros. When the host does not have specific information for a route, it sends the packet to the default gateway, which in this entry is 192.168.1.1. When you enter a default gateway address in your TCP/IP configuration, this routing entry is always created.

NETWORK DESTINATION	NETMASK	GATEWAY	INTERFACE	METRIC
127.0.0.0	255.0.0.0	127.0.0.1	127.0.0.1	1

This second entry is the route for the loopback network. All packets sent to any IP address in the loopback address range are treated as incoming packets to the IP stack. Pinging the loopback gateway 127.0.0.1 is good method of determining that the IP stack is functioning properly.

NETWORK DESTINATION	NETMASK	GATEWAY	INTERFACE	METRIC
192.168.1.0	255.255.255.0	192.168.1.100	192.168.1.100	1

If you recall the previous discussion about the "This" network address, you might have noticed immediately that this third entry is the route entry for it. This routing entry tells the IP stack that the network destination of 192.168.1.0

is accessible locally through its own interface of 192.168.1.100. Any route entry where the gateway and the interface are the same indicates that the network destination is locally accessible. When the IP stack receives a packet with a destination on network 192.168.1.0, it ARPs for the MAC address of the host instead of sending it to its default gateway.

NETWORK DESTINATION	NETMASK	GATEWAY	INTERFACE	METRIC
192.168.1.100	255.255.255.255	127.0.0.1	127.0.0.1	1

This fourth entry is called a *host route*. All host routes have a subnet mask of all ones (255.255.255.255). Because the mask has all ones, you know that the network destination represents a host address. You also know that this address is assigned to a connection local to the IP stack because its gateway and interface are set to the IP loopback address.

NETWORK DESTINATION	NETMASK	GATEWAY	INTERFACE	METRIC
192.168.1.255	255.255.255.255	192.168.1.100	192.168.1.100	1

The routing table also contains an entry for the IP broadcast address or the all ones address. This route entry tells us that the broadcast address is reachable locally because the gateway and interface entries are the same. When an application needs to send an IP packet to all IP hosts on the local subnet, it forwards the packet with the IP broadcast address, in this case 192.168.1.255, onto the local subnet. At the data link layer, ARP is not utilized because the packet's MAC address is the data link broadcast address of FF-FF-FF-FF-FF-FF.

NETWORK DESTINATION	NETMASK	GATEWAY	INTERFACE	METRIC
224.0.0.0	224.0.0.0	192.168.1.100	192.168.1.100	1

This network destination is the IP multicast network address range. It is contained in the routing table in the event that an application will use this range. There are many uses for the multicast address range, including routing protocols, multimedia, and so on. Table 3-4 lists several reserved multicast addresses.

NETWORK DESTINATION	NETMASK	GATEWAY	INTERFACE	METRIC
255.255.255.255	255.255.255.255	192.168.1.100	2	1

The last entry in this routing table is called a *black hole route*. It indicates that our interface 2 is down and any traffic destined for it should be discarded.

Table 3-4   Reserved IP Multicast Addresses

ADDRESS	DESCRIPTION
224.0.0.1	All Systems on this subnet
224.0.0.2	All Routers on this subnet
224.0.0.5	OSPFIGP all routers
224.0.0.6	OSPFIGP designated routers
224.0.0.9	RIP2 routers
224.0.0.10	IGRP routers
224.0.0.22	IGMP
224.0.0.102	HSRP
224.0.1.24	microsoft-ds

Whether you are troubleshooting the routing table of a host or a router, the table entries of both are essentially the same. Once you understand how a host uses routing information for its own uses in reaching destination networks, you can understand how a router uses the same information. Routing is a complex subject requiring many more pages than are available in this text to explain. However, the basics of routing are essentially the same. As with IP addressing, starting small and building on top of the basics is a guaranteed model for success in network troubleshooting knowledge and techniques.

Route Types

There are several types of route entries. Where the information about the route originated determines what kind of route type it is. The following are different ways a route could be originated:

- **Static.** Static routes are manual routes added by a network administrator. They are usually used in circumstances where a routing protocol cannot provide information about specific routes.

- **Connected.** Connected routes are routes that are known because the host or router has a direct connection to the network. A network card with an IP address of 192.168.1.0 and mask of 255.255.255.0 is an example of a connected route, the route being a NIC connection directly to the 192.168.1.0 network.

- **Default.** Default routes are used when there is not enough information in the routing table to know specifically where a packet should be forwarded. In the case of a table not having any specific route entries for a network, packets are forwarded to the default gateway. The default gateway is also called the *gateway of last resort* because it is sometimes truly the last resort routing decision for processing a packet.

- **Advertised.** In large networks (like the Internet) where it is not feasible to statically configure a route entry for every network in every router, a method of obtaining routing information through listening to advertisements is used. For this to work, routers must run what is called a routing protocol. *Routing protocols* advertise information from one router to another so that every router on a network knows how to forward packets destined to other networks. In Chapter 1, I showed a very simple example of how a routing protocol works and briefly discussed its function. Each router on a network first gathers its own information as it's connected and statically configured routes. It then advertises to other routers on the network the information that it knows about. Those routers in turn create routing entries in their route tables to point to that router as the next-hop gateway to reach those networks. Figure 3-18 illustrates how this works.

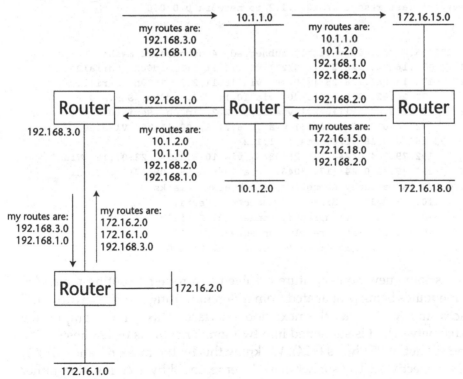

Figure 3-18   Routing protocol example.

Router Routing Tables

Unlike nodes such as desktop computers or servers, a router has to handle processing and forwarding traffic on many more nodes than just itself. A router also has more interfaces. Depending on the type of network, a router may have Ethernet, Token Ring, serial interfaces, or even ATM (Asynchronous Transfer Mode) connections. Due to the nature of its job, a router's route table will be slightly more complex than that of a Windows 2000 workstation. The following Telnet output illustrates a routing table from a Cisco MSFC (Multi-layer Switch Feature Card) and the network diagram of the route locations.

```
Router_1#sho ip route
Codes: C - connected, S - static, I - IGRP, R - RIP, M - mobile, B - BGP
       D - EIGRP, EX - EIGRP external, O - OSPF, IA - OSPF inter area
       N1 - OSPF NSSA external type 1, N2 - OSPF NSSA external type 2
       E1 - OSPF external type 1, E2 - OSPF external type 2, E - EGP
       i - IS-IS, L1 - IS-IS level-1, L2 - IS-IS level-2, ia - IS-IS
inter area
       * - candidate default, U - per-user static route, o - ODR
       P - periodic downloaded static route

Gateway of last resort is 10.1.1.2 to network 0.0.0.0


       172.16.0.0/16 is variably subnetted, 4 subnets, 2 masks
O E2    172.16.240.128/25 [110/20] via 10.11.2.2, 1d00h, Serial0
O E2    172.16.243.128/25 [110/20] via 10.11.2.2, 1d00h, Serial0
O E2    172.16.227.0/24 [110/20] via 10.11.2.2, 1d00h, Serial0
O E2    10.11.2.4/30 [110/20] via 10.11.2.2, 1d00h, Serial0
O E1    172.16.0.0/16 [110/13] via 10.6.21.2, 00:11:38, Vlan100
S    192.168.0.0/16 [1/0] via 10.1.1.2
D EX    192.79.244.0/24 [170/2690816] via 10.6.3.58, 22:07:16, Vlan1
D EX    192.79.32.0/24 [170/30464] via 10.6.3.58, 08:37:37, Vlan1
10.0.0.0/8 is variably subnetted, 4 subnets, 1 masks
C       10.6.3.0/32 is directly connected, Serial1
C       10.11.2.0/32 is directly connected, Serial0
C       10.1.1.0/24 is directly connected, Vlan10
C       10.6.21.0/24 is directly connected, Vlan100
```

There is some new nomenclature involved in a router's routing table. You now have routes being propagated from different routing protocols with serial interfaces and VLANs as the next hop interfaces. Take, for example, the 172.16.0.0 network. It is subnetted into two smaller subnets of 128 hosts (/25) and one subnet of 254 hosts (/24). We know this by the mask notation of /25 and /24 respectively. The subnet mask is represented by a /n notation rather than a dotted decimal mask. The subnet mask is now indicated by how many bits are in the network portion of the address. For example, the 10.11.2.4 network has a mask notation of /30. This means that 30 bits of subnet masking are being used. This leaves only two bits out of 32 for the host portion. Two host bits allows us only four bit combinations: 00,01,10, and 11. Because 00 is reserved for the network ID and 11 is reserved for the broadcast address, you have only two addresses left for use by hosts. Table 3-5 shows the conversion between the dotted decimal mask notation and the /n notation. A subnet mask of 255.255.255.0 can also be represented as /24 because the first three octets of the mask are being used as the network portion. Because each octet is 8 bits, 8 times 3 equals 24, hence 24 bits. The slash (/) notation indicates how many bits are in the network portion.

Table 3-5   Subnet Mask Notation Conversions*

DECIMAL MASK NOTATION	/N MASK NOTATION	NETWORK/HOST BITS
255.0.0.0	/8	nnnnnnnn.hhhhhhhh.hhhhhhhh.hhhhhhhh
255.128.0.0	/9	nnnnnnnn.nhhhhhhh.hhhhhhhh.hhhhhhhh
255.192.0.0	/10	nnnnnnnn.nnhhhhhh.hhhhhhhh.hhhhhhhh
255.224.0.0	/11	nnnnnnnn.nnnhhhhh.hhhhhhhh.hhhhhhhh
255.240.0.0	/12	nnnnnnnn.nnnnhhhh.hhhhhhhh.hhhhhhhh
255.248.0.0	/13	nnnnnnnn.nnnnnhhh.hhhhhhhh.hhhhhhhh
255.252.0.0	/14	nnnnnnnn.nnnnnnhh.hhhhhhhh.hhhhhhhh
255.254.0.0	/15	nnnnnnnn.nnnnnnnh.hhhhhhhh.hhhhhhhh
255.255.0.0	/16	nnnnnnnn.nnnnnnnn.hhhhhhhh.hhhhhhhh
255.255.128.0	/17	nnnnnnnn.nnnnnnnn.nhhhhhhh.hhhhhhhh
255.255.192.0	/18	nnnnnnnn.nnnnnnnn.nnhhhhhh.hhhhhhhh
255.255.224.0	/19	nnnnnnnn.nnnnnnnn.nnnhhhhh.hhhhhhhh
255.255.240.0	/20	nnnnnnnn.nnnnnnnn.nnnnhhhh.hhhhhhhh
255.255.248.0	/21	nnnnnnnn.nnnnnnnn.nnnnnhhh.hhhhhhhh

(continued)

Table 3-5   *(continued)*

DECIMAL MASK NOTATION	/N MASK NOTATION	NETWORK/HOST BITS
255.255.252.0	/22	nnnnnnnn.nnnnnnnn. nnnnnnhh.hhhhhhhh
255.255.254.0	/23	nnnnnnnn.nnnnnnnn. nnnnnnnh.hhhhhhhh
255.255.255.0	/24	nnnnnnnn.nnnnnnnn. nnnnnnnn.hhhhhhhh
255.255.255.128	/25	nnnnnnnn.nnnnnnnn. nnnnnnnn.nhhhhhhh
255.255.255.192	/26	nnnnnnnn.nnnnnnnn. nnnnnnnn.nnhhhhhh
255.255.255.224	/27	nnnnnnnn.nnnnnnnn. nnnnnnnn.nnnhhhhh
255.255.255.240	/28	nnnnnnnn.nnnnnnnn. nnnnnnnn.nnnnhhhh
255.255.255.248	/29	nnnnnnnn.nnnnnnnn. nnnnnnnn.nnnnnhhh
255.255.255.252	/30	nnnnnnnn.nnnnnnnn. nnnnnnnn.nnnnnnhh
255.255.255.254	/31	Illegal subnet mask
255.255.255.255	/32	nnnnnnnn.nnnnnnnn. nnnnnnnn.nnnnnnnn

*n = network portion, h = host portion

The Forwarding Process

Figure 3-19 describes the forwarding process a router goes through when it receives a packet. The following are the questions a router must ask itself about how to route an IP packet it has received. These questions make up the routing decision process.

- Is the destination a locally attached IP address?
- Is the destination on a locally connected network?
- Is the destination on a nonlocal network?
- Is there a default route?

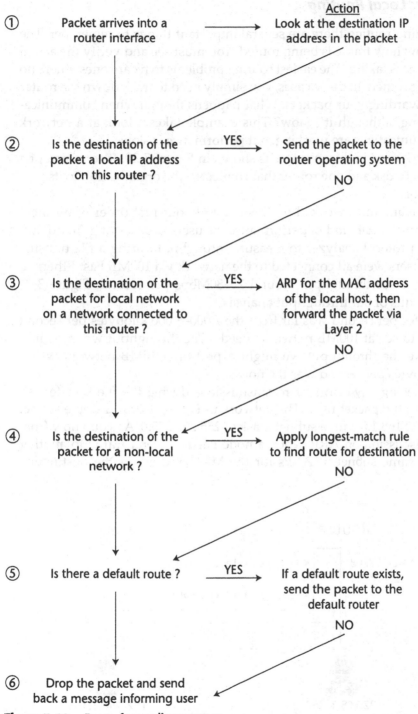

Action

① Packet arrives into a router interface ⟶ Look at the destination IP address in the packet

② Is the destination of the packet a local IP address on this router ? — YES ⟶ Send the packet to the router operating system

NO

③ Is the destination of the packet for local network on a network connected to this router ? — YES ⟶ ARP for the MAC address of the local host, then forward the packet via Layer 2

NO

④ Is the destination of the packet for a non-local network ? — YES ⟶ Apply longest-match rule to find route for destination

NO

⑤ Is there a default route ? — YES ⟶ If a default route exists, send the packet to the default router

NO

⑥ Drop the packet and send back a message informing user

Figure 3-19   Route forwarding process.

Case Study: Local Routing

When analyzing routing there are several important things to remember. The first is to know how traffic is being routed. You must see and verify the actual path that traffic is taking. The easiest routing problems to fix are ones where no traffic is being routed. In those cases, you simply need to track down the router that isn't forwarding your packets. What happens though when communication is working, although it's slow? This example takes a look at a network where communications are working, but performance is slow.

The network used in this example is shown in Figure 3-20. It consisted of a flat Layer 2 network and one router that connected the organization to its parent corporation.

When my team and I worked on this network, our first order of business was to determine what kind of performance the users were getting. To do this, we used our protocol analyzer to measure throughput during a file transfer. Because the users were all connected to the network via 100MB Fast Ethernet, we expected to see throughput around 70–80Mbps per second. Figure 3-21 shows the results of our throughput analysis.

743 kilobytes per second was far from the 7,000–8,000 kilobytes per second we expected to see at 100MB network speeds. The throughput we measured was more like the throughput we might expect on a 10MB network where 700–800 kilobytes per second was the norm.

After not seeing any errors or retransmissions during the file transfer, we started tracing the packet flow. The network in Figure 3-20 is a single subnet network of 192.168.1.0 with a subnet mask of 255.255.255.0. As you know from the earlier discussion on ARP, when a node needs to send traffic to another node on the same subnet, it ARPs for the MAC address of the destination

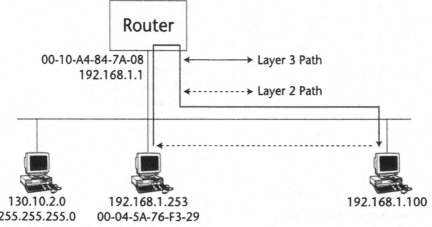

Figure 3-20 Sample network.

THROUGHPUT EXPECTATIONS

How do you determine what kind of throughput to expect? The best way to judge is to use the lowest common denominator, the media. Between any two endpoints the lowest link speed is going to determine your maximum throughput. Here's the math for a 10-Mb network:

10MB is equal to 10 million bits per second. That's 10,000,000 bits that can be transferred across the media in a single second. Dividing that by 8 bits, you get the maximum bytes per second (10,000,000 / 8) = 1,250,000 bytes per second or 12.5 KB/sec or about 1.2 MB/sec. Due to several reasons that I discuss in Chapter 6, you never get the maximum throughput, so the maximum is really the maximum theoretical throughput. However, you should expect to receive at least 70 percent of the maximum if not more. 70 percent of 12.5 KB/sec is roughly 875KB/sec. On a T1 link of 1,536 bits per second you should be getting at least 134 KB/second. By analyzing throughput over different media speeds you can get a rough idea of what is normal for your network.

node. Once it receives the ARP response, it builds a packet directly to that station's MAC address (and IP address in the network layer). In this case, when we looked at the ARP cache for the 192.168.1.253 node, we didn't see an entry for 192.168.1.100. How then could it be communicating with it if it didn't have an IP to MAC address resolution?

When tracing the packet flow in a routed network, it is important to look at both the data link layer and the network layer at the same time, so on our analyzer we activated columns for the network layer address and also the physical layer address (that is, the MAC address). When we looked at the MAC address that the source station was communicating with, we found out it wasn't the destination node's MAC address but that of the router. It then dawned on us what was happening. 192.168.1.253 was sending all of its traffic through the router instead of ARPing and using the Layer 2 path to 192.168.1.100. Figure 3-22 illustrates the packet flow seen on the analyzer.

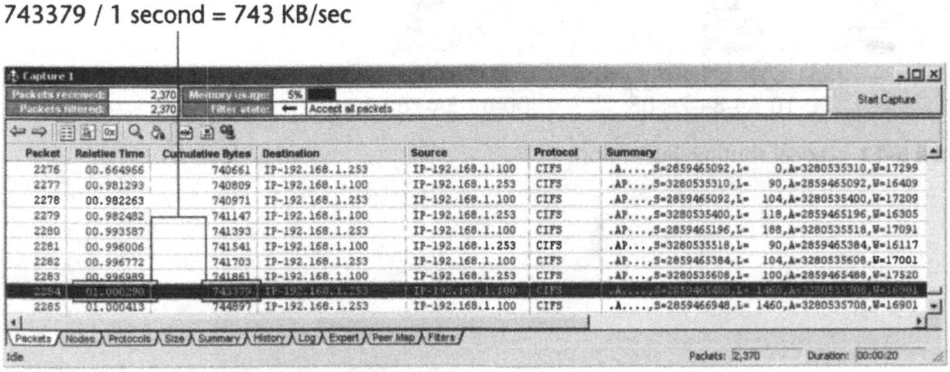

743379 / 1 second = 743 KB/sec

Figure 3-21 File transfer throughput.

If you look at the packet flow, you will notice that 192.168.1.253 is sending its packets to the router, while 192.168.1.100 is sending them directly to the MAC address of 192.168.1.253. Think back to the earlier discussion on IP addressing and ask yourself, "What would cause this type of anomaly?" If you guessed an incorrect subnet mask, you are right. Further investigation yielded the information that the 192.168.1.253 node had an incorrect subnet mask of 255.255.255.252 instead of 255.255.255.0. When it performed the logical AND operation on the destination address, it determined that 192.168.1.100 was on a nonlocal network and therefore sent its packets to the default router, in this case 192.168.1.1. 192.168.1.100 had a correct subnet mask, so when it performed its logical AND operation, it determined 192.168.1.253 was on the same local network and, therefore, ARPed for its MAC addresses. The degradation of performance was due to the router having only a 10MB interface rather than a 100MB interface on the local network. All communication through it was limited to 10MB. After correcting the subnet mask on the node, we reanalyzed, and suddenly throughput was back into the normal range.

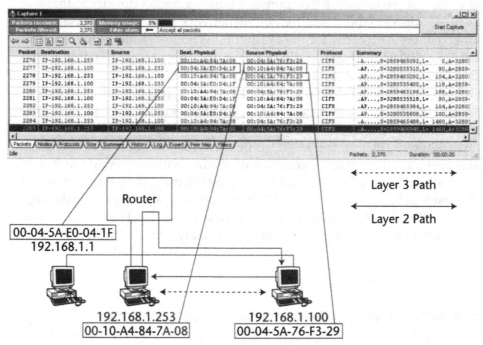

Figure 3-22 Local routing illustration.

IP Packet Format

I began my discussion of the Internet Protocol with IP addressing and the communications process. With the basics of IP out of the way, I can now move into the internals of the protocol and discuss its packet formats and fields. IP uses 14 separate fields in the packet to do its job. The fields fall into three basic categories. Header management fields handle the packet structure, version, data length, and protection of the IP header. Packet flow fields, such as Type of Service, Fragmentation, and Time to Live, handle the end-to-end delivery of packets and problems with their transfer. Multiplexing is provided by the IP protocol field, telling IP where to deliver the data it's carrying. IP also provides for several options discussed later. A detailed description of the fields follows.

Version

This field specifies the current version of the IP protocol. Unless you are using very outdated networking equipment or doing testing with IP version 6, you will almost always see this set to 4.

Header Length

The header length field contains the number of 32-bit words in the header. A word is simply a grouping of bits, in this case 32 bits. The IP header length is normally 20 bytes, which in the header length field would read 5 because the header is made up of five 32-bit words (32 bits = 4 bytes, 5 × 4 = 20 bytes). The only time the length of the IP header would change is when IP options are used. IP options are rarely used in today's networks; furthermore, many firewalls and routers disallow their use for security reasons.

Type of Service

The type of service (TOS) field allows routers to make routing decisions on the type of service a sender would like to receive. The type of service field is actually an 8-bit field divided into a precedence field and a type of service field.

■■ The *precedence bits* let a router determine how to handle the frame while it is being queued in a router's buffer for forwarding. Depending on the value of the precedence field, a router can select certain packets to be forwarded before other packets. The precedence bit values (bits 0–2) are as follows:

  ■ 000—Routine

  ■ 001—Priority

  ■ 010—Immediate

- 011—Flash
- 100—Flash override
- 101—CRITIC/ECP
- 110—Internetwork control
- 111—Network control

- The *type of service field* lets a router make a decision on routing based on the values of the field. The field values are as follows:

  - Bit 4—Delay
  - Bit 5—Throughput
  - Bit 5—Reliability
  - Bit 6—Cost

It is rare to see either the precedence or the TOS bits set in packets today. TOS and precedence bits were designed for use in a time where bandwidth and processing power was at a premium. Your network won't be affected by them unless you explicitly configure a router to check for the presence of these

---

DIFFERENTIATED SERVICES

TOS bits are now being used for what is called Differentiated Services. DiffServ, as it's called, renames and reallocates the usage of the TOS bits into DiffServ traffic classifications. The following is a decode of the new DiffServ bit classification:

```
Differentiated Services Field:0x00 DSCP 0x00: Default; ECN: 0x00
    0000 00.. = Differentiated Services Codepoint: Default (0x00)
    .... ..0. = ECN-Capable Transport (ECT): 0
    .... ...0 = ECN-CE: 0
```

Bits 7 to 2 are known as the DS Codepoint, which indicates what is called the per hop behavior, or PHB. The PHB indicates how packets are handled at each router hop. The following DS Codepoints are defined:

- ◆ Relative Priority Marking
- ◆ Service Marking
- ◆ Label Switching
- ◆ Integrated Services/Resource Reservation
- ◆ Protocol
- ◆ Static per-Hop Classification

Bits 1 and 0 are the Explicit Congestion Notification indicators. Bit 1 indicates if the node is capable of setting the Congestion Indication bit. Bit 0 is set when a router experiences congestion.

bits being set. In most cases, if you see they are set, you can safely ignore it unless you know that type of service routing is implemented on the network.

Datagram Length

The datagram length is the entire length of the IP datagram, including the data. IP has a maximum datagram length of 65,535 bytes, although it is rare to see a packet that big on the network. IP queries the data link layer as to the maximum data size it can carry and adjusts its sizes accordingly. For example, the maximum length you typically see on this field for Ethernet is 1,500 bytes.

Fragment ID

The fragment ID is used when an IP datagram is too large for the outgoing Layer 2 link and needs to be fragmented into smaller packets to be transmitted. A single large IP datagram is actually fragmented into several smaller IP datagrams, each containing its own fragment ID. The receiving host then assembles all the fragments and uses the fragment ID fields to piece back together the fragments into the original IP datagram. If you see fragmentation occurring on your networks, it is probably a good idea to investigate why. The fragmentation process can severely tax router processors and add to the time it takes to send and receive data.

CROSS-REFERENCE In Chapter 4, I discuss how routers can handle a frame that is too large for the outgoing media.

Fragmentation Flags

The fragmentation flags field indicates whether an IP datagram is a full datagram or just a fragment of a larger one. The bit values for this field are as follows:

- Bit 0—Reserved
- Bit 1—1=Don't Fragment, 0=May Fragment
- Bit 2—1=More Fragments, 0=Last Fragment

Fragment Offset

The fragment offset specifies the location of the individual fragment within the whole larger IP datagram. For example, a 1,556-byte IP datagram being fragmented into two smaller IP datagrams would have an offset first of zero as it sends the first 1,500 bytes (the maximum IP datagram on Ethernet). The second 56 bytes would be sent with a fragment offset of 185. Why 185, you might ask, when it's sending only another 56 bytes? The way the fragment offset works is that it simply orders the fragments with offsets that cover the entire maximum size. The fragment offset is in bits, so $185 \times 8 = 1,480$ bytes. Because the IP header is 20 bytes itself, you need to subtract that from the total data size it can carry, which would be $1500 - 20 = 1,480$ bytes.

Time to Live

The time to live field, also called the TTL field, serves two purposes.

- Its first purpose is to provide a countdown timer for IP fragment reassembly. When a host receives the first fragment of series of datagrams, it starts a countdown timer based on the TTL value. If all fragments of an IP datagram have not been received by the expiration of the TTL timer, the fragments are discarded. The sending host then has to retransmit the data.

- The second purpose of the TTL field is to act as a mechanism that ensures IP datagrams are not endlessly forwarded back and forth around a network. Sometimes during a routing problem, bad routing information is propagated causing packets to endlessly loop around a network. This TTL loop-prevention mechanism works by having hosts send each datagram with a starting value in the TTL field. When a router forwards a frame, it decrements the value in the TTL field. When a packet's TTL field value reaches zero, a router discards the frame. Depending on the operation system, the starting TTL value may be different. Common starting values include 255, 128, 84, and 60. When looking at the TTL field, this difference in starting value is important because you never know what the starting value was that the host was using. A TTL value of 126 could mean that a packet passed through two routers if the starting TTL was 128, or 129 routers if the starting TTL was 255.

  When troubleshooting IP connectivity problems, it is always important to validate the TTL field value with the number of routers in the infrastructure path. For example, if you know that your starting TTL is 128 and your network has only seven routers, a packet with a TTL of 101 would indicate something is amiss.

Protocol

The protocol field contains the protocol ID of the upper-layer protocol from which the data originated and to what protocol it needs to be sent. Common values for this field are UDP, TCP, and ICMP.

Header Checksum

The header checksum protects the 20-byte IP header from corruption. It does not calculate the checksum over any of the data because that is covered by the Layer 2 CRC. A router discards any packets with an invalid IP checksum. The header checksum is recalculated by routers when they forward the datagram to the next-hop address. Recalculation is needed because the TTL field is decremented.

Source IP Address

This is the 32-bit IP address of the source station.

Destination IP Address

This is the 32-bit IP address of the destination station.

Options

IP datagrams can be sent with several options enabled. I don't go into them here because their descriptions are listed in RFC 1122. They are rarely used anymore because most routers and firewalls disallow them. Not all hosts and routers even support them. The options that are currently defined are as follows:

- Security and handling restrictions
- Record route
- Timestamp
- Loose source routing
- Strict source routing

Data

The last of the fields is the data field, which is the data that the IP packet is carrying. The Layer 2 protocol determines how much data is contained in this field. On Ethernet, you usually see a maximum of 1,480 bytes, on Token Ring and FDDI networks, over 4,000 bytes. The data field doesn't always contain user data. Remember, there are four more layers of the OSI model that the IP layer has to transfer data for. The data field will contain other protocol headers such as UDP, TCP, ICMP, NetBIOS, and more.

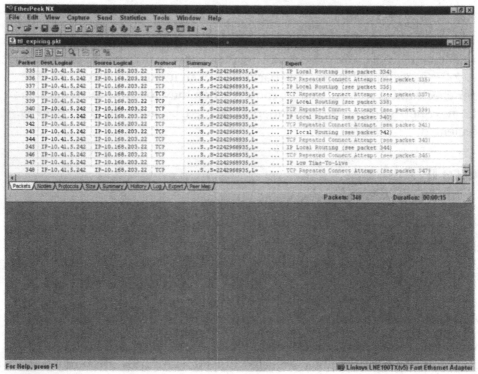

Figure 3-23 Expert mode analysis of TTL problem.

Case Study: TTL Expiring

Now that you have some knowledge of the IP packet format, I want to use that knowledge to start solving some real problems. The following problem occurred when users in the remote New York office couldn't send print jobs to a printer located in the corporate office in Philadelphia.

We knew that the users' print jobs in New York were spooled to a local print server on-site in their own building. From there the print server would handle sending the jobs to the printer in Philadelphia. We set up a capture filter between the IP address of the print server and the IP address of the printer and watched when users attempted to print. Figure 3-23 shows what we saw.

This is where the analyzer's expert mode comes in handy. Even though at this point in the book I haven't talked about TCP, it's pretty obvious by the symptom "TCP Repeated Connect Attempt" in the figure that something wasn't working right. You can also see the symptom "IP Local Routing." With these two symptoms, we had a pretty good idea of what was happening. There is also another symptom displayed in Frame 347 called "IP Low Time-To-Live." On seeing that symptom, we then knew immediately what was happening. The packets were bouncing back and forth between two routers until the TTL value reached zero and the packets were discarded. The cause of the problem was a bad route entry in one of the routers, causing it to forward all packets for that subnet back to the originating router. With the expert mode it was relatively easy to spot the problem. But what if you didn't have an expert mode? How would you go about analyzing the problem?

At first look, the analyzer's capture buffer contained over 350 packets. Since we already knew the users couldn't print, we knew that the packets probably weren't making it to the printer, although the summary display made it look as though hundreds of packets were being sent to the printer, and it was the printer that wasn't responding. Luckily, in this case, we had placed our analyzer between the two routers that connect the WAN locations.

Because the problem was an IP problem, our next step was to trace the path of a single IP datagram as it came out of the remote office router and went into the corporate office router. We created a pattern match filter on the IP identification value of one of the packets. Since each IP datagram has a different identification value, we should have seen only one packet when we activated our display filter. Instead what we saw were many packets, all with the same IP identification field. This meant that our IP datagram was doing a bit more traveling than we thought. But where was it going?

We then activated our source and destination MAC address display columns. Figure 3-24 shows the result of what we saw.

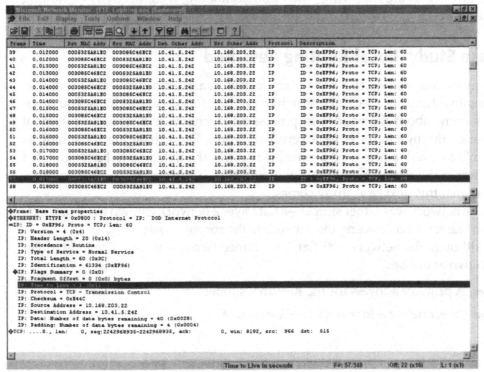

Figure 3-24 Non-expert mode analysis of TTL problem.

By looking at the source and destination MAC addresses, we knew that our IP datagram was bouncing back and forth between two routers. Every time one of the routers forwarded the packet, it would decrement the TTL field. In Frame 57, you can see where the TTL field eventually reaches 1.

TIP While you don't required an expert mode to diagnose problems like these, it sure is helpful.

By the way, can you guess what the starting TTL value was of the print server in New York? If you guessed 60, you guessed right. The 57 frames in the capture filter means that the original frame's TTL started at 57 when it hit the problem router. With a little bit of knowledge of the network architecture, my team knew that there were only three more hops to the subnet where the print server was located giving us a total of 60 for the starting TTL value.

This example illustrates the basic methodology of how to troubleshoot IP connectivity problems. Our analzyer told us that the packets were being transmitted out onto the wire, but were never being received by the printer. By using a pattern match filter to track a single packet, we were able to confirm that the single packet was showing up again and again on our network, each time the TTL field being decremented. Finally, by using our MAC layer address display, we were able to see the Layer 2 path and knew that packets were bouncing between two routers. It is important to always trace the path that IP packets are following when troubleshooting a connectivity or routing problem.

Case Study: Local Routing Revisited

If any of you reading this have ever worked in a pharmaceutical or chemical company that does medical research or produces medical products, you probably know about the validation process all machines and testing equipment must go through in order to be certified for use. Even changing something as simple as the IP address on a machine requires the machine to be revalidated for use in the research and development cycle. It is from this sort of environment that this next case study comes.

The network was rather simple—a flat Layer 2 network (shown in Figure 3-25) with one router connecting the network to the corporate site.

Although the network was flat, it contained two IP subnets. The local router had two addresses:

- A primary address for the Research subnet
- A secondary address for the Test subnet

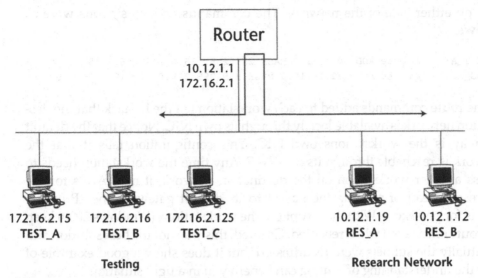

Figure 3-25   Local router network.

Each subnet had a 24-bit mask, giving it 254 hosts each. Up until this point, either subnet used the router only for communications to the corporate network. They never needed to communicate with each other until users on the Test subnet needed access to a database server that resided on the Research subnet. This access was not a problem because all nonlocal traffic was sent to the default gateway. The router simply handled the routing between the two local subnets. Even though the router had only one physical connection, it was able to forward traffic between the two subnets because it had two logical connections, one to each IP network.

Things were working fine until the use of the Research database server by the Test users started to tax the capabilities of the router. The router was a smaller model only designed to forward traffic at WAN speeds over a T1, not full wire transfer speeds between two Ethernet stations. Performance was degrading at a very rapid rate, and the users needed an answer as to when a new router would be purchased.

The suggestion to change the IP address scheme so that all devices were on the same subnet was not an option because changing any parts of the configuration on those machines, including the IP address, would invalidate the machine's certification for testing and research. They needed another solution. It didn't seem as if there was any other solution other than purchasing a bigger, faster router to handle all of the routing between the two subnets. When I was presented with this problem I realized that if we could somehow convince each computer on both networks that the other subnet was local, then it would ARP for the MAC address instead of using the router. In effect, we could communicate via Layer 2 to the device instead of having our traffic pass through the router. I solved the problem by adding a persistent route statement to each host on either side of the network. The commands on two stations were as follows:

```
TEST_A:     route ADD 10.12.1.0 MASK 255.255.255.0  172.16.2.15    -P
RES_A:      route ADD 172.16.15.0 MASK 255.255.255.0  10.12.1.19   -P
```

The route commands added to each workstation tell the IP stack that the destination network is available locally through its own NIC. Notice that the default gateway is the workstations own NIC. This configuration tells it that the network is reachable through its own NIC. Any time the workstation needs to access another workstation on the destination network, it now ARPs for the address instead of sending the packet to its default gateway. The –P option stands for persistent. With the –P option, the workstations (Windows 2000) keep the route entry even when rebooted. Granted, this was not the best solution and eventually the subnets were readdressed, but it does show a good example of how the understanding of routing can benefit you in a tight situation.

A Word about IP Version 6

This chapter has focused solely on the most common version of the IP protocol, version 4. The most current version, while not widely implemented, is version 6. IPv6, as it's commonly referred to, is the newest upgrade to the IP protocol suite. IPv6 changes IPv4 in several ways, but the most significant change is the increase of the address length from 32 bits to 128 bits. This increase in address length greatly expands the available address space available on the Internet and provides a solution for the shortage of addresses for a long time to come. One might think that this increase in address space would have long ago motivated most ISPs and organizations to move to IPv6. Unfortunately, the timing of IPv6's release into the market couldn't have been worse. At the time that IP addressing availability was becoming a problem, two things happened:

- Classless Interdomain Routing (CIDR) was introduced.
- Proxy servers and Network Address Translation (NAT) became widely available.

CIDR eliminated the concept of fixed class based subnet masks. No longer were IP addresses in the range from 128.0.0.0 to 191.255.255.255 required to use a Class B mask of 255.255.0.0. This change allowed ISPs to allocate smaller blocks of addresses with a prefix mask. Also during this process, as I mentioned previously in this chapter, ISPs were readdressing their networks for aggregation. These two things recovered a lot of wasted address space on the Internet. While the Internet was fixing its own addressing mess, router vendors were adding NAT abilities to their products. Using Port Address Translation (PAT), an organization technically needed only a /30-bit network supporting two hosts, their own router, and the ISPs router. A single public PAT address could support the entire inside network. Proxy servers gave organizations the same ability because the proxy server did all of the communication for the inside clients. The combination of CIDR and NAT did a great job of extending the life of IPv4, so great of a job that very few organizations will move to IPv6 anytime soon.

Now that you know why you aren't using IPv6, I want to talk about how it differs from IPv4.

Several factors drove the development of IPv6:

- **Addressing.** As I mentioned before, IPv4 uses a 32-bit address length. IPv6 increases this length to 128 bits, providing for substantially more addresses.

- **Performance.** IPv4 has a header length of 20 bytes, not including any IP options that may be present. With IPv6's increase in address length, the IP header grows to 44 bytes, with 32 of those bytes being the address fields alone. Because of this, IP implemented a next header identifier in the new IP header. The next header identifies any extensions or options existing after the IP header. The following extension headers have been defined:

  - **Hop-by-hop options header.** Defines options that require hop-by-hop processing

  - **Routing header.** Used for extended routing options

  - **Fragment header.** Contains IP fragmentation and reassembly information

  - **Authentication header.** Provides packet integrity and authentication

  - **Encapsulating security payload header.** Provides privacy

  - **Destination options header.** Defines any optional information that needs to be processed by the destination host

- **Security.** Security options in IPv6 provide for authentication, whereby an end system can verify the identity of the sender, and also for privacy, which allows a sending host to encrypt the data it sends across the network. IPv6 uses the same security methods defined in the IPsec standards for IPv4.

- **Network Service.** IPv6 retains IPv4's ability to prioritize a packet's transmission by a router, but redefines the types of priority, as I will show in the header definitions. IPv6 also includes a flow label that uniquely identifies a conversation between two IP hosts. Flow labels allow routers to easily identify what services a conversation receives without looking at the addressing or upper-layer port information to identify the conversation.

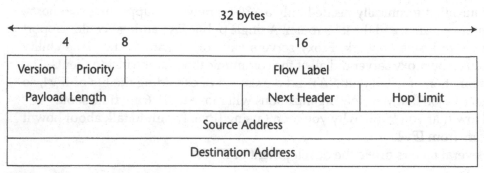

Figure 3-26   IPv6 header format.

The IPv6 Header

Figure 3-26 shows the format of the IPv6 header.

The following shows an EtherPeek NX decode of the IPv6 header.

```
IP Version 6 Header - Internet Protocol Datagram
  Version:             6 [14 Mask 0xF0]
  Priority:            0 Uncharacterized Traffic  [14 Mask 0x0F]
  Flow Label:          0x000000 [15-17]
  Payload Length:      1024 [18-19]
  Next Header:         0x8A Static [20]
  Hop Limit:           10 [21]
  Source Address:      FE80:0000:0000:0000:0000:0000:0014:001A  [22-37]
  Destination Address: FE80:0000:0000:0001:0000:0800:2076:93D7  [38-53]
Static
  IP Data Area:
  ;.....              3B 00 00 00 00 00  [54-59]
```

The following describes the definitions of the IP header fields:

- **Version.**   Specifies the IP version.

- **Priority.**   The Priority field is set to zero for uncharacteristic traffic. The priority field has the following values:

    - 0—Uncharacteristic Traffic

    - 1—Filler Traffic

    - 2—Unattended Data Transfer

    - 3—Reserved

    - 4—Attended Bulk Transfer

    - 5—Reserved

    - 6—Interactive Traffic

- 7—Internet Control Traffic
- 8—Non–Congestion Controlled Traffic
- 9—Non–Congestion Controlled Traffic

Flow Label.   The Flow Label field is set to zero, indicating that the packet has not been identified as a flow.

Payload Length.   The Payload Length field indicates how much data, not including the IP header, is being carried by the IP packet. The Next Header field value indicates what follows the IP header. A value of static (as shown in the previous EtherPeek decode of the header) indicates that no header extensions exist after the end of the IP header.

Next Header.   The Next Header field functions exactly as IPv4's protocol ID field. It tells the IP stack what protocol is next after the IP header. In the case of IPv6, this protocol could be either a standard protocol ID, such as TCP, or one of the new IP headers mentioned previously. A complete listing of Next Header values can be found on the Internet at www.iana.org/assignments/protocol-numbers.

Hop Limit.   The Hop Limit is similar to IPv4's Time to Live field. It specifies how many router hops remain that the packet can pass through.

Source Address.   This is the address of the source station that sent the packet.

Destination Address.   This is the address of the destination station that sent the packet.

> **NOTE** The current version of the IPv6 specification is RFC2460 and can be found at www.ietf.org/rfc/rfc2460.txt.

IPv6 Address Format

You might notice in the IPv6 decode in the previous section that the source and destination addresses are in a new format. They are hex instead of decimal and also are separated by colons instead of decimals. Each hexadecimal digit separated by colons is 16 bits in length. With 8 digits comprising the entire IP address, the total length is 128 bits ($16 \times 8 = 128$). IPv6 also gives us two additional ways to express an address.

- The first way allows you to truncate repeating parts of the address with a double colon "::".The double colon enables you to shorten an address with repeating zeros. For example, the address DEAD:BEEF:0000:0000:0000:0074:FEED:FOOD could be shortened to DEAD:BEEF::74:FEED:FOOD. The :: represents the missing zeros.

■ The second way of expressing IP addresses is used when you need to express an IPv4 address in IPv6 format, which is done by simply using the standard IPv4 decimal notation. The address 172.16.34.1 can be expressed in IPv6 as 0000:0000:0000:0000:0000:0000:172.16.34.1 or by using the colon descriptor ::172.16.34.1.

Both of these methods give you the ability to easily express long IP addresses with a minimum of effort.

Other Changes to IPv6

Along with changes to the core IP header, there were changes to IP's supporting protocols, such as Internet Control Message Protocol (ICMP). The current version of ICMPv6 can be found at `www.ietf.org/rfc/rfc2463.txt`.

Along with ICMP, any protocol using IPv4's 32-bit addresses need to be upgraded to support IPv6's 128-bit address length.

CROSS-REFERENCE An excellent reference to the changes in IPv6 is Mark Miller's *Implementing IPv6: Supporting the Next Generation Internet Protocols, Second Edition*, from Wiley Publishing.

Summary

IP provides an end-to-end path for all upper-layer network protocols. When troubleshooting IP connectivity, it is the first protocol that should be examined. Command-line tools such as ARP, ROUTE, and PING can give you many quick views into how things are working on the network. It is these tools that I turn to first when analyzing a problem, only breaking out a protocol analyzer when I have exhausted all possibilities with the command-line tools. IP is one of the few protocols you can do a lot of troubleshooting of with simple command-line tools. As you move into the higher layers, you will see that you will rely more and more on the protocol analyzer as your tool of choice.

Internet Control
Message Protocol

Chapter 3 introduced the Internet Protocol (IP), its addressing, and how IP traffic gets from a source to a destination. But what happens if there is a problem along that path? What if a router doesn't have a route to the destination? What if the IP datagrams are too large to be transmitted onto an outgoing link? What if the destination host doesn't respond?

IP is what is called an unreliable connectionless protocol. Although it is responsible for getting our data from one place to another, it does not guarantee that it will make it. When transmitting traffic across a Layer 2 link, such as Ethernet, the data link layer is responsible for guaranteeing the integrity of the data. For example:

- If a user on a shared Ethernet segment transmits at the same instant as another station, a collision results. Both stations "hear" the collision and attempt to transmit again.

- If a cable connecting a next-hop router is faulty and corrupts a packet that is being transmitted over the link, a CRC error results. The destination station (or router) checks the CRC on the frame; when it sees that it is incorrect, it drops the packet. Eventually the sending station will notice that it hasn't received a response, and it will transmit the data again.

Both of these examples illustrate how the data link layer handles events that occur in the physical layer. Collisions and CRC errors are manifestations of problems that occur in the physical layer of the network. What happens, though, when Layer 2 is operating without any problems, and there is a problem in Layer 3? Is IP responsible for dealing with the problem? As I stated above, IP is an unreliable, connectionless protocol. In Chapter 3, I talked in detail about how the IP protocol works, but I really didn't discuss its responsibilities. I avoided that discussion in Chapter 3 on purpose. Many books jump right in and immediately start discussing what a protocol does, how it works, and what its lines of responsibility are. I chose not to do this in order to first give you an understanding of the protocol. Once you understand its operations, you are better suited to discuss what it does and doesn't do. There are a lot of functions needed to handle certain network situations that IP does not have. For example, what happens if a router can't pass an IP packet because it's too big. IP has no way of giving feedback to the source host to tell it to reduce its packet size. In this chapter, I am going to discuss several situations that IP does not have the inherent functionality to handle. Instead, this functionality is implemented in a helper protocol called Internet Control Message Protocol (ICMP). As ARP "helps" the IP protocol with respect to MAC (Media Access Control) address resolution, ICMP "helps" IP with other functions that I will discuss.

Reliability in Networks

Networks by themselves are unreliable. As I have already stated, there are a number of events that can occur and cause communications to fail. To circumvent these problems, you need a protocol that can handle these events. You actually need more than one protocol because errors may occur at each layer. Layer 4, or the transport layer, is responsible for ultimately guaranteeing your data transfers. Regardless of any other events that occur in Layers 1 to 3, it is the transport layer that must guarantee that your data is delivered to its destination.

CROSS-REFERENCE I discuss how it does this in Chapter 6.

Connection-Oriented versus Connectionless Networks

Protocols can be classified as either connection-oriented or connectionless. Connection-oriented protocols have several attributes. First, they send data via organized methods. Each packet of data that is sent has a sequence number attached to it. In this way, a destination host can examine the sequence number of the frame and send back an acknowledgment message to the source host, indicating that it received the data. This process is how reliability is implemented. To implement this sequence and acknowledgment functionality, the protocol must set up a connection with its peer destination protocol.

This connection allows both sides to agree on attributes, such as which sequence number to start with, the frame size, and other options. This connection is what makes a protocol a *connection-oriented protocol.*

Conversely, the IP protocol has no method of connection setup or frame sequencing and acknowledgment functionality, so it has no ability to provide reliability. Therefore, IP is a *connectionless protocol.*

Another aspect of connection-oriented protocols is the method by which they forward data through the network. Connection-oriented networks determine their path before the first packet is even transmitted. A perfect example of a connection-oriented protocol is Asynchronous Transfer Mode (ATM). When a user on an ATM network wants to transmit data to a destination host, the ATM network must first set up an end-to-end connection between the nodes. When packets (actually called cells) arrive at each ATM switch, the switch immediately knows how to forward those packets to the next ATM switch. There is no routing table lookup process as in IP. IP routers must make their routing decisions based on the information contained in their routing tables hop by hop through the network. The chances that a packet arriving into an IP router has no destination are just as high as the chances of a router being able to properly forward the packet. On ATM networks, a frame would never leave the source host if an end-to-end route didn't exist.

Feedback

Because IP isn't a reliable protocol, and it isn't a connection-oriented protocol, what can it do if there is a problem with end-to-end data transfer? The answer is not much. The designers of the IP protocol purposely left the functionality of providing reliability to the transport layer. However, instead of letting the transport layer handle every situation that may occur in the lower layers, they created a method of letting intermediate systems, such as routers and destination stations, provide feedback to a source host about certain situations on the network. They did this by implementing the *Internet Control Message Protocol (ICMP).*

There are two types of feedback that a host can receive from the network. (When I say network I mean the routers and other hosts that forward and receive packets sent by a source host.)

- The first type of feedback is *passive feedback.* Collisions are a method of passive feedback. In passive feedback, the source host is not explicitly notified about a network problem. For example, when the data link layer of the source host "hears" a collision on the wire after transmitting its data, it knows it must retransmit its data.

- The second type of feedback is called *active feedback.* With active feedback, the source host receives explicit information about its data transfer. On Frame Relay networks, routers receive active feedback about congestion on the Frame Relay network by the use of the Forward

Explicit Congestion Notification (FECN) and Backward Explicit Congestion Notification (BECN) bits in the Frame Relay packets. Hosts on an IP network receive active feedback from the ICMP protocol.

Exploring the Internet Control Message Protocol

ICMP is the protocol that handles events that occur in the network layer. ICMP does not operate by itself; it uses the IP protocol to deliver its messages. ICMP's main responsibility is to provide feedback to a source node about problems occurring along the network layer path. To use an analogy, consider the post office:

- You drop a letter in a mailbox to be delivered. The next step in the process occurs when the mailman comes to pick up the mail. The mail then is taken to the local post office for routing to other post offices, and then finally it is delivered to the destination address specified on the envelope. What happens though if a post office is too busy and can't process your mail? What if your letter was simply thrown in the garbage? You would never know. Of course, if your letter were actually a bill payment to your credit card company, you would hear feedback pretty quickly from them indicating that they did not receive your payment.

- For another example, suppose that you sent a large envelope full of papers to someone, and you didn't put enough postage on the envelope. In most cases, you would receive back the letter stamped with an indication that you need more postage stamps.

These examples show the types of scenarios that occur within data networks. These are the network events that ICMP is responsible for providing a source host feedback about. Imagine if instead of the post office or mailman being responsible for handling these events, that another organization was. That organization would handle all feedback that was necessary about mail delivery. If you look at IP as the postal system, you could consider ICMP as the postal feedback system. It handles any messages about what is going on in the post office and with your mail delivery.

ICMP Header

Now that I have talked about the responsibilities of ICMP, I want to discuss how the protocol actually functions. Figure 4-1 shows the ICMP header.

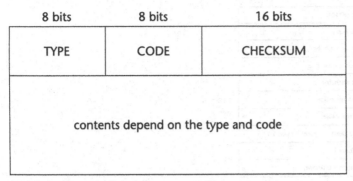

8 bits	8 bits	16 bits
TYPE	CODE	CHECKSUM
contents depend on the type and code		

Figure 4-1 ICMP header.

ICMP has several *types* of messages that provide the active feedback to the source node. Each message type has several codes associated with it. The *codes* specify more detail about the nature of the message. Because ICMP messages are sometimes critical to the proper functioning of a network, ICMP provides its own 16-bit checksum field.

NOTE Unlike IP's checksum, which only protects the IP header, ICMP's checksum field is calculated over the entire contents of the ICMP message.

Every ICMP header is followed by more-specific details, depending on the type and code in the header. Following the message detail information is, strangely enough, another 28 bytes of information. These 28 bytes contain the 20-byte IP header of the packet that caused the ICMP message to be sent along with an additional 8 bytes of that packet's data.

ICMP Types and Codes

When a router or host wants to send an ICMP message back to a source host, it uses a specific type and code combination to indicate the message type. Figure 4-2 illustrates the combinations of types and codes that a node may use to notify a host of a specific message.

Not all types and codes are important. Out of the list in Figure 4-2, I have seen only about 10 of them out of several hundred different networks.

NOTE Most of the other ICMP types and codes are specific to certain configurations on routers. For example, if a router is using type of service (TOS) routing, you may see ICMP messages indicating feedback about the availability of TOS routing. Other messages, such as timestamp requests and replies, are used by programs that use those features of ICMP. In short, most of the messages besides the ones I mention here are seen only when specific network configurations or applications exist.

TYPE	CODE	DESCRIPTION
0	0	Echo Reply
3		*Destination Unreachable*
	0	Network Unreachable
	1	Host Unreachable
	2	Protocol Unreachable
	3	Port Unreachable
	4	Fragmentation Needed and Don't Fragment Bit was Set
	5	Source Route Failed
	6	Destination Network Unknown
	7	Destination Host Unknown
	8	Source Host Isolated
	9	Communication w/ Dest Network Administratively Prohibited
	10	Communication w/ Dest Host Administratively Prohibited
	11	Destination Network Unreachable for Type of Service
	12	Destination Host Unreachable for Type of Service
	13	Communication Administratively Prohibited
	14	Host Precedence Violation
	15	Precendence cutoff in effect
4	0	Source Quench
5		*Redirect Codes*
	0	Redirect Datagram for Network
	1	Redirect Datagram for Host
	2	Redirect Datagram for Type of Service and Network
	3	Redirect Datagram for Type of Service and Host
	4	
6	0	Alternate Address for Host
7		Unassigned
8	0	Echo
9	0	Router Advertisement
10	0	Router Advertisement
11		*Time Exceeded*
	0	Time to Live Exceeded in Transit
	1	Fragment Reassembly Time Exceeded
12		*Parameter Problem*
	0	Pointer indicates error
	1	Missing a Required Option
	2	Bad Length
13	0	*Timestamp Request*
14	0	*Timestamp Reply*
15	0	*Information Request*
16	0	*Information Reply*
17	0	*Address Mask Request*
18	0	*Address Mask Reply*

Figure 4-2   ICMP types and codes.

However, the 10 that I mention are very important to understand. Because it takes very little extra coding to have an analyzer parse ICMP messages, most analyzers notify you of at minimum the 10 I talk about, if not all of them.

ICMP messages are broken up into five categories:

- **Destination Unreachable Messages (Type 3, Code 0–15).** Destination messages consist of messages that inform a host about the reachability of the destination it is trying to reach. Examples of destination messages include routers that don't have routes for a destination, a host that is not running a specific application, or even a host that is not running a specific upper-layer protocol.

- **Diagnostic Messages (Type 8, Code 0 and Type 0, Code 0).** The most popular diagnostic message in the ICMP protocol is PING. There are varying stories of where the term PING came from. Many believe it is from submarine terminology where one submarine would send an audible ping and then wait for it to bounce off of another submarine so the first submarine could determine distance and angle. Another popular definition is that PING stands for Packet Internet Groper. Whatever the origin, the PING message type is a powerful troubleshooting tool for IP networks.

- **Redirect Messages (Type 5, Code 0–4).** Redirect messages inform hosts about the best path to use for reaching a destination host.

- **Time Exceeded Messages (Type 11, Code 0–1).** Chapter 3 contains an example showing how the Time to Live field in the IP header is used to prevent a packet from endlessly looping around a network. ICMP notifies you about when the TTL field reaches zero and a packet is dropped.

- **Informational Messages (Type 12, 13, 14, 15, 16, 17, 18).** ICMP contains a number of informational messages about parameter problems, lengths, and other information.

ICMP Message Detail

In this next section, I discuss the types of messages you see on a network in detail. I discuss what they mean and review several case studies about how they can aid in troubleshooting.

Destination Unreachable (Type 3)

There are six important Destination Unreachable messages that are commonly seen on a network.

Network Unreachable (Code 0)

Network Unreachable messages are sent back to a host when a router receives datagrams for which it does not contain a valid route or default route. In Chapter 3, I discuss how the last step in the route forwarding process is to send any datagrams for which there is not a specific route to the gateway of last resort, also known as the default route. If a specific route for a datagram does not exist and there is no default route, the router has no choice but to drop the packet and inform the source host. The router does so via the Network Unreachable message. In Figure 4-3, Router A does not contain a specific route for the 172.16.1.0 network, but because it has a default route it forwards the packet to Router B. The default route, also known as the gateway of last resort, is represented by the route entry 0.0.0.0 0.0.0.0 192.168.1.2. Router B does not have a specific or default route so it drops the packet and sends back an ICMP Network Unreachable message to the source host at 10.1.2.11.

Host Unreachable (Code 1)

Host Unreachable messages are the same as Network Unreachable messages, except that they refer to a host instead of a network. A Network Unreachable message indicates that the router does not have a route for a specific network. A Host Unreachable message indicates that, although the router has a valid route for the destination, it is unable to reach the host on that network. Thinking back to the discussion on IP communications in Chapter 3, what process would a router use in order to determine that a host on a network is unreachable? If you guessed ARP, you're right. Host Unreachable messages are sent by routers when they send out an ARP resolution request for an IP address on a specific subnet but do not receive a reply. Figure 4-4 illustrates a Host Unreachable message being sent back to a host from a router because the router does not receive a response when it sends out an ARP for the host at 172.16.1.5.

NOTE Not all routers are enabled to send back host unreachable messages by default. Cisco routers, for example, do not send back Host Unreachable messages when they are unable to resolve the MAC address of a node via ARP. I recommend enabling ICMP Host Unreachable messages on routers because the explicit feedback from the router will aid in troubleshooting. On Cisco routers, Host Unreachable messages can be enabled by the `ip unreachables` command.

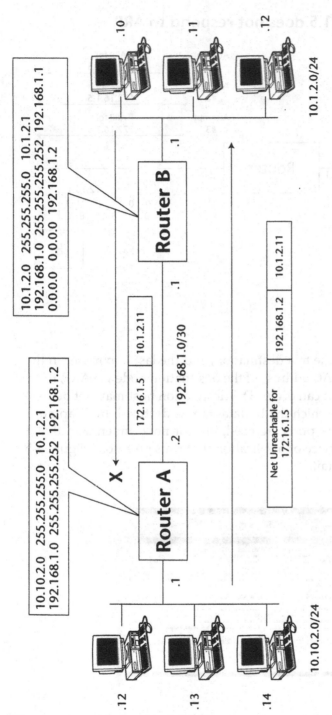

Figure 4-3   Network Unreachable.

Host 172.16.1.5 does not respond to ARP

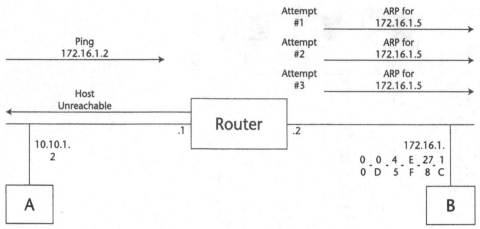

Figure 4-4   Host Unreachable.

Port Unreachable (Code 3)

If all routers have a valid route to a destination, and the last hop router in the path is able to resolve the MAC address of the destination node via ARP, there is still one more problem that can occur. The destination host may not be running the specific service for which the IP datagram is destined. In Chapters 5 and 6, I discuss in detail how ports are used, but for now understand that a port represents a specific service or application that runs on a host. Figure 4-5 illustrates this concept in detail.

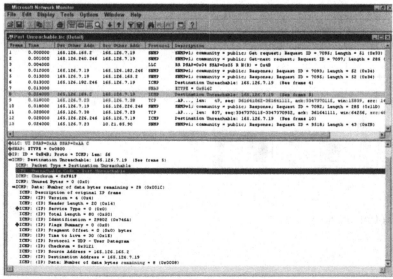

Figure 4-5   ICMP Port Unreachable.

1. In Frame 1, you have a network management station sending an SNMP Get request to the host at 165.126.165.2.

2. In Frame 5, you see 165.126.165.2 responding to the SNMP request.

3. Everything seems fine, except for the fact that in Frame 8 you see 165.126.7.19 sending back an ICMP Port Unreachable message to 165.126.165.2.

This example is actually a very interesting case study because normally when an ICMP Port Unreachable message is sent it means that a host has received data for an application that it is not running. In this case, however, we saw a response from that host in Frame 5. The strange behavior of the network management station encouraged us to investigate it further, whereupon we found out it was a vendor bug. The bug caused the station to sometimes send erroneous Port Unreachable messages unnecessarily. A simple software patch fixed the problem.

Fragmentation Needed and Don't Fragment Bit Was Set (Code 4)

In Chapter 3, I discuss the flags field of the IP header and how it indicates if a single large datagram was fragmented into several smaller datagrams due to an outgoing link maximum transmission unit (MTU) size being too small for the datagram. Those flags are also used to let a host indicate its desire to have its packets fragmented or not. In Figure 4-6, you see that the host KEVIN is initiating a TCP connection to www.tracemasters.com.

Notice that the host has set the Don't Fragment bit, indicating its wishes to not have its datagrams fragmented. How then, you might ask, does a host know the correct size datagrams to send out onto a network? Hosts can't possibly know the MTU size of every link on the network. ICMP is used to inform hosts about the correct size they need to use in order to traverse a link. When a router receives a datagram that is too big for it to forward out onto an outgoing link, the router normally fragments the datagram into several small datagrams. When an IP packet has the Don't Fragment bit set, the router is not allowed to fragment the datagram, so instead it sends back an ICMP Destination Unreachable message with Type 3 and Code 4, indicating that fragmentation is needed but the Don't Fragment bit was set.

Case Study: MTU Problem

Users on a network were having some very strange problems. When they were transferring files they were sometimes unable to complete the file transfer. Even though the clients were on a Token Ring segment and the servers were on Ethernet, it shouldn't have mattered because ICMP would allow them to discover the correct MTU to use when sending data to the server segment. Strangely enough, the problem was intermittent; sometimes file transfers would fail, and sometimes they would be completed with no problem.

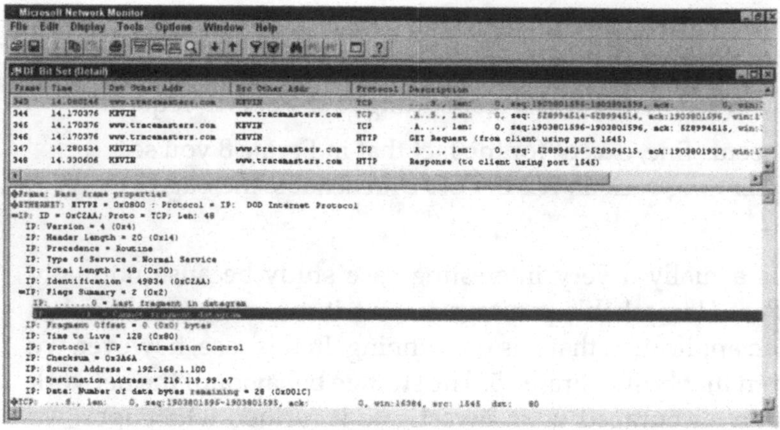

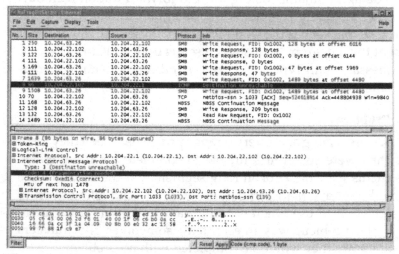

Figure 4-6   TCP connection request.

As my team started analyzing the problem, it wasn't long before we were able to capture a trace of the problem occurring. As the file transfer progressed, the host eventually sent a datagram that was too big for a router to forward. Most file transfer protocols, like SMB in this example, start with a smaller data size and slowly ratchet their way up. One of the routers in between the client and the server had the MTU on one of its interfaces set to a smaller size than the Token Ring client segment. Since these were Microsoft clients, they were setting the Don't Fragment Bit, meaning that the router was not permitted to fragment their datagrams. The router was also not sending back ICMP Fragmentation Needed messages to inform the client that it needed to fragment its packets but couldn't because the Don't Fragment bit was set. Someone had inadvertently turned off the router's ICMP function so it was unable to provide feedback to hosts on the network.

Figure 4-7   Fragmentation needed, but Don't Fragment bit is set.

Figure 4-7 shows the trace file after we turned back on the router's ICMP functionality. (Notice the analyzer showing an IP and TCP decode after the ICMP header. This is the extra 28 bytes of the offending IP packet after the ICMP header and message in Frame 8.) Now, the router is sending ICMP Destination Unreachable messages indicating that fragmentation of the packet is needed before it can be sent on the outgoing link.

1. In Frames 1 to 6, you see the client writing a file to the server using the SMB protocol. Notice that from Frames 1 to 6 the frame sizes are relatively small.

2. In Frame 7, you see that the client attempts to write a significantly larger amount of data to the server, 1,639 bytes to be exact. Because the router in between the client and the server cannot handle this large frame size, the router needs to inform the client of the correct datagram size to send. It does this by placing the correct size inside of the ICMP message.

3. Looking at Figure 4-7, you can see that the correct size the client needs to use is 1,478.

Figure 4-8 shows the decode of Frame 9, where the client is using the correct size as specified in the ICMP Fragmentation message.

Communication Administratively Prohibited (Code 13)

The last of the ICMP Destination Unreachable messages concerns itself with security. Routers, when set up with access lists, can be configured to drop and accept certain kinds of traffic. For example, an Internet router may let only the HTTP protocol into certain Web servers inside the company or perhaps only SMTP into certain mail servers. Administrators have the option to allow routers to send back ICMP messages about their packet-filtering security policies. These

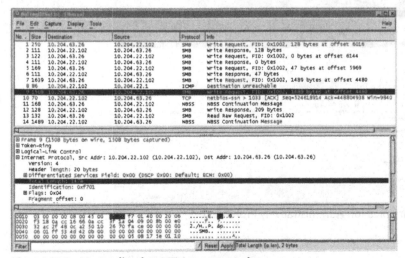

Figure 4-8   Host adjusting MTU to correct size.

ICMP messages are called Communication Administratively Prohibited messages. They derive their name from the fact that an administrator most likely is the one who has configured the packet filters that drop certain kinds of traffic.

In Figure 4-9, you can see several DNS queries being sent from host 10.117.101.92.

In Frames 2, 4, and 6, the host receives back ICMP Communication Administratively Prohibited messages for all three queries, indicating that there is an access list blocking DNS traffic. You can also can tell which router is blocking the DNS traffic because the packet trace shows the ICMP messages coming from the IP address 10.99.146.1.

> **WARNING** Communication Administratively Prohibited messages are excellent aids in troubleshooting, but can also be a helpful tool to a hacker attempting to access your network. I recommend enabling them only on routers located internally to an organization.

Diagnostic Messages

ICMP is the workhorse of the most commonly used diagnostic tool ever made for computer networks, the PING program. PING uses two ICMP types.

- Type 8, Code 0 is used for the ICMP Echo requests, which are the PING packets that are sent out to a destination host.

- Type 0, Code 0 are the ICMP Echo Replies, which hosts send back in response to a PING packet.

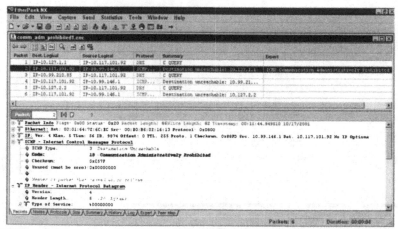

Figure 4-9 Communication Administratively Prohibited.

In Chapter 2 I discuss how the PING program can be used to measure latency on a network. The delta time between the PING request and response gives us the round-trip response time (RTT). It is the amount of time it takes for the PING request to be sent, turned around and acknowledged by the destination host, and sent back to the source. The ICMP request packet contains a certain data pattern that the destination host echoes back to the source host. The data pattern varies, depending on the implementation of the PING program. Windows 2000 machines use a repeating alphabet pattern; other hosts use number sequences. Cisco routers have an option called Extended PING. It lets you control specific details about how the PING packet is formed and what data patterns are used in the Echo message. The following illustrates the usage of the Cisco Extended PING command.

```
Router1#ping
Protocol [ip]:
Target IP address:172.16.12.7
Repeat count [5]: 100
Datagram size [100]: 1000
Timeout in seconds [2]:
Extended commands [n]: y
Source address or interface:
Type of service [0]:
Set DF bit in IP header? [no]:
Validate reply data? [no]:
Data pattern [0xABCD]: 0000
Loose, Strict, Record, Timestamp, Verbose[none]:
Sweep range of sizes [n]:
Type escape sequence to abort.
Sending 100, 1000-byte ICMP Echos to 172.16.12.7, timeout is 2 seconds:
Packet has data pattern 0x0000
!!!!!!!!!!!!!!!!!!!!!!!!!!!!!!!!!!!!!!!!!!!!!!!!!!!!!!!!!!!!!!!!!!!!!!!!!
!!!!!!!!!!!!!!!!!!!!!!!!!!!!!!!!!
Success rate is 100 percent (100/100), round-trip min/avg/max = 52/59/92 ms
```

You must have enable rights to the router in order to perform an Extended PING.

TIP Extended PING is an excellent tool for testing T1 and T3 circuits. The type of encoding used on T1 and T3 circuits replaces a certain series of zeros with something called Bi-Polar violations. This substitution, called B8ZS and B3ZS, respectively, ensures that timing slips do not occur on the circuit. By using Extended PINGs, you can put all zeros in your data pattern to test the ability of a WAN circuit to perform this zero substitution properly. A success rate of 100 percent indicates the substitution function is working correctly.

Redirect Codes (Type 5)

ICMP Redirect messages allow routers to inform hosts about a better route to a destination. There are two kinds of Redirect messages:

- The *Network Redirect* message informs a host that there is a better way to reach a network.

- The *Host Redirect* message informs a host that there is a better way to reach a host.

Routers send redirects based on information contained in their routing tables. In effect, a redirect is when a router says, "Do not use me to reach the destination, use another router." Redirects are best illustrated by the examples provided in the next few sections.

Redirect Datagrams for Network (Code 0)

Figure 4-10 illustrates an example of an ICMP Network Redirect.

Host 10.6.3.222 has a subnet mask of 255.255.248.0 putting it on a network with a host range of 10.6.0.1 to 10.6.7.254. In Frame 5, host 10.6.3.222 sends a NetBIOS Name Query out to the broadcast address of 10.6.7.255, addressing all IP hosts on the subnet. The host is sending out a NetBIOS Name Query because it wants the IP address for a specific NetBIOS name. In Frame 6, you see a router at 10.6.3.249 returning an ICMP Network Redirect message to the host. Looking at the frame detail, you can see that the router is directing the host to use the gateway of 10.6.7.255 in order to reach the destination network.

Figure 4-10   ICMP Network Redirect.

NOTE If you are scratching your head wondering why the router was doing this, you're not alone. ICMP messages should never be returned for a broadcast frame (see the "When ICMP Messages Should Not Be Sent" sidebar in this chapter). This router is breaking a cardinal rule of ICMP. The reply also makes no sense, as the gateway specified in the frame is the broadcast address for the subnet. Upon further research, we found out that this router had a corrupt routing table.

Case Study: Incorrect Routing

In this case study, I am going to revisit the ICMP Network Redirect method to illustrate another example of how Network Redirect messages can indicate routing problems.

1. In Figure 4-11, host MARIE sends a single PING packet (ICMP Echo) to host JINXIE.

2. The path of the Echo packet is through Router C and Router A and eventually to host JINXIE. The response from host JINXIE is sent to JINXIE's default gateway 10.41.4.4, which is an interface on Router A. (In this case, as shown in Figure 4-11, host JINXIE has a default route of 10.41.4.4, Router A has a next hop of 10.41.4.1 for network 10.41.0.0 via a configured default route, and Router B has a next hop of 10.41.4.4 for network 10.41.10.0/24 via a configured specific route.)

TIP A detailed understanding of what routes exist in the routing tables of each host and router is important in diagnosing routing problems.

3. When Router A receives the ICMP Echo Response from host JINXIE, it forwards the frame to the next hop in its route table, which would be Router B. It also sends an ICMP Network Redirect message to JINXIE because Router B is on the same subnet as JINXIE, and JINXIE should be sending its packets to Router B instead of Router A. Unfortunately, Router B is not the correct path to get packets back to host MARIE.

4. When Router B examines the frame and sees it is destined for network 10.41.10.0, it sends an ICMP Network Redirect to host JINXIE because it believes JINXIE should have sent the frame to Router A. It then forwards the frame back to 10.41.4.4 (Router A), which corresponds to the entry it has in its route table for network 10.41.10.0.

5. When Router A receives the packet, it sends it back to Router B because its routing table tells it that Router B is the way to reach network 10.41.0.0.

6. Router B repeats the same actions, and the entire process starts over repeatedly, until eventually the Time-To-Live field of the packet hits zero and the frame is dropped.

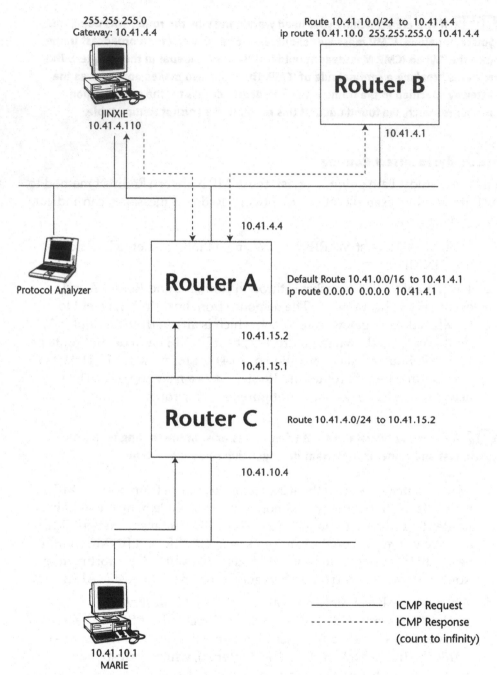

255.255.255.0
Gateway: 10.41.4.4

Route 10.41.10.0/24 to 10.41.4.4
ip route 10.41.10.0 255.255.255.0 10.41.4.4

Router B

JINXIE
10.41.4.110

10.41.4.1

Protocol Analyzer

10.41.4.4

Router A

Default Route 10.41.0.0/16 to 10.41.4.1
ip route 0.0.0.0 0.0.0.0 10.41.4.1

10.41.15.2

10.41.15.1

Router C

Route 10.41.4.0/24 to 10.41.15.2

10.41.10.4

ICMP Request
ICMP Response
(count to infinity)

10.41.10.1
MARIE

Figure 4-11　Incorrectly routed traffic.

Figure 4-12 shows the trace file capture of this sequence of events.

To make reading the trace file easier, I modified the name table so I could represent the MAC addresses with the names of the hosts and routers. This

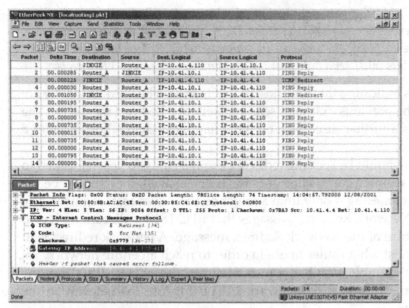

Figure 4-12 Incorrect routing trace file.

technique makes it much easier to follow the path of traffic. Without knowing the routing tables of Router A and Router B, it is easy to deduce which router has the incorrect route by looking at the ICMP Redirect messages. The keys to the riddle are in Frames 3 to 14. In Frame 3, Router A sends a redirect message to host JINXIE. Routers send ICMP Redirects based on information in their routing tables. In Frame 4, after sending the Redirect message, Router A, being a router, then routes the PING Reply from JINXIE and forwards it to Router B. Router B, upon receiving the packet, does the same thing as Router A, sends an ICMP Redirect message to host JINXIE and routes the frame back to Router A. Frames 6 to 14 show the PING Reply endlessly bouncing back between Router A and Router B. It will bounce back and forth until the TTL value reaches zero and one of the routers discards the frame. The key to finding out who the culprit is in a situation like this is to look at who forwarded the packet incorrectly the first time. Here, it was easy to see that this was Router A. The solution to the problem was to put a more specific route for 10.41.10.0 in Router A.

Redirect Datagrams for Host (Code 1)

Host redirects are similar to network redirects except that they inform about the best router to use to reach a host. A very interesting fact exists about ICMP network and host redirects. You saw in the previous section an example of routers using Network Redirect messages. Strangely enough, RFC 1812: *Requirements for IP Version 4 Routers* states the following:

Routers MUST NOT generate the Redirect for Network or Redirect for Network and Type of Service messages (Codes 0 and 2). . . . In a CIDR environment, it is difficult to specify precisely the cases in which network Redirects can be used. Therefore, routers must send only host (or host and type of service) Redirects.

If RFC 1812 is indicating that only host redirects should be used, then why are the routers in the previous examples sending Network Redirect messages? The answer requires a further discussion on what happens when a host receives a redirect message.

First, a router should be sending redirect messages only to hosts attached to one of its local segments. The same goes for hosts, as well; they should be listening to redirect messages only from a router on their own local segment. The problem with Network Redirect messages that RFC 1812 is discussing has to do with the nature of the Network Redirect message. A network redirect is in effect telling a host what router to use in order to reach an entire network. So, in the previous example, you had a router telling a host (Host JINXIE in the example) that in order to reach network 10.41.0.0 to use the gateway in the redirect message.

But, what if, for example, network 10.41.0.0 actually was subnetted further into multiple Class C addresses? Those subnets could easily be located behind other local routers on the users local network. The danger in the Network Redirect message is that a router (like the one in the example) configured with a static route for a larger supernet could incorrectly redirect hosts to another router that is unable to reach all of those hosts itself. RFC 1812 recommends that routers, instead of using network redirects, use host redirects. Using host redirects would tell hosts that they could reach a single host via another router, not the entire subnet. However, you might think the fact that routers use network redirects instead of host redirects would cause a problem. It doesn't. Here is why. RFC 1122 Section 3.3.1.2 states:

Since the subnet mask appropriate to the destination address is generally not known, a Network Redirect message SHOULD be treated identically to a Host Redirect message.

When a host receives either a Network or Host Redirect message, it will update its local routing table with a host route and not a network route. Host routes, as discussed in Chapter 3, are route entries for a single destination host.

NOTE Redirects are sent only by routers to hosts. A router should never send a redirect message to another router. Routers do not need to utilize redirect messages because all of their path information is obtained through the use of routing protocols.

Time Exceeded (Type 11)

Time-to-Live messages prevent IP datagrams from endlessly cycling around a network. In cases of incorrect routing (as I have shown in the previous example), packets sometimes get forwarded back and forth between routers. The TTL field makes sure that eventually after a period of time (that is, the time to live) they get discarded.

Time to Live Exceeded in Transit (Code 0)

I talk about the TTL field in some detail in Chapter 3. ICMP TTL Exceeded in Transit messages let routers inform us when they have received a packet that has a TTL value of zero. This ICMP message is normally the result of a routing problem whereby packets cycle endlessly around a network or, as in the case study earlier in this chapter, they bounce back and forth between two routers (known as count to infinity). Expert modes, such as the one in EtherPeek NX, will report this symptom as a Low Time-To-Live (also shown in Frame 9 of Figure 4-10). The expert symptom is letting you know that there are packets on the network that are being endlessly routed around until the TTL value hits zero and they are dropped.

Fragment Reassembly Time Exceeded (Code 1)

The Fragment Reassembly Time Exceeded message is similar to the Time to Live Exceeded message, except that it deals with how long it takes a host to receive all packets from a fragmented IP datagram. When a router has to fragment an IP datagram into several smaller IP datagrams, there is the possibility that they all might arrive at a destination out of order. A host cannot reassemble the original IP datagram until all fragments have been received. Each host will wait a specific amount of time to receive them before giving up and notifying the source host with a Fragment Reassembly Time Exceeded message.

Informational Messages

Informational messages are largely unused except in specific applications that implement them. I personally have not seen any of these types and codes on the networks I have analyzed, but this does not preclude their use.

Parameter Problem (Type 12)

The ICMP Parameter Problem is a catchall for any IP errors not covered by the rest of the defined types and codes. A code of 0 indicates that there was a problem with the IP header. A pointer field in the message points to the location in the IP header that was the cause of the problem. Code 1 indicates a missing option and Code 2 a bad length.

Timestamps (Type 13, 14)

The Timestamp message request and reply allows the measurement of latency between two hosts. Hosts will stamp packets within units of milliseconds since midnight Universal Time.

Information Request/Reply (Type 15, 16)

Information requests are another method for a diskless workstation to obtain an IP address. Information requests/responses have been made obsolete by RFC 1122, which states that hosts should not support these messages.

Address Mask Request/Reply (Type 17, 18)

ICMP address mask requests and replies are used by a host that knows its own IP address, but not its subnet mask. Routers respond to address mask requests indicating the subnet mask for the local network.

Network Diagnostics with ICMP

ICMP is basically a diagnostic protocol. It helps hosts make better routing decisions and tells them when things aren't working as they should be on the network. Most protocol analyzers do a good job of decode ICMP messages, at least the most common ones. Expert modes do an even better job of quickly informing us of ICMP messages. I've already discussed one very common utility that uses ICMP messages to do its job, PING. By modifying the value of the TTL field, you can use PING to discover the path that a packet would take across a network. This method is exactly the one used by the traceroute program.

WHEN ICMP MESSAGES SHOULD NOT BE SENT

There are several packets that routers should never send an ICMP message in response to. The following list describes packets that should never generate an ICMP message from a router or host.

- ◆ **ICMP Error Message.** Responding to an ICMP message with an ICMP message could easily spiral out of control causing an infinite exchange of ICMP messages between two hosts.

- ◆ **IP datagram addressed to the broadcast address.** Because every host processes broadcasts, a packet sent in error to the broadcast address causes all hosts on a network to attempt a response at the same time, flooding the network with unnecessary traffic and also burdening the source of the broadcast with many ICMP messages.

- ◆ **IP fragments other than the first fragment.**

- ◆ **A datagram with a nonunicast source address.** This prevents ICMP replies from being accidentally sent to a multicast or broadcast address.

The traceroute program operates by sending ICMP echo requests to the destination host with the TTL field initially set to one. The application sends three echo requests every time it increases the TTL field by one. The intervening routers in the path towards the destination decrement the TTL field by one, and when it reaches zero, they drop the datagram and send back an ICMP TTL Exceeded message to the source host. By looking at the returned ICMP errors sent by the router, the traceroute program can build a hop-by-hop map of the path to the destination. Figure 4-13 illustrates the traceroute program in action.

To keep it simple, I ran the traceroute program with the -d option, which turns off reverse DNS lookups. You can see how the traceroute program starts at a TTL value of one and then increases it every three packets until eventually it reaches 15 and does not receive TTL Exceeded in Transit anymore. The example in Figure 4-13 uses Windows 2000 traceroute, which is actually called Tracert. It uses ICMP echo requests (that is, PING) as its packet of choice to discover the path. Unix systems typically use random UDP ports to do the same thing. It doesn't matter what protocol is used as long as the intervening routers are sending back ICMP TTL Exceeded messages.

It is important to be wary of the output you receive when doing a traceroute. Figure 4-14 shows a perfect example of this.

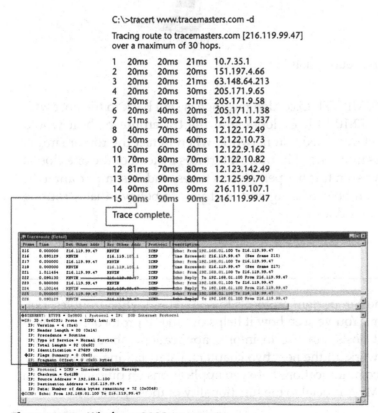

Figure 4-13 Windows 2000 traceroute.

```
C:\>tracert 192.168.17.9

Tracing route to KEVIN [192.168.17.9]
over a maximum of 30 hops:

  1   20 ms   20 ms   21 ms  10.7.35.1
  2   20 ms   20 ms   20 ms  10.112.5.3
  3   20 ms   30 ms   21 ms  172.168.182.15
  4   20 ms   20 ms   30 ms  172.10.13.1
  5   20 ms   20 ms   21 ms  192.168.17.9

Trace complete.
```

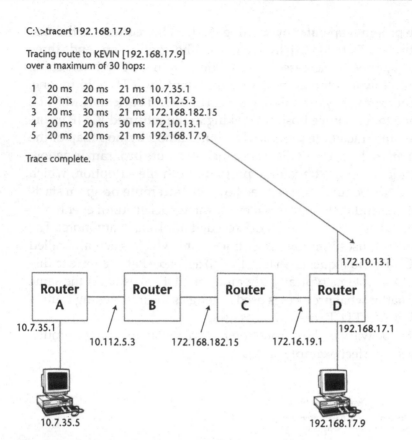

Figure 4-14   Strange traceroute results.

On Router D, the ICMP TTL Exceeded message is sent back to the host with a source address of 172.10.13.1. By looking at the traceroute path, it would appear that the packet traversed that network, when in fact the router simply used a source address from one of its other interfaces instead of the one closest to the source host. I've seen this happen several times, and it is important to be aware of because it can be confusing and lead you to believe that a routing problem exists when one doesn't.

Summary

ICMP is one of the most important protocols to understand when troubleshooting a TCP/IP problem. You've seen how it helps out the IP protocol by providing information that hosts can use to inform applications about conditions occurring on the network. In the next two chapters, I start talking about protocols that handle the communications between applications on our network. An understanding of ICMP is crucial to the functionality of those protocols.

User Datagram Protocol

UDP stands for User Datagram Protocol. Its name reflects the type of service it provides. The term *datagram* is defined by the Free Online Dictionary of Computing (FOLDOC) (http://foldoc.doc.ic.ac.uk/foldoc/index.html) as:

A self-contained, independent entity of data carrying sufficient information to be routed from the source to the destination computer without reliance on earlier exchanges between this source and destination computer and the transporting network.

UDP does not use a connection setup to transfer data nor does it rely on any other processes, as would a protocol like TCP. Hence, UDP is referred to as an unreliable and connectionless datagram service. Similar to IP, UDP does not guarantee the delivery of data. IP's responsibility is to forward upper-layer data throughout the IP network but it does not make a guarantee that it will arrive at the destination. UDP is a Layer 4 transport layer protocol. In Chapter 1, I briefly discussed the roles of the transport layer, but before moving on to the details of the UDP protocol, it is important I revisit those roles to convey a solid understanding of the transport layer.

Revisiting the Transport Layer

As I state in Chapter 1, the transport layer can provide reliable or unreliable service to an application or other upper-layer protocol. Depending on the type of application, the services of the transport layer required will be different. The term *transport* does not mean that the transport layer *will* guarantee the end-to-end delivery of data but only that it *may* guarantee it. The TCP/IP suite of protocols contains two important transport layer protocols, UDP and TCP.

CROSS-REFERENCE I talk about TCP in Chapter 6.

The transport layer provides two important functions, regardless if the protocol in use is TCP or UDP.

- **Data Protection.** Data protection is implemented in the transport layer by use of checksums. These checksums provide another layer of data integrity besides the data link layer checksum implemented as the CRC field in such protocols as Ethernet. The transport layer calculates its own checksum value over its own header and data. That checksum value is recalculated upon receipt of the data by the destination.

- **Multiplexing.** The multiplexing function of the transport layer allows an application to communicate with another application residing on a destination. The transport layer identifies the source and destination application processes by something called a port, which I will discuss in the next section, on the UDP header.

UDP provides only the two functions above, data protection and multiplexing. It is a very simple protocol designed for applications that do not need the services of a complex protocol such as TCP. Applications using UDP in almost all cases implement their own methods of reliability and connection setup with the destination host. Functions such as flow control are usually not required, but in some cases when they are, can be implemented by the use of the ICMP Source Quench message. ICMP Source Quenches allow a destination to inform a host that it is receiving datagrams faster than they can be processed. Each host allocates a certain amount of buffer space for each transport-layer connection. As I show in Chapter 6, TCP lets each host constantly inform the other about how much buffer space it has left; UDP has no such functionality. When a host is running out of buffers for a UDP-based application, it will send an ICMP Source Quench message to the host to tell it to slow down.

NOTE The TCP/IP stack on Microsoft Windows Operating Systems will not send ICMP Source Quench messages, but it will act on them if they are received.

UDP Header

Figure 5-1 shows the UDP header. The fields of the UDP header are defined in the sections that follow.

Source Port

The source port is a 16-bit number greater than 1023 that is chosen by a user of a UDP based application. These ports are known as *ephemeral* ports because they are only used for the lifetime of the connection (*ephemeral* means short-lived). Ephemeral source port numbers are chosen by the IP stack and used by the transport layer for the delivery of data to upper-layer applications. They function essentially the same as the Ethernet Ethertype and the IP Protocol ID field. When a source host sends data using UDP to a destination host, it chooses an unused source port greater than 1023 to be placed into the UDP Source Port field. The application on the destination station in turn uses this port number in the Destination Port field when it sends data back to the host.

Destination Port

The destination port is also a 16-bit number, which may be greater or less than 1023. In the early ages of TCP/IP, most applications used what are called well-known port numbers. Unlike ephemeral ports, applications will keep a well-known port open for as long as the application is running. Well-known port numbers are in the range of 0 to 1023. Hosts using these applications would use a source (ephemeral) port greater than 1023 and a destination port (well-known) between 0 and 1023. For example, DNS uses UDP port 53. A DNS server allocates the use of port 53 on the local server. When a client sends a DNS request to that server, it will use a source ephemeral port and a destination port of 53. When the DNS server replies to the request, it will use the client's ephemeral port as the destination UDP port and port 53 as the source port. So many applications now use TCP and UDP that the defining line between which ports applications use is blurred. It is typical to see applications using ports ranging from 0 to 65535. Table 5-1 shows some typical UDP well-known application ports.

Table 5-1 Common UDP Application Ports

APPLICATION	UDP PORT
NetBIOS Name Service	137
Simple Network Management Protocol	161
Domain Name Services	53
Routing Information Protocol	521

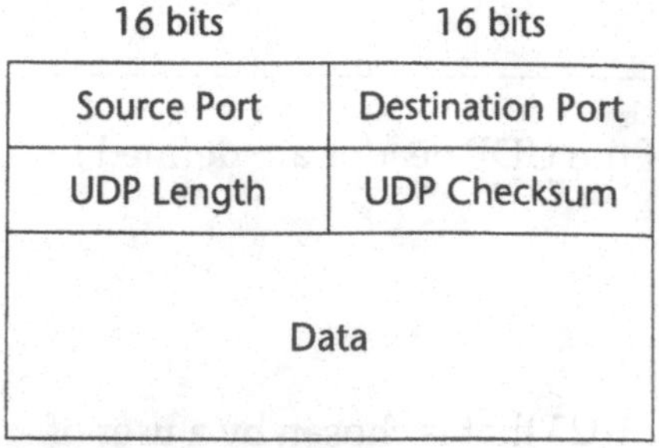

16 bits   16 bits

Source Port	Destination Port
UDP Length	UDP Checksum

Data

Figure 5-1   UDP header.

NOTE A listing of all UDP and TCP ports can be found on the Internet Ports Database at www.portsdb.org/.

UDP Length

The value of the UDP length field is the sum of the length of the UDP header (8 bytes) and the length of the data it is carrying. A quick way of determining the UDP length field is to subtract 20 bytes from the value in the IP length field. Because the IP header is always 20 bytes long, the resulting value will always be equal to the length of the UDP header and its data. For example, if IP is carrying 1,480 bytes, you know that UDP is carrying 1,452 bytes (1,480 – 20(IP) – 8(UDP Header) = UDP data). Of course, you can always look at the UDP length field, but sometimes it's easier to just perform the subtraction in your head.

UDP Checksum

The UDP checksum field covers the entire UDP header and the data being carried by UDP. The UDP header checksum is optional; an application does not have to use it. Eliminating the UDP checksum calculation can sometimes speed up packet processing on slow hosts. If the checksum is not used, the sender must transmit the checksum as all ones. When a receiving station sees all ones in the checksum field, it will not attempt to recalculate the checksum.

WARNING When you are making the decision to turn off UDP checksums, it is important that an application have the ability to guarantee data integrity. There is always the possibility that data could become corrupted after it is received by the MAC layer. In that case, if UDP checksums are not enabled and the application has no data integrity functions, then the data will be passed to the application, which will have no knowledge that the data it is receiving is corrupted.

The UDP checksum includes something called the UDP pseudo-header. The pseudo-header is a virtual extension to the UDP header, which the entire UDP checksum is computed across. The pseudo-header is not included in the actual header but used to provide another guarantee that the UDP data has been received by the correct host. Figure 5-2 shows the UDP psuedo-header. When a source transmits a UDP packet, it builds a virtual UDP packet including the source and destination IP addresses, the IP Protocol ID, and the UDP Length field. The UDP checksum field includes these virtual fields when it calculates the checksum value. When the destination UDP layer receives the UDP datagram, it takes the source IP address, destination IP address, and protocol ID from the IP header for use in recreating the virtual UDP psuedo-header. The destination host literally rebuilds the same virtual UDP packet that the source host used to calculate its UDP checksum. It then compares the checksum it calculated to the checksum received in the packet to make sure they are the same. Although you never actually see the pseudo-header in the UDP packet, it is important to understand that this process exists. Psuedo-headers make the UDP checksum more resilient in guaranteeing data integrity between hosts. By disabling the UDP checksum, you may gain performance, but lose the ability to provide data integrity to your applications, unless of course, the application has a way of providing it.

Data

The data field of the UDP datagram contains the data the destination application is to receive, the application being defined by the destination UDP port number.

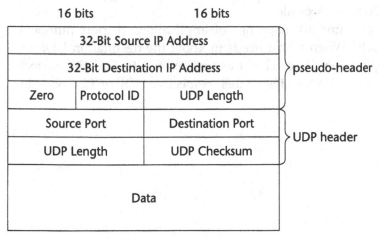

Figure 5-2 The UDP psuedo-header.

UDP Communication Process

Communications at the transport layer are sometimes called client/server communications. Typically one host (the client) needs to use an application on another host (the server).

> **NOTE** Although there is no requirement for either host to actually be a server-type machine, it is easier to view the communications processes in terms of a client and a server.

When a client needs to use an application on a remote host using the UDP protocol, it needs to know a couple pieces of information.

- The IP address of the host where the application resides
- The destination UDP port number of the application

There are several different methods through which a host can obtain the IP address of a destination host. One is the Domain Name System (DNS); another is the Windows Internet Naming System (WINS).

> **CROSS-REFERENCE** I talk about these methods in Chapters 7 and 8.

For now, assume that a host knows that an application resides on another host with the IP address of 172.16.1.15. After obtaining the IP address, it now needs to know what the applications destination UDP port number is. All UDP and TCP port numbers are stored in a file named the *services file*. On Unix systems, the services file is typically located in /etc/services. On Windows 2000 hosts, it can be found in c:\windows\system32\drivers\etc. Figure 5-3 shows a typical Windows 2000 services file.

The services file contains all mappings of applications to port numbers for both TCP and UDP. When a host needs to know the destination UDP or TCP port of an application, it searches the services file to find the correct port number. Custom applications install their respective UDP or TCP ports in this file.

```
# Copyright (c) 1993-1999 Microsoft Corp.
#
# This file contains port numbers for well-known services defined by IANA
#
# Format:
#
# <service name>   <port number>/<protocol>   [aliases...]   [#<comment>]
#

echo              7/tcp
echo              7/udp
discard           9/tcp     sink null
discard           9/udp     sink null
systat            11/tcp    users              #Active users
systat            11/tcp    users              #Active users
daytime           13/tcp
daytime           13/udp
qotd              17/tcp    quote              #Quote of the day
qotd              17/udp    quote              #Quote of the day
chargen           19/tcp    ttytst source      #Character generator
chargen           19/udp    ttytst source      #Character generator
ftp-data          20/tcp                       #FTP, data
ftp               21/tcp                       #FTP. control
telnet            23/tcp
smtp              25/tcp    mail               #Simple Mail Transfer Protocol
time              37/tcp    timserver
time              37/udp    timserver
rlp               39/udp    resource           #Resource Location Protocol
nameserver        42/tcp    name               #Host Name Server
nameserver        42/udp    name               #Host Name Server
nicname           43/tcp    whois
domain            53/tcp                       #Domain Name Server
domain            53/udp                       #Domain Name Server
bootps            67/udp    dhcps              #Bootstrap Protocol Server
bootpc            68/udp    dhcpc              #Bootstrap Protocol Client
tftp              69/udp                       #Trivial File Transfer
gopher            70/tcp
finger            79/tcp
http              80/tcp    www www-http       #World Wide Web
kerberos          88/tcp    krb5 kerberos-sec  #Kerberos
kerberos          88/udp    krb5 kerberos-sec  #Kerberos
hostname          101/tcp   hostnames          #NIC Host Name Server
iso-tsap          102/tcp                      #ISO-TSAP Class 0
rtelnet           107/tcp                      #Remote Telnet Service
pop2              109/tcp   postoffice         #Post Office Protocol - Version 2
pop3              110/tcp                      #Post Office Protocol - Version 3
sunrpc            111/tcp   rpcbind portmap    #SUN Remote Procedure Call
sunrpc            111/udp   rpcbind portmap    #SUN Remote Procedure Call
auth              113/tcp   ident tap          #Identification Protocol
uucp-path         117/tcp
nntp              119/tcp   usenet             #Network News Transfer Protocol
ntp               123/udp                      #Network Time Protocol
epmap             135/tcp   loc-srv            #DCE endpoint resolution
epmap             135/udp   loc-sr             #DCE endpoint resolution
netbios-ns        137/tcp   nbname             #NETBIOS Name Service
netbios-ns        137/udp   nbname             #NETBIOS Name Service
netbios-dgm       138/udp   nbdatagram         #NETBIOS Datagram Service
netbios-ssn       139/tcp   nbsession          #NETBIOS Session Service
imap              143/tcp   imap4              #Internet Message Access Protocol
pcmail-srv        158/tcp                      #PCMail Server
snmp              161/udp                      #SNMP
snmptrap          162/udp   snmp-trap          #SNMP trap
print-srv         170/tcp                      #Network PostScript
bgp               179/tcp                      #Border Gateway Protocol
irc               194/tcp                      #Internet Relay Chat Protocol
ipx               213/udp                      #IPX over IP
ldap              389/tcp                      #Lightweight Directory Access Protocol
```

Figure 5-3   Windows 2000 services file. *(continues)*

```
https              443/tcp       MCom
https              443/udp       MCom
microsoft-ds       445/tcp
microsoft-ds       445/udp
kpasswd            464/tcp                            # Kerberos (v5)
kpasswd            464/udp                            # Kerberos (v5)
isakmp             500/udp       ike                  #Internet Key Exchange
exec               512/tcp                            #Remote Process Execution
biff               512/udp       comsat
login              513/tcp                            #Remote Login
who                513/udp       whod
cmd                514/tcp       shell
syslog             514/udp
printer            515/tcp       spooler
talk               517/udp
ntalk              518/udp
efs                520/tcp                            #Extended File Name Server
router             520/udp       route routed
timed              525/udp       timeserver
tempo              526/tcp       newdate
courier            530/tcp       rpc
conference         531/tcp       chat
netnews            532/tcp       readnews
netwall            533/udp                            #For emergency broadcasts
uucp               540/tcp       uucpd
klogin             543/tcp                            #Kerberos login
kshell             544/tcp       krcmd                #Kerberos remote shell
new-rwho           550/udp       new-who
remotefs           556/tcp       rfs rfs_server
rmonitor           560/udp       rmonitord
monitor            561/udp
ldaps              636/tcp       sldap                #LDAP over TLS/SSL
doom               666/tcp                            #Doom Id Software
doom               666/udp                            #Doom Id Software
kerberos-adm       749/tcp                            #Kerberos administration
kerberos-adm       749/udp                            #Kerberos administration
kerberos-iv        750/udp                            #Kerberos version IV
kpop               1109/tcp                           #Kerberos POP
phone              1167/udp                           #Conference calling
ms-sql-s           1433/tcp                           #Microsoft-SQL-Server
ms-sql-s           1433/udp                           #Microsoft-SQL-Server
ms-sql-m           1434/tcp                           #Microsoft-SQL-Monitor
ms-sql-m           1434/udp                           #Microsoft-SQL-Monitor
wins               1512/tcp                           #Microsoft Windows Internet Name Service
wins               1512/udp                           #Microsoft Windows Internet Name Service
ingreslock         1524/tcp      ingres
l2tp               1701/udp                           #Layer Two Tunneling Protocol
pptp               1723/tcp                           #Point-to-point tunnelling protocol
radius             1812/udp                           #RADIUS authentication protocol
radacct            1813/udp                           #RADIUS accounting protocol
nfsd               2049/udp      nfs                  #NFS server
knetd              2053/tcp                           #Kerberos de-multiplexor
man                9535/tcp                           #Remote Man Server
```

Figure 5-3   Windows 2000 services file. *(continued)*

MICROSOFT PORT QUERY TOOL

Microsoft has a tool called Port Query (portqry.exe) that allows you to query other hosts to see if the host is running a specific application over a well-known UDP or TCP port. This tool is a great way to confirm that an application is listening on a port and also to confirm that a firewall or router isn't filtering out traffic destined to certain ports. It can be downloaded at www.microsoft.com. The following output shows the Port Query tool being used to verify that my ISPs DNS server is in fact listening for DNS Name Resolution Requests on UDP port 53:

```
C:\apps>portqry -n 151.197.0.39 -e 53 -p UDP

Querying target system called:

 151.197.0.39

Attempting to resolve IP address to a name...

IP address resolved to home4.bellatlantic.net

UDP port 53 (domain service): LISTENING
```

After an application finds out the destination UDP port of the application, the following happens:

1. It chooses a port number greater than 1023 for use in the source UDP port field.

2. Upon reception of the packet, the destination host examines the destination UDP port number to determine what application should receive the UDP data.

3. When the application responds to the source host, it reverses the UDP port numbers, placing the destination stations source UDP port in the destination UDP port field and its own source UDP port in the source field.

Figure 5-4 illustrates this process.

A DNS name resolution request is sent from host 192.168.1.100 to the DNS server at 151.197.0.39. In frame 1 of the trace, the source UDP port is 3422 and the destination port is the well-known DNS port for UDP of 53. In Frame 2 the response from the DNS server to the client is from the source DNS port 53 to the client's UDP port 3422.

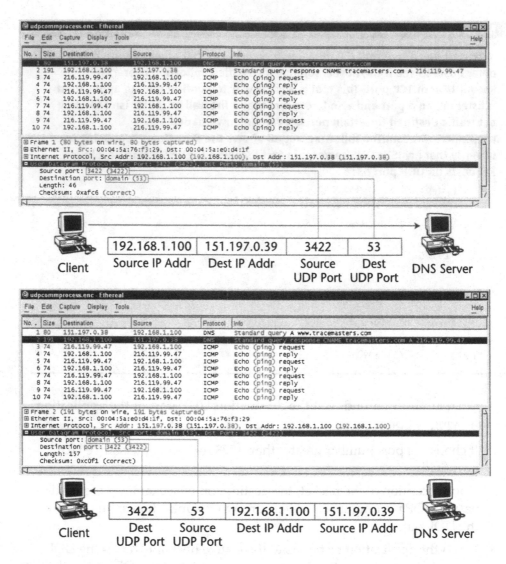

Figure 5-4   UDP communication process.

Case Studies in UDP Communications

As I have discussed, UDP is a very simple protocol, providing only multiplexing and data protection services to upper-layer applications. In a very simple sense, it either works, or it doesn't work. Its simplicity makes it very dependent on the lower-layer networking services to operate without errors. UDP has no methods to retransmit lost data or handle more than minimal flow control issues via ICMP Source Quench messages.

Given all that, it is important to understand the reasoning behind why applications use UDP over TCP when troubleshooting a problem. In this section, I take a look at several application protocols that use UDP. I discuss the basic functionality of the application and try to illustrate how the application handles reliability services that UDP does not provide.

Name Resolution Services

In Chapters 7 and 8, I discuss two kinds of name resolution services in IP networks. One is used to resolve NetBIOS names, and the other is used to resolve IP host names. Both are similar in nature. Both of these application protocols use UDP as their method of transport rather than TCP. There are a couple of reasons that UDP is a good choice for these applications:

- The first reason is that they are request/response applications. A single request is sent and a single response is received. In file transfer applications, a server often sends multiple segments of data back to a client. A protocol such as TCP can gather multiple small data segments and group them into a single large TCP segment. This method of grouping small segments together into one larger segment prevents wasting network bandwidth on multiple small packets (see the sidebar "Packet Efficiency" in this chapter). UDP has no such functionality. Every time an application writes data to the UDP layer, a packet is generated. UDP doesn't provide segment assembly services, and therefore, is much faster. Every time UDP receives data, it creates a UDP header and passes its data down to the IP layer. For request/response applications, UDP is fast and efficient because it doesn't provide any reliability.

- Second, most request/response applications will retry their requests if they don't receive an answer. For example, if a client sends a DNS name resolution request to a DNS name server and does not receive a response, it will attempt the resolution process again and again, until it eventually gives up. In Figure 5-5, you see a client sending repeated DNS requests to a DNS server that is not responding. After the first attempt in Frame 1, the client tries again after 1 second, 2 seconds, 5 seconds, and 9 seconds, and then finally gives up and displays the Unknown host www.tracemasters.com message. Notice also that the attempts are roughly doubled after each name resolution request. The client host waits a little bit longer each time before making another request in the hope that the network problem, which is preventing name resolution, will be resolved. Here, the reliability is built into the protocol itself. There is no need to use a protocol (like TCP) that provides reliability. The nature of most protocols like DNS is that they will perform their own retransmissions of data.

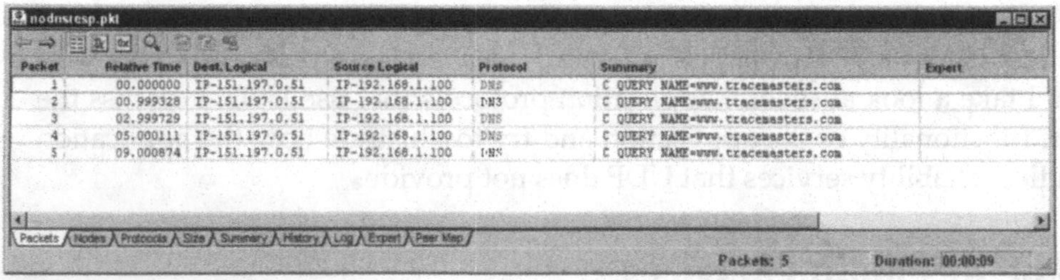

Figure 5-5 No DNS response.

Routing Information Protocol

The *Routing Information Protocol*, or *RIP* as it is commonly known, is used to distribute routing information among routers on an IP network. It operates by sending routing information in one or more IP broadcast packets. Routers using the RIP protocol send out routing advertisements every 30 seconds. Each packet can contain multiple route entries. When there are more route entries than can fit in a single RIP packet, the routes are sent in consecutive RIP packets. Each router sends out as many RIP packets during a single advertisement interval as are necessary to advertise its entire routing table.

RIP is what is known as a distance vector routing protocol. A *distance vector routing protocol* simply advertises what routes it knows to other routers, with those routers passing on information they have heard to other routers. The process continues until all routers have built a routing table of all routes in the network.

Since hosts depend on the network to provide end-to-end routing of data, it would seem that it would be important enough for routing protocols such as RIP to use a reliable protocol like TCP for advertising routing information. However, RIP does not; it uses UDP. If a single RIP packet is lost, UDP will not retransmit the data. Fortunately, because of the way RIP works, the loss of a single packet does not affect the routing process. Routers listening to RIP broadcasts will not automatically flag a route as unreachable if they miss a single RIP packet containing the route entry. Listening routers typically wait a multiple of several advertisement intervals before declaring a route unreachable. For example, RIP advertises route entries every 30 seconds. A router listening for RIP advertisements will delete a route from its route table only after not hearing an advertisement for the route after three route advertisement intervals. In the case of RIP, this amounts to 90 seconds until a router declares a route unreachable.

So why then doesn't RIP use a reliable protocol like TCP? To understand why a reliable protocol like TCP is unnecessary, examine Figure 5-6. The router at 10.239.1.81 is advertising 109 separate route entries every 30 seconds via the RIP protocol. In its second advertisement, you see only 100 route entries being advertised, as the last RIP packet containing the last 9 entries is lost. 30 seconds

PACKET EFFICIENCY

All packet transmissions over a network have overhead associated with them. For example, a user's password may consist of only 20 bytes of data, but it takes 46 bytes of overhead to transmit it over the network. Each protocol layer adds its own overhead needed to do its job. *Overhead* is anything added to a data transmission besides the data. Here is the amount of overhead at each layer needed to carry a simple 20 bytes of data across the network using the UDP protocol.

```
Ethernet (addressing, Ethertype, CRC) = 18 bytes
Internet Protocol Header = 20 bytes
UDP Header = 8 Bytes
Data = 20 bytes


Total Overhead = 46 bytes
Total Packet Length = 66 bytes
```

Packet efficiency is the percentage of the total packet length that is being utilized for data. The more that is utilized, the better the efficiency is. Packet efficiency is calculated by dividing the data length by the packet length.

```
10 bytes / 66 bytes = 15% Packet Efficiency
```

As you increase the amount of data that each packet is carrying, your packet efficiency increases. If you start carrying the maximum amount of data in each UDP packet, your efficiency is maximized. Here is the packet efficiency for 1,452 bytes of UDP data.

```
1,452 bytes / 1,518 bytes = 95% Packet Efficiency
```

The bottom line is that it is better to fill your packets with as much data as possible before transmitting them across the network.

later you can again see the full 109 routes being advertised. There is no need to retransmit this lost RIP broadcast because this is done automatically at the next advertisement interval.

In essence, the reliability needed for the routing information is already built into the protocol itself by way of its advertisement interval. Routing protocols like RIP use UDP because of this built-in "reliability." By its nature, RIP is going to broadcast its routes whether or not a destination router receives them. It simply doesn't need a reliable transport to do what it is already going to do. OSPF, another routing protocol, uses neither UDP nor TCP because it runs directly over IP. Only in the most critical situations does a routing protocol use a reliable protocol. BGP-4, the routing protocol behind the Internet backbone, is one such protocol. BGP-4 uses TCP as its reliable transport protocol.

Frame	Time	Dst Other Addr	Src Other Addr	Protocol	Description
1	31.036494	255.255.255.255	10.239.1.81	RIP	Response, 25 Entries (ver. 1)
2	32.03772	255.255.255.255	10.239.1.81	RIP	Response, 25 Entries (ver. 1)
3	33.042707	255.255.255.255	10.239.1.81	RIP	Response, 25 Entries (ver. 1)
4	34.040045	255.255.255.255	10.239.1.81	RIP	Response, 25 Entries (ver. 1)
5	35.044908	255.255.255.255	10.239.1.81	RIP	Response, 9 Entries (ver. 1)
6	51.632907	255.255.255.255	10.239.1.82	RIP	Response, 25 Entries (ver. 1)
7	52.435522	255.255.255.255	10.239.1.80	RIP	Response, 25 Entries (ver. 1)
8	52.637429	255.255.255.255	10.239.1.82	RIP	Response, 8 Entries (ver. 1)
9	53.436705	255.255.255.255	10.239.1.80	RIP	Response, 25 Entries (ver. 1)
10	54.437882	255.255.255.255	10.239.1.80	RIP	Response, 25 Entries (ver. 1)
11	55.440118	255.255.255.255	10.239.1.80	RIP	Response, 25 Entries (ver. 1)
12	56.443953	255.255.255.255	10.239.1.80	RIP	Response, 9 Entries (ver. 1)
13	65.07658	255.255.255.255	10.239.1.81	RIP	Response, 25 Entries (ver. 1)
14	66.077872	255.255.255.255	10.239.1.81	RIP	Response, 25 Entries (ver. 1)
15	67.078963	255.255.255.255	10.239.1.81	RIP	Response, 25 Entries (ver. 1)
16	68.080116	255.255.255.255	10.239.1.81	RIP	Response, 25 Entries (ver. 1)
17	82.669596	255.255.255.255	10.239.1.82	RIP	Response, 25 Entries (ver. 1)
18	83.674185	255.255.255.255	10.239.1.82	RIP	Response, 8 Entries (ver. 1)
19	86.475979	255.255.255.255	10.239.1.80	RIP	Response, 25 Entries (ver. 1)
20	87.477196	255.255.255.255	10.239.1.80	RIP	Response, 25 Entries (ver. 1)
21	88.478409	255.255.255.255	10.239.1.80	RIP	Response, 25 Entries (ver. 1)
22	89.479547	255.255.255.255	10.239.1.80	RIP	Response, 25 Entries (ver. 1)
23	90.484427	255.255.255.255	10.239.1.80	RIP	Response, 9 Entries (ver. 1)
24	99.121799	255.255.255.255	10.239.1.81	RIP	Response, 25 Entries (ver. 1)
25	100.123108	255.255.255.255	10.239.1.81	RIP	Response, 25 Entries (ver. 1)
26	101.124185	255.255.255.255	10.239.1.81	RIP	Response, 25 Entries (ver. 1)
27	102.125813	255.255.255.255	10.239.1.81	RIP	Response, 25 Entries (ver. 1)
28	103.130192	255.255.255.255	10.239.1.81	RIP	Response, 9 Entries (ver. 1)
29	113.706383	255.255.255.255	10.239.1.82	RIP	Response, 25 Entries (ver. 1)
30	114.710654	255.255.255.255	10.239.1.82	RIP	Response, 8 Entries (ver. 1)
31	120.516427	255.255.255.255	10.239.1.80	RIP	Response, 25 Entries (ver. 1)

Annotations: 109 route entries from 10.239.1.81 (frames 1–5); 100 route entries from 10.239.1.81 (frames 13–16); 109 route entries from 10.239.1.81 (frames 24–28). 30 second interval between groups.

Figure 5-6   Router RIP advertisements.

Simple Network Management Protocol

Simple Network Management Protocol (SNMP) is another application-layer protocol that does not require a reliable transport. Used by network management stations to query the status of devices, SNMP actually relies on failures in the network in order to build its uptime statistics. Like RIP, it queries devices on the network for information contained in their MIB tables. SNMP can gather from devices such information as uptime, error counts, and interface bandwidth statistics. The values it collects are stored in a database on the management station for further use in reports or alarms. When an SNMP network management station does not receive a response from an SNMP query, it attempts to query the device several more times before flagging the device as down. It then, depending on its configuration, possibly creates an alarm condition and notifies network administrators that the device is down. SNMP, like RIP, by its nature is going to query network devices regardless of whether or not they respond. When they respond, the management station knows that it will be able to continue querying the device for various values in its MIB tables. When a device stops responding, it will still query the device periodically to make sure it hasn't come back online.

UDP and Firewalls

Unlike TCP, UDP is stateless. State refers to the ability of a protocol to provide information about its connection status with another station. TCP does this with something called sequence numbers and connection flags. The sequence numbers and flags make it easy to track a TCP application through a firewall. It is important to track where conversations are initiated to prevent the spoofing of an application conversation. With UDP, this is difficult to do. Most firewall administrators limit UDP traffic through their firewalls for exactly this reason. Some applications, though, use UDP. DNS is one important protocol that uses UDP and that cannot be filtered from most firewalls. Sometimes it is difficult to determine what protocols and ports an application uses without manually analyzing a packet trace of the application. Many times I have seen applications using protocols and ports that the administrators didn't even know about. A simple packet capture during the execution of an application can quickly reveal which protocols and ports it depends on.

CROSS-REFERENCE I talk about TCP sequence and acknowledgement numbers in Chapter 6.

TIP When troubleshooting connections through a firewall, a protocol analyzer is an excellent tool to have on hand because by using it you can immediately determine what ports and protocols are being blocked by a firewall.

The following case studies illustrate why you sometimes need to utilize proper analysis techniques in order to diagnose application problems. When an application fails due to a firewall or router blocking the traffic it requires, I very often see time-consuming knowledge base searches performed on the vendor's Web sites in search of the answer. Sometimes the answer is that a registry entry or configuration parameter needs to be changed, but it is important to first understand what is happening that causes the application to fail. I illustrate how to use a protocol analyzer to do just that in the following cases.

Case Study: Failed PCAnywhere Session

Upon the implementation of a new third-party firewall, my team and I immediately received calls from the server administration group about their not being able to access PCAnywhere sessions on their servers.

After getting an administrator on the phone and our protocol analyzer's filters set up, we were able to capture a session between the administrator and the server on which that person was trying to access a PCAnywhere session. What we saw was several UDP packets from the client with no response from the server. The UDP packets had a destination UDP port of 5632. It was immediately obvious that the firewall was dropping these UDP packets. Unfortunately, the firewall policy mirrored the corporate security policy that no UDP packets are allowed through the firewall except for protocols that absolutely needed UDP, protocols like DNS, which were critical to the functioning of the network.

After doing a little research on Symantec's Web site, we discovered that UDP port 5632 was used only for obtaining the status of the PCAnywhere service. The actual PCAnywhere sessions ran over TCP port 5631. We also found a small registry entry that could be configured on PCAnywhere client machines that told the software to continue connecting with TCP even if it did not receive a response on the UDP status port (see the sidebar "PCAnywhere Registry Fix"). Once the local administrators configured their machines with this registry entry, they were able to access PCAnywhere because the local software continued the connection processing using TCP even after never receiving a UDP status response.

PCANYWHERE REGISTRY FIX

To disable the pcAnywhere UDP status packets you need to modify the following registry key:

HKEY_LOCAL_MACHINE\SOFTWARE\Symantec\pcAnywhere\CurrentVersion\System

You need to add the DWORD value TCPIPConnectIfUnknown and set the value of this new entry to 1.

I've seen this situation more times than I care to count on networks that use PCAnywhere for remote administration. It is a fine example of how understanding an application protocols and ports can aid in problem solving. Figure 5-7 illustrates how PCAnywhere sessions work. In Frame 1 the client sends a UDP status frame to the server running PCAnywhere on port 5632. Only after the server responds to the status frame does the client continue the connection process using TCP port 5631.

Case Study: NFS Failures

Network File System (NFS) is another protocol that uses UDP. NFS is primarily used on Unix systems and uses UDP port 2049. Unix systems also use other UDP port services for several other applications known as Remote Procedure Calls, or RPC. Clients using these RPC services do not know off-hand what port the remote service will be running on. They use an RPC feature called Port Mapper to find out. Figure 5-8 illustrates a situation we ran into after migrating several Unix systems to a different location and putting them behind a firewall.

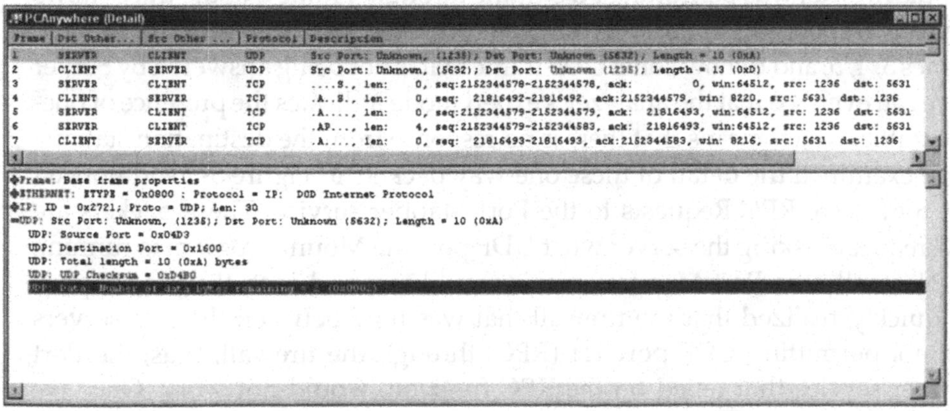

Figure 5-7 PCAnywhere session.

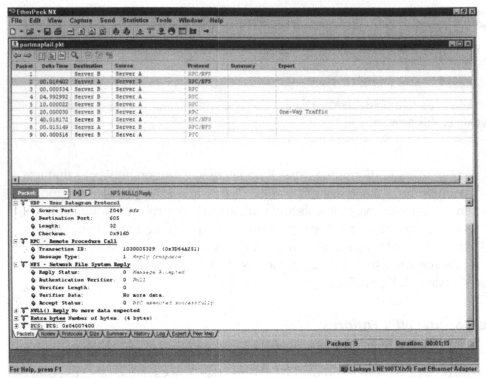

Figure 5-8 NFS in action.

Unix administrators notified us that they could no longer mount remote Unix volumes across the network. Figure 5-8 shows a packet capture of what happened while we watched as they attempted to mount a remote Unix file system volume.

Since we knew that Unix uses the NFS protocol, we could immediately see that the firewall was permitting NFS traffic through. Frame 2 of the trace shows Server B responding to an NFS call from Server A that was sent in Frame 1. Frames 3, 4, 5, and 6 show some UDP traffic that is not being answered by Server B. We can even see that the analyzer's expert mode indicates the presence of one-way traffic, which means that there is no response from the destination station.

We examined the detail of these one-way packets in Figure 5-9 and noticed that they were RPC Requests to the Port Mapper service. These packets are RPC requests asking the server what UDP port the Mount program is running on. Normally the Port Mapper service would respond with the proper port. We quickly realized that the firewall that was now between the two servers was not permitting UDP port 111 (RPC) through the firewall; thus, the Port Mapper service that relied on the RPC function, would not work. Once we modified the firewalls ruleset to allow UDP port 111, the Unix administrators were able to mount remote volumes.

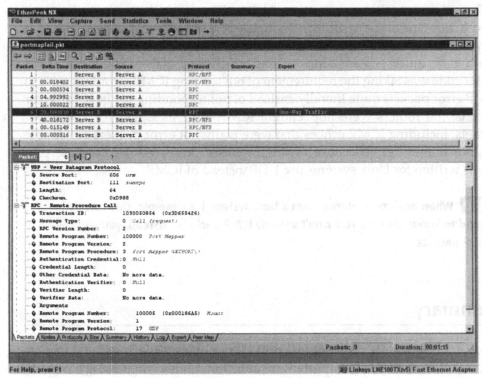

Figure 5-9 RPC dropped.

I would like to reinforce once again how important it is to properly analyze an application's traffic during a problem. The previous case studies clearly show the definitive diagnosis and solution to the problems. Many times similar results can be obtained by making multiple configuration changes until the application starts working. The drawback to this random guesswork is that when a similar problem occurs, you might try the same fix without any result. Different problems sometimes manifest themselves with the same symptoms. Without knowing the real cause of the problem by way of proper analysis, you will never be able to translate that knowledge to other situations.

Traceroute Caveats

In Chapter 4, I discussed how the PING program uses ICMP Echo and Echo Reply messages to query if a host is responsive or not. I also show how the traceroute program uses these ICMP Echo messages to build a list of routers along the path of the packets using TTL Expired messages. The traceroutes I use in the Chapter 4 section on TTL are from the *tracert* program on a Microsoft Windows 2000 station. If you happen to be analyzing a Unix system traceroute, you might be scratching your head as to why you don't see any ICMP Echo Requests. You don't see them because most Unix systems use UDP instead of ICMP for traceroute.

To explain actually requires some history. The original traceroute program used ICMP. One of the first times the developers tested the traceroute program they noticed that routers were not sending back ICMP TTL Expired messages. After some quick conversations to router vendors, they found out that the router code was taking the requirement of not sending ICMP error messages to ICMP error packets quite literally. Instead of not responding to just ICMP error packets, the routers were not sending ICMP error messages for any ICMP packets, including ICMP echoes that were really not error packets but simple diagnostic messages. Because of this problem, the original traceroute programs written for Unix systems use UDP instead of ICMP.

TIP When analyzing latency from a Unix system, for example, this history is good to know because you won't see any ICMP packets. Instead, you will see UDP packets.

Summary

UDP is a very simple protocol that provides only multiplexing and data protection functionality. It is important to understand how, when using a nonreliable transport protocol, an application must take on the responsibility of reliability itself. In the next chapter, on TCP, I take a look at how reliability, flow control, and myriad other features are implemented to provide functionality that UDP, or even IP, cannot provide.

Transmission Control Protocol

As you move up higher and higher into each layer of the OSI model, protocols become more complex. TCP is no exception to this statement. Its complexity derives from TCP's rich set of features and functionality. By not learning its inner functions, you risk missing the ability to completely understand the protocol, which, in troubleshooting scenarios, can be deadly. This chapter seeks to help you understand TCP from the inside out.

Introduction to TCP

Chapter 6 is broken down into four main sections.

- First is the one you are reading, the introduction. In it I discuss TCP at the 10,000-foot level, briefly glancing over its many intricacies. TCP is a difficult protocol to explain without getting into its many intricate details. I have purposely left out many of these details in the first section. I simply want you to be familiar with their existence before we talk about their use. Thus, I immediately describe the TCP Header, which will be the basis for our discussion on the rest of the protocol's functionality. I also talk about what a reliable transport protocol does and what it needs to be able to do its job. Again, these subjects will be at a very broad level so that the reader may glean a look at what is to come later in the chapter.

- Second, I talk about the connection-oriented nature of TCP, how it opens, closes, and handles connection problems between hosts.

- Third, I talk in depth about how TCP handles flow control between two hosts and what happens if packets are lost during a data transfer.

- Finally, I wrap up the chapter on TCP with examples analyzing applications that run over TCP.

Each of these four sections includes numerous case studies. The best way to illustrate a protocol is by example. Many a skilled network administrator has gained his experience from configuring workstations, building servers, and configuring routers. As you move up into the higher layers, however, there is often nothing to configure. The only way to learn is by example, by watching the protocols themselves in action. TCP cannot be understood without taking the time to analyze packet by packet the transactions occurring between hosts. TCP takes time.

NOTE I whole-heartedly encourage readers to pick up a copy of W. Richard Stevens' *TCP/IP Illustrated*, Volume 1 (Addison-Wesley January 1994). Stevens does an excellent job of extrapolating on almost every nuance of the TCP protocol. The book is an invaluable reference for the protocol and should be a part of any network analyst's book collection.

Requirements for a Reliable Transport Protocol

In Chapter 5, I discussed how UDP provides only multiplexing and data protection services to upper-layer protocols and data. TCP also provides the same services as UDP, using source and destination port numbers, a TCP checksum, and even the same pseudo-header that UDP uses to verify the data's destination endpoint and to ensure data integrity. However, unlike UDP, TCP is a connection-oriented, reliable transport protocol. TCP has the ability to track data transmissions and, if necessary, retransmit them. It has the ability to manage flow control between a sender and receiver. Unlike UDP, which was only able to utilize ICMPs Source Quench message, TCP can inform an endpoint of its data reception capabilities in a very granular manner. TCP has other functionality that allows it to provide better service to applications regardless of their traffic type. The next sections present several scenarios that a reliable, connection-oriented transport protocol needs to handle.

Fast Sender and Slow Receiver

A host that is receiving data from another host may need to inform the sending host of the need to adjust its rate of transmission. There may be several reasons that a host cannot receive data at the same rate as a sender transmits it.

- The host may have less processing power than the sender.
- Its TCP/IP stack may be busy servicing many other concurrent communications.
- It also may have an application that is not retrieving data from the transport layers buffers quickly enough.

An application using UDP has only the ability to use the ICMP Source Quench message to inform a host to slow down its rate of transmission. Unfortunately, the ICMP Source Quench message does not contain any information that would allow it to tell a host how long it needs it to slow down for. Congestion conditions inside of a host can change very quickly. A host unable to receive any data could be ready to receive more data in under a half a second. ICMP Source Quench messages are a brute force method of congestion control. A reliable transport protocol needs a granular feedback mechanism to inform senders of exactly how much data they are able to accept at any given time. With this information, a sending host can adjust its rate of transmission to suit the needs of a receiving host. Later in the chapter, you will see how TCP's window size advertisement does just this.

Packet Loss

In some of the previous chapters I mention several conditions, such as congestion or media errors, that may cause packets to be dropped on their way from a sender to a receiver. Any number of circumstances could cause packet loss on a network. Whether packet loss occurs on the network, inside of a router, or on the way up the stack to an application is not a concern to the transport layer. A reliable transport layer is concerned only with the end-to-end data transfer. Reliability by the transport layer is provided by its ability to retransmit data that has not been received by a destination host. So, in order for a host's TCP stack to recognize packet loss, it must have a method of tracking individual segments of data that it transmits. It does this by sending with every segment a unique sequence number. When a destination host's TCP stack receives the data segment, it sends back an acknowledgment message telling the sender that it received the data segment sent by the host. This acknowledgment message tells the source that the host's TCP stack, in fact, received the data with a specific sequence number. If a sending host does not receive an acknowledgment for a sequenced data segment, it assumes that the data segment was lost in route to the destination. After waiting a certain time interval, the sending host's TCP stack will retransmit the last data segment.

> **NOTE** Remember, however, that reliability in a reliable protocol does not mean that data transmission is guaranteed. Although a reliable protocol will do its best to mitigate problem conditions on a network, it cannot handle every situation that is likely to occur. For example, an interface on a router may be intermittently dropping data packets. If a packet is dropped, the TCP protocol will retransmit the packet. Assuming that the interface problem is intermittent, there is a good chance that the retransmitted packet will make it to the destination host. If the interface fails completely and stops passing all traffic, the TCP protocol on the sending host can retransmit lost data indefinitely and it will not be successful until the routers interface module is replaced. This situation is what we call *best effort*. A reliable transport protocol can really only provide a best effort attempt at data transmission because it, like other protocols, also relies on the layers below it to do their job correctly.

Data Duplication

I want to expand on the topic of packet loss. Assume that a packet on a network is lost. TCP retransmits the lost data segment, and all is well. Maybe. What happens if the destination host receives the original segment a split second after TCP retransmits the lost segment? Now the destination host is going to receive the same data twice, and unless the application has some way of also sequencing data, it is also going to receive the same data twice. This situation could possibly corrupt an application if there isn't some way to detect duplicate data. Fortunately, there is. As I said previously, TCP sends every data segment with a unique sequence number. When a receiving host's TCP stack notices the same sequence number being received a second time, it simply drops the duplicate data. This example is a fine illustration of the types of services that TCP provides to an application. If not for TCP's data sequencing function, an application would have to provide the same functionality. And in order for an application to perform the same services as TCP, the programmers would have to include code in the application that would, in effect, do the exact same thing that TCP does already. So, why not just write applications to take advantage of the services that TCP already offers?

Priority Data

Often when two hosts are transferring data between them it is through an interactive user application. Telnet is a fine example of an interactive application. Telnet uses control characters to handle screen formatting, keystroke echoing functions, and other data manipulation. It is sometimes imperative for real-time applications like Telnet to prioritize certain data, such as control characters, over regular data. The TCP protocol allows an application to do this with something called the urgent pointer. The urgent pointer lets an application specify data that is urgent. The application then is able to retrieve that data and process it before other data in the stream. Applications that make use of data that is by nature a priority would never be able to operate over a simple unreliable transport protocol like UDP. The urgent pointer is not often used because TCP has a function called the Push bit that provides similar functionality to the urgent pointer. I discuss the Push bit in a later section of this chapter.

Out-of-Order Data

In redundant networks, it is not uncommon to have more than one possible network path between a sender and receiver. Because of this, it is quite possible that packets could take different paths upon traveling to their final destination. Some networks utilize parallel links that transmit packets in a round-robin fashion across both links. This type of transmission allows equal distribution of traffic over both links.

Assume that an application that transmits files between a source and destination host is using UDP as its transport protocol. Further, assume that the network between the source and destination has multiple network paths. What happens when a stream of data packets arrives in a different order from which they were sent? Unless the source application provided some method of numbering each data segment with a unique sequence number, the destination application will have no way of telling that the data segments it has received are in the wrong order. This situation could lead to serious data corruption because the data will be written to the application in the wrong order. Imagine a situation where each packet contains financial bank data for individual bank accounts. It's pretty easy to see what a disastrous affect this could have on application data. A requirement for the proper ordered delivery of data is precisely why application developers choose to write their applications over a reliable protocol like TCP. TCP adds a sequence number to each segment of data before sending it. These sequence numbers allow the receiver to easily reorder the data segments into the proper order before delivering them to the upper-layer application.

Each of the situations discussed in the previous sections has led to the requirements for developing the TCP protocol as it exists today. In the next section, I discuss where these requirements are implemented in the TCP packet header. Then, after you understand where these services are implemented, I discuss how each of them actually works.

The TCP Header

The TCP header is 20 bytes long and contains a number of data fields. Figure 6-1 illustrates these fields. Their descriptions are given in the sections that follow.

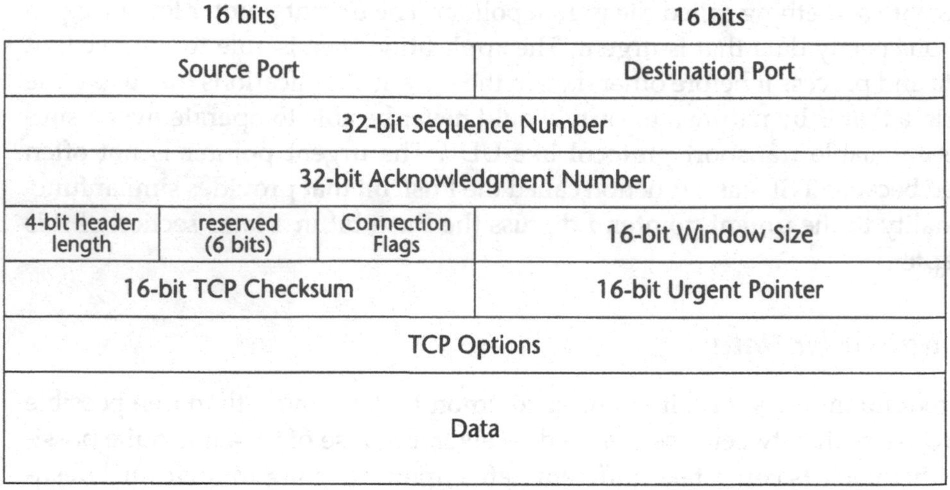

16 bits   16 bits

Source Port	Destination Port
32-bit Sequence Number	
32-bit Acknowledgment Number	

4-bit header length	reserved (6 bits)	Connection Flags	16-bit Window Size

16-bit TCP Checksum	16-bit Urgent Pointer
TCP Options	
Data	

Figure 6-1   TCP header.

Source Port

The source port is a 16-bit number greater than 1023 that is chosen by a user of a TCP-based application. As is the case with UDP, these ports are ephemeral ports—they are short-lived. The source port number is used by the transport layer in delivering data to upper-layer applications. It functions essentially the same way as the Ethernet Ethertype and the IP Protocol ID field. When a source host uses TCP to send data to a destination host, it chooses an unused port number over 1023, which is placed in the TCP Source Port field. The application on the destination station will, in turn, use this port number in the Destination Port field when it sends data back to the host.

Destination Port

The destination port is also a 16-bit number, which may be greater or less than 1023. In the early ages of TCP/IP, most applications used what are called well-known port numbers. Well-known port numbers were in the range of 0 to 1023. In early versions of TCP on Unix systems, only superuser or root-level users were able to create ports in the well-known range (0–1023). Although not a standard, this convention has stayed with developers of TCP applications. Users of these applications running on well-known port numbers will use ephemeral port numbers greater than 1023. Table 6-1 shows some typical TCP well-known application ports.

Table 6-1   Example of TCP Ports

APPLICATION	TCP PORT
Hypertext Transport Protocol (HTTP)	80
File Transfer Protocol	21, 20
Telnet	23
NetBIOS session	139

NOTE Due to the growth in the number of applications running over TCP, it is not uncommon for applications to run on ports outside of the 0–1023 range. You will, however, usually only see clients allocate source ports that are greater than 1023.

Sequence Number

The sequence number is a 32-bit number that identifies the first byte of data being sent in a TCP data segment. Unlike other block-based transport protocols that sequence packets, TCP sequences bytes. Each byte being transmitted contains its own unique sequence number.

Acknowledgment Number

The acknowledgment number is a 32-bit number that indicates to a sending station the next byte sequence that it expects to receive from the sender. When TCP receives a sequence of bytes from a sender, it adds the data segment's sequence number to the amount of bytes received to come up with the acknowledgment number.

Header Offset

The Header Offset field is 4 bits long and represents the length of the TCP header in the number of 32-bit words (4 bytes). A TCP header without any options has a length of 20 bytes, which would be indicated by a header offset value of 5 (5 × 4 = 20 bytes).

Reserved Bits

The current IP version 4 specification reserves the 6 bits after the 4-bit header offset. These reserved bits are usually set to all zeros. There is a current proposal to use these bits for the purposes of Explicit Congestion Notification.

Specified in RFC 3168, Explicit Congestion Notification allows the use of bits 8 and 9 in the reserved space for notifying a source host of congestion. As specified in section 6.1 of RFC 3168, bit 8 is used to notify the source of the congestion and bit 9 is used for notifying a source of its ability to indicate congestion. If you see bit 9 being set, then you know a host has the ability to indicate congestion conditions.

Connection Flags

TCP connection flags indicate the state of a TCP connection. There are six state flags that are used during the lifetime of a TCP connection.

- **URG.** The urgent flag is used to notify a host of urgent data inside of the TCP data field.
- **ACK.** The acknowledgment field is used by a host to indicate an acknowledgment of TCP data to another host.
- **PSH.** The push field informs TCP to *push* data immediately to the upper layer protocol.
- **RST.** The Reset bit indicates that a TCP connection has been reset by a host.
- **SYN.** The Synchronize bit is used to open a TCP connection with another host.
- **FIN.** The Finish bit is used by a host to close a TCP connection.

Window Size

The 16-bit window size field indicates to a peer TCP host how many TCP buffers it has left to accept data. Hosts will constantly adjust this field, depending on their ability to accept new data.

TCP Checksum

The TCP checksum functions exactly like the UDP checksum. It protects the TCP header as well as the data that TCP is carrying.

CROSS-REFERENCE For more about the UDP checksum, see Chapter 5.

Urgent Pointer

The urgent pointer is used in conjunction with the Urgent bit to notify a host of where urgent data is located in the TCP data field.

Options

The TCP options fields are options that allow a host to specify parameters for a TCP connection. Parameters that I discuss later in this chapter include the Maximum Segment Size and Window Scaling options.

Data

The data field is the actual upper-layer data that is being carried by TCP.

TCP Implementation

By utilizing the fields described in the previous section, TCP implements the required functionality for a reliable connection-oriented transport protocol. The next sections take a look into which of these fields are used in providing which functionality of the protocol.

Multiplexing

Application multiplexing is handled by the same method that UDP uses, ports that identify each individual upper-layer application or protocol. For example, a user may have several open connections to different servers. The user may be opening a Web page on the Internet with TCP Port 80, transferring a file from a local Windows NT server with Port 139, and updating a router configuration over a Telnet session on Port 23. All three of these tasks can occur at the same time using a single host's source IP address and multiple port and destination IP address pairs.

Data Sequencing and Acknowledgment

The 32-bit sequence and acknowledgment fields are used by TCP on hosts that are communicating with each other. These fields allow two hosts to track the data they are sending to each other and to inform the sending host that they have received (or not received) TCP data. The sequence and acknowledgment fields are what enable TCP to be a reliable protocol.

Flow Control

Flow control in TCP is implemented by the TCP Window Size field. Each host advertises the amount of TCP data that it can accept from another host. As a host receives data, it informs the sending host of its window size in the next acknowledgment frame it sends. You will see how TCP sequence acknowledgment, and window size fields work together in later sections of this chapter.

Besides multiplexing, data sequencing and acknowledgment, and flow control, TCP offers upper-layer applications and protocols myriad other services. These services are sometimes known as TCP Options. Although they are not necessary or mandatory to use, it is to the advantage of an application program to use these options to further maximize communication using TCP. I discuss TCP options later in the chapter.

TCP Connection Management

Okay, I've mentioned it several times now. TCP is a connection-oriented protocol. What does that mean?

TCP operates in what are called connection states. In short, you either have a connection or you don't; however, in between opening a connection and closing a connection, there are several different states that TCP goes through. The complete details of the TCP connection states are described in texts like W. Richard Stevens' *TCP/IP Illustrated,* Volume 1, which I mentioned earlier in the chapter, but you don't need to know all that detail in order to troubleshoot TCP. What you do need to know I am going to explain here.

Using TCP is analogous to making a phone call. By picking up the phone and dialing a number, you are in effect bringing up a Layer 3 path from a source (your phone number) to a destination (someone else's phone number). What happens when you make a call? Usually the other person picks up the phone and says, "Hello." At this point you know that the Layer 3 path is active, and you can initiate your conversation. The conversation represents the data you wish to transmit upon the wire, for example, a user saving a file onto a remote network server. You want to transmit your voice "data" across the phone line to another person. Upon hearing the word *hello* from your calling destination, you begin your conversation attempt. Most likely your next step will be to cordially tell the person on the other end who you are and why you're calling. Usually it's something like "Hello, this is Kevin. Is Marie there?" This is your connection setup. Now, you need Marie to come to the phone. When she does, you will most likely hear her say, "Yes this is Marie, can I help you?" The destination's response is the acknowledgment of your connection setup. It is also its own connection setup because you know that it's going to be sending you data also (that is, conversation data in the phone call example). You now have a two-way conversation opened up with both parties fully ready to communicate.

TCP performs the same type of connection setup with something called the TCP three-way handshake. I will refer to it as the first TCP connection state, the TCP Open.

TCP Open

The TCP Open refers to the actions performed by the TCP layer of a host wishing to open a communications channel to another host using the TCP protocol. The TCP Open performs the three-way handshake using the SYN and ACK connection flags. The TCP Open has two purposes:

- To exchange initial sequence numbers
- To negotiate TCP options

Figure 6-2 illustrates the TCP Open. In Frame 3, you can see the source station KEVIN opening a connection to the destination www.tracemasters .com. The source TCP port is 4270, allocated on the source station. The destination port is port 80, which is HTTP. Just by looking at the source and destination IP addresses and the ports, you can see you have a single station attempting to open a connection to a remote Web server. You know that this is a TCP Open request because the SYN bit is set to 1. The SYN bit is set to 1 only during a TCP Open request. You will never see it set to 1 any other time. You also see the value of 554776182 in the TCP sequence number field. This is the starting sequence number for the data connection from host KEVIN to host www.tracemasters.com. We can also see that there are two TCP options specified. The first is called the Maximum Segment Size, the second the SACK (Selective Acknowledgment) Permitted Option. I discuss TCP options in an upcoming section in this chapter.

Initial Sequence Number (ISN)

The initial sequence number is used in conjunction with the acknowledgment number. To illustrate, look at Figure 6-3, which contains the decode for Frame 4, the second part of the TCP Open procedure. In Frame 4, you can see that along with the SYN bit being set to 1, you now also have the Acknowledgment bit set to 1. The SYN bit indicates that this host (216.119.99.47) is opening up a TCP connection to host KEVIN. Looking down farther, you can see that it is also negotiating two TCP options for Maximum Segment Size and Selective Acknowledgments. This connection allows host 216.119.99.47 to send TCP data to host KEVIN.

But what about this acknowledgment bit? The acknowledgment bit indicates that besides establishing its own connection, the host is also acknowledging data from another host. What data though, you may ask, because I haven't even finished setting up the connection. The host is actually acknowledging that it received the SYN segment from host KEVIN. Notice in Frame 3 what host KEVIN's initial sequence number was. It was 554776182. You can see in Frame 4 that the acknowledgment field contains the number

554776183, which is exactly the original initial sequence number sent by host KEVIN plus 1. This is the method used by TCP to acknowledge data. SYN and FIN flags all consume one sequence number. When a host wants to acknowledge them it must respond with the ISN plus 1. Frame 4 utilizes what are called piggybacked acknowledgments. It acknowledges the SYN request from host KEVIN, but also opens its own TCP connection in the same packet. I will show you later on in the chapter how this technique allows TCP to operate as a full-duplex protocol.

Now, take a look at Figure 6-4. In Frame 5, you may quickly notice that the ACK bit is set, so you know that this is an acknowledgment frame. Looking at the acknowledgment sequence number, you see that it is the ISN of host 216.119.99.47 plus 1 (ISN + 1). This frame is a TCP acknowledgment of the TCP Open request (SYN) by host 216.119.99.47. Notice though that in Frame 5 there are no TCP options present. TCP options are negotiating only when SYN segments are sent. You will not see them in any other TCP segments.

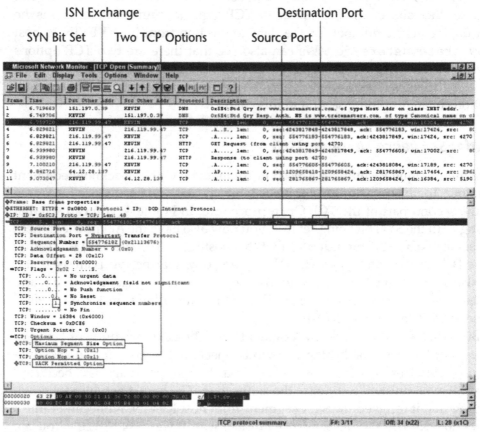

Figure 6-2 TCP Open.

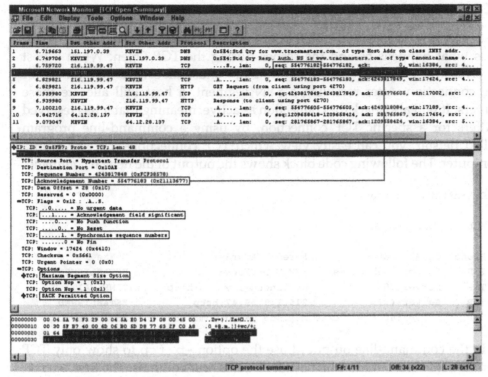

Figure 6-3   SYN with piggybacked ACK.

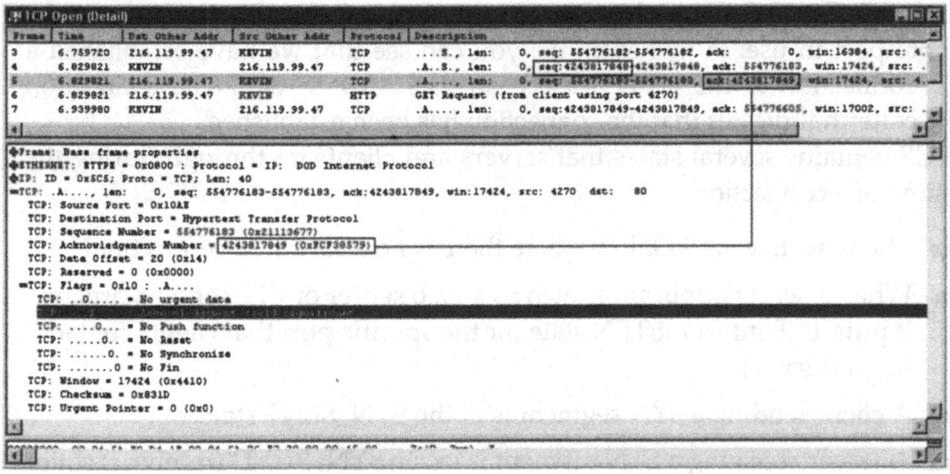

Figure 6-4   ACK of SYN.

TCP Connection States

You have now seen how the TCP Open procedure works. Now, I want to discuss what happens behind the scenes during the TCP Open. When a host receives a TCP Open request, it knows that it must allocate certain buffers for the connection. After receiving a SYN segment, a host will allocate those buffers. It will also mark the connection as active, meaning that it has reserved buffers for a specific TCP connection. By using a command-line program called netstat, you can easily view which TCP connections are active on a computer. The following code block shows the output of the netstat command:

```
C:\>netstat -p tcp

Active Connections

  Proto  Local Address        Foreign Address            State
  TCP    Server:netbios-ssn   KEVIN_98:1044              ESTABLISHED
  TCP    Server:1089          worldnetdaily.com:http     TIME_WAIT
  TCP    Server:4270          216.119.99.47:http         ESTABLISHED
  TCP    Server:4008          cs44.msg.sc5.yahoo.com:5050 ESTABLISHED
```

In the command-line output , I use the option –p tcp to show only TCP connections. The output from netstat contains four columns. The first, Proto, is short for protocol, indicating whether the protocol is TCP or UDP. The Local Address column contains the local hostname and local port number allocated for the connection. If you look back at Figure 6-2, you'll see that the source port allocated for the connection was 4270. The Foreign Address column shows the remote hostname or, in this case, the IP address and the remote port in use. In this example, you can see that we have established a TCP connection to the HTTP service on 216.119.99.47. The connection state column indicates that the connection has been established.

TCP contains several states that servers and clients go through during the lifetime of a connection.

- The first state is CLOSED, where there is no active TCP connection.

- When a server application such as a Web server or FTP server starts up, it puts TCP into a LISTEN state for the specific port that clients contact the service on.

- A client sending a SYN segment is in the SYN_SENT state.

- A server receiving a SYN segment is in the SYN_RCVD (received) state.

- When both sides send and acknowledge their respective SYN segments, only then does the connection go into the ESTABLISHED state on both ends.

There are several other TCP connection states, such as FIN_WAIT, TIME_WAIT, CLOSE_WAIT, and LAST_ACK. While it is nice to know these states exist, they are rarely needed in troubleshooting TCP problems. Please refer to Stevens' book, which I mentioned earlier in the chapter if you are interested in their details.

TCP Options

Besides the fact that TCP options are sent only during SYN segments, so far I've said very little about them. TCP options allow a host to negotiate specific parameters that it wishes to use during the life of the connection. A very common option used by all hosts is the Maximum Segment Size (MSS) option. MSS is the largest amount of data TCP is willing to accept in a single packet. In Figure 6-5, I have expanded the TCP options decode section to examine the size of data segments that host KEVIN is willing to accept.

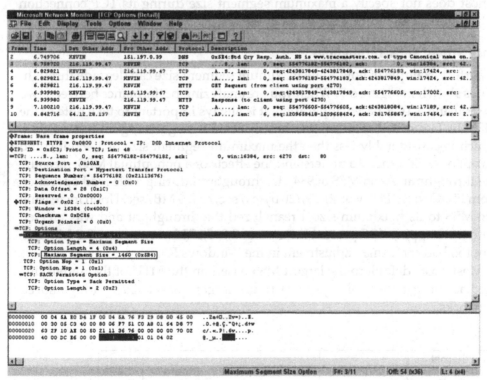

Figure 6-5   Maximum Segment Size.

You can see in the figure that the host is willing to accept 1,460 bytes of data in a single TCP segment. You might ask yourself why 1,460 bytes? What is magical about this number? Nothing actually, but it does represent the largest amount of data that TCP can carry on an Ethernet network. If you examine the length of the different headers that encapsulate TCP, the size 1,460 becomes obvious. Figure 6-6 illustrates the different header sizes that make up an Ethernet frame. The source and destination MAC addresses in the Ethernet header take up 6 bytes each. The Ethertype takes up 2 bytes. Both the IP and TCP headers take up 20 bytes each. Because the maximum Ethernet frame size is 1,518 bytes, once you add the 4-byte CRC to the frame, you have only 1,460 bytes left over for the data. So in this case, the host is negotiating the maximum size data segments it wants to receive. It is generally better for a host to use larger data segments whenever possible. Because every packet is going to contain 58 bytes of overhead (Ethernet + IP + TCP headers) you are going to have to transmit that 58 bytes of overhead across the wire whether you're transmitting 10 bytes of data or 1,460 bytes of data. It benefits a host to fill the frame. If a host does not specify a maximum segment size during its TCP connection setup, the size defaults to 536 bytes of data.

Case Study: Slow Throughput

A perfect example of how a low maximum segment size can degrade throughput is shown in Figure 6-7. When you are analyzing performance between two hosts using a TCP-based application, it is always important to take note of the MSS. In Figure 6-7, you see that host RUFUS is negotiating an MSS of 984, which is considerably less than the maximum segment size of 1,460 it could accept over Ethernet. To understand the effects of a nonoptimal MSS, measure the throughput. At an MSS of 984, the throughput during a file read operation from FIDO to RUFUS was 2,679,120 bytes/sec, or 2.6 MB/sec. Upon increasing the MSS to its maximum size, I reanalyzed the throughput and was greeted with a whopping 68.7 percent increase of 3,895,875 bytes/sec, or 3.8 MB/sec. Not too bad for a small adjustment in the Windows Registry.

Most hosts default to the largest MSS based on the MTU of the underlying media. You generally always want to use larger packet sizes on high-speed networks.

Ethernet DA(6) SA(6) Etype(2)	IP	TCP	Data	CRC
14	20	20	1,460	4 = 1,518 bytes

Figure 6-6   Ethernet header overhead.

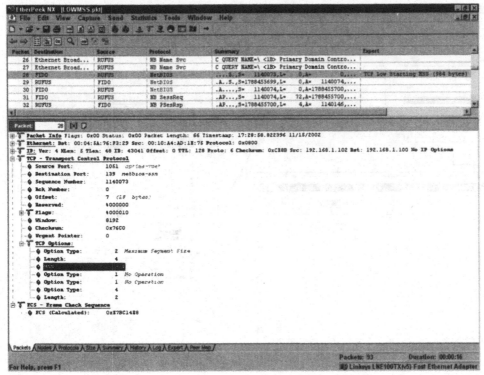

Figure 6-7 Low MSS.

MSS Filtering

When performing network health assessments at an organization, one of the things I like to do is search for nonoptimal maximum segment size values. An analyzer like EtherPeek NX has an expert mode that will tell you immediately if it sees a nonoptimal MSS value. Even if you don't have an expert mode, you can still search for nonoptimal MSS values. An easy way to do this is to create a pattern match filter to search maximum segment size values that are not equal to 1,460 (on Ethernet). To create a filter that will do this, there are several offsets in the TCP header that you want to look for. Because you know that the TCP MSS is negotiated only during the opening SYN-SYN-ACK procedure, you can filter for the SYN flag being set to 1 and the MSS value to anything other than 1,460. To do this, you need to have an analyzer with the ability to search for bit patterns at specific offsets. EtherPeek NX allows you to do this with its value filter. For Microsoft NetMon users, this procedure is even easier. By using the display filter's property sheet, you can simply choose a value that you would like to filter for in the MSS field. Figure 6-8 illustrates how I created both filters using Ethernet NX and Microsoft NetMon.

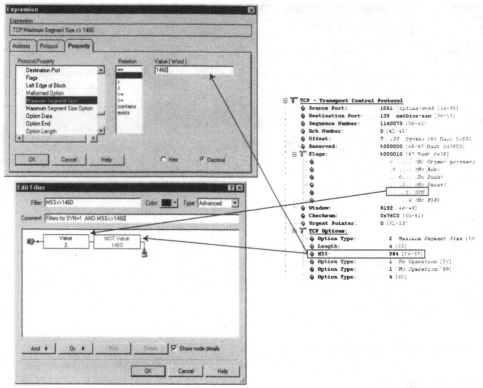

Figure 6-8 MSS filtering.

There are several other TCP options, such as the Selective Acknowledgment option that I discuss at a later point in the chapter. The MSS option is by far the most common and important of all TCP options you will run across in the TCP Options field.

TCP Close

After two stations open a TCP session and transfer their respective data, they must close the TCP session to release the reserved buffer space that was allocated for that connection. When a host wishes to close a TCP session, it uses the FIN, or FINish, flag. The TCP Close is very similar to the TCP Open, although you sometimes may see it occur in four frames instead of only three. The key to recognizing a TCP Close is to watch for the FIN flag being set and also for the sequencing and acknowledgment values, just as you did when you analyzed the TCP Open.

Take a look at an example. Figure 6-9 shows a TCP Close in action. In Frame 89, you see host RUFUS sending a TCP segment with the FIN bit set to 1. You might also notice that the ACK bit is set. In this case the ACK bit is simply an acknowledgment of the previous TCP segment sent by FIDO, another fine example of how TCP piggybacks its acknowledgments. In Frame 90 you see host FIDO responding to RUFUS's TCP Close request. It sets the ACK bit, indicating that it is acknowledging TCP data. If you look at the acknowledgment value, you see that it is one more than the TCP sequence number sent by RUFUS in Frame 89. You now know that this is FIDO's acknowledgment of RUFUS's TCP Close request. Like SYN bits, FIN bits also consume a single sequence number. Looking further into Frame 90 you can see that FIDO is also sending its own close request using the FIN bit. If you look ahead at Frame 91, you will see that RUFUS acknowledges FIDO's FIN bit with a sequence number of 1790069232, one plus the original sequence sent by FIDO.

Half-Close

There is another TCP state that you may sometimes see, called the TCP Half-Close. Normally, when a host receives a FIN segment it responds with a FIN to close its side of the connection. This occurrence is called an orderly release. The Half-Close occurs when a host sends another host a FIN segment requesting that the TCP session be closed. Normally, the receiving station acknowledges the close request and also sends a FIN segment to close its session. But sometimes hosts never close their side of the connection. By not doing so they waste buffer space that could be used for other TCP connections. Some TCP implementations actually support a call that allows an application to close one-half of the connection if it has no more data to send. Hosts closing their half of a TCP connection can still receive data and acknowledge data sent to them, but they can no longer send data because the host at the other side of the connection most likely terminated their connection and reserved buffer space on receipt of the FIN segment.

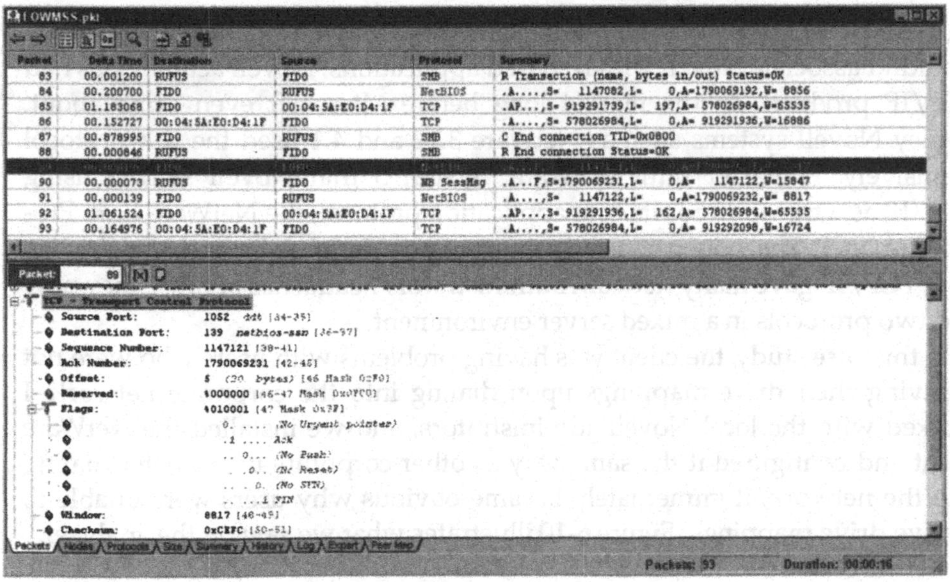

Figure 6-9   TCP Close.

TCP Reset

Besides opening and closing a connection, TCP has another little trick up its sleeve that allows an application to immediately abort a connection in midstream. It's called the TCP Reset. For example, what would happen if an application crashed in the middle of a data transfer? It certainly wouldn't be up to TCP to close the connection in an orderly fashion. Connection open and close events are initiated strictly by an application. TCP's job is to make sure that data is passed between two applications on different hosts. The Reset allows TCP or an application to abruptly close a connection when the application has crashed or for some reason can no longer continue with the connection. TCP Resets are also known as *abortive* releases. The TCP Reset is one of the most important parameters of the TCP protocol to understand. When applications do not function, the behavior will most likely be exhibited in the TCP Reset segment.

There are three reasons that a TCP Reset might be sent by a host.

- There is no listening process on the IP/port pair on which an application is attempting to make a connection.

- An application may abort the connection in the middle of a data transfer due to an application anomaly or crash.

- A host may disconnect its side of the TCP connection if it does not receive acknowledgments from a host to which it was sending TCP data.

The best way to understand TCP Resets is to illustrate them in case studies as I do in the sections that follow.

Case Study: Missing Drive Mappings

This first case study on TCP Resets involves Novell. While most people wouldn't associate Novell with IP-based applications, Novell actually has had TCP/IP products on the market long before Microsoft even came about. Legacy Novell systems such as NetWare 3.12 and 4.1 used the IPX protocol exclusively. It wasn't until NetWare version 5 that Novell started using TCP/IP as a transport for its core application protocol, the NetWare Core Protocol, or NCP. The integration and mixing of pre-NetWare 5.*x* and NetWare 5.*x* with TCP/IP gave many network administrators headaches because they now had two protocols in a mixed server environment.

In this case study, the client was having problems with users who were not receiving their drive mappings upon dialing into the corporate network. I worked with the local Novell administrators, and we installed the NetWare client and configured it the same way as other corporate users. After dialing into the network, it immediately became obvious why users were unable to receive drive mappings. Figure 6-10 illustrates what we saw on the analyzer.

Frame	Delta Time	Destination	Source	Summary
1	0.000.000	Darth_Vadar	RAS User	TCP: D=524 S=1098 SYN SEQ=74910778 LEN=0 WIN=8192
2	0.200.106	RAS User	Darth_Vadar	TCP: D=1098 S=524 RST ACK=74910779 WIN=0
3	0.414.882	Darth_Vadar	RAS User	TCP: D=524 S=1098 SYN SEQ=74910778 LEN=0 WIN=8192
4	0.165.042	RAS User	Darth_Vadar	TCP: D=1098 S=524 RST ACK=74910779 WIN=0
5	0.434.975	Darth_Vadar	RAS User	TCP: D=524 S=1098 SYN SEQ=74910778 LEN=0 WIN=8192
6	0.165.018	RAS User	Darth_Vadar	TCP: D=1098 S=524 RST ACK=74910779 WIN=0
7	0.434.967	Darth_Vadar	RAS User	TCP: D=524 S=1098 SYN SEQ=74910778 LEN=0 WIN=8192
8	0.175.050	RAS User	Darth_Vadar	TCP: D=1098 S=524 RST ACK=74910779 WIN=0
9	0.009.866	CAB1BABE.0200000	0 CAB1BABE.FFFFFFFF	RIP: request: find 1 network, 347253AD"
10	0.197.618	CAB1BABE.347253A	D CAB1BABE.02000000	RIP: response: 1 network, 347253AD at 1 hop"
11	0.012.466	CAB1BABE.02000000	347253AD.1	NCP: C Create service connection N=0 Cx=255
12	0.165.047	347253AD.1	CAB1BABE.02000000	NCP: R OK
13	0.005.015	CAB1BABE.02000000	347253AD.1	NCP: C Get file server info
14	0.165.019	347253AD.1	CAB1BABE.02000000	NCP: R OK

TCP Connection Attempt to Port 524 being rejected

Figure 6-10 Analyzing an IP NetWare server.

In Frames 2, 4, 6, and 8 you can see TCP RST (Resets) being returned from the NetWare 5 server whenever a RAS user makes a connection attempt. I first asked the administrators why the client was attempting to connect to this server. My second question was: What was port 524? After looking at our Net-Ware client configuration we noticed that Darth_Vadar was listed as the preferred NetWare server to connect to. Looking up TCP 524, we found that it was the TCP port for the NetWare Core Protocol.

My third question was why wasn't the server responding? Upon a quick inspection of the server, we found out it wasn't running NetWare IP. Even though this was a NetWare version 5 server and had IP on it, the NCP protocol was configured to run only over IPX. Apparently the RAS administrators assumed that because the server was NetWare 5 that the clients would be using TCP/IP to connect to it. The problem was resolved after the help desk assisted 500 some odd users with changing their default NetWare client configurations to make sure that they were connecting to the correct NetWare server, one that allowed use of the NCP protocol over TCP/IP.

Whenever possible, try to recreate the exact circumstances in which a problem occurs. In this case, mirroring the client's configuration on my own laptop allowed me to experience the same network issues as the corporate users.

Case Study: No Telnet

TCP Resets are a great way to prove that an application is not functioning properly. Often an application will appear to be functioning. Its administration console may work, it may be listed as active in the list of Windows services, but for all intents and purposes, the application will not accept new connections. Often users will blame the network when they receive a message that they are unable to connect to a service or server. Listing 6-1 shows a typical Windows command-line response when an application isn't working properly:

```
C:\>telnet 10.41.10.130
Connecting To 10.41.10.130...Could not open a connection to host:
Connect failed
```

Listing 6-1   TCP Reset response on a Windows client.

The response message isn't very helpful, is it? If you have the luxury of Telnetting to an application from a router, you will get a slightly better message. Listing 6-2 shows the message a Cisco router will give you when it receives a TCP Reset:

```
Router>telnet 10.41.10.130
Trying 10.41.10.130 ...
% Connection refused by remote host
```

Listing 6-2   TCP Reset response on a Cisco router.

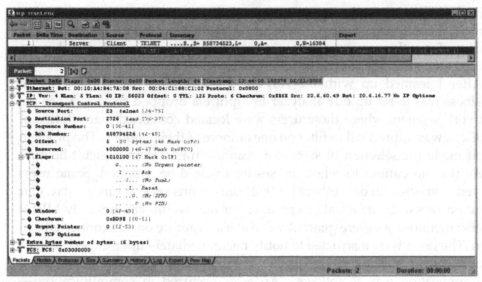

Figure 6-11 TCP Reset decode.

Figure 6-11 shows a client's attempt at Telnetting to a remote server. You see in Frame 2 that the server sends back a TCP Reset to the client, indicating that the service or application is not listening on the application's port. Even the expert mode in Frame 2 shows us that the TCP Connection was refused. A TCP Reset is undeniable proof that an application is not functioning properly.

Case Study: Dropped Sessions

One of the more interesting troubleshooting sessions I have been on involved TCP/IP and a little-known IBM protocol called MPTN. MPTN stands for Multi-Protocol Transport Networking. It is an IBM-developed protocol designed to allow legacy SNA applications to run over TCP/IP without modification. MPTN uses TCP sessions as a logical pipe between a client and an application server. There are two steps to an MPTN session setup.

1. The first is the TCP three-way handshake that connects the clients ephemeral port to the MPTN port (397) on the application server, in this case an AS400.

2. The next step is to set up an IBM-type 5250 terminal session between the client and the AS400. When you set up a 5250 session, each client must be configured with a unique device name, in this case the device name is KEVINB.

Users began experiencing problems upon the installation of a firewall between the network where the users were located and the network where the AS400 was located. The application was used for shipping and receiving. It was a Visual Basic GUI front end using preconfigured Reflections terminal configurations. When the application needed to communicate with a remote server, it would run a macro that would start the respective 5250 Reflections session. Everything seemed fine until the firewall was installed and users started experiencing dropped 5250 sessions.

After I teamed up with the AS/400 administrators, our first order of business was to set up our analyzer to capture a dropped session. Since the network segment where these users were located contained many forms of traffic, it was impractical to filter on one or more of their stations. The problem itself made the selection of stations to capture traffic from difficult because there was no pattern to when the sessions would be dropped. Some users stayed connected all day, others lost the connections several times a day. Our solution was to create a pattern match filter that would capture only MPTN traffic; therefore, we were guaranteed to at least capture one disconnected session. The users were instructed to notify me immediately upon experiencing a dropped session. The message users were receiving when attempting to use the application was as follows: "An error occurred in communications— Device KEVINB not available."

As I discussed in the previous case study, sometimes messages are of little value when troubleshooting a problem. In this case, we were initially confused. Why was the message telling us that our own station KEVINB was not available? After speaking with the AS400 administrators, we learned that the AS400 uses our device name to associate us with an active session. So the AS400 was telling us that our session was unavailable. Upon further research, we found out that although the error message told us our session wasn't available, when we looked at the AS400 session screen, it showed that our 5250 terminal session, as well as the TCP session, was still active on the AS400. Only when the administrators cleared the active session was the client application able to create a new session. This puzzled us even more. The problem then was clearly on the client end, or was it?

Preferring not to guess, we deployed our analyzers and captured our first session disconnection. Figure 6-12 shows a normal MPTN TCP session proceeding until the end of the capture, where a TCP Reset is sent by host KEVINB to the AS400 in Frame 291. Notice the R flag in the summary column of Frame 291. This indicates the TCP Reset.

This would seem to confirm our suspicions that the problem is on the clients. But how could 20 clients suddenly stop working? Were their machine configurations changed somehow? Was new software upgraded or loaded that would possibly cause their MPTN sessions to start disconnecting? This solution didn't sit well with us; we knew that the problem had to be elsewhere. Could the firewall be causing it?

Packet	Relative Time	Destination	Source	Protocol	Summary
74	00.000000	AS400	KEVINB	TCP	.A....,S= 238458,L= 0,A= 691519407,W= 9492
75	07.314064	AS400	KEVINB	TCP	.AP...,S= 238458,L= 48,A= 691519407,W= 9492
76	07.439778	KEVINB	AS400	TCP	.AP...,S= 691519407,L= 20,A= 238506,W= 8192
77	07.450674	AS400	KEVINB	TCP	.AP...,S= 238506,L= 1270,A= 691519427,W= 9472
78	07.466596	KEVINB	AS400	TCP	.AP...,S= 691519427,L= 890,A= 239776,W= 8192
79	07.504312	AS400	KEVINB	TCP	.AP...,S= 239776,L= 27,A= 691520317,W= 8582
80	07.526940	KEVINB	AS400	TCP	.AP...,S= 691520317,L= 36,A= 239803,W= 8192
81	07.539512	AS400	KEVINB	TCP	.AP...,S= 239803,L= 20,A= 691520353,W= 8546
82	07.593988	KEVINB	AS400	TCP	.AP...,S= 691520353,L= 1270,A= 239823,W= 8192
83	07.619130	AS400	KEVINB	TCP	.AP...,S= 239823,L= 20,A= 691521623,W= 9492
84	07.623320	KEVINB	AS400	TCP	.AP...,S= 691521623,L= 705,A= 239843,W= 8192
85	07.724730	AS400	KEVINB	TCP	.AP...,S= 239843,L= 27,A= 691522328,W= 8787
86	07.916654	KEVINB	AS400	TCP	.AP...,S= 691522328,L= 0,A= 239870,W= 8192
87	08.085112	KEVINB	AS400	TCP	.AP...,S= 691522328,L= 1023,A= 239870,W= 8192
88	08.170598	AS400	KEVINB	TCP	.AP...,S= 239870,L= 27,A= 691523351,W= 9492
89	08.176464	KEVINB	AS400	TCP	.AP...,S= 691523351,L= 474,A= 239897,W= 8192
90	08.278712	AS400	KEVINB	TCP	.A....,S= 239897,L= 0,A= 691523825,W= 9018
290	01:08.744826	AS400	KEVINB	TCP	.A....,S= 691523824,L= 1,A= 239897,W= 8192
291	01:08.847074	AS400	KEVINB	TCP	.A.R..,S= 239897,L= 1,A= 691523824,W= 8192

Figure 6-12   MPTN reset.

We dug back into the packet trace. Looking again at the information in Figure 6-12, we noticed something: The TCP Reset in Frame 291 occurred in response to a TCP segment from the AS400 in Frame 290. We also noticed that no MPTN traffic passed between the host KEVINB and the AS400 for over an hour. You can see this by looking at the Relative Time column in Frame 290. Between Frame 90 and Frame 290 you can see that an hour had passed. The AS400 administrators informed us that when an unused session is left open on the AS400 for an extended period of time the AS400 will poll the station to see if it's still active. The packet in Frame 290 was one of those polls. A quick check on our firewall revealed that it kept inactive sessions open only for the period of one hour. After one hour the firewall tore down the state entry for the TCP connection. Now, we knew the problem was with the firewall. When users did not have any shipping information to enter into the application, the session would sit idle. After one hour, the firewall would clear the entry from its tables, and all packets from the clients to the AS400 would be dropped. But how could we fix the problem? Asking users to remember to hit a key every hour just because our firewall had an idle connection time-out of one hour would probably be asking too much. We could increase the idle time-out to its maximum setting, but this would just be masking a problem that the firewall didn't create. What we needed was a keep-alive function on the client that would periodically send a packet to the AS400 in order to reset the connection timers on the firewall. TCP actually has a keep-alive function, but unfortunately, the Reflections MPTN client did not allow us to enable it.

What was the solution then? Very simple. By editing users' Reflections sessions, we created an automatic keystroke macro that would refresh the terminal screen every 15 minutes. By doing so we were able to generate traffic every 15 minutes to keep the connection alive across the firewall.

It is always important to understand the communication characteristics of all devices along a path. This case study shows how correlating client application idle time with the connection time-out on a firewall led to the solution.

TCP Data Flow Management

The previous section discussed how TCP handles connection states—how it opens, closes, and resets connections if necessary. This section concentrates on what happens during a TCP connection. How does it handle things like flow control, buffer management, and flagging priority data?

Data Sequencing and Acknowledgment

Since Chapter 1, I have been telling you that TCP is a reliable protocol—that it makes a best effort to guarantee data delivery. In order for a protocol to be reliable, it must posses a method of data acknowledgment. In the previous section, you saw how TCP uses the sequence and acknowledgment fields to track receipt of the SYN and FIN connection flags. TCP also uses the sequence and acknowledgment fields to track the receipt of data. Transport protocol transfer data in two ways:

- As blocks
- As bytes

TCP is a byte-oriented protocol meaning that it transfers data as a stream of bytes. The receiving host application never knows how many bytes it is going to receive. The TCP data transfer is transparent to the application; it simply processes the received stream of bytes as TCP passes them up to it. During a TCP Open and Close transaction, TCP acknowledges the SYN and FIN flags by adding one to the original sequence number. TCP acknowledges bytes the same way. For each byte received by a host it will add one to the sender's sequence number and send it back in an acknowledgment packet. Figure 6-13 illustrates how this works.

In Frame 5, host ROLLINS opens a file and begins to write data to it starting in Frame 7. After receiving a positive write acknowledgment from host BRUCE, the file transfer continues over the NetBIOS session protocol. NetBIOS in this instance actually uses TCP as its transport. For the rest of the file transfer NetBIOS is actually dropping blocks of data down to TCP for transmission across the network. TCP simply treats these blocks as a stream of bytes. In Frames 12 and 13, you can see host ROLLINS sending 2,920 bytes of data. How do you know this? Well, if you captured the TCP three-way handshake, you would have seen host BRUCE negotiate an MSS of 1460. A sending host will almost always send the maximum amount of data up to the destination's maximum segment size.

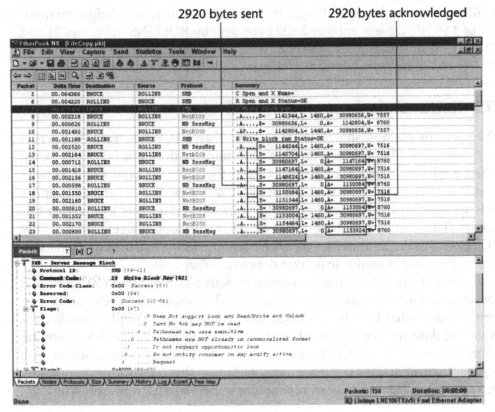

Figure 6-13   TCP sequencing and acknowledgment.

There is another simple way of determining how much data TCP is carrying in a segment. Simply look at the packet summary. In Frame 12, the analyzer shows the amount of TCP data with the L=1460 notation. The two 1,460-byte segments of data sent in Frames 12 and 13 equal 2,920 bytes. In Frame 14, you see host BRUCE sending an acknowledgment. You know by the value of the acknowledgment field that BRUCE has acknowledged all bytes sent to it by host ROLLINS. If you take the original sequence number sent by ROLLINS in Frame 12 and add 2,920 bytes to it, you get an acknowledgment number of 1147164. TCP acknowledgments indicate to the host receiving the acknowledgment that the host has received all bytes up to but not including the sequence number contained in the acknowledgment field. Another way to put this is that the acknowledging host expects the sending host to use that sequence number next in its transmissions.

Look at Frame 15. What sequence number does host ROLLINS use? If you guessed 1147164, you were right. Look at the next two segments sent by ROLLINS in Frames 15 and 16. They also are 1460 bytes each for a total of 2,920 bytes of data over two packets. Their acknowledgment by host BRUCE indicates that BRUCE received both segments and expects the next TCP segment to have a sequence number of 1150084. Next, two more segments of

1460 bytes are each acknowledged by BRUCE with an acknowledgment number of 1153004. Next, another 2,920 bytes sent by ROLLINS in Frames 21 and 22 are acknowledged by BRUCE with an acknowledgment number of 1155924. I think you get the picture now.

TCP Retransmissions

The previous example shows what happens when a TCP data transfer is occurring normally. Many times though a data transfer does not occur normally. Being a reliable transport protocol, TCP has the ability to handle situations in which data does not flow over the network in a neat and orderly fashion, as was the case in the previous example. Sometimes data gets lost. When this occurs TCP will retransmit the data. I want to take a look at an example of how TCP does this. In Figure 6-14, you see what happens when a host with an existing TCP session is unable to deliver data to another host.

Frame 1 is a data transmission during an active TCP session. You know that the session is active because the ACK bit is set. The sequence number of the currently transmitted byte is 2195533. You would expect DORIA to acknowledge this data with an ACK number of 2195548 because ANDREA is sending 15 bytes of data. Instead, in Frame 2 you see ANDREA sending another TCP segment with the same sequence number. In fact, this occurs four more times, in Frames 3, 4, 5, and 6. These are what are known as TCP retransmissions.

Retransmission Time-Out

When TCP sends a segment of data to a host, it will wait a set period of time called the retransmission time-out (RTO). If it does not receive an acknowledgment from the host during that time, it will retransmit the data segment. Implementations vary as to how long they will wait before retransmitting a data segment. Most implementations determine the RTO by something called the smooth round-trip time (SRTT). The speed at which acknowledgments are returned by a host determines the SRTT upon which the RTO is based. The faster acknowledgments are returned, the lower the RTO, and vice versa. If a TCP acknowledgment is not received in roughly double the SRTT, TCP will retransmit the segment. In Figure 6-14, you can see that TCP makes five attempts to retransmit the data. With each retransmission, TCP will double the time it waits before sending the next retransmission. Look at the delta time; notice that the retransmissions occur at 373ms, 871ms, 1.72sec, 3.53sec, and 7.12ms. The retransmission intervals are not exact, but they are roughly doubled each time. This rough interval is due to how the TCP/IP stack uses a computer clock interval to tell time. After five unsuccessful attempts to retransmit a data segment, TCP informs the application that it was unable to deliver the data. Depending on the application, it may decide to keep trying or disconnect the session.

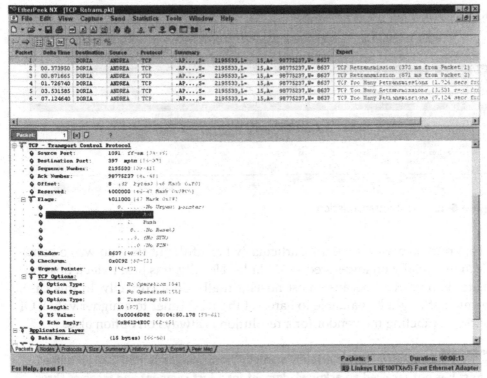

Figure 6-14 TCP retransmissions.

Case Study: Bad RTO

Figure 6-15 shows what happens when a host calculates the retransmission time-out incorrectly. In Frame 6, you see the expert system complaining about a Fast Retransmission by host Printer. Using Wildpacket's Set Relative Packet feature, I was able to, at Frame 4, reset the relative time to zero and let it count upward. Why Frame 4? Because that is the original TCP segment that was retransmitted in Frame 6. The TCP sequence number in Frame 4 is 2589; you can see that this sequence number is also contained in Frame 6. Furthermore, both packets are transmitting the same amount of data, 1 byte. The analyzer flags this as a fast retransmission because it is within the threshold set by the analyzer.

How do you know that the analyzer is correct? Previously I discussed how the RTO is based on how fast acknowledgments are returned by a host (the SRTT). Look at the delta time in Frame 3. This tells you that the Server acknowledged the Printer's SYN segment in 44 milliseconds (0.044288). This is the first and only SRTT calculation performed by the printer. The Relative Time in Frame 6 is the RTO being used by the server. The server waited only 3 milliseconds (0.003362) before retransmitting the segment it sent in Frame 4. Considering its first SRTT measurement of 44 milliseconds, a 3 millisecond RTO is much too fast.

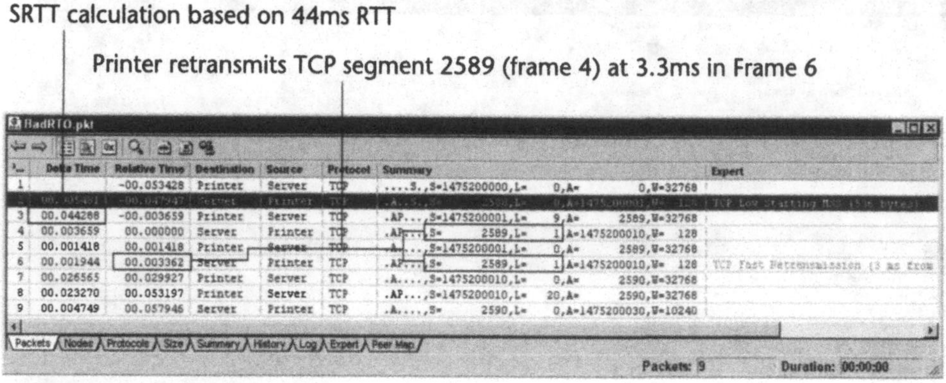

SRTT calculation based on 44ms RTT

Printer retransmits TCP segment 2589 (frame 4) at 3.3ms in Frame 6

Figure 6-15   Fast retransmission.

Fast retransmissions are not particularly harmful, but they do waste bandwidth, especially on low-speed WAN links. Usually, it is best to let a host calculate its own RTO because most hosts actually do it correctly. In this case, however, it might be valuable to hard-set the RTO timer to a higher value. Of course, contacting the vendor for a resolution is always on option also.

NOTE Fast Retransmit is actually an algorithm specified in RFC 2001. When a host has not received an acknowledgment for a lost segment and receives three acknowledgments in a row with the same acknowledgment number, it will retransmit the lost segment before the the retransmit timer expires.

Delayed Acknowledgments

TCP does not always acknowledge data immediately upon receiving it. Because TCP is a full-duplex protocol, you almost always have data traveling both ways, even on a largely one-way transaction. During a file read operation, most of the data will be coming from a server towards a client. But there is almost always some upper protocol control information that needs to be sent back to the client every so often. It is to TCP's advantage to send this data at the same time it is acknowledging data it has received from a host. This is called the piggyback ACK.

For example, assume that Host A has sent Host B a file open request. Host B is going to have to send a reply back to Host A indicating that the file is open. Host B is also going to have to acknowledge Host A's TCP segment containing the file open request. By combining the upper-layer reply with the TCP acknowledgment, TCP can do in one packet what would otherwise take two. Figure 6-16 illustrates how this works. Instead of immediately sending an acknowledgment, TCP waits to see if there might be any data from the application that could be sent in the direction of the acknowledgment. If TCP sends

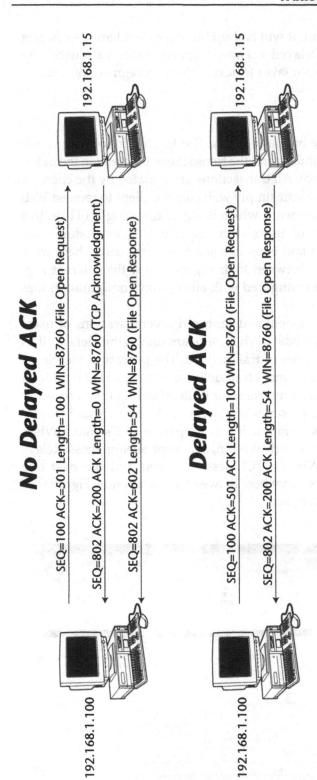

Figure 6-16   Delayed acknowledgment.

an immediate acknowledgment, it will end up having to send another packet containing the host's data. Delayed acknowledgment saves bandwidth by reducing the amount of packets it takes to acknowledge a segment of data.

Case Study: Slow Surfing

Delay in a transaction can take on many forms. The key to pinpointing where the delay is coming from is to understand the transactions involved in the delay.

Take Web surfing, for instance. All transactions are initiated by the client. A server does not initiate any traffic; it simply waits for the client to request Web pages, graphics, and other documents, which it serves up using HTTP. In this case study analysis, a group of users were experiencing very slow Web response times on the Internet and even to some sites internally. There were multiple routers and switches between their segment and the Internet segment, and their browsers were configured with auto-proxy configuration files to provide redundancy.

I took an analyzer to their segment and captured several sessions of users surfing during the normal workday. When you are analyzing delays, it is important to view traffic as a series of transactions. The process of viewing a Web page is really just a series of small transactions. I discuss HTTP more in the next chapter, but for now it's important for understanding this case study to know that Web pages are just a series of objects or elements. Your browser downloads each object such as a graphic file in a separate TCP session. When analyzing one particular user's Web session, we kept seeing these delays between object downloads. When a TCP session ended and the next one began, I was seeing long delays, anywhere between 2 to 8 seconds. Figure 6-17 illustrates what I saw on the analyzer.

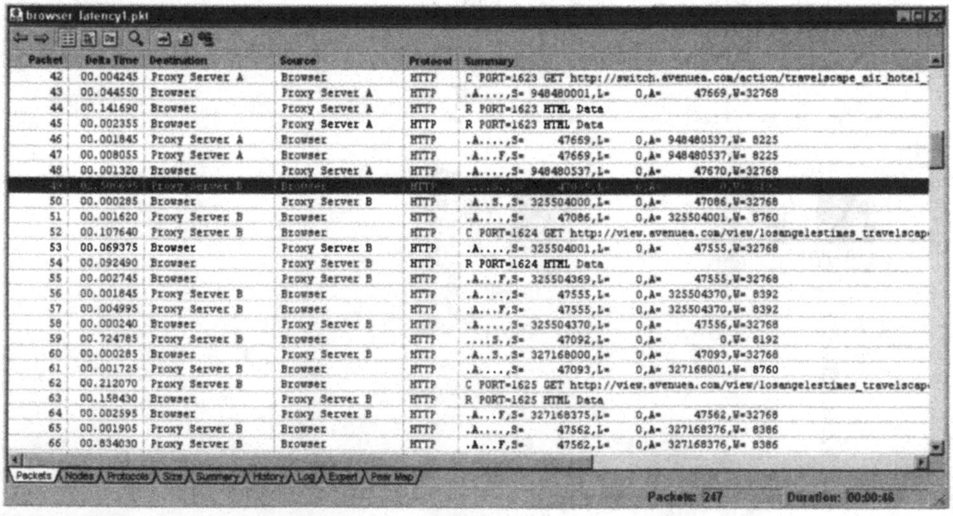

Figure 6-17   Browser latency.

NOTE Newer Web browsers support a technique called pipelining whereby the browser can request multiple objects using a single TCP connection.

Between Frames 43 and 48, you can see the browser finishing the down-loading of a Web object and disconnecting that TCP session. After 2.5 seconds, the browser opens another TCP connection to start the downloading of the next Web object. From the receipt of Frame 48 until the browser initiates the next TCP connection, the host waits 2.5 seconds. If a Web page contains 20 graphics files as well as links, pictures, and other elements, a 2.5 second delay between each object's downloading could cause the entire process to take min-utes to complete.

Besides the 2.5-second wait between the close of the old session and the establishment of the new one, I noticed that the browser was also using a new proxy server. Why? What I discovered was that every time the host would open a new element, it would consult an auto-proxy.pac file to find out what proxy server it should use. Auto-proxy.pac files are configuration files that contain a small bit of code to randomize which proxy server is used during each connection. This is the reason that the browser was choosing a new proxy server on the next connection. Unfortunately, this small process was adding seconds to each TCP connection. Once again, a call to the vendor and a soft-ware upgrade on the client's browser software fixed the problem.

When analyzing delays such as this one, it is important to always confirm that the client is not waiting for any more data from a server. If you look at the sequence number in Frame 47 where the Browser client sends the Proxy Server a FIN for the current session, it is 47669. In Frame 48, Proxy Server A acknowl-edges the FIN with an ACK number of 47670. This information told me that the browser was finished with the current session and would not be receiving any more data from it. In client/server applications, the client is always responsible for the requesting of data from the server, not the other way around. When the server has no more data to send the client, any delays at that point are always due to the client.

The Push Flag

When an application using UDP passes data down to the transport layer, UDP will immediately pass the data down to the network layer for transmission onto the network. When a host receives UDP data, it will immediately pass the data up to the application. There is no wait, no reassembly of data, and no bundling of acknowledgments with outgoing data as there is in TCP. When TCP receives data from a peer TCP stack, it does not always pass the data up to the application. TCP will sometimes wait to see if more data is sent to it so that it may acknowledge more data with a single ACK. This process converses bandwidth.

However, sometimes this delay can affect an application, for example, a Telnet session where quick screen updates are critical to the functioning of the application. If an application needs a receiving host's TCP stack to immediately pass data up to the application without delay, it sets the Push (PSH) flag (also known as the Push bit). When TCP receives data segments with the PSH flag set, it will not wait to see if other data is on the way. It will immediately pass the data to the upper-layer application or protocol. You may also see the Push flag set on the last segment of a large data transfer.

In Figure 6-18, you can see a host whose browser has aborted an HTTP session by sending TCP Reset segments to the Web Server. Starting in Frame 314, the browser aborts the connection and sends a Reset every time the Web server attempts to deliver it more data. This example really shows the robustness of the TCP protocol. The Web server continues to send the data in its buffers to the client. On the last TCP segment it sends, it sets the PSH bit to notify the receiving application that it should pass any data waiting in its buffers to the application. Setting the PSH bit is very common when a server is sending the last segment of data to a client, even more so when it hasn't received an acknowledgment from the client for any of its sent data. Setting the PSH bit is almost like a last-ditch effort to tell the client to please process the previous data it has sent. Unfortunately, in this case, the receiving application hung and most likely never saw any of that data.

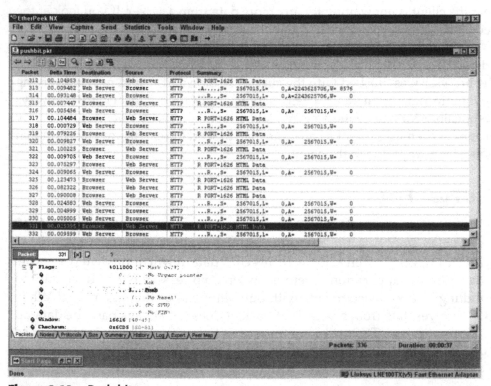

Figure 6-18   Push bit.

TCP Sliding Windows

TCP has another method of buffer control called the TCP window. If you've been wondering what all of those W=8760 statements in the summary panes of the examples were, you're going to find out now. TCP allocates a finite number of buffers for receiving data from a peer TCP host. The TCP Window field lets TCP inform the peer TCP host how much buffer space it has to receive data. The W=8760s are the decodings of the value in the Window field.

At the beginning of a TCP connection, both hosts will announce their window size in the SYN segments they send to each other. As data flow progresses, the hosts will inform each other of how much buffer space they have left to accept data. Hence, the TCP window slides back and forth as it adjusts itself to how much buffer space is left.

> **NOTE** A complete understanding of the TCP window is unnecessary in most troubleshooting situations. For those interested in the semantics, I would refer you to W. Richard Stevens' *TCP/IP Illustrated, Volume 1*, which I've mentioned before, or J. Scott Haugdahl's *Network Analysis and Troubleshooting* (Addison-Wesley, January 2000). Both offer excellent descriptions of the TCP sliding window operation.

The TCP Window's main purpose is flow control between sender and receiver. The best way to think of the TCP Window is to think of it as a physical window. When a window is open, it lets more air in; when it's closed, it allows less air in. Thinking of data as air is a great way to view how the TCP window operates. Bigger window, more data; smaller window, less data. The amount of data that will pass through the window is called the window size. Three things affect the TCP Window size:

- One is the rate at which TCP is receiving data. A fast sender can easily overwhelm the TCP buffers of a slower receiver. In that case, the receiving station's TCP stack should reduce the window size, informing the sender it cannot accept more data.

- Second is the speed at which an application processes the data inside of TCP's buffers. Just because TCP has received data does not mean that the application has processed it. A slow application could easily cause TCP's buffers to fill up quickly.

- The third thing that can affect the TCP window is the amount of TCP buffers available on the receiver. The lower the amount of buffers, the lower the window size. Often very small PDA-type network devices do not have the memory that a larger desktop-based system would have. To conserve memory then, they may have a lower amount of TCP buffers available to them.

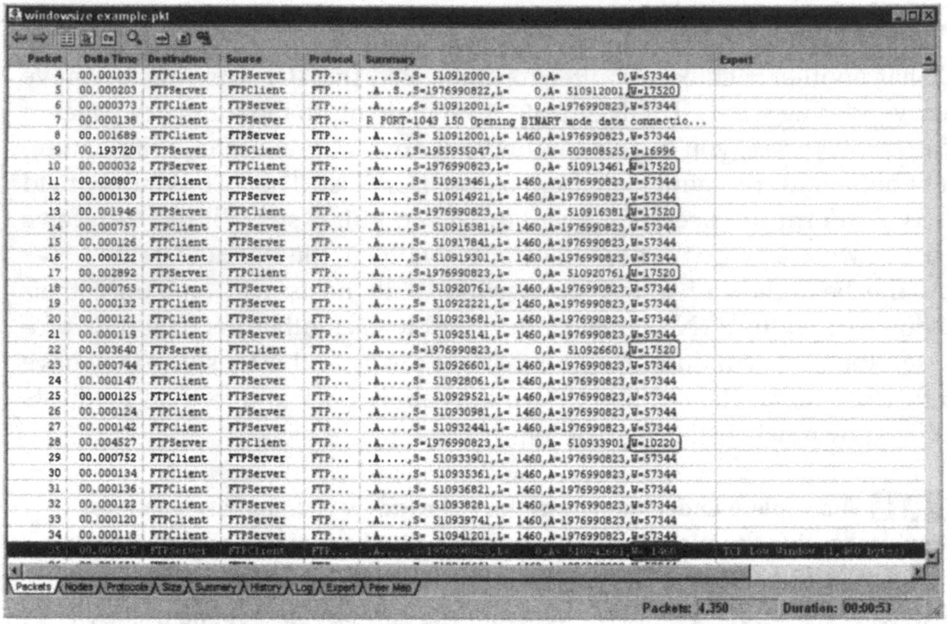

Figure 6-19 TCP window operation.

Now, take a look at an example of how the TCP Window operates. In Figure 6-19, you can see an FTP session start up in Frame 4. Both the FTP client and server advertise their TCP windows, 17520 and 57344 bytes, respectively. Frame 8 starts the data transfer from the server to the client. In the next 34 frames, the server continues to send FTP data to the client. The acknowledgments in Frames 10, 13, 17, and 22 all contain the same original window size advertisement of 17520.

However, the situation changes in Frame 28. In Frame 28, the client is telling the FTP server that now it can accept only 10220 bytes of data. Also, notice that in the same packet the client has acknowledged, so far, all data that the server has sent to it. Once again, you can tell by the acknowledgment number in the frame. The ACK number of 510933901 indicates that all bytes up to, but not including, 510933901 have been received and that the client expects the next TCP sequence number to be 510933901. In Frames 29 to 34, the FTP server sends the client 8760 more bytes of data. (The six packets of 1,460 bytes each equal 8,760 total bytes of data sent.) Then in Frame 35 you can see something very interesting. The client has drastically reduced its window size, now advertising only 1460 bytes of data. This means that the FTP server is permitted to send only one more full-sized TCP segment of 1,460 bytes before the receiver's buffers become filled. Why the sudden drop in window size?

Consider the three reasons for the adjustment in window size I just outlined. It's doubtful that the receiving station has a minimal amount of buffer space because it started out with 17,520 bytes of buffer. With that eliminated, the problem could be one of two things, that the sender is sending data too rapidly or that the application is not processing the data in the TCP buffers quickly enough.

Let's go on to the next sequence of frames to find out. In Frame 36 of Figure 6-20, you can see that the FTP server did, in fact, send only one more full-sized segment of 1460 bytes to the client.

In Frame 37, the client acknowledges that segment and updates its window size back to 17520 bytes. The reduction in window size was due to the time it took the FTP client to process the data in its buffers. Sudden changes in a host's window size advertisements are indicative of this behavior. The server is now allowed to send the client 17,520 bytes of data. In Frames 38 to 45, the server sends 11680 bytes of data to the client. Now, look closely and you can really see how TCP operates. In Frame 46, the client acknowledges the TCP data sent to it. But this time it does not acknowledge all of the data. The acknowledgment number it sends back to the server is 510949961, indicating to the server that the client has received 5,840 more bytes of data. Its acknowledgment number acknowledges only bytes 510944121 through 510949960 as having been received. Doing some math will help you here. If the original window advertisement was 17,520 bytes and the server sent 11,680 bytes of data, the server can send only 5,840 more bytes of data before exceeding the window size advertised by the client. However, in Frame 46 the client acknowledges 5,840 of those 11,680 bytes. So, now the window slides open 5,840 more bytes for an advertisement of 11680 bytes.

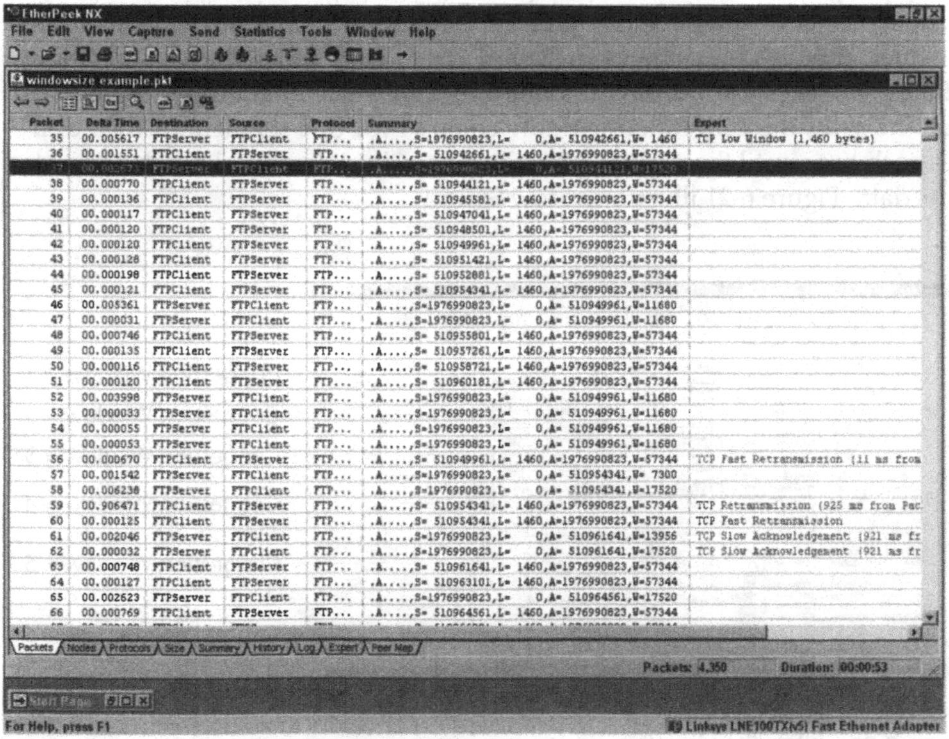

Figure 6-20 TCP window operation continued.

TCP's sliding window mechanism is not easy to understand, but with practice you can master it. It is critical to understand it when troubleshooting performance problems between hosts. Watching how fast a host acknowledges data it receives gives you a good idea of its processing power and, further, how efficient an application is at processing received data. You will not always see the same types of results every time you analyze a TCP data transfer. I recommend analyzing data transfers between different kinds of hosts over different networks, with different applications. All three or any combination of the three will usually yield different results. The important thing to do is to establish a baseline as to how a host processes data during normal operation. This baseline gives you a reference to use in the future if problems arise.

Slow Start and Congestion Avoidance

There is actually another type of window that exists in TCP that you don't see explicitly advertised in the packets. It is called the congestion window. The congestion window exists because of something called TCP Slow Start.

In Figure 6-19, the FTP client immediately advertises 17520 bytes of data in its window size. You'll notice in that example, though, that the FTP server does not immediately send 17,520 bytes of data; it sends only 1,460 bytes of data. The reason it does this is because of something called Slow Start. Slow Start is a congestion avoidance algorithm implemented in TCP stacks to avoid unnecessary packet loss. Instead of sending out the exact amount of data advertised in the receiver's window, the sender starts out sending one segment at a time and then doubles the amount of data it sends each time. It uses something called the congestion window to determine how much data to send out each time. Initially, the congestion window equals 1 for one segment; it then doubles each time until the receiving host stops sending timely acknowledgments to its data. Figure 6-21 illustrates Slow Start.

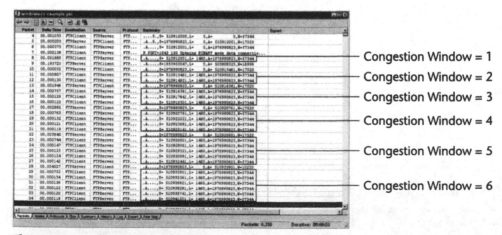

Figure 6-21   Slow Start in action.

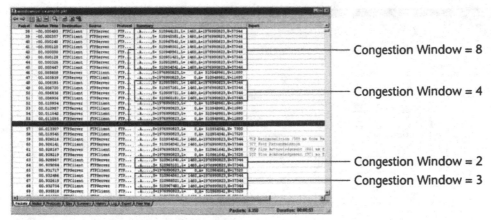

- Congestion Window = 8
- Congestion Window = 4
- Congestion Window = 2
- Congestion Window = 3

Figure 6-22   Reduced congestion window.

Even though the receiving window is 17520, the sender's congestion window is initialized at one segment. You can see how upon successful transmission and acknowledgments, the sender slowly increases its congestion window and sends out more segments. The congestion window is adjusted based on how fast acknowledgments are returned by the receiving host. In Figure 6-22, you can see that the congestion window has increased even more, up to 8, but when only half of the data sent in the last congestion window is acknowledged (Frame 46), the host quickly reduces the congestion window to half of its original value.

You can also see in Figure 6-22 that in Frame 56 the FTP server has retransmitted segment 510949961, which was originally sent in Frame 42. Whenever a sender experiences a segment loss (or one that has not been ACK'd quickly enough) it will reduce the congestion window by half, so in this example the congestion window is cut from 4 to 2. After all data has been successful received, you can see it starting to increase the congestion window again to 3. The TCP window and the congestion window constantly change during the lifetime of a connection, which allows a host to send the optimal amount of data based on network conditions and the ability of the host to receive that data.

Nagle Algorithm

Some applications, by their nature, transmit very small amounts of data. Sometimes these data segments are considerably smaller than a receiving hosts MSS. The Nagle Algorithm states that a host may have one only TCP segment less than the MSS that is unacknowledged. This algorithm prevents a host from flooding the network with very small packets. Hosts implementing the Nagle Algorithm will buffer all small data writes from an application and send them as one large segment. Figure 6-23 shows how the Nagle Algorithm works.

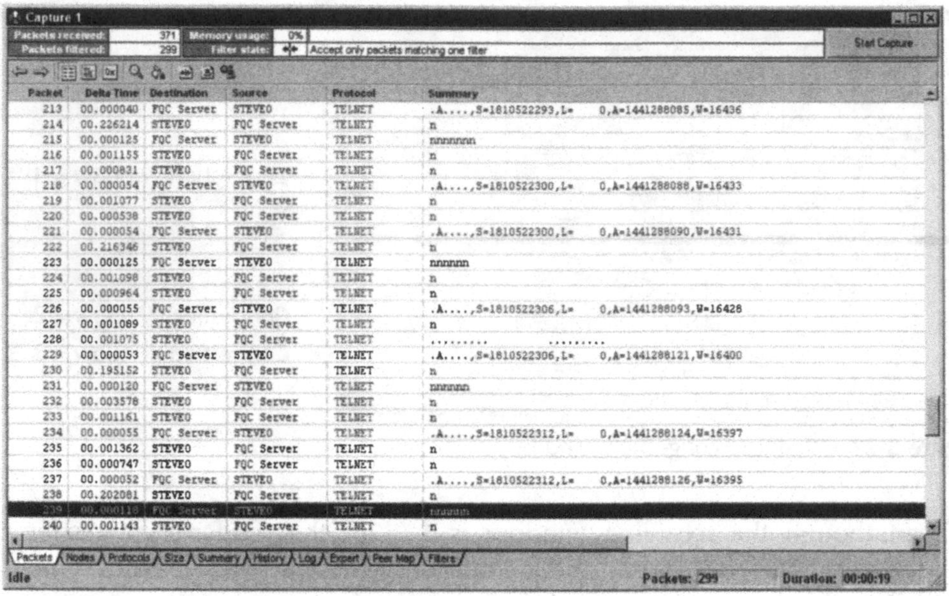

Figure 6-23 Nagle Algorithm in action.

From my host STEVEO, I Telnetted to a Unix server FQC Server. While capturing a Telnet session, I held the *n* key down for several seconds to force our host to send out multiple *n* characters. Instead of sending one character per packet, you can see that in Frames 215, 223, 231, and 239 the TCP stack is bundling the data and sending it as a single larger packet. This saves bandwidth because you don't have one packet per character being sent across the network.

NOTE Some applications need to disable the Nagle Algorithm because it is critical that destination hosts receive the data without any delay. XWindows is one of those applications. Another is an application called Virtual Network Computing, which functions similar to XWindows, and applications like PCAnywhere that allow a user to control the mouse and keyboard of another computer.

In Figure 6-24, I established a VNC session between two computers. Both computers negotiated their MSS to be 1460 bytes. Once the VNC session was established, I moved the mouse around constantly for about 20 seconds. This forced the VNC host to have to update my local VNC application constantly with mouse movement and position data. You can see in the trace that the host machine has disabled the Nagle Algorithm for the connection. You can see it sending out more than one small segment of data that is not acknowledged.

Although you may never run into a situation where understanding the Nagle Algorithm is necessary, it is important to understand its existence and why it is enabled or disabled. Unless an application disables the Nagle Algorithm, it is active by default on almost all TCP/IP stacks.

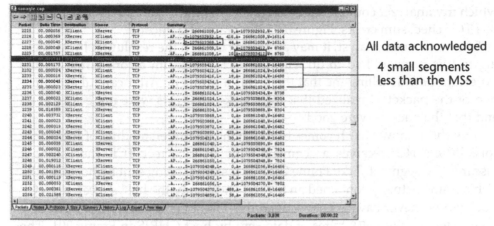

All data acknowledged

4 small segments
less than the MSS

Figure 6-24 Nagle Algorithm disabled.

Data Protection

The TCP protocol guarantees data integrity by the implementation of a check-sum. The checksum is calculated over the entire contents on the TCP data. Just as with UDP's checksum, if the checksum value the receiving host calculates is different from the value in the checksum field, the data segment is discarded. A valid checksum guarantees that the receiving host's application is getting exactly the same data the source host sent it. If for some reason a packet is received with a correct data link layer CRC and an incorrect TCP checksum, the chances are that the packet's data was corrupted somewhere between Layers 2 and 4, either that or (in one case I have seen) the sending host was actually miscalculating the TCP checksum.

Case Study: TCP Checksum Errors

While analyzing a connection time-out issue between two groups of geographically dispersed users on a LAN, I employed the use of RMON probes to perform data captures.

> **TIP** RMON probes are generally not good analyzers, but in this case the problem was so difficult to capture that I used the RMON probes to capture and store large volumes of traffic data until I could, at a later time, download the traffic into capture files for analysis.

The RMON probe used a proprietary trace file format that the analyzers were unable to read. Fortunately, the probe management software had a conversation utility so that I was able to convert the traces into Sniffer enc format, which my analyzer could read. Upon analyzing the capture, I noticed numerous TCP checksum errors. Figure 6-25 illustrates the tracefile.

To an untrained analyst, it may appear as though the resolution I was seeking to this problem had to do with the TCP checksum errors. After all, the expert mode was telling me that there was a problem. After careful examination of the packets, I realized that the checksum errors were not errors at all and that the packets were good.

How did I know this? It comes from having an understanding of the protocols. When TCP receives a segment with an incorrect TCP checksum, it discards the segment. Take Frame 201, for instance, being sent by host CHRIS. If this frame actually contained an invalid checksum, the host's receiving TCP stack would never have acknowledged the data. In Frame 205, host CHRISSY acknowledges the 1078 bytes of data sent by host CHRIS in Frame 201. The data is being acknowledged and passed on to upper layers, which means that the packets are good.

But why the TCP checksum symptoms then? Was the analyzer wrong? No, in fact, the analyzer was right; the checksum values in the fields are incorrect. What was happening was that the conversation program I was using to convert the trace files into Sniffer format was periodically corrupting the values in the TCP Checksum field. The receiving host was not receiving incorrect checksum values, but in the traces they were incorrect.

Figure 6-25   TCP checksum errors.

This is a fine example of how an analyzer's expert mode can lead you astray as to the true source of the problem. When you see TCP checksum errors, data should not be passing. In this example, when I matched up the sequence and acknowledgment numbers, I could see that the host was acknowledging frames that the analyzer said were corrupt. However, if they were truly corrupt, the host would have discarded them, not sent an acknowledgment. Never blindly trust your tools; always base your analysis on your knowledge of the protocol's operation.

TCP Expert Symptoms

The TCP protocol is probably responsible for more misdiagnosis of protocol analyzer symptoms than any other protocol. The reason is that it is so dynamic. The functions built into TCP have made it a fantastic protocol capable of tuning itself to meet the needs of almost any network or network condition. It is also the reason that analyzers' expert modes seem to constantly notify you of every small symptom relating to a TCP data transfer. There are two categories of TCP expert symptoms.

- One category you should pay attention to. I call these *symptoms to watch for*:
  - TCP Transport Retransmissions
  - TCP Reset Connection
  - TCP Repeated Connection Attempt
  - TCP Low Starting MSS
  - TCP Invalid Checksum
  - TCP Connection Refused
  - TCP Lost Connection

  This first group of symptoms deals primarily with whether something is working or not working. Lost Connection, Reset Connection, Repeated Connection Attempt, and Connection Refused all indicate something wrong with the TCP connection. Invalid Checksum and Retransmission symptoms affect a session because they indicate that packets are going to be dropped or are already being dropped. Repeated connection attempts are a type of retransmission that occurs during the establishment phase of the connection. The Low Starting MSS symptom is important in that you may be able to increase performance by simply changing a variable on a host.

- The other category of symptoms you should take note of but not let concern you greatly. I call this category *symptoms to take note of*:
  - TCP Zero Window
  - TCP Stuck Window

- TCP Low Window
- TCP Idle Too Long
- TCP Long ACK

The second group of symptoms deals with how TCP is transferring data. These are the most confusing symptoms to an untrained analyst. None of the symptoms in and of themselves indicates that anything is horribly wrong. These symptoms could be showing up because of how a TCP stack does (or does not) implement certain TCP functions such as window sizing or delayed acknowledgments.

WARNING Expert symptoms are fantastic flags to let you know that something *might* be wrong. However, they should never be taken at face value as indicating that there is a problem on the network. A general rule about analyzer expert symptoms is that if you see a symptom, you should be able to understand why the analyzer is giving you the symptom. No matter how good an expert symptom is, never blindly trust it without first verifying the reasons behind the symptom.

TCP Application Analysis

There are numerous applications that utilize the TCP protocol. It is imperative to have an understanding of how TCP performs its functions independently from the responsibility of the application. In this section, I take a look at some examples of analyzing application-specific attributes of TCP data transfers. In this section, I review what I have discussed in the previous sections on the TCP protocol and its operations with respect to how applications and TCP integrate to maximize performance and overcome latency.

TCP and Throughput

There are three things that determine the throughput of an application:

- Segment size
- Latency
- Window size

Segment Size

Having each host use a maximum segment size that is as large as possible helps eliminate inefficiency due to sending multiple small segments over the wire.

Since each small segment incurs the same amount of overhead from the data link, network, and transport protocol headers, it is much more efficient to transfer those multiple small segments as one large segment across the network.

For example, take a host that uses the default TCP segment size of 536 bytes. The overhead of the lower-layer protocols is going to be 58 bytes, bringing the total packet size to 594 bytes. At 536 bytes of data, the overhead contributes 9.7 percent of data to the entire frame. However, if you increase the segment size to 1,460 bytes (on Ethernet), the percentage of overhead drops to 3.9 percent of the total frame size. While a 5.8 percent reduction of data might not seem like a lot, remember that each 536 bytes of data is going to need a separate packet in order to be transmitted. A maximum segment size of 1,460 bytes can be sent in one packet. The same 1,460 bytes would need three packets in order to be transmitted across the network and incur an extra added overhead of 12 percent. During a large file transfer, that 12 percent can add up quite quickly and inhibit performance over lower-bandwidth WAN links.

CROSS-REFERENCE Overhead and packet efficiencies are discussed in more detail in Chapter 5.

Latency

Latency is the total amount of delay between a sender sending data and a receiver receiving it. TCP helps overcome latency. A good analogy is grocery shopping. Say you live 3 miles away from the local grocery store. Between you and the store is a highway with a speed limit of 60 mph. Traffic is normally light, so you are able to travel at the maximum speed limit to reach the store in 3 minutes. While you are there you buy a single item, for example, milk. You then get in your car and travel 60 mph home again in 3 minutes. You drop off the milk, get in the car, drive 60 mph to the store in 3 minutes. While you are there, you buy eggs. After purchasing the eggs, you get in the car and drive home, arriving there in 3 minutes. Assume that you have 10 items to buy. Using this technique, it would take you at least 60 minutes to get home with all 10 items (10 items × 6-minute round trip per item = 60 minutes). Wouldn't it be to your advantage to buy all 10 items at once and make one single round trip to the store? If you did so, you would dramatically reduce the time it would take you to shop. Although this seems to be a ridiculous example in real life, it is a very realistic example of how some applications operate over TCP. Instead of handing TCP multiple blocks of data to transmit all at once, they send small amounts of data back and forth across the network. The Nagle Algorithm (discussed earlier in the chapter) was specifically designed to prevent applications from doing this by forbidding them to have more than one outstanding small-sized segment on the network at a time.

Latency can also occur on other places besides the network. In *Network Analysis and Troubleshooting*, Haugdahl refers to the kinds of latency transactions you may face in what he calls the "latency wedge." He views the three basic parts of a transaction—request, processing, and reply—as making up a triangular wedge-shaped object.

- **Request.** Latency can occur on a client when it doesn't request data quickly enough.

- **Processing.** Processing delay takes place once a packet reaches a host. It must be processed by all layers of the OSI model before being handed off to the application. (Later in this section, I present an example that shows you how to determine the status of a TCP segment once it is inside a host.)

- **Reply.** A server application may not respond to a request in a timely fashion.

Window Size

TCP window sizes allow hosts to give each other feedback concerning the amount of buffers they posses to accept TCP data. The TCP sliding window keeps data flowing at the fastest possible rate by constantly informing the sender of how much data it can accept. The congestion window makes sure that the network or the destination host is not overwhelmed by data too quickly. Along with data acknowledgments, both windows work in harmony to provide the best possible performance.

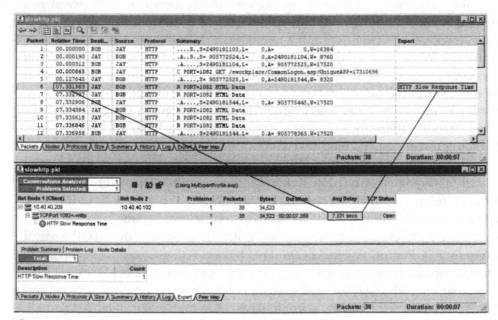

Figure 6-26 HTTP delay.

As I present the following case studies, keep in mind the three factors that affect throughput. Their understanding is critical when diagnosing the reasons behind poor throughput.

Case Study: Slow Web Server

This first example illustrates how to discern delay inside of a host.

In this case, user complaints as to how long it took to load a Web page led my team to analyze the transactions during the HTML page loading process. After watching the client browser (JAY) download the entire page, we concentrated on each individual TCP session to determine which session was causing the delay. Figure 6-26 shows a filtered-down trace with the session causing the problem.

You can see the TCP session start normally with SYNs and ACKs being exchanged. In Frame 4, you can see the client send a request to open an Active Server Page. In Frame 6, you can see it takes exactly 7.331 seconds for the server to send back the first of several HTTP data segments. So, how do you know if the problem is with the network or the application? After all, if the network connection had gone down in the time between Frames 5 and 6, the HTTP reply in Frame 6 could have been the last retransmission attempt by the server that just happened to make it through. The TCP acknowledgment segment in Frame 5 gives you a clue. Figure 6-27 shows a decode for Frame 4.

In Frame 4, the client (JAY) is making an HTTP request to server BOB to open an Active Server Page (asp) file. The TCP sequence number sent along with this request is 2490181104. The HTTP request data is 440 bytes in length (IP Length of 480 – 40 for IP, TCP headers = 440). In Frame 5 you see that 126 milliseconds later the server sends a TCP acknowledgment for that data. You know that the server is acknowledging the 440 bytes of client data because it sends an acknowledgment number of 2490181544. This tells you two things:

- The network round-trip time is 126 milliseconds or less. If server BOB's TCP stack can return an acknowledgment in 126 milliseconds, you know that the network is capable of delivering the data in that time.

- The TCP stack on the server has received the request and has notified the application that it has data waiting to be processed.

The rest of the 7.331 seconds it took to turn around the HTTP request is the result of application delay. TCP has done its job, acknowledging the data in 126 milliseconds; the only other job left is for the application to process it. Figure 6-28 shows a more simplistic view of this process.

> **NOTE** The 126 millisecond time for TCP to acknowledge the data segment includes the TCP Delayed Ack time for TCP to wait and see if it can piggyback its acknowledgment onto some data being sent back to the client.

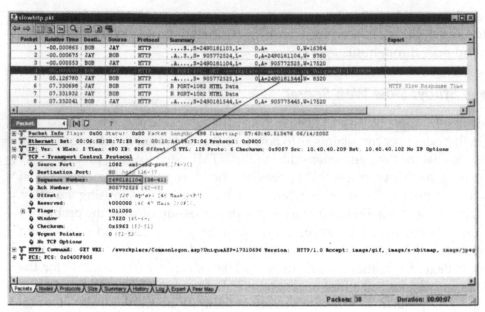

Figure 6-27   Fast ACK, slow application.

Case Study: Bad Windowing

When TCP transfers and acknowledges data it should do so in a fashion that enables a smooth constant flow of data. A good TCP stack will exhibit very few windowing symptoms such as Stuck Windows or Zero Windows messages in an analyzer. A good stack will use its window advertisements effectively to avoid the need for a receiving host to stop the data transfer all together until it catches up. Figure 6-29 shows one such TCP stack that didn't use any window advertisements.

The receiving host began with an advertised window of 17520 bytes and left it at the same value during the life of the data transfer. By not using window advertisements, a receiving host has no other choice but to not acknowledge data in a timely fashion. Normally, a host will inform a sender that its window has been reduced. This causes the sender to adjust the number of data bytes it is currently sending out. Without this feedback, a sending host will keep sending the full window size of data every single time. Notice in Frame 14 that the receiving host starts acknowledging, frame by frame, all the preceding data sent to it. It would have been much more efficient to wait and acknowledge all of the data with a single TCP acknowledgment rather than waste network bandwidth on individual ACKs.

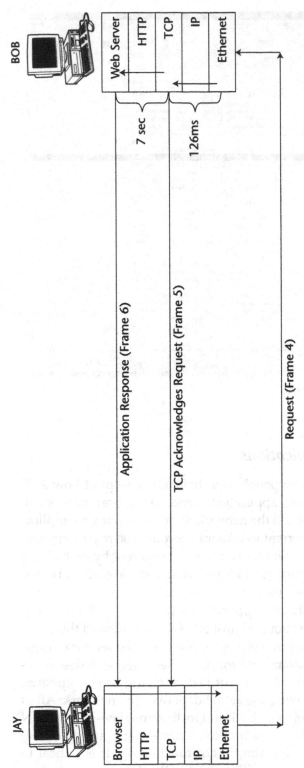

Figure 6-28   TCP and application processing.

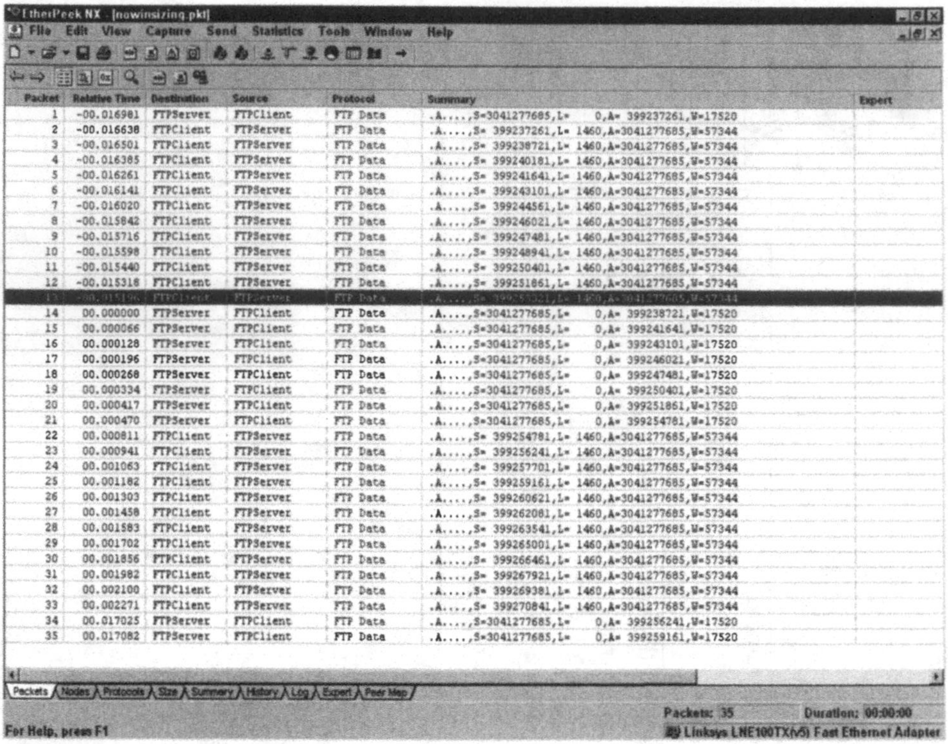
EtherPeek NX - [nowinsizing.pkt]
File Edit View Capture Send Statistics Tools Window Help
Packet Relative Time Destination Source Protocol Summary Expert
1 -00.016981 FTPServer FTPClient FTP Data .A....,S=3041277685,L= 0,A= 399237261,W=17520
2 -00.016638 FTPClient FTPServer FTP Data .A....,S= 399237261,L= 1460,A=3041277685,W=57344
3 -00.016501 FTPClient FTPServer FTP Data .A....,S= 399238721,L= 1460,A=3041277685,W=57344
4 -00.016385 FTPClient FTPServer FTP Data .A....,S= 399240181,L= 1460,A=3041277685,W=57344
5 -00.016261 FTPClient FTPServer FTP Data .A....,S= 399241641,L= 1460,A=3041277685,W=57344
6 -00.016141 FTPClient FTPServer FTP Data .A....,S= 399243101,L= 1460,A=3041277685,W=57344
7 -00.016020 FTPClient FTPServer FTP Data .A....,S= 399244561,L= 1460,A=3041277685,W=57344
8 -00.015842 FTPClient FTPServer FTP Data .A....,S= 399246021,L= 1460,A=3041277685,W=57344
9 -00.015716 FTPClient FTPServer FTP Data .A....,S= 399247481,L= 1460,A=3041277685,W=57344
10 -00.015598 FTPClient FTPServer FTP Data .A....,S= 399248941,L= 1460,A=3041277685,W=57344
11 -00.015440 FTPClient FTPServer FTP Data .A....,S= 399250401,L= 1460,A=3041277685,W=57344
12 -00.015318 FTPClient FTPServer FTP Data .A....,S= 399251861,L= 1460,A=3041277685,W=57344
13 -00.015196 FTPClient FTPServer FTP Data .A....,S= 399253321,L= 1460,A=3041277685,W=57344
14 00.000000 FTPServer FTPClient FTP Data .A....,S=3041277685,L= 0,A= 399238721,W=17520
15 00.000066 FTPServer FTPClient FTP Data .A....,S=3041277685,L= 0,A= 399241641,W=17520
16 00.000128 FTPServer FTPClient FTP Data .A....,S=3041277685,L= 0,A= 399243101,W=17520
17 00.000196 FTPServer FTPClient FTP Data .A....,S=3041277685,L= 0,A= 399246021,W=17520
18 00.000268 FTPServer FTPClient FTP Data .A....,S=3041277685,L= 0,A= 399247481,W=17520
19 00.000334 FTPServer FTPClient FTP Data .A....,S=3041277685,L= 0,A= 399250401,W=17520
20 00.000417 FTPServer FTPClient FTP Data .A....,S=3041277685,L= 0,A= 399251861,W=17520
21 00.000470 FTPServer FTPClient FTP Data .A....,S=3041277685,L= 0,A= 399254781,W=17520
22 00.000811 FTPClient FTPServer FTP Data .A....,S= 399254781,L= 1460,A=3041277685,W=57344
23 00.000941 FTPClient FTPServer FTP Data .A....,S= 399256241,L= 1460,A=3041277685,W=57344
24 00.001063 FTPClient FTPServer FTP Data .A....,S= 399257701,L= 1460,A=3041277685,W=57344
25 00.001182 FTPClient FTPServer FTP Data .A....,S= 399259161,L= 1460,A=3041277685,W=57344
26 00.001303 FTPClient FTPServer FTP Data .A....,S= 399260621,L= 1460,A=3041277685,W=57344
27 00.001458 FTPClient FTPServer FTP Data .A....,S= 399262081,L= 1460,A=3041277685,W=57344
28 00.001583 FTPClient FTPServer FTP Data .A....,S= 399263541,L= 1460,A=3041277685,W=57344
29 00.001702 FTPClient FTPServer FTP Data .A....,S= 399265001,L= 1460,A=3041277685,W=57344
30 00.001856 FTPClient FTPServer FTP Data .A....,S= 399266461,L= 1460,A=3041277685,W=57344
31 00.001982 FTPClient FTPServer FTP Data .A....,S= 399267921,L= 1460,A=3041277685,W=57344
32 00.002100 FTPClient FTPServer FTP Data .A....,S= 399269381,L= 1460,A=3041277685,W=57344
33 00.002271 FTPClient FTPServer FTP Data .A....,S= 399270841,L= 1460,A=3041277685,W=57344
34 00.017025 FTPServer FTPClient FTP Data .A....,S=3041277685,L= 0,A= 399256241,W=17520
35 00.017082 FTPServer FTPClient FTP Data .A....,S=3041277685,L= 0,A= 399259161,W=17520
Packets Nodes Protocols Size Summary History Log Expert Peer Map
Packets: 35 Duration: 00:00:00
For Help, press F1
Linksys LNE100TX(v5) Fast Ethernet Adapter

Figure 6-29 Bad window adjustment.

Case Study: Inefficient Applications

A lot of applications are written by people who have no concept of how TCP works. These network "unaware" applications tend to transfer very small amounts of data back and forth across the network. When analyzing an application that runs over TCP, it is important to take into account the maximum segment size being used and also the window advertisements sent by each client. This information will give you a very good idea of what hosts on each end of the connection are capable of. If you see packets that are smaller than the MSS being sent back and forth, you can bet that the application is not using TCP effectively.

In the early days of SQL applications, almost all of them exhibited this same behavior, which led to countless problems when these databases were transferred from terminal-based mainframe platforms to client/server-based architectures over wide area networks. Instead of just receiving screen updates, the client applications were receiving the actual data over the network. All of those small segments making their way back and forth across low-speed WAN circuits caused innumerable delays and increased application latency, sometimes to the point of the application simply not functioning. It is critical to understand how an application works with respect to the data sizes and send-to-receive ratios it uses between clients and servers.

High-Performance Extensions to TCP

From its inception, TCP has not changed very much. Besides some modifications to behind-the-scenes algorithms, the basic format and function of the protocol has been the same for the last 10 years. The designers of the protocol left room for improvements and changes. The TCP Options field is one aspect that has enabled newer TCP functions to be implemented, while still providing for backward compatibility with older TCP stacks. In this section, I want to take a look at these new options.

Selective Acknowledgments

TCP is a byte-acknowledged transport protocol. As you have seen in previous sections, a receiving host acknowledges each byte of TCP data it has received. It does so with an acknowledgment number. TCP acknowledgments may acknowledge a single segment of data or multiple segments of data. The ability to acknowledge multiple segments of data with a single packet allows TCP to conserve bandwidth and avoid ping-pong type protocol actions. However, the acknowledgment scheme used by TCP also has limitations in certain situations that could actually cause more data to be sent than necessary when a packet is lost on the network. Figure 6-30 illustrates why.

Host JAY is in the process of transmitting 2500 bytes of application data. JAY has just sent five TCP segments of 500 bytes each to host BOB. Due to a network anomaly, the packet containing bytes 8,000–8,499 has been lost. Because TCP is able to acknowledge data only from a byte perspective, it has no choice but to send an acknowledgment for bytes up to and including 7999. Even though it has received the last two packets, containing bytes 8,500–9,999 it has no way of informing host JAY of this. Host JAY, upon receiving the acknowledgment, believes that BOB has received only the first two segments. Based on the acknowledgment number from BOB, host JAY will retransmit all bytes starting with 8000. As you can see in the figure, this process wastes bandwidth due to the sending of two extra segments that have already been received by the destination.

Enter the Selective Acknowledgment, or SACK, option. SACK allows TCP to inform a host that it has received a range of bytes and that the host should retransmit only the lost segment. Figure 6-31 illustrates how this works. Host BOB, upon receiving all data segments except 8,000–8,500, sends an acknowledgment packet with the TCP SACK option. The SACK option contains two extra fields called the Left Edge Block and the Right Edge Block. The acknowledgment field will contain the value of the last sequential segment of data received. The SACK block fields will contain a range of bytes that the host has also already received. In Figure 6-31 the acknowledgment number is 7999, indicating that it has received up to and including bytes 7,000 to 7,999. The left block field contains the value of the next byte of data that TCP has received, in

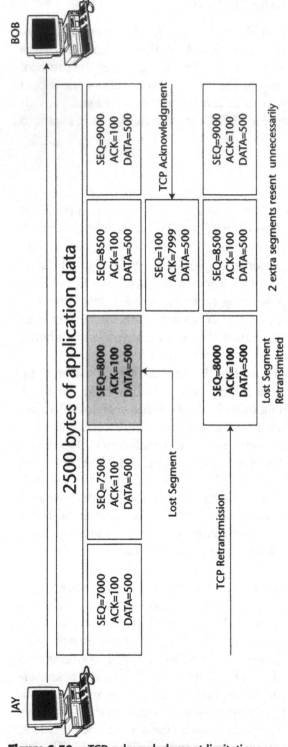

Figure 6-30   TCP acknowledgment limitations.

this case 8500. The right edge block field contains the ending byte of that series of bytes received by TCP, in this case 9500. The SACK option allows a host, BOB in this example, to tell a sending host that it has received bytes 7,000 through 7,999 and bytes 8,500 through 9,500 but not bytes 8,000–8,500. Upon receiving the SACK frame, JAY retransmits only the lost segment, thus saving the time and bandwidth of sending extra unnecessary segments that have already been received by the destination.

Window Scale Option

When TCP was designed, the designers could never have imagined the need for a window field longer than 16 bits. Sixteen bits limits a host to advertising a window of no larger than 65,535 bytes. With today's large multiprocessor gigabit connected servers, this 64K window size actually becomes the limiting factor in TCP data transfer throughput. At Gigabit Ethernet speeds, a buffer of 64K could be emptied in less than a microsecond. Ten years ago at 10MB speeds, it would take a host 50 milliseconds to empty the same 64K buffer. Hosts today can handle considerably higher TCP buffers, but TCP had no way of informing a destination host of available buffers higher than 64K.

It had no way, that is, until the Window Scale option was implemented. Using fields in the TCP Options section of the TCP header allows two hosts to advertise window sizes up to 30 bits in length with a maximum advertisement of 1GB. The TCP window scale contains a 14-bit scale factor field that is used to tell a host how many bit positions it should shift the current window size to the left. For example, a window size of 65,535K would translate into 16 ones in binary. In order to increase the scale factor of the window size, a host would negotiate a scale factor value of 3, or 00000000000011. This tells a host that the value in a window advertisement should be left-shifted two bit places. More simply stated, the decimal value of the window size should be converted to binary, have two zeros added to the end of the value, and then converted back into decimal. The following example shows how this is performed:

Window Size = 65,535 decimal or 1111111111111111 binary

Scale Factor = 00000000000011

New Window Size = 262,143 or 111111111111111100

The TCP window scale factor breathes new life into the limited 16-bit window field.

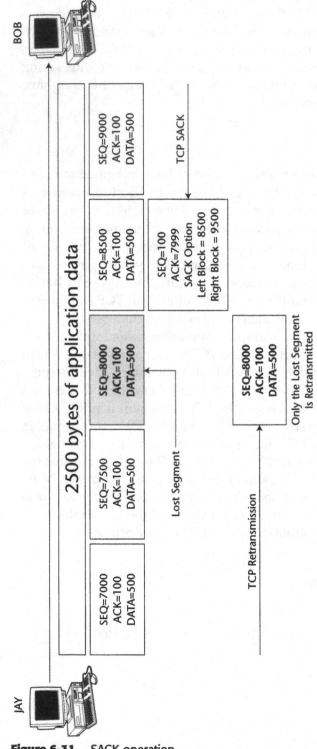

Figure 6-31   SACK operation.

Timestamp Option

During the lifetime of a connection, TCP constantly needs to keep track of the round-trip time to make adjustments for the retransmission time-out interval. The TCP timestamp feature allows a host to mark packets with explicit time information showing when they were transmitted or received. This feature also makes your life as an analyst easier because you are able to infer from the timestamps how much longer host processing will take on each end of a connection. TCP will eventually also use the timestamp feature to make better decisions on RTO and other timers it uses.

Summary

TCP is a complicated dynamic protocol. It is not easy to master. It is critical to understand the different features of its implementations so that you can quickly spot their use in a trace analysis. This chapter should leave you with a better understanding of how TCP handles the transfer of data between hosts. It is important to understand the many processes that TCP uses during a connection. It takes a failure of only one of these processes to cause problems. Once you understand them, it becomes second nature to verify them during your analysis. The complexity of TCP rivals some application-layer protocols. Once you acquire a firm foundation of TCP, an understanding of application dynamics is made that much easier. The only way to understand a protocol is to see it in action. No other protocol epitomizes this statement like TCP.

Related TCP/IP Protocols

CHAPTER 7

Upper-Layer Protocols

In the previous six chapters, I have laid the groundwork for discussing the bottom four layers of the OSI model. Upon reading those, you should have a firm grasp on the operations and functions performed by the core protocols of the TCP/IP stack. These protocols, though, have almost no use without the existence of upper-layer protocols. The top three layers of the OSI model consist of protocols that support the very software that runs on PCs and servers. In this chapter, I am going to discuss those protocols that allow the software to take advantage of the network.

Introduction to Upper-Layer Protocols

Before moving into a discussion of the upper-layer protocols, I want to review the functions of the lower four layers.

- The *physical layer* handles the transformation of binary ones and zeros into actual signaling such as electrical or optical pulses. It uses specific types of media such as copper or fiber-optic cable. In some cases, water pressure, or even air pressure, could be used to transport signaling information.

- The *data link layer* handles access to the media. Protocols like Ethernet and Token Ring control how hosts actually put the ones and zeros on the local network.

- The *network layer* handles the end-to-end delivery of data. Since a large internetwork may consist of multiple types of Layer 2 networks, such as Ethernet, Frame Relay, or ATM, the network layer allows you to have a common data path over all types of media. Addressing between two network-layer hosts stays the same no matter how many Layer 2 networks the packets have traversed.

- The *transport layer* attempts to guarantee the data delivery between a source and destination host on a network. If packets are dropped or corrupted along the way, the transport layer will do its best to retransmit them and ensure proper arrival.

So why do you need the next three upper layers? Assume that you have only the four previously mentioned layers to work with. This would allow you only the four functions of the layers described in the previous bulleted list. Assuming this, an application developer would need to implement all other functionality he or she would need in each application. Consider the following:

- Anyone who has worked for a help desk knows how hard it is sometimes to walk a user through running ipconfig and to obtain the user's IP address. Imagine if each user needed the IP address of all other users and servers in order to communicate over the network.

  Luckily, this isn't the case. Human beings tend to think of things as nouns, as a person, place, or thing. To simplify this, each user's computer could be given a name. Microsoft networks do this with the implementation of the Computer Name. After clicking on Network Neighborhood, a user only needs to search for the Computer Name rather than an unfriendly IP address in order to access remote resources on another host. If each application developer had to implement his or her own method of naming, each application could possibly have a different name for each host, a situation that is very similar to client SNA sessions that are configured with a separate SNA session name on each computer. Now that IP has become the standard, most applications take advantage of the Computer Name.

- What about data representation? In multivendor networks there are different types of files. A file may be stored using ASCII, EBCDIC, or even simple binary. One host's method of file representation may be different than another's. A method of handling the way data is presented to an application must be implemented on each host. Instead of each application developer writing the functions to handle every type of file format, wouldn't it be easier to implement this functionality in a presentation-layer protocol? This way each application could use the services of the protocol to handle the exchange of different file formats between hosts.

■ What about security? Similarly to file formats, a common method of security could be implemented in the application layer so that developers do not have to implement their own methods. Many applications today take advantage of the inherent security systems inside of Microsoft NT, 2000, and XP servers rather than writing their own methods.

The methods just discussed form the basis of functions that exist in protocols that occupy the upper three layers of the OSI model. Table 7-1 illustrates the location of each function.

Analyzing Upper-Layer Protocols

When analyzing upper-layer protocols, it is important to understand the interactions and dependencies between the protocols and the application. Each layer performs a specific function along the data path originating from the user's application. When you troubleshoot an application, you are actually troubleshooting all the layers the application is dependent on. The application layer itself is commonly misunderstood. The application layer is not the application itself but the entry point into the network. Figure 7-1 illustrates the integration between applications and the OSI model. User applications do not normally talk directly to an application-layer protocol. Instead, they use function calls from what is called the application program interface, or API. The API contains multiple functions, which allows an application to use lower-layer functions of the operating system and protocol stack. The API interacts directly with application-layer protocols such as Server Message Block (SMB), Remote Procedure Call (RPC), or terminal emulation protocols such as Telnet.

Table 7-1 Protocol Functions by Layer

FUNCTION	LAYER
Name resolution	Session
Data representation	Presentation
Security	Application

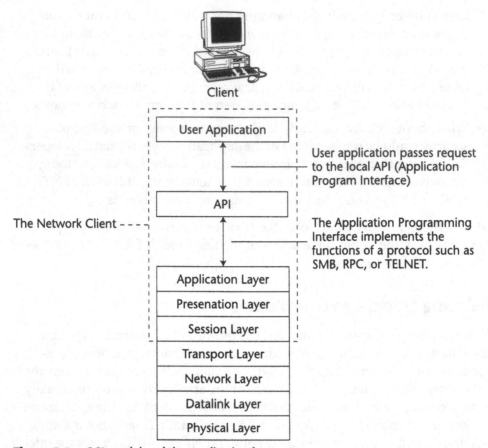

Figure 7-1   OSI model and the application layer.

Most of the time, your analysis will be not only of the application-layer protocol but of an application itself. The upper three layers of the OSI model sometimes present the most complicated challenges to a network analyst because of their complexity and obscurity. In order to properly analyze the upper layers and the applications that use them, it is important to do the following:

- **Understand the dependencies.**   An application will rely not only on the application-layer protocol but also on the processes performed by the lower layers. Take Figure 7-2 for example. Opening a simple Web page utilizes three layers of the OSI model.

  1. First, the session protocol DNS is used to resolve the hostname www.tracemasters.com to an IP address.

  2. Second, the transport protocol TCP initiates a connection to the destination host.

  3. Third, the application protocol, HTTP, sends requests for HTML (HyperText Markup Language) data from the Web server.

  A failure of any one of these protocols would cause the Web page not to load.

No.	Delta	Destination	Source	Protocol	Info
1	0	mail4.bellatlantic.net	Server	DNS	Standard query A www.tracemasters.com
2	0.027991	Server	mail4.bellatlantic.net	DNS	Standard query response CNAME tracemasters.com A 216.119.99.47
3	0.001716	tracemasters.com	Server	TCP	1794 > http [SYN] Seq=24040503 Ack=0 Win=16384 Len=0
4	0.078319	Server	tracemasters.com	TCP	http > 1794 [SYN, ACK] Seq=1394751226 Ack=24040504 Win=17424 Len=0
5	0.000081	tracemasters.com	Server	TCP	1794 > http [ACK] Seq=24040504 Ack=1394751227 Win=17424 Len=0
6	0.00263	tracemasters.com	Server	HTTP	GET / HTTP/1.1
7	0.107057	Server	tracemasters.com	TCP	http > 1794 [ACK] Seq=1394751227 Ack=24040926 Win=17002 Len=0
8	0.005104	Server	tracemasters.com	HTTP	HTTP/1.1 304 Not Modified
9	0.161553	tracemasters.com	Server	TCP	1794 > http [ACK] Seq=24040926 Ack=1394751462 Win=17189 Len=0

Figure 7-2 Layer association of Web browsing session.

- **Understand what the application is doing.**　It is easy to get caught up in the details of a protocol. As you move farther and farther up the OSI stack, the protocols you will be dealing with are increasingly complex. In order to simplify your understanding of what's happening on the network, you need to have a good understanding of exactly what an application is trying to accomplish. It does no good to spend hours analyzing a complex protocol command if the command has no relation to the problem at hand.

  However, many times it is impossible to completely understand an application. Unless you are the programmer who wrote the actual code, you will never truly understand all the details of how an application functions. The good news is that you most likely won't have to. How then can you solve a problem if you can't completely understand what an application is doing? Take, for example, a file transfer failure. If you are seeing TCP Resets in the middle of the transfer, you know that the host has either aborted or closed the connection, or perhaps the application itself has crashed. If you see very small amounts of data being transmitted back and forth while the window size is large and the MSS is being used, you know that the application is responsible for the poor performance.

- **Associate packets to processes.**　Even if an analyzer cannot decode the application-specific data that you need to analyze, you still have ways to determine what an application is doing. One of the ways to do this is to examine the raw data display panel of your analyzers. Often the hex data can clue you in on what is happening in the packet. For example, in Figure 7-3, if you look at the bottom of the trace in the ASCII hex portion, you can see that the application is asking the user to enter a password. From there, you could determine the next process of the packets by watching the application in action.

TIP　When I analyze an application problem, I try to capture the actual user packets while the problem is occurring. Sometimes, the best place you can have your analyzer hooked up is right next to a user who is experiencing a problem. This lets you see the packets on the user's side of the network connection and associate them with the actions a user is performing.

Chapter Goals

I have two goals in this chapter:

- To explain the functionality of each upper-layer protocol.
- To take a look at techniques to analyze these protocols and the types of problems often seen in the upper layers.

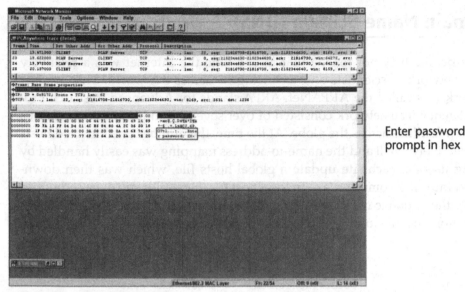

Enter password prompt in hex

Figure 7-3   Hex data decode.

It is impossible in the space of this text to illustrate all the details about the upper-layer protocols I will be discussing. Instead, I will be using these protocols to illustrate how the analyzer and other tools can be utilized to resolve problems quickly and decisively. The case studies I will be reviewing will illustrate the different types of solutions to problems in the upper layers. Not all solutions will be found in the three upper layers. The techniques of protocol analysis stress the proper analysis of each and all layers in the quest for a solution.

I will be reviewing three distinct types of situations:

- **Positive application responses.**   Positive application responses indicate that the application-layer protocol is functioning normally. They are usually no cause for concern.

- **Negative application responses.**   Negative application responses indicate that the application layer has either rejected a request or sent back a response that indicates the failure of a specific request.

- **Transport layer responses.**   Many times an application responds by disconnecting the current session. Session disconnects appear as transport-layer messages such as a TCP Reset.

I will also be covering some new tools and techniques for analyzing these upper-layer protocols and the applications that use them. In many cases, a protocol analyzer is an overly complex tool to use when a simple answer is needed. I will make note of when a simpler tool can be substituted for a protocol analyzer.

Domain Name System (DNS)

Many people may not realize that at one time the Internet was a relatively small network of scientists and technologists across the world. This original network was called the ARPANet. ARPA stands for Advanced Research Projects Agency. The network consisted of over several hundred hosts at various research facilities across the globe. At the time, the number of connected hosts was relatively small and the name-to-address mapping was easily handled by having users at each site update a global hosts file, which was then downloaded into each computer's own local host file. Host files still exist today and give us the option to maintain our name-to-address mappings locally. Below is a common host file found on Windows and Unix hosts alike:

```
127.0.0.1           localhost
64.97.37.170        mail.tracemasters.com   # old mail web site
20.6.1.56           router.ispnet.com       # backbone router
198.156.45.33       webserver.pdocs.com     # main research web server
12.45.22.6          research.scinet.com     # main lab server
177.33.19.94        stubrtr.xmsnet.com      # backup xms router
```

NOTE On Windows NT/2000/XP operating systems, the host file can be found in the `c:/<winnt>/system32/drivers/etc` directory. On Unix systems, it can be found in `/etc`.

When users of the original ARPANet referred to a resource by name instead of IP address, their computer would search the host file to see if an address-to-name mapping entry existed. If an entry existed, it would know which IP address to use to contact the destination host.

Host files were easy to manage when the number of hosts on the ARPANet was still in the several hundred range. When the Internet grew larger, the ARPANet needed a more scalable dynamic method of resolving hostnames to IP addresses. Thus was born the Domain Name System, or DNS. DNS is a distributed database of host information contained on various servers around the world. DNS servers allow users to obtain various information about hosts on the Internet.

One of the most basic pieces of information that can be retrieved from a DNS server is the IP address of a host, because users will need this address in order to communicate with a host. Another piece of information is where to send mail for a specific domain. In order to email `kevin@tracemasters.com`, your local mail server will need to know where to forward the mail. DNS contains the host information for that domain, which tells your mail server what server on the `tracemasters.com` domain to send mail to.

DNS also allows a hierarchical namespace. For example, a fictional newspaper company called `analysistimes.com` could be broken up into several domains of authority.

- The editorials department could have its own domain called `editorials.analysistimes.com`

- The sports department could have a domain named `sports.analysistimes.com`

- The business department could have a domain called `business.analysistimes.com`

A *domain* is a part of the DNS database, the authority for which falls under the administration of a single group or organization. Even though the editorial, sports, and business domains are part of a larger domain called `analysistimes.com`, they can be *authoritative* for their own domain name information. The possibility exists also that one group or organization could manage the entire `analysistimes.com` namespace. I discuss how these namespaces are broken down and stored in the database later in this chapter.

Name servers are the hosts where namespace information is stored. Name servers contain complete host information for at least some part of a domain. Name servers, like organizations, can be authoritative for a domain. Look at the example in Figure 7-4.

`Analysistimes.com` contains four domains managed by four separate organizations. Any hosts that reside in each of the domains have host information contained in the respective name servers in each of the domains. You might notice that each of the name servers has the same name, ns. This situation is fine because they are in separate domains; you refer to each host by its fully qualified domain name (FQDN). So, the name server in the sports department would have a name of `ns.sports.analysistimes.com`, making it dissimilar to the name server in the editorials department, which has a name of `ns.editorials.analysistimes.com`. Each name server contains only the host information for hosts in the domain it is authoritative for. When you make a name server authoritative for some part of a domain, you configure it for what is called a zone. A *zone* is the part of a domain database that a name server is authoritative for.

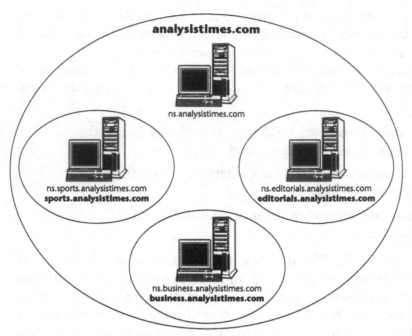

Figure 7-4   Domain space authority.

DNS Database

The DNS database is organized very much like a directory structure. There is a top-level directory or domain that contains several lower domains called subdomains. The Internet domain database contains several top-level domains that contain all lower subdomains. These top-level domains are organized in two ways:

- One way is by generic top-level names that attempt to categorize the type of subdomains they contain.

- The second way is by country code, where each country in the world is assigned its own top-level domain, and organizations become subdomains of the top-level country domain.

Figure 7-5 illustrates the two types of domains. In the generic category of top-level domains, organizations are categorized by their organizational type. Table 7-2 shows a partial list of the existing generic top-level domains and their descriptions.

Table 7-2 Common Internet Top-Level Domains

TOP-LEVEL DOMAIN	DESCRIPTION
.com	Commercial
.org	Organizations
.net	Network
.tv	Television
.biz	Business
.gov	Government
.mil	Military
.edu	Education

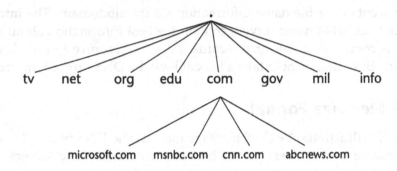

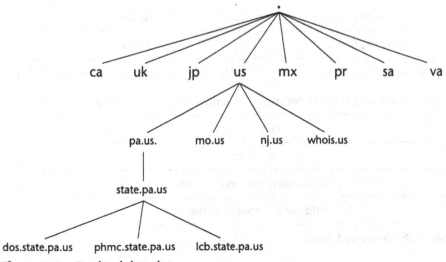

Figure 7-5 Top-level domains.

Top-level domains are expanding all of the time to allow the categorization of information contained in specific sites. In Figure 7-5, you see how Web sites like `msnbc.com` and `microsoft.com` are located in the `.com` top-level domain. Generically speaking, they are both commercial Web sites but serve entirely different purposes. `msnbc.com` is strictly a news site and would possibly be better categorized in a separate `.news` top-level domain.

NOTE The `.com` domain is a generic top-level domain where almost any Web site or organization can exist. Unfortunately, the creation of newer more specific top-level domain descriptions such as `.tv` and `.biz` have arrived too late. Internet users are so used to typing in the `.com` after a domain name that most Web sites are usually put into the `.com` domain.

The country code top-level domains are typically used by state and educational organizations. You can see in Figure 7-5 that the state of Pennsylvania has several subdomains inside of the top-level `.us` domain. Each of these subdomains can be managed by a different organization, with its own name server containing the name information for its subdomain. The information that tells us what name servers contain the best information about a subdomain is contained in resource records. I discuss resource records later in the chapter. But I first want to take a look at how the DNS protocol operates.

DNS Message Format

Figure 7-6 illustrates the DNS message format. The DNS protocol is made up of questions and answers passed between hosts and name servers on a network. These questions and answers are referred to as messages.

16 bits	16 bits
Identification	Flags
Number of questions	Number of answers/resource records
Number of authoritative resource records	Number of additional resource records
Questions	
Answers	
Authoritative resource records	
Additional resource records	

Figure 7-6   DNS message format.

The following is a description of the fields in the DNS message format.

- **Identification.** The 16-bit identification field allows a host to match DNS questions with responses.

- **Flags.** The Flags field is broken down into several smaller field entries:

  - **QR (Bit 16).** A 0 in the question response (QR) field indicates that the DNS message is a question; a 1 indicates it is a response.

  - **Opcode (Bits 17–20).** A 0 indicates a standard query, a 1 indicates an inverse query, and a 2 indicates a server status request.

  - **AA (Bit 21).** The authoritative answer (AA) field is the DNS authority field. This indicates that the answer is from an authoritative server for the particular domain.

  - **TC (Bit 22).** The truncated (TC) bit indicates that the reply is truncated to 512 bytes.

  - **RD (Bit 23).** The Recursion Desired (RD) bit allows two types of DNS questions, recursive and nonrecursive. A *recursive* question indicates to a name server that it should handle the resolution of the information asked for in the question section of the message. A *nonrecursive* question indicates to the name server that it should only return information to the host about where best to locate an answer for information about the domain in question.

  - **RA (Bit 24).** The Recursive Available (RA) bit is set to 1 if a server supports recursion. This bit will be set on all recursive answers.

  - **Zero field (Bits 25–27).** These three bits are set to 0.

  - **RC (Bits 28–31).** The Return Code (RC) indicates the status of the returned answer from a name server. A 0 indicates no error, and a 3 indicates an error. Name errors are sent only by servers that are authoritative for a domain. They indicate that the name does not exist.

- **Number of questions.** The number of questions is typically only 1.

- **Number of answers/resource records.** This indicates the number of resource records present in the answer.

- **Number of authoritative resource records.** This indicates the number of authoritative resource records present in the answer.

- **Number of additional resource records.** This indicates the number of additional resource records present in the answer.

- **Questions.** This section contains the questions in the message.

- **Answers.** This section contains the answers in the message.

- **Authoritative resource records.** This section contains the authoritative resource records in the answer.

- **Additional resource records.** This section contains the additional resource records in the answer.

Figure 7-7 shows a DNS question decode.
Figure 7-8 shows a DNS answer decode.

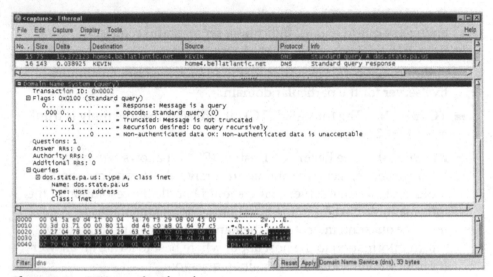

Figure 7-7   DNS question decode.

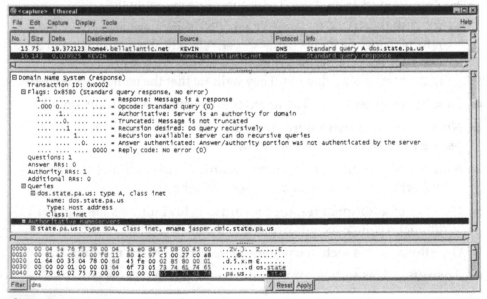

Figure 7-8   DNS answer decode.

Using NSLookup

There are several different types of questions or queries that a host may ask a name server. There are also different methods of analyzing these messages. While a protocol analyzer easily displays the decoded DNS messages, there is a far simpler method of analyzing these messages. NSLookup, the perfect DNS analysis tool, is included right on your own computer. NSLookup is a tool included with almost all Windows and Unix systems on the market. NSLookup allows a user to query a DNS name server about specific information it has about a host or a domain.

Using NSLookup, I want to analyze the first of several DNS resource records I intend to discuss in this chapter. My first resource record type is called the Start of Authority (SOA). An SOA record indicates where the best source of information about a domain can be found. Figure 7-9 illustrates this example.

First, you start the NSLookup program by simply typing **nslookup** at the Windows command prompt. Next, you need to set the type of resource record you are looking for. You do this by typing **set type=SOA**. This configures NSLookup to query the default name server for SOA records only. Now, all you have to do is type in the name of the domain for which you want the SOA record. The response from the default name server, `home4.bellatlantic .net`, shows that the primary name server for the `dos.state.pa.us` domain is `jasper.cmic.state.pa.us`. This name server, `jasper`, contains the best source of information for the `dos.state.pa.us` domain. You can also see some other records, which I discuss later in this chapter.

Now, take a look at the `dli.state.pa.us` domain. After querying the default name server for its SOA record, you receive a primary name server name of `linux1.pal2.state.pa.us`. This is interesting because you now have a case of a subdomain under `dli.state.pa.us` that is managed by a different organization and also has another primary source of name information for its domain. Although both subdomains fall under the larger domain `dli.state.pa.us`, they both have different sources of "best" information about the hosts in their domain.

NOTE Some domains use what is called a *hidden master*, which is simply a bogus entry in the SOA record so that it is impossible to determine the real primary name server. Such an entry is used for security reasons, because a denial-of-service attack is best performed on the primary DNS server for the domain. Yahoo!, for example, implements the hidden master by the following SOA entry:

```
Type=SOA, Class=1, TTL=262 (4 Minutes 22 Seconds), RDLENGTH=59
    Name Server=hidden-master.yahoo.com, Mailbox=hostmaster.yahoo-inc.com
```

```
Microsoft Windows 2000 [Version 5.00.2195]
(C) Copyright 1985-1999 Microsoft Corp.

C:\>nslookup
Default Server:  home4.bellatlantic.net
Address:  151.197.0.39

> set type=SOA  ◄─────────────────────────  Set the lookup type to SOA
>
> dos.state.pa.us.  ◄──────────────────────  Lookup SOA for domain dos.state.pa.us
Server:  home4.bellatlantic.net
Address:  151.197.0.39

state.pa.us
      primary name server = jasper.cmic.state.pa.us ◄───  Start of Authority Name
      responsible mail addr = security.state.pa.us        Server for dos.state.pa.us
      serial  = 971681
      refresh = 21600 (6 hours)
      retry   = 1800 (30 mins)
      expire  = 259200 (3 days)
      default TTL = 3600 (1 hour)
>
> dli.state.pa.us.  ◄──────────────────────  Lookup SOA for domain dli.state.pa.us
Server:  home4.bellatlantic.net
Address:  151.197.0.39

dli.state.pa.us
      primary name server = linux1.pal2.state.pa.us ◄───  Start of Authority Name
      responsible mail addr = crenshaw.pal2.state.pa.us   Server for dli.state.pa.us
      serial  = 2002100800
      refresh = 14400 (4 hours)
      retry   = 3600 (1 hour)
      expire  = 604800 (7 days)
      default TTL = 86400 (1 day)
dli.state.pa.us nameserver = linux1.pal2.state.pa.us
dli.state.pa.us nameserver = sunws02.cmic.state.pa.us
linux1.pal2.state.pa.us internet address = 164.156.232.37
sunws02.cmic.state.pa.us      internet address = 164.156.27.5
>
```

Figure 7-9   NSLookup SOA query.

Name Servers

Now that you know the process of finding the best source of information about a domain (that is, the SOA record), I can talk more in detail about how name servers function.

As I mentioned previously, a zone is the part of a domain's database for which a name server is authoritative. When you set up a name server, there are two types of zones that must be configured. These are called forward lookup zones and reverse lookup zones.

- *Forward lookup zones* contain information for what is called forward resolution. *Forward resolution* is the term for resolving any type of information for a hostname. For example, a DNS client querying a server for the IP address of www.analysistimes.com is performing a forward lookup. Forward lookup zones are used for finding out the IP address from a hostname.

- *Reverse lookup zones* are zones used to hold a special type of resource record called pointer records. *Pointer records* point you back to the original domain name from which the IP address originates. This feature allows you to determine the source from which an IP address originates. So, if you need to find out a hostname for a specific IP address, DNS allows you to do this by using the features of reverse lookup zones.

For each host in a forward lookup zone, there also exists a reverse lookup zone for the Class C network where the host is located. For example, the Internet-connected host on which this book is being written resolves to an IP address of 151.197.255.128. The Class C subnet of 151.197.255.0 is represented as a subdomain in a larger domain called in-addr.arpa. The name of the Class C subdomain for this reverse lookup zone would be 255.197.151 .in-addr.arpa. The network address in this case is octet reversed because a lookup of the zone would actually be done from right-to-left (.arpa, in-addr, 151, 197, 255). These entries in the reverse lookup zone are known as *reverse mappings*. When a Web site or firewall logs activity, it will do reverse lookups on the IP addresses that it sees coming through its network. In Figure 7-10, you can see an NSLookup resolution for the IP address of my workstation.

You can see in the figure that it maps to a hostname of `pool-151-197-255-128.phil.east.verizon.net`. This simple reverse mapping allows an administrator to review security logs that contain domain names instead of IP addresses. Any issues with access from a particular IP address could easily be taken up with the administrative contact for the domain.

How would you find that administrator though? On the Internet, the reverse lookup zone `in-addr.arpa` is administered by an organization called the American Registry for Internet Numbers (ARIN). By using a utility called Whois, you can look up administrative contact information for any of the Class C networks for which a reverse lookup zone exists. By using ARIN's online Whois utility, you can find out the administrative contact for hosts on that network. Figure 7-11 shows the output received when I performed a Whois search on my Class C network using ARINs Web site.

NOTE ARIN's WHOIS can be found online at www.arin.net/whois/.

ROOT Name Servers

Now that you know how to find out what name servers are authoritative for the specific domains, I want to climb back up the ladder and discuss more about top-level domains. Each top-level domain, such as .com, .edu, or .org, also has specific authoritative name servers where its domain information is stored. If you were setting up a new DNS name server, what servers would you use to resolve this top-level domain information? It just so happens that the Internet contains several top-level name servers whose only job is to help other name servers resolve information on these top-level domains. These top-level name servers are called the Internet *root* name servers, because they are the last resort for resolving the location of domain host information.

If you look back to Figure 7-5, you will see that the top-level domain actually begins with a period or dot (.). This dot is the highest level of domain information on the Internet. In order to find the top-level domain name servers on the Internet, all one has to do is search for all name servers authoritative for ".". In Figure 7-12, I use nslookup to search for all name servers on the "." domain. First, I set the record type to NS (name server), then I simply type "." and press enter. The result is a listing of all root name servers on the Internet. As mentioned, these 13 name servers are the last resort for resolution of any domain information on the Internet. If these 13 servers can't find the information, chances are nobody can.

```
C:\>nslookup
Default Server:  home4.bellatlantic.net
Address:  151.197.0.39

> set type=PTR
> 47.99.119.216.in-addr.arpa
Server:  home4.bellatlantic.net
Address:  151.197.0.39

*** home4.bellatlantic.net can't find 47.99.119.216.in-
omain
> quit
Server:  home4.bellatlantic.net
Address:  151.197.0.39

*** home4.bellatlantic.net can't find quit: Non-existen
> exit

C:\>nslookup
Default Server:  home4.bellatlantic.net
Address:  151.197.0.39

> 151.197.255.128
Server:  home4.bellatlantic.net
Address:  151.197.0.39

Name:    pool-151-197-255-128.phil.east.verizon.net
Address:  151.197.255.128

>set type=PTR
> 151.197.255.128
Server:  home4.bellatlantic.net
Address:  151.197.0.39
```

Reverse Lookup Zone Mapping

```
128.255.197.151.in-addr.arpa    name = pool-151-197-255-128.phil.east.verizon.net
255.197.151.in-addr.arpa        nameserver = ns1.bellatlantic.net
255.197.151.in-addr.arpa        nameserver = ns2.bellatlantic.net
ns1.bellatlantic.net   internet address = 199.45.32.40
ns2.bellatlantic.net   internet address = 199.45.32.41
>
```

Figure 7-10   IP address lookup.

Search results for: 151.197.255.128

Verizon Internet Services VIS-151-196 (NET-151-196-0-0-1)
                151.196.0.0 - 151.205.255.255
Verizon Internet Services VZ-DSLDIAL-PHLAPA-5 (NET-151-197-249-0-1)
                151.197.249.0 - 151.197.255.255

Search results for: ! NET-151-196-0-0-1

OrgName: Verizon Internet Services
OrgID: VRIS

NetRange: 151.196.0.0 - 151.205.255.255
CIDR: 151.196.0.0/14, 151.200.0.0/14, 151.204.0.0/15
NetName: VIS-151-196
NetHandle: NET-151-196-0-0-1
Parent: NET-151-0-0-0-0
NetType: Direct Allocation
NameServer: NSDC.BA-DSG.NET
NameServer: GTEPH.BA-DSG.NET
Comment:
RegDate:
Updated: 2002-08-22

TechHandle: ZV20-ARIN
TechName: Verizon Internet Services
TechPhone: +1-703-295-4583
TechEmail: noc@gnilink.net

OrgAbuseHandle: VISAB-ARIN
OrgAbuseName: VIS Abuse
OrgAbusePhone: +1-703-295-4583
OrgAbuseEmail: abuse@verizon.net

OrgTechHandle: ZV20-ARIN
OrgTechName: Verizon Internet Services
OrgTechPhone: +1-703-295-4583
OrgTechEmail: noc@gnilink.net

ARIN Whois database, last updated 2002-12-20 20:00
Enter ? for additional hints on searching ARIN's Whois database.

Figure 7-11   WHOIS search.

Microsoft Windows 2000 [Version 5.00.2195]
(C) Copyright 1985-1999 Microsoft Corp.

C:\>nslookup
Default Server: home4.bellatlantic.net
Address: 151.197.0.39

>
> set type=NS
> . ◄─────────────────────────────── Name Server Search for "."
Server: home4.bellatlantic.net
Address: 151.197.0.39

Non-authoritative answer:
(root) nameserver = G.ROOT-SERVERS.NET
(root) nameserver = H.ROOT-SERVERS.NET
(root) nameserver = I.ROOT-SERVERS.NET
(root) nameserver = J.ROOT-SERVERS.NET
(root) nameserver = K.ROOT-SERVERS.NET
(root) nameserver = L.ROOT-SERVERS.NET
(root) nameserver = M.ROOT-SERVERS.NET   All Root Name Servers returned
(root) nameserver = A.ROOT-SERVERS.NET
(root) nameserver = B.ROOT-SERVERS.NET
(root) nameserver = C.ROOT-SERVERS.NET
(root) nameserver = D.ROOT-SERVERS.NET
(root) nameserver = E.ROOT-SERVERS.NET
(root) nameserver = F.ROOT-SERVERS.NET

G.ROOT-SERVERS.NET   internet address = 192.112.36.4
H.ROOT-SERVERS.NET   internet address = 128.63.2.53
I.ROOT-SERVERS.NET   internet address = 192.36.148.17
J.ROOT-SERVERS.NET   internet address = 192.58.128.30
K.ROOT-SERVERS.NET   internet address = 193.0.14.129
L.ROOT-SERVERS.NET   internet address = 198.32.64.12
M.ROOT-SERVERS.NET   internet address = 202.12.27.33
A.ROOT-SERVERS.NET   internet address = 198.41.0.4
B.ROOT-SERVERS.NET   internet address = 128.9.0.107
C.ROOT-SERVERS.NET   internet address = 192.33.4.12
D.ROOT-SERVERS.NET   internet address = 128.8.10.90
E.ROOT-SERVERS.NET   internet address = 192.203.230.10
F.ROOT-SERVERS.NET   internet address = 192.5.5.241

Figure 7-12   Root name server lookup.

Name Server Caching

Name servers perform DNS lookups all day long. A typical ISP name server services thousands, if not millions, of DNS client requests per day. When a name server resolves a piece of information for a host, it keeps this information in its memory for further use. This memory is called the *cache*.

All name servers build up a cache of resolved host information over time. When a duplicate request is made for that data, the name server first searches its local cache for the information instead of forwarding the request on to higher-level name servers. If it finds the information in its cache, it responds to the DNS client with what is called a nonauthoritative request. This means that although it has replied to the query with the information requested, it is not the authoritative DNS server for the domain. In Figure 7-13, I show how a server caches information by exploring the two types of DNS questions, recursive and nonrecursive queries.

1. First I set nslookup for no recursion. This tells our local name server to *not* resolve the information I request, but to simply point me to a name server that can resolve the information. The response I receive is a listing of the root Internet name servers.

2. Next, I turn recursion on to force our local name server to resolve the IP information I desire for www.thetechfirm.com. It responds as a name server should with the correct IP address.

3. Then, I turn recursion back off again with the set norecurse command. This time, instead of answering with the list of root Internet name servers, the local name server responds with the IP address I asked for. Notice though that the response is non-authoritative, meaning that the name server responding is not authoritative for the domain.

This simple example shows how, after a name server resolves a hosts IP address (or other information), it caches it and uses the cached information to answer future queries.

Resource Records

DNS name servers contain several types of host information. This information is held in what are called *resource records*. There are several different types of resource records. Each contains a specific piece of information that is used by DNS clients to utilize Internet resources. Table 7-3 contains the list of DNS resource record types.

```
> set norecurse  ◄──────────────────────────    No Recursion Desired
> www.thetechfirm.com
Server:  home4.bellatlantic.net
Address:  151.197.0.39

com    nameserver = A.GTLD-SERVERS.NET
com    nameserver = G.GTLD-SERVERS.NET
com    nameserver = H.GTLD-SERVERS.NET
com    nameserver = C.GTLD-SERVERS.NET          Local name server has no
com    nameserver = I.GTLD-SERVERS.NET          cached information for
com    nameserver = B.GTLD-SERVERS.NET          www.thetechfirm.com
com    nameserver = D.GTLD-SERVERS.NET          so it returns the list of ROOT
com    nameserver = L.GTLD-SERVERS.NET          Internet Name Servers
com    nameserver = F.GTLD-SERVERS.NET
com    nameserver = J.GTLD-SERVERS.NET
com    nameserver = K.GTLD-SERVERS.NET
com    nameserver = E.GTLD-SERVERS.NET
com    nameserver = M.GTLD-SERVERS.NET
A.GTLD-SERVERS.NET      internet address = 192.5.6.30
G.GTLD-SERVERS.NET      internet address = 192.42.93.30
H.GTLD-SERVERS.NET      internet address = 192.54.112.30
C.GTLD-SERVERS.NET      internet address = 192.26.92.30
I.GTLD-SERVERS.NET      internet address = 192.43.172.30
B.GTLD-SERVERS.NET      internet address = 192.33.14.30
D.GTLD-SERVERS.NET      internet address = 192.31.80.30
L.GTLD-SERVERS.NET      internet address = 192.41.162.30
F.GTLD-SERVERS.NET      internet address = 192.35.51.30
J.GTLD-SERVERS.NET      internet address = 192.48.79.30
K.GTLD-SERVERS.NET      internet address = 192.52.178.30
E.GTLD-SERVERS.NET      internet address = 192.12.94.30
M.GTLD-SERVERS.NET      internet address = 192.55.83.30
> set recurse  ◄───────────────────────────    Recursion Desired
>
> www.thetechfirm.com
Server:  home4.bellatlantic.net
Address:  151.197.0.39


> www.thetechfirm.com
Server:  home4.bellatlantic.net
Address:  151.197.0.39
                                                www.thetechfirm.com
Name:    www.thetechfirm.com                    IP Address Resolved by
Address:  216.251.32.98  ◄──────────           local bellatlantic.net
                                                name server

> set norecurse  ◄──────────────────┐
>                                    │
> www.thetechfirm.com                │
Server:  home4.bellatlantic.net      │
Address:  151.197.0.39               │
                                     │           Even though recursion is not requested
Non-authoritative answer:            │           the local bellatlantic name server
Name:    www.thetechfirm.com         │           is still able to resolve the IP address
Address:  216.251.32.98  ◄───────────┘           since it now has it cached.
```

Figure 7-13   Caching example.

Table 7-3   DNS Resource Record Types

RECORD TYPE	DESCRIPTION
A	Address
AAAA	Ipv6 address
ALL	All records
CNAME	Canonical name
HINFO	Host information
MAILB	Mailbox
MB	Mailbox domain name
MG	Mailbox group member
MX	Mail exchanger
NS	Name server
PTR	Pointer
RP	Responsible person
SOA	Start of authority
TXT	Text
WKS	Workstation information

The following list briefly explains the most important resource record types you need to understand. The other resource records are mostly outdated and no longer used. In the case of the Ipv6 Address record type, it will become more important as ISPs and other organizations move to IP Version 6.

- **Address (A).**   The address record contains the IP address for a host.
- **Canonical Name (CNAME).**   A canonical name is simply another name for an already existing host. This record type is used extensively with the MX record type.
- **Mail Exchanger (MX).**   The MX record type contains the hostname of a mail server that will accept mail for a specific domain.
- **Name Server (NS).**   The NS record contains name servers that are authoritative for a specific zone.
- **Pointer (PTR).**   The PTR record contains the reverse mapping of IP address-to-hostname information.
- **Start of Authority (SOA).**   The SOA record contains the server that is the best source of information for a domain. The SOA record also contains several parameters, which name servers use in storing the domain information.

The use of the DNS resource records above are best illustrated by examples using nslookup. In the following examples, I take a look at how each record is utilized using nslookup.

```
Address (A)
> set type=A
> www.tracemasters.com
Server:  home4.bellatlantic.net
Address:  151.197.0.39
Name:     tracemasters.com
Address:  216.119.99.47
Aliases:  www.tracemasters.com
```

In this first code example, you can see the IP address record being returned by our local name server for www.tracemasters.com.

```
Mail Exchanger (MX)
> set type=MX
> tracemasters.com
Server:  home4.bellatlantic.net
Address:  151.197.0.39
tracemasters.com        MX preference = 10, mail exchanger =
mail.tracemasters.com
```

In this second example, setting the type to MX, I query the name server for the tracemasters.com domain. By issuing a MX query, I am asking the name server to tell me the host to where mail should be sent for the tracemasters.com domain. You can see it responds with mail .tracemasters.com. Now, I simply need to look up the A record for this host, which I do in the following example:

```
Canonical Name (CNAME)
> set type=A
> mail.tracemasters.com
Server:  home4.bellatlantic.net
Address:  151.197.0.39
Non-authoritative answer:
Name:     mail7.crystaltech.com
Address:  216.119.106.105
Aliases:  mail.tracemasters.com
```

When I look up the A record for mail.tracemasters.com, you can see that the name server responds with a nonauthoritative answer that includes something called an alias. An *alias* is another name for a canonical name. When a name server encounters a CNAME record, it will replace the alias with the canonical name. In this case the name server will replace mail.tracemasters .com with mail7.crystaltech.com, which is the true hostname of the mail server. Aliases allow you to have more than one hostname for a single IP address. You can also look up only the CNAME by setting the CNAME type in NSLookup. The following example shows how to do this using NSLookup.

```
> set type=CNAME
> mail.tracemasters.com
Server:  home4.bellatlantic.net
Address:  151.197.0.39
Non-authoritative answer:
mail.tracemasters.com    canonical name = mail7.crystaltech.com
```

Name Server (NS)
```
> set type=NS
> tracemasters.com
Server: home4.bellatlantic.net
Address:  151.197.0.39
Non-authoritative answer:
tracemasters.com           nameserver = dns30.register.com
tracemasters.com           nameserver = dns29.register.com
```

By setting the record type to NS, I can retrieve a list of all authoritative name servers for a domain. In the preceding example, you can see that `tracemasters.com` has two authoritative name servers.

Pointer (PTR)
```
> set type=PTR
> 216.119.106.105
Server:  home4.bellatlantic.net
Address:  151.197.0.39
105.106.119.216.in-addr.arpa    name = mail7.crystaltech.com
105.106.119.216.in-addr.arpa    name = web104.crystaltech.com
```

The pointer resource record shows us the reverse `in-addr.arpa` mapping for the address being looked up. In the preceding example, it appears there are two reverse mappings for `216.119.106.105`.

Start of Authority (SOA)
```
> set type=SOA
> tracemasters.com
Server: home4.bellatlantic.net
Address:  151.197.0.39
Non-authoritative answer:
tracemasters.com
        primary name server = dns29.register.com
        responsible mail addr = root.register.com
        serial  = 200010268
        refresh = 10800 (3 hours)
        retry   = 3600 (1 hour)
        expire  = 604800 (7 days)
        default TTL = 86400 (1 day)
```

In this final example, the SOA record type gives us the following new information:

- **Primary Name Server.** This is the primary authoritative name server for the domain.

- **Responsible Mail Address.** This is the email address of the authoritative person or group for the domain.

- **Serial Number.** The serial number indicates to secondary name servers whether or not they should obtain a new copy of the domain records.

- **Refresh.** Tells secondary name servers how often they should check the accuracy of their data.

- **Retry.** If for some reason a secondary name server is not able to reach the primary name server, it will attempt to reconnect every retry interval.

- **Expire.** If for some reason a secondary name server is unable to contact the primary name server. It will keep its data records only for an interval no longer than the expire value. In the preceding example, if the primary name server, dns29.register.com, became unavailable, the secondary name server, dns30.register.com, would wait 7 days before deleting its records. After the expire timer interval, a secondary name server will return name error messages to any requests it receives.

- **Default TTL.** The TTL, or Time-to-Live, value tells other name servers how long they should cache data records resolved for a particular domain. For instance, the preceding example causes any name server to keep data such as www.tracemasters.com in its cache for no longer than 1 day before it must reresolve the data from the primary authoritative name server for the domain.

CACHING CONFIGURATION

The default TTL field allows a name server administrator great latitude in telling other Internet name servers how long they should cache specific domain record data. If a low TTL value is configured, it will cause name servers to constantly reresolve records with the primary domain name server. If a high TTL value is configured, then resource record changes on the primary name server will take time to replicate to other name servers around the Internet due to their long usage of the already cached local domain data.

Analyzing DNS

DNS is the first protocol I deal with in this book that allows you to utilize a simple command-line utility rather than a protocol analyzer to troubleshoot it. There are several other tools at your disposal that allow you to see behind the scenes at how DNS is operating, and because of caching, you need to know how it has been operating because responses cached several hours ago could still be used by a name server.

IPCONFIG

If you are using Windows NT, 2000, or XP, the command-line program ipconfig allows you several new DNS options. `IPCONFIG /displaydns` will display the DNS domain information that is currently cached by your Windows 2000 host. The following illustrates the output from the `/displaydns` command.

```
C:\>ipconfig /displaydns

Windows 2000 IP Configuration

    www.tracemasters.com.
    --------------------------------------------------------
       Record Name . . . . . : www.tracemasters.com
       Record Type . . . . . : 5
       Time To Live  . . . . : 68687
       Data Length . . . . . : 4
       Section . . . . . . . : Answer
       CNAME Record  . . . . :
                        tracemasters.com

       Record Name . . . . . : tracemasters.com
       Record Type . . . . . : 1
       Time To Live  . . . . : 68687
       Data Length . . . . . : 4
       Section . . . . . . . : Answer
       A (Host) Record . . . :
                        216.119.99.47

       Record Name . . . . . : tracemasters.com
       Record Type . . . . . : 2
       Time To Live  . . . . : 68687
       Data Length . . . . . : 4
       Section . . . . . . . : Authority
       NS Record   . . . . . :
                        dns29.register.com

       Record Name . . . . . : tracemasters.com
       Record Type . . . . . : 2
```

```
Time To Live  . . . . : 68687
Data Length . . . . . : 4
Section . . . . . . . : Authority
NS Record   . . . . . :
                dns30.register.com

Record Name . . . . . : dns29.register.com
Record Type . . . . . : 1
Time To Live  . . . . : 68687
Data Length . . . . . : 4
Section . . . . . . . : Additional
A (Host) Record . . . :
                216.21.234.85

Record Name . . . . . : dns30.register.com
Record Type . . . . . : 1
Time To Live  . . . . : 68687
Data Length . . . . . : 4
Section . . . . . . . : Additional
A (Host) Record . . . :
                216.21.226.85
```

I have used the /displaydns option several times when I was unable to connect to a host due to a DNS server responding with incorrect address records.

NOTE ipconfig also allows you the use of the /flushdns option, which deletes all cached DNS records and forces the client to reresolve all host records.

CyberKit

Cyberkit is a very useful Windows-based tool that includes a visual nslookup utility. Figure 7-14 shows CyberKit's nslookup functionality.

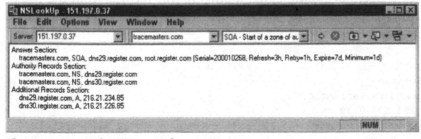

Figure 7-14 CyberKit example.

NOTE CyberKit can be downloaded at:

www.cyberkit.net/archives/cyber30.zip.

DNS Expert

DNS, although simple in nature, can become very complicated. Of all protocols I have worked with, DNS can have the greatest impact when misconfig-
ured. In large complex multizone domains managed by many groups of
people, it is often very easy to make simple mistakes in a DNS configuration. I
have seen examples of the smallest configuration changes having network-
wide impact on an infrastructure. These small mistakes are sometimes very
easy to overlook during a minor configuration change. A company called Men
and Mice makes an excellent product called DNS Expert that allows you to
fully analyze a zone for errors and common configuration problems. When I
first heard of this utility, I ran it against my own domain to see what it came up
with. Figure 7-15 shows the result.

The first two warnings from DNS Expert tell me that my primary name
server has older information than my secondary name server. DNS Expert is
able to tell this by looking at the serial numbers of the resource record data. A
higher serial number indicates newer or more current data. Serial numbers are
very important when making resource record changes. A secondary name
server will frequently poll a primary name server to see if the serial number
has changed. If the primary name server has a larger value, it will transfer a
new copy of the zone data from the primary name server. If the serial number
is lower, then the secondary name server will assume that it has the latest or
most current copy of zone data.

The zone errors in the DNS Expert analysis are of no concern because most
DNS servers will allow only authoritative servers to perform zone transfers.

The last error, concerning only one MX record, is, in fact, a concern. MX
records contain the name of a mail server that can accept mail for a domain.
MX records are configured by preference, with a lower preference value
indicating first usage. For example, the following MX records from the Men
and Mice Corporation indicate which mail servers can receive mail for
menandmice.com.

```
> set type=MX
> menandmice.com
Server:  home4.bellatlantic.net
Address:  151.197.0.39
menandmice.com  MX preference = 10, mail exchanger = mail.menandmice.is
menandmice.com  MX preference = 20, mail exchanger = mx1.mmedia.is
menandmice.com  MX preference = 30, mail exchanger = mx2.mmedia.is
```

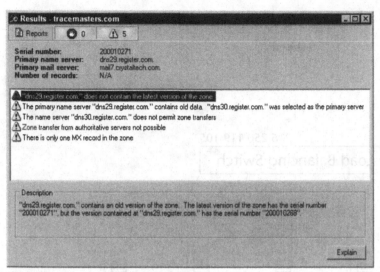

Figure 7-15 DNS Expert analysis.

As is shown in the preceding example, the first mail server that will be contacted will be the `mail.menandmice.is` server. If that mail server is unreachable, the `mx1.mmedia.is` and then `mx2.mmedia.is` servers will be tried.

However, in the case of my domain, `tracemasters.com`, there exists only a single MX record entry, as can be seen in the following:

```
> tracemasters.com
Server:   home4.bellatlantic.net
Address:  151.197.0.39
Non-authoritative answer:
tracemasters.com          MX preference = 10, mail exchanger =
mail7.crystaltech.com
```

Being curious about this single MX record entry, I contacted my ISP and inquired about email redundancy for my site. I was gladly surprised when I found out that there are several email servers sitting behind a load-balancing switch. `mail7.crystaltech.com` is actually the IP address of a load balancer that will redirect email traffic (port 25) to another email server if one mail server becomes unavailable.

Many Web sites are also architected this way. A single DNS entry actually points to a virtual IP address on a load-balancing switch. The switch then handles redirection of the Web site traffic to multiple servers behind the load balancer. Figure 7-16 illustrates this type of architecture.

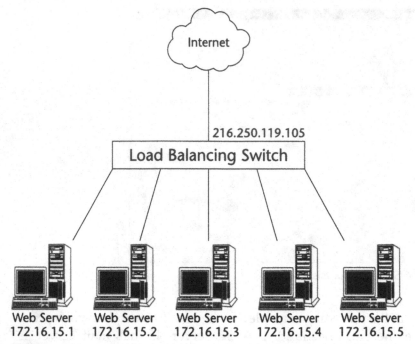

Figure 7-16   Application load-balancing architecture.

Common DNS Configuration Mistakes

I have taken the most common DNS configuration mistakes and listed them here. When analyzing DNS architectures, I typically check the following list to see if any of these issues exist. More often than not, you will find at least one of the following problems on a network using DNS:

- **Default TTL too Low.**   Low TTL values cause name servers to cache host data only for a short period of time. While this might be useful when making IP address changes on a domain, it will dramatically increase the amount of DNS requests your domain servers must handle because remote Internet name servers will be expiring your record data after a short period of time.

- **Refresh Interval too Low.**   Secondary name servers must initiate zone transfers after the refresh interval has expired. Large zone databases may take long periods of time to transfer, therefore increasing the load on the DNS servers.

- **Incorrect Serial Numbers.** Serial numbers allow secondary name servers to determine if the primary name servers have a more current copy of domain data. If updates are made on a primary name server, the serial number should always be updated so that the secondary name servers will initiate a zone transfer as soon as possible.

- **Incorrect MX Record Configuration.** MX name server records are very often configured with the same preference values or sometimes with only a single MX record. If you are running a backup mail server, you must have an MX record for that mail server with its own unique preference value.

- **Missing "." in record entry.** The "." in an entry tells a name server that it should not append the domain name to the end of the answer. If you have ever seen a DNS response similar to www.tracemasters.com.tracemasters.com, then you know that there is an A record in the zone data that has the "." omitted from its record entry.

File Transfer Protocol (FTP)

The File Transfer Protocol (FTP) was designed to allow hosts with different operating systems and different file systems the ability to transfer files. FTP historically did (and still does) offer several methods of data representation and file format controls. These methods and file formats allowed a variety of hosts that had different file systems to transfer files. For example, a host using the EBCIDIC file format would be able to transfer ASCII-based files from another host even though they used different character sets. Today, the only options for file transfer formats using FTP are ASCII mode and binary mode.

FTP Commands and Responses

FTP uses what are known as Network Virtual Terminal (NVT) ASCII codes to send commands between two hosts. The NVT commands allow the configuration of FTP file transfer options. Each NVT command is followed by the ASCII carriage return and line feed character pairs (CR, LF). Table 7-4 contains a listing of commonly used FTP commands. Each FTP command is acknowledged by a host with a reply code. Reply codes are categorized by the value of their first and second digits. FTP reply code categories from RFC 959 are listed in Table 7-5.

Table 7-4   FTP Command Code Descriptions

COMMAND	DESCRIPTION
ABOR	Abort previous FTP command
LIST	List files or directories
PASS	Send password to server
PORT	Specify client IP address and port
QUIT	Log off from FTP server
RETR	Retrieve file command
STOR	Store (transmit) command
SYST	Request system type from server
TYPE	Set file type (ASCII or Image)
USER	Send username to server

Table 7-5   Generic FTP Reply Code Descriptions

REPLY (FIRST DIGIT)	DESCRIPTION
1yz	Positive preliminary reply. The requested action is being initiated; expect another reply before proceeding with a new command.
2yz	Positive completion reply. The requested action has been successfully completed. A new request may be initiated.
3yz	Positive intermediate reply. The command has been accepted, but the requested action is being held in abeyance, pending receipt of further information. The user should send another command specifying this information.
4yz	Transient negative completion reply. The command was not accepted and the requested action did not take place, but the error condition is temporary and the action may be requested again.
5yz	Permanent negative completion reply. The command was not accepted and the requested action did not take place. The user process is discouraged from repeating the exact request.

Table 7-5 *(continued)*

REPLY (SECOND DIGIT)	DESCRIPTION
x1z	Syntax—these replies refer to syntax errors, syntactically correct commands that don't fit any functional category, unimplemented or superfluous commands.
x2z	Information—these are replies to requests for information, such as status or help requests.
x3z	Authentication and accounting—these are replies for the login process and accounting procedures.
x4z	Unspecified.
x5z	File system—these replies indicate the status of the server file system vis-a-vis the requested transfer or other file system action.

For the most part, you need to understand only a few FTP reply codes. Unless you are using uncommon exotic FTP options, you will most likely see only a small subset of the entire reply code list. I have included the most common FTP reply codes in Table 7-6.

Table 7-6 Specific FTP Reply Code Descriptions

REPLY CODE	DESCRIPTION
150	File status OK; about to open data connection
200	PORT command successful
220	FTP service ready
226	Transfer complete
227	Entering passive mode
230	User logged in, proceed
331	User name okay, need password
425	Can't open data connection
500	Command not understood
530	Not logged in
550	No such file or directory

The FTP protocol uses two separate TCP connections when performing a file transfer.

- The first TCP connection is on TCP port 21 and is used for FTP control data. FTP control data contains the commands in Table 7-4.

- A second connection on port 20 is used to transfer the actual file data between hosts.

Figure 7-17 illustrates what happens on the wire as a user transfers a file using the Windows 2000 command-line FTP program.

In Frame 1, the first TCP connection was opened to port 21. This is the control connection. The control connection allows you to send FTP commands and receives replies like those in Frames 6 through 12, where you enter your username and password to gain access to the FTP server. In Frame 14, I set the file transfer type to image (or binary). After setting the file transfer type, I issued the get command to retrieve the test.pkt file from the FTP server.

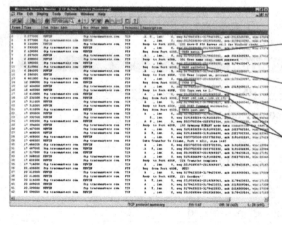

```
C:/>ftp
ftp> open ftp.tracemasters.com
Connected to tracemasters.com.
220 Serv-U FTP Server v4.0 for
Winsock ready...
User (tracemasters.com: (none)) :
kevin
331 User name okay, need password.
Password:
230 User logged in, proceed.
ftp> bin
200 Type set to I.
ftp> get test.pkt
200 PORT Command successful.
150 Opening BINARY mode data
connection for test.pkt (1440 bytes).
226 Transfer complete.
ftp: 1440 bytes received in
0.02Seconds 72.00bytes/sec.
ftp> quit
221 Goodbye!
```

Figure 7-17 FTP file transfer process.

In Frame 18, you see the host sending an FTP PORT command. The PORT command reveals an interesting aspect of how the FTP protocol uses data connections to transfer files. Control connections over port 21 are initiated by the client, while data connections are initiated by the server. This is what the PORT command is used for. The PORT command tells the FTP server what IP address and port it should use to initiate its data connection. In Frame 18, you see the FTP client (KEVIN) sends the PORT command with an IP address of 192.168.1.100. It also includes the comma-separated numbers 15 and 171 after the IP address. These two numbers actually specify the 16-bit port number. To calculate the port number, you multiply 15 by 256 and then add 171 (15 * 256 + 171). This equals a port number of 4011, which you can see in the decode of Frame 23 in Figure 7-18. After the PORT command is sent, the FTP data connection is opened by the server (in Frame 23), and the file transfer process beings. After the file transfer is complete, the FTP server disconnects the TCP session on port 20 and sends a reply code of 226 telling the client that the transfer is complete. You can then type the **QUIT** command, which disconnects the FTP session and closes the port 21 connection.

Case Study: Active Transfer Failure

Figure 7-19 illustrates a common problem with FTP file transfers.

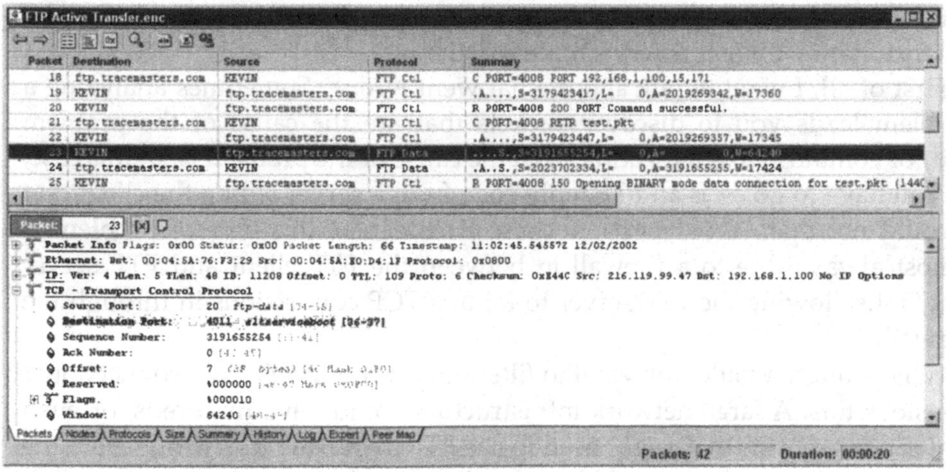

Figure 7-18   FTP data connection active open.

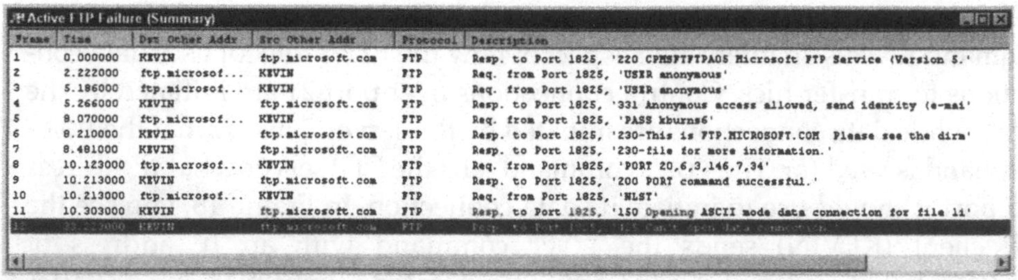

Active FTP Failure (Summary)

Frame	Time	Dst Other Addr	Src Other Addr	Protocol	Description
1	0.000000	KEVIN	ftp.microsoft.com	FTP	Resp. to Port 1825, '220 CPMSFTFTPA05 Microsoft FTP Service (Version 5.'
2	2.222000	ftp.microsof...	KEVIN	FTP	Req. from Port 1825, 'USER anonymous'
3	5.186000	ftp.microsof...	KEVIN	FTP	Req. from Port 1825, 'USER anonymous'
4	5.266000	KEVIN	ftp.microsoft.com	FTP	Resp. to Port 1825, '331 Anonymous access allowed, send identity (e-mai'
5	8.070000	ftp.microsof...	KEVIN	FTP	Req. from Port 1825, 'PASS kburns6'
6	8.210000	KEVIN	ftp.microsoft.com	FTP	Resp. to Port 1825, '230-This is FTP.MICROSOFT.COM Please see the dirm'
7	8.481000	KEVIN	ftp.microsoft.com	FTP	Resp. to Port 1825, '230-file for more information.'
8	10.123000	ftp.microsof...	KEVIN	FTP	Req. from Port 1825, 'PORT 20,6,3,146,7,34'
9	10.213000	KEVIN	ftp.microsoft.com	FTP	Resp. to Port 1825, '200 PORT command successful.'
10	10.213000	ftp.microsof...	KEVIN	FTP	Req. from Port 1825, 'NLST'
11	10.303000	KEVIN	ftp.microsoft.com	FTP	Resp. to Port 1825, '150 Opening ASCII mode data connection for file li'
12	33.223000	KEVIN	ftp.microsoft.com	FTP	Resp. to Port 1825, '425 Can't open data connection.'

Figure 7-19 FTP active transfer failure.

The figure shows the following:

1. In Frames 1 to 9, you see the normal FTP command and reply activity, with the last command set being the `PORT` command to tell the FTP server the IP address and port pair on which to initiate the connection back to the FTP client.
2. In Frame 10, the `NLST` command is being sent as a result of a user typing the `ls` (LIST) command.
3. In Frame 11, the server is responding that it is opening up the FTP data connection.
4. Then in Frame 12, you see the FTP server respond back with a reply code of 425, indicating that it cannot open the data connection.

For a newcomer to the FTP protocol, this problem can be very frustrating, but fortunately there is a very simple solution.

First of all, I want to talk about what went wrong. Sometimes analyzing a problem leads you to discover packets that are the cause of the problem and/or contain errors indicating what the cause of the problem is. In this case, all you have to go on is an FTP reply code from a server telling the client that it could not open the data connection. Fortunately, this type of problem is almost always due to a firewall in between the FTP client and FTP server that is disallowing the FTP server to initiate TCP connections in through the firewall.

Why, though, would you want to filter out incoming FTP data connections? Consider this: A large network infrastructure could have hundreds, or even thousands, of hosts that might need to use FTP to transfer files to and from the Internet. Administrators would have to allow any hosts on the Internet to initiate the FTP port 20 data connection into an organization's network. By opening up the entire network to incoming data connections, any host running FTP is vulnerable to attack. It's pretty easy to see why most organizations wouldn't want to allow this.

How then can you block out incoming TCP port 20 connections and still be able to use FTP? The solution is to use an FTP command called PASV. Almost all FTP programs support it. When an FTP server initiates the data connection to the client, it is performing what is known as an *active* file transfer. The PASV command allows you to use what is called a *passive* file transfer, whereby the client initiates the port 20 connection to the server. Nearly all good FTP programs enable you to turn on passive mode somewhere in the settings. In my favorite FTP program, FileZilla, you open up the firewall settings from the edit menu. Figure 7-20 shows how you enable Passive FTP using the open-source FileZilla FTP client.

Figure 7-21 illustrates how the PASV command works.

1. The FTP process starts in Frame 1, where the FTP control connection to port 21 is opened.

2. Then the FTP process progresses normally until, instead of sending the PORT command, the client sends the PASV command in Frame 21. This PASV command is exactly opposite of the PORT command.

3. In Frame 23, you see the server responding with the port and IP address pair for the client to use in making its port 20 connection to the server ($16 * 256 + 197 = 4293$).

4. In the decode panel of Frame 25 we see our FTP client initiating a connection to TCP port 4293 to begin the data transfer.

By enabling Passive FTP, you can circumvent security problems with using active FTP file transfers.

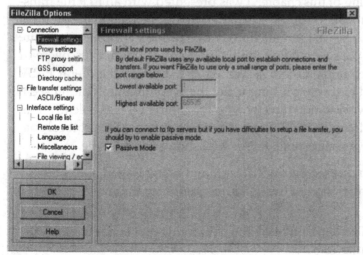

Figure 7-20 Enabling FTP passive mode.

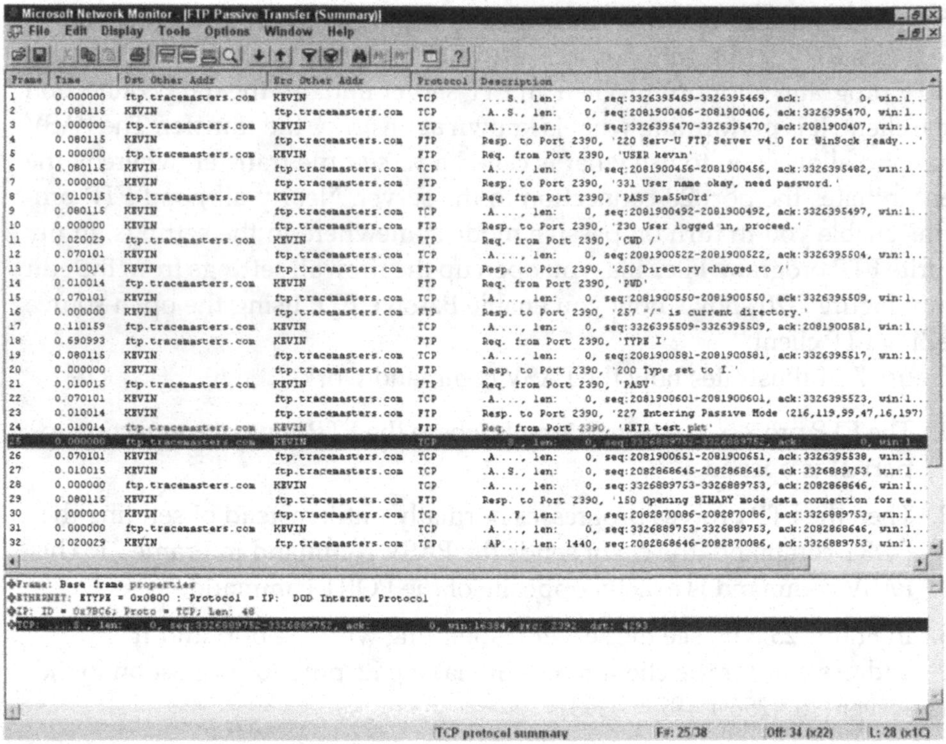

Figure 7-21   FTP passive mode trace.

Case Study: Passive Transfer Failure

As recently as the writing of this chapter, I was presented with an FTP file transfer problem using Microsoft's Windows 2000 FTP client. Seeing that the problem was obviously a firewall issue, I studied the command-line FTP options to figure out a way to use FTP passive mode. With the literal command, I discovered I could send raw FTP commands to a server. After executing the literal PASV command, I attempted a directory listing using the ls command. It didn't seem to work. Moving my workstation directly onto the Internet, I was able to study the actions of the Windows 2000 FTP client. After breaking out the protocol analyzer, I realized what was happening. Figure 7-22 shows the trace file.

1. In Frame 14, you can see the PASV command being issued and the server responding to it with the IP address and port pair for the client to use.

2. Instead of the FTP client initiating the data transfer, it sends a PORT command in Frame 18.

3. Then in Frame 23, you can see the FTP server initiating the data connection.

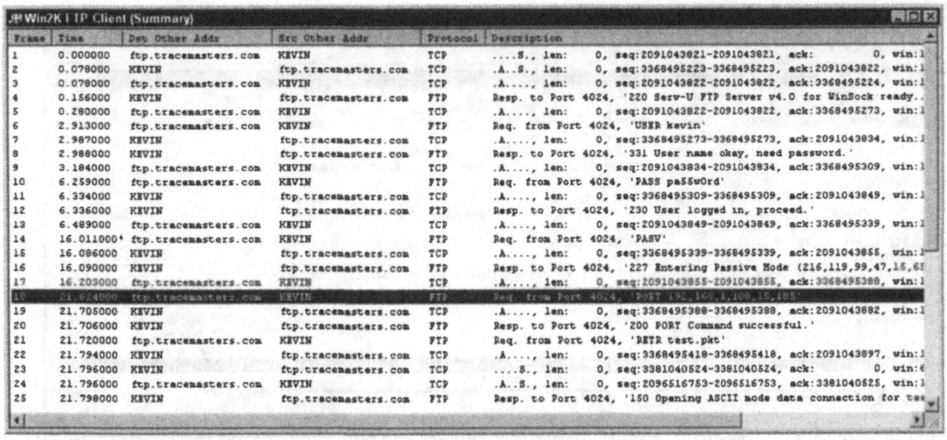

Frame	Time	Dst Other Addr	Src Other Addr	Protocol	Description
1	0.000000	ftp.tracemasters.com	KEVIN	TCP	....S., len: 0, seq:2091043821-2091043821, ack: 0, win:1
2	0.078000	KEVIN	ftp.tracemasters.com	TCP	.A..S., len: 0, seq:3368495223-3368495223, ack:2091043822, win:1
3	0.078000	ftp.tracemasters.com	KEVIN	TCP	.A...., len: 0, seq:2091043822-2091043822, ack:3368495224, win:1
4	0.156000	KEVIN	ftp.tracemasters.com	FTP	Resp. to Port 4024, '220 Serv-U FTP Server v4.0 for WinSock ready..
5	0.280000	ftp.tracemasters.com	KEVIN	TCP	.A...., len: 0, seq:2091043822-2091043822, ack:3368495273, win:1
6	2.913000	ftp.tracemasters.com	KEVIN	FTP	Req. from Port 4024, 'USER kevin'
7	2.987000	KEVIN	ftp.tracemasters.com	TCP	.A...., len: 0, seq:3368495273-3368495273, ack:2091043834, win:1
8	2.988000	KEVIN	ftp.tracemasters.com	FTP	Resp. to Port 4024, '331 User name okay, need password.'
9	3.184000	ftp.tracemasters.com	KEVIN	TCP	.A...., len: 0, seq:2091043834-2091043834, ack:3368495309, win:1
10	6.259000	ftp.tracemasters.com	KEVIN	FTP	Req. from Port 4024, 'PASS pa55w0rd'
11	6.334000	KEVIN	ftp.tracemasters.com	TCP	.A...., len: 0, seq:3368495309-3368495309, ack:2091043849, win:1
12	6.336000	KEVIN	ftp.tracemasters.com	FTP	Resp. to Port 4024, '230 User logged in, proceed.'
13	6.489000	ftp.tracemasters.com	KEVIN	TCP	.A...., len: 0, seq:2091043849-2091043849, ack:3368495339, win:1
14	16.011000	ftp.tracemasters.com	KEVIN	FTP	Req. from Port 4024, 'PASV'
15	16.086000	KEVIN	ftp.tracemasters.com	TCP	.A...., len: 0, seq:3368495339-3368495339, ack:2091043855, win:1
16	16.090000	KEVIN	ftp.tracemasters.com	FTP	Resp. to Port 4024, '227 Entering Passive Mode (216,119,99,47,15,65
17	16.203000	ftp.tracemasters.com	KEVIN	TCP	.A...., len: 0, seq:2091043855-2091043855, ack:3368495388, win:1
18	21.624000	ftp.tracemasters.com	KEVIN	FTP	Req. from Port 4024, 'PORT 192,168,1,100,15,185'
19	21.705000	KEVIN	ftp.tracemasters.com	TCP	.A...., len: 0, seq:3368495388-3368495388, ack:2091043882, win:1
20	21.706000	KEVIN	ftp.tracemasters.com	FTP	Resp. to Port 4024, '200 PORT Command successful.'
21	21.720000	ftp.tracemasters.com	KEVIN	FTP	Req. from Port 4024, 'RETR test.pkt'
22	21.794000	KEVIN	ftp.tracemasters.com	TCP	.A...., len: 0, seq:3368495418-3368495418, ack:2091043897, win:1
23	21.796000	KEVIN	ftp.tracemasters.com	TCP	....S., len: 0, seq:3381040524-3381040524, ack: 0, win:6
24	21.796000	ftp.tracemasters.com	KEVIN	TCP	.A..S., len: 0, seq:2096516753-2096516753, ack:3381040525, win:1
25	21.798000	KEVIN	ftp.tracemasters.com	FTP	Resp. to Port 4024, '150 Opening ASCII mode data connection for tes

Figure 7-22 Passive transfer failure.

It was no wonder I was having failures. Since the client's firewall doesn't allow incoming TCP connections to port 20, the transfers won't work. Unfortunately, even though I enabled passive mode on the client, it still attempted to perform an active transfer. After further research, I found out the Windows 2000 FTP client supports only active FTP transfers. Solution: Use another FTP program like FileZilla.

Case Study: FTP Failures through Firewall

This next case study was interesting as the file transfer progressed normally until all of a sudden it would fail. Once again, a protocol analyzer saved the day.

Sometimes, troubleshooting connections between a firewall can be very complex. Most firewalls perform some sort of network address translation (NAT) and/or port address translation (PAT) where the TCP sequence numbers of a single connection will be different on either side of the firewall. NAT uses a static list or pool of public IP addresses that it dynamically maps to private IP addresses. PAT is when a single public Internet-side address is used to represent multiple private inside addresses. Each inside address is mapped to a specific IP destination and source port.

In this case study, hosts on the inside of the firewall talk directly to the IP address of hosts on the Internet, but hosts on the Internet use the PAT address on the firewall. To analyze a connection problem through a firewall using NAT or PAT, it is important to obtain simultaneous packet captures on both sides of the firewall. Figure 7-23 shows two simultaneous captures from inside the firewall and from outside the firewall.

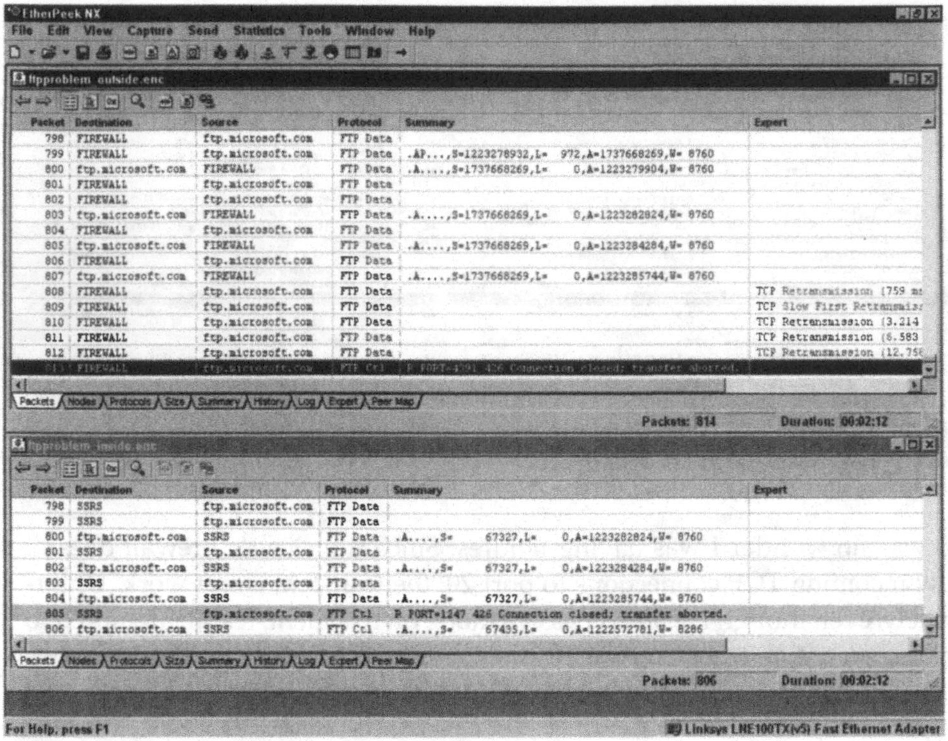

Figure 7-23 Inside/outside firewall captures.

When you analyze any type of disconnected session, it is important to find out where in the packet trace the session is disconnected and then work backwards into the trace. In Figure 7-23 it is relatively easy to determine where the disconnection is. On the outside trace you see the FTP server aborting the connection in Frame 813; on the inside trace, in Frame 805. The packets in between where the transfer was working properly and the disconnection will reveal the cause of the problem.

By looking at the outside trace, you may notice something that is not present in the inside trace: TCP Retransmissions. You can see five TCP retransmissions in Frames 808 to 812 that are not seen in the inside trace. The retransmissions tell you that the firewall is dropping one or more TCP segments, which causes the FTP server to abort the connection. But why is the firewall dropping packets?

When analyzing a connection problem through a firewall, I like to create what I refer to as a *connection flow diagram*. Figure 7-24 is a connection flow diagram created from the trace files on either side of the connection. A connection flow diagram lets you easily see the state of TCP transmissions and acknowledgments. Rather than scratching sequence and acknowledgment numbers down on paper as you move back and forth through two packet traces, you can see the TCP connection flow on one single piece of paper. On the left hand side of Figure 7-24, I show the TCP connection flow on the outside of the firewall, on the right hand side, the inside of the firewall. The thick black line separating the two sides is the firewall. The `ftp.Microsoft.com` server talks to the firewall address and the inside host SSRS talks to `ftp.Microsoft.com`.

NOTE When you see packets being dropped, never assume that it is normal. Packets can and will be dropped due to normal circumstances, such as congestion or bandwidth utilization, but until you can confirm the reason for the drops, always investigate.

You already know that the FTP server is retransmitting a specific TCP segment that is being dropped by the firewall. What you now need to know is whether or not the segment even previously reached the firewall. Using the connection flow diagram and tracking back to Frame 798 on the outside, you find that the FTP server did indeed send the segment, which it retransmits in Frame 808, but did you receive it?

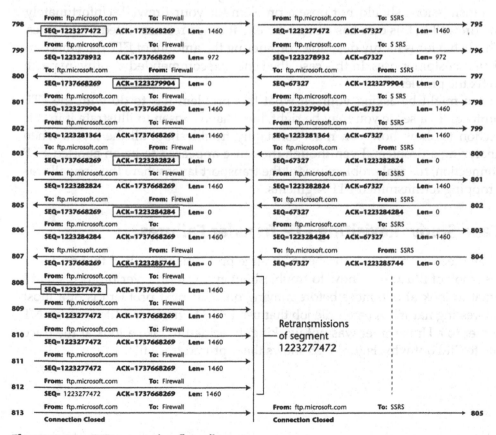

Figure 7-24 TCP connection flow diagram.

By adding the data length to the sequence number in Frame 798, you come up with an acknowledgment number of 1223279904. In Frame 800, you can see the client sending an acknowledgment number of 1223279904. This tells us that the SSRS client inside the firewall received the TCP segment. Why then did the `ftp.microsoft.com` server retransmit the segment in Frame 808?

If you have read Chapter 6 of this book already, you may recall a discussion on TCP segment sequencing and acknowledgment. How does a host know if its TCP segments have been received? The acknowledgment number, right? On the outside connection, Frames 800, 803, 805, and 807 all cumulatively acknowledge data segments that have been sent by the FTP server. Even if acknowledgment frames 800, 803, and 805 were lost, the last acknowledgment frame, Frame 807, would have been sufficient enough to acknowledge all previous TCP segments sent by the FTP server. By its retransmitting TCP segment `1223277472` in Frame 808, you know that the FTP server has not received any of the acknowledgments sent by the host SSRS. So in Frame 808 through Frame 812, it attempts to retransmit the segment.

So who is at fault here? Is it the firewall, is it the Internet, or is it Microsoft? Packet loss, while undesirable, is completely normal on the Internet. Any retransmissions should not pose a problem for your firewall. Unfortunately, the firewall in this case has a bug whereby it drops retransmitted FTP frames. This behavior is hardly desirable considering the amount of FTP data this particular customer uses. In this case, the vendor recommended a software patch to fix the problem.

You might be asking yourself what this problem has to do with the FTP protocol. In a sense you may be right, but I have chosen to illustrate it in this section to show how you must constantly troubleshoot all the layers when analyzing a problem. Even though the cause appeared to be an aborted FTP connection, the real problem was at the transport layer where the firewall was dropping retransmitted FTP segments.

Case Study: Revisiting FTP Transfer Failures

I have seen such a good number of strange problems using FTP that do a fantastic job of illustrating how to troubleshoot application-layer protocols that I want to look at one more before moving on. This next problem is of a most interesting nature. A batch file job that used FTP to transfer a file from an NT server to a Unix server was not working. I decided to take a look at the trace file to find out why. Figure 7-25 shows the captured trace file.

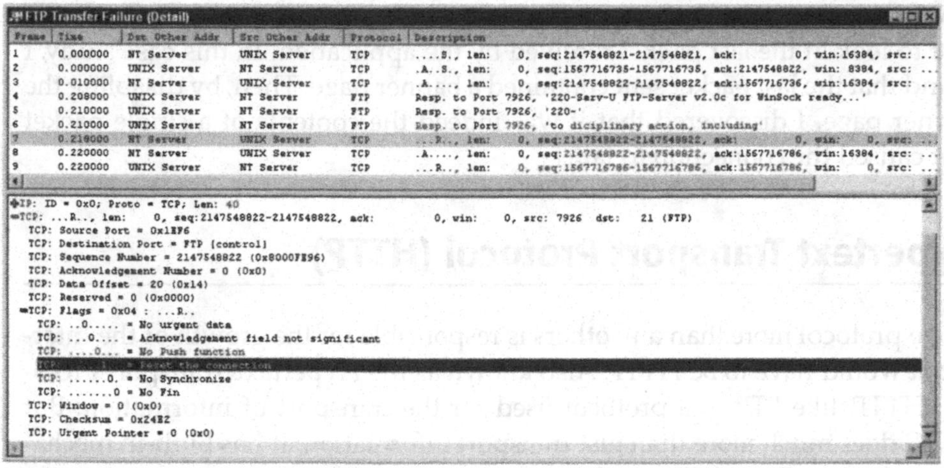

Figure 7-25 FTP transfer failure.

You can immediately see that in Frame 7 the Unix server is sending a TCP Reset to the NT server that disconnects the session. To determine the cause of the TCP Reset, I asked the users on the Unix side of the connection to send me a screenshot of their FTP command-line program during the failed transfer. Below was what they saw:

```
ftp. unix2.tracemasters.com
Connected to tracemasters.com.
220 Serv-U FTP Server v4.0 for WinSock ready...
```

Alone, the screenshot information is not much use in determining the problem. But when it is combined with what you see in the trace file, it puts you one step closer in determining the cause of the problem. Notice in the trace file that Frame 4 contains the response from the NT server containing the reply code and message: 220 Serv-U FTP Server v2.0 for WinSock ready. Because this appeared on the screen, you know that Frame 5 was indeed received by the Unix system. However, the trace contains two more frames before the Unix system sends a reset. By analyzing a successful FTP connection, I was able to determine that the server was using an FTP banner page containing a security disclaimer message. The banner page never appeared on the Unix system console during the FTP session, which told us that the FTP client on the Unix system never received the frames, or did it?

I decided to check, so for my next step, I disabled the banner page and, amazingly, everything worked fine. For some reason, the FTP client software on the Unix system had a big problem with FTP banner pages. After further research, I found out that it was certain characters inside of the banner page that the Unix system deemed illegal. A simple rewrite of the banner message without the illegal characters fixed the problem.

When an application disconnects a seemingly normal session, it is important to look at the last packet received by the application. In this case study, I found that the last packet sent contained a banner page. Then, by disabling the banner page, I discovered that it was indeed the contents of a single packet that caused the connection to fail.

Hypertext Transport Protocol (HTTP)

If one protocol more than any others is responsible for the growth of the Internet, it would have to be HTTP. Also known as the Hypertext Transport Protocol, HTTP, like FTP, is a protocol used for the transport of information. But HTTP does much more than just transport information. It has built-in mechanisms for handling different data formats, provides connection persistence, and includes indicators for caching. HTTP works in conjunction with the HyperText Markup Language or HTML. HTML is a code format that handles the formatting and construction of Web pages. HTML contains references to text, graphics, and other data. When used in conjunction with specific Web servers, HTML can contain other code, such as Active Server Page (ASP) or Java. These types of code extensions allow Web servers and clients to provide extra functionality such as back-end database connectivity or other offloaded processes. HTTP is the protocol that handles retrieving and transporting the code and data that makes a Web page show up on a user's Web browser.

HTTP Requests

HTTP is a client/server protocol. The client, most likely a Web browser, sends HTTP requests to an HTTP server, also known as a Web server. The Web server responds with the HTML or other code contained in the Web page that was specified in the HTTP request. Once an HTTP client (or browser) obtains the code, it processes the code to determine what further action it needs to take. HTML or other code is simply instructions that tell your Web browser what actions to take in order to build a Web page. HTTP allows your Web browser to obtain those instructions.

Figure 7-26 shows a packet trace of a simple HTTP GET operation:

1. In Frames 1 and 2, you see DNS doing its job by resolving the IP address of the Web site www.tracemasters.com.

2. Frames 3, 4, and 5 show the TCP three-way handshake to set up the connection.

3. In Frame 6, you see the HTTP GET operation. The decode of Frame 6 contains several lines that list the parameters of the GET request.

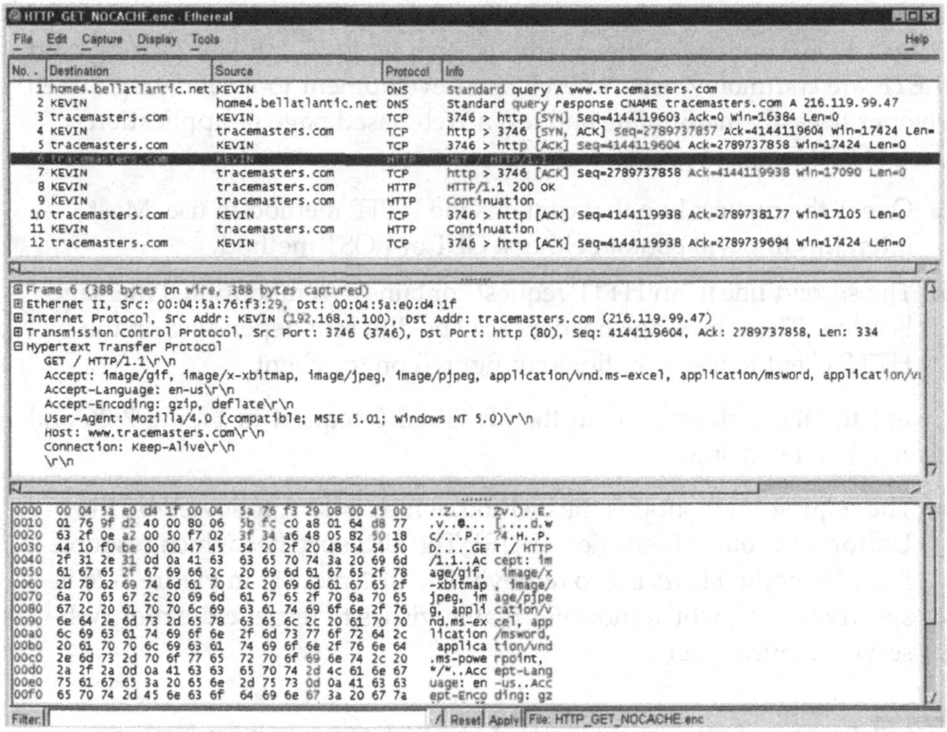

Figure 7-26 HTTP GET operation.

A GET request is part of a larger group of what are called HTTP methods. Each method provides the HTTP client with some functionality pertaining to retrieving, transferring, or diagnosing a page or pages on a Web server. Table 7-7 lists some common HTTP methods.

Table 7-7 HTTP Methods

METHOD	DESCRIPTION
GET	Requests an object from a Web server
CONNECT	Provides support for tunneling
DELETE	Deletes an object from a Web server
HEAD	Checks for the existence of an object
POST	Sends data to a Web server object for processing
PUT	Sends data to be stored inside of a Web server object
TRACE	Traces path to server
OPTIONS	Query Web server capabilities

The most common HTTP methods that are used by Web browsers are the GET and POST options. Other methods such as PUT, HEAD, TRACE, and DELETE are commonly used in Web site development tools allowing a Web developer to easily manipulate and test a Web-based page or application. Each HTTP request has two parts.

- One is the request line that contains the HTTP method in use. Most often this line will contain either a GET or POST method.

- The second line in an HTTP request contains several optional message headers. These message headers may be different depending on the HTTP client in use or options configured on the client.

I want to take a closer look at the HTTP GET request in Figure 7-26 and analyze what it is doing.

- The request line contains the method, which is GET, followed by the Uniform Resource Identifier, or URI. The URI specifies which resource the GET method is trying to retrieve. The GET request in Figure 7-26 is specifying "/", which indicates that it wishes to retrieve the root Web server resource page.

NOTE Root pages are commonly stored on a Web server as index.html or a default.html. Either an html or htm extension may be used on most Web servers.

- In the decode for Frame 6 in Figure 7-26, you can also see six message headers.
    - The Accept header lets the client specify the type of content it can accept. The order in which the content types are listed indicates the client's preference for the type of content. Here you can see that the client prefers GIF, bitmaps, JPEG, PJPEG, MS-Excel, MS-Word, and several others.
    - The Accept-Language field specifies a language preference of English.
    - The Accept-Encoding field specifies a content-encoding type of either gzip or deflate.
    - The User-Agent field includes the type of browser that the HTTP client is running.
    - The host message included is www.tracemasters.com.
    - The connection type specified is Keep-Alive.

I could easily write several chapters on every intricacy of the HTTP protocol. As of this writing, it contains well over 50 separate message headers. Space doesn't permit that in this text. Instead, I will be reviewing the most common message types to give you a basic understanding of HTTP. Once you understand the basic operations of a protocol, you will find it easy to extend that knowledge to more complex protocol interactions or even other protocols completely. Eventually, you will discover that all protocols tend to share the same types of operations. An understanding of these key operations takes you a long way in the analysis of complex problems. Knowledge of what is supposed to happen is the key to problem solving.

HTTP Responses

When an HTTP client sends a request, it receives an HTTP response. When a client requests a new resource, the first response will always be an HTTP status code. Looking back at Figure 7-26, you can see in Frame 8 that the Web server responds with an HTTP 200 OK status code. There are several categories of HTTP status codes. I refer to them throughout the HTTP section of this chapter. Table 7-8 contains a list of HTTP status codes.

Table 7-8   HTTP Status Codes

CATEGORY	CODE	DESCRIPTION
1xx		Informational
	100	Continue
	101	Switching protocols
2xx		Successful
	200	OK
	201	Created
	202	Accepted
	203	Nonauthoritative information
	204	No content
	205	Reset content
	206	Partial content
3xx		Redirection
	300	Multiple choices

(continued)

Table 7-8 *(continued)*

CATEGORY	CODE	DESCRIPTION
	301	Moved permanently
	302	Found
	303	See other
	304	Not modified
	305	Use proxy
	306	Unused
	307	Temporary redirect
4xx		Client error
	400	Bad request
	401	Unauthorized
	402	Payment required
	403	Forbidden
	404	Not found
	405	Method not allowed
	406	Not acceptable
	407	Proxy authentication required
	408	Request time-out
	409	Conflict
	410	Gone
	411	Length required
	412	Precondition failed
	413	Request entity too large
	414	Request-URI too long
	415	Unsupported media type
	416	Requested range not satisfiable
	417	Expectation failed
	426	Upgrade required

Table 7-8   *(continued)*

CATEGORY	CODE	DESCRIPTION
5xx		Server error
	500	Internal server error
	501	Not implemented
	502	Bad gateway
	503	Service unavailable
	504	Gateway time-out
	505	Version not supported

After the Web server sends a status OK message, it will continue with transferring the contents of the page to the client. Frames 9 and 11 of Figure 7-26 contain the actual HTML code contained in the default page on the Web server. Once the Web browser receives the HTML page data, it reads the data to find out what other actions it needs to take in order to fully display the Web page.

NOTE Remember, a Web page may contain code such as Active Server Scripts or even functions that call other pages. Not all information that you see on a screen is necessarily contained in a single Web page.

Now that you've watched the loading of the Web site's default page at www.tracemasters.com, I want to open up the Web page again so you can watch what happens. Figure 7-27 shows a slightly different transaction than you saw the first time I opened up the Web page. This time, you see only a single HTTP packet being returned from the server. It is an HTTP status code 304, indicating that the Web page has not been modified.

This status code is most useful in speeding up your Web browsing and cutting down on unnecessary traffic. After you visit a Web page for the first time, your Web browser (if configured to) will cache all HTML pages and page objects in a local directory on your hard drive. This permits your Web browser to create a Web site's content from this local directory instead of transferring it a second time over the Internet. If a Web browser knows it has cached data, it will ask a Web server when its content was last modified. If the content is still the same as when the browser visited the site previously, it will use the local content it has stored in its cache. In Figure 7-27, you can see that the content of the default page of www.tracemasters.com hasn't changed since January 1, 2003, at 5:32:15 eastern standard time (22:32:15 GMT). Any Web page requests since that time will be able to use the Web objects located in their local Web browser's cache directory. Understanding how browsers use the local cache helps you troubleshoot Web content that appears to be out of date.

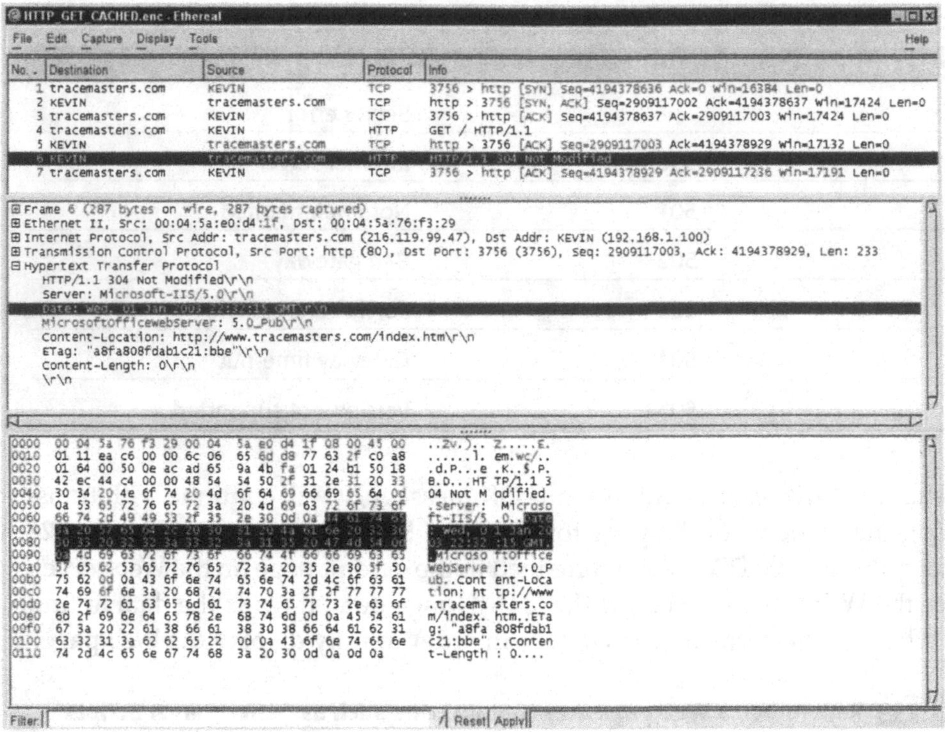

Figure 7-27 If-Modified header.

HTTP Headers and Messages

The IP-Modified header is one example of the types of headers HTTP uses. As I have previously indicated, unfortunately, HTTP contains too many headers and messages to completely cover in this chapter. I have chosen several types of headers to give you an understanding of how headers operate and how these headers and messages are used on HTTP clients and servers alike.

By gaining a basic understanding of several headers, you can translate that knowledge into understanding the more complex headers. Headers enable the operations that allow HTTP to perform its job. Without an understanding of the headers, you will never be able to analyze exactly what is happening during an HTTP transaction. And as I've mentioned, understanding what is supposed to happen is the key to problem solving.

NOTE Stephen A. Thomas's excellent book, *HTTP Essentials: Protocols for Secure, Scaleable Web Sites,* by Wiley Publishing, covers in detail all headers and messages used by the HTTP protocol.

Host Header

HTTP host headers are used to allow what is known as virtual hosting, or sometimes virtual Web services. When multiple Web servers are running under a single IP address there must be a way to separate Web pages with the same name. For instance, two servers could not have the same index.html name because the Web server would not know which Web page to deliver. Figure 7-28 shows how HTTP host headers work to allow multiple Web servers to run on a single IP address.

Even though both clients are requesting the same root object of "/", the Web server knows which Web site to return to the client because they are specifying the full Web site name in the host header portion of the HTTP packet. Without the host header, the Web server would have no idea which Web site to return because they both are running under a single IP address.

Redirection

The redirection message allows a Web server to inform a client that the object it has requested is located at another URI. This is useful if an administrator needs to temporarily redirect clients to another Web server for maintenance or administrative reasons. Figure 7-29 shows how the redirection process works.

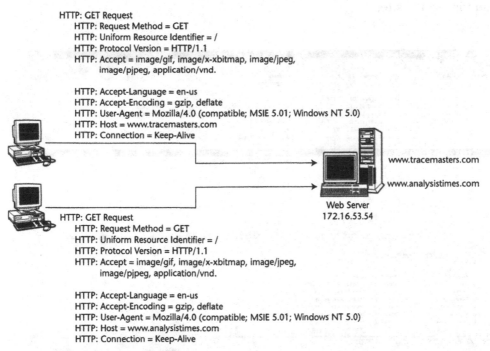

HTTP: GET Request
    HTTP: Request Method = GET
    HTTP: Uniform Resource Identifier = /
    HTTP: Protocol Version = HTTP/1.1
    HTTP: Accept = image/gif, image/x-xbitmap, image/jpeg,
           image/pjpeg, application/vnd.

    HTTP: Accept-Language = en-us
    HTTP: Accept-Encoding = gzip, deflate
    HTTP: User-Agent = Mozilla/4.0 (compatible; MSIE 5.01; Windows NT 5.0)
    HTTP: Host = www.tracemasters.com
    HTTP: Connection = Keep-Alive

www.tracemasters.com

www.analysistimes.com

Web Server
172.16.53.54

HTTP: GET Request
    HTTP: Request Method = GET
    HTTP: Uniform Resource Identifier = /
    HTTP: Protocol Version = HTTP/1.1
    HTTP: Accept = image/gif, image/x-xbitmap, image/jpeg,
           image/pjpeg, application/vnd.

    HTTP: Accept-Language = en-us
    HTTP: Accept-Encoding = gzip, deflate
    HTTP: User-Agent = Mozilla/4.0 (compatible; MSIE 5.01; Windows NT 5.0)
    HTTP: Host = www.analysistimes.com
    HTTP: Connection = Keep-Alive

Figure 7-28   Host header operation.

I have used one of my favorite news sites as an example; you can see that after typing in the URI of **www.londontimes.com,** a DNS lookup is performed, a TCP connection is made, and then an HTTP GET request is sent to the Web server. Instead of receiving a status 200 code for OK, I receive a status code of 301, indicating that the Web site has been permanently moved. The HTTP message headers also tell me where it has been moved. The location field gives me a new URI of http://www.the-times.co.uk. In Frames 13 through 18, you can see the DNS lookup for the new URI and the TCP connection, as well as the GET request in Frame 19.

Cookies

Cookies are pieces of information that are created by Web servers and stored on a client's computer. Cookies allow a Web server to track a client based on the information contained in its cookie. Simply put, a *cookie* is a file stored on a user's hard drive. It contains certain information that lets a Web server track a client across multiple connections. For example, an e-commerce site will use a client's cookie information to track the user as it puts items in its shopping cart. An online bookstore will keep a shopping cart of all the books you select. Amazon.com, for example, maintains a list of books a user has looked at. When you revisit the amazon.com site, it immediately knows who you are by your cookie. It shows you the books you were browsing through the last time you visited the site.

Figure 7-29   Web site redirection.

Cookies are set by the Web server on the first HTTP response to a GET request. They are enabled by the Set-Cookie header. Figure 7-30 shows a Web server at amazon.com performing a cookie placement on my local computer.

When a cookie is received by a Web browser, it saves the cookie in a special cookie directory. It also writes an entry to a cookie cache index, which it searches to find out if a cookie exists for a specific Web site. When a Web site is revisited, the cookie is inserted into the HTTP request header, as shown in Figure 7-31.

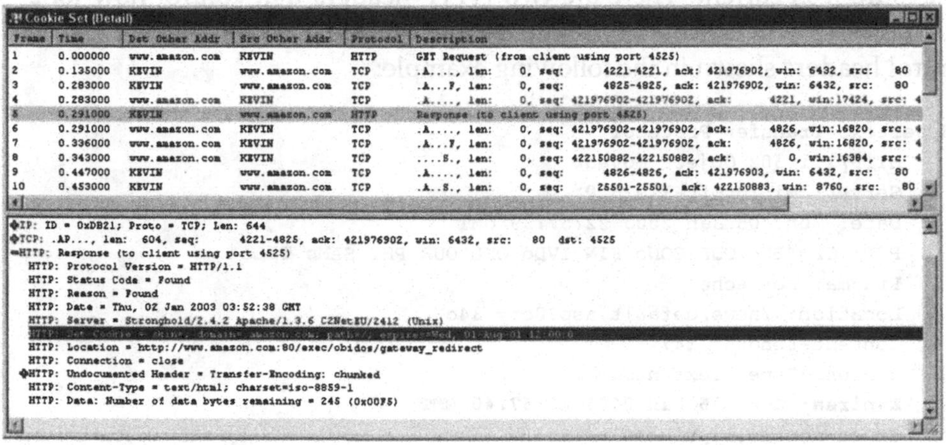

Figure 7-30 Cookie set.

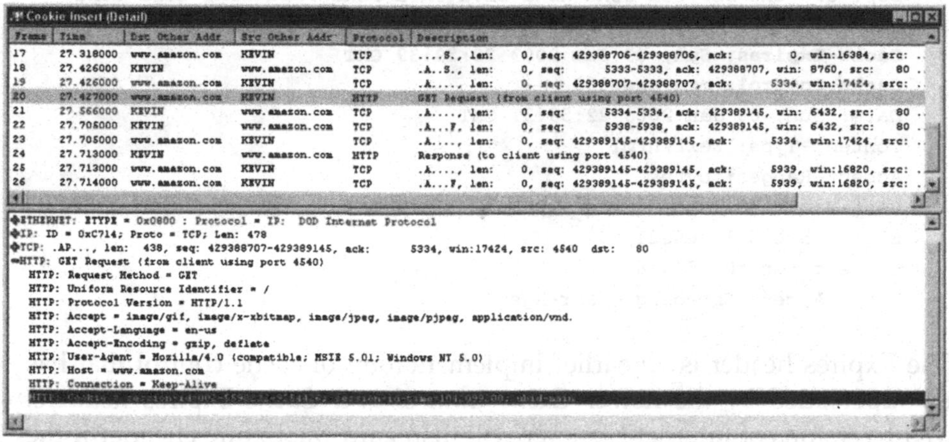

Figure 7-31 Cookie insert.

Cache Control Headers

Chances are you are going to visit the same Web sites more than once. Web browser designers understand this fact as well and have built in mechanisms to speed up your response time the second or subsequent times you access a site. They do this by caching the contents of the Web sites you visit on your local hard drive. Microsoft calls these cached Web objects, temporary internet files. They are temporary because they are used only a limited amount of times before the browser reloads and restores the information from a Web site to make sure it is current. There are two HTTP headers that control how long your browser will cache Web objects. These are the Expires and the Cache Control headers shown in the following example:

```
Hypertext Transfer Protocol
    HTTP/1.1 302 Object moved
    Server: Microsoft-IIS/5.0
    Date: Sun, 05 Jan 2003 22:57:39 GMT
    P3P: CP="BUS CUR CONo FIN IVDo ONL OUR PHY SAMo TELo"
    Pragma: no-cache
    Location: /news/default.asp?0ct=-34o
    Content-Length: 147
    Content-Type: text/html
    Expires: Sun, 05 Jan 2003 10:57:40 GMT
    Cache-control: private


Hypertext Transfer Protocol
    HTTP/1.1 200 OK
    Server: Microsoft-IIS/5.0
    p3p: CP="CAO DSP COR CURa ADMa DEVa TAIa PSAa PSDa IVAi IVDi CONi
OUR BUS
    Cache-Expires: Sun, 05 Jan 2003 22:59:39 GMT
    Cache-Control: max-age=300
    Date: Sun, 05 Jan 2003 22:59:31 GMT
    Content-Type: text/html
    Accept-Ranges: bytes
    Last-Modified: Sun, 05 Jan 2003 22:59:27 GMT
    ETag: "5cb95d19eb5c21:898"
    Content-Length: 54416
    Vary: Accept-Encoding, User-Agent
```

The Expires header is an earlier implementation of cache control that has been superceded by the newer Cache-Control and Cache-Expires headers. Current versions of Internet Explorer will disregard the Expires header if the newer Cache Control headers are present. In the previous example a browser will use the cached Web object no later than 10:57:40 Greenwich mean time for the Expires header and 22:59:39 GMT for the Cache-Expires header.

HTTP Proxies

Proxy servers allow an organization to save bandwidth by funneling all Internet traffic through a single (or multiple) Internet-connected host. A proxy server gets its name by the operation it performs. Instead of an HTTP client making requests to a Web site directly, the client sends the requests to a proxy server that handles retrieving the Web objects on the site and returning them to the client. Proxy servers are typically dual-homed servers containing two NIC cards. They may or may not be running firewall software to protect an internal network. If they are not, then the outside Internet connection is typically configured with a firewall that contains rulesets allowed access only to and from the proxy server and the Internet. In a proxy server configuration, inside clients have no knowledge of the outside network. All requests are sent to the IP address of the proxy server. Proxy servers do not allow end-to-end IP communication. On a single Web session through a proxy server, there are actually two TCP connections:

- One from the client to the proxy server
- One from the proxy server to the Web site on the Internet

Figure 7-32 illustrates the functionality of a proxy server.

Notice how the source and destination addresses on the inside portion of the network change as the request is sent to the proxy server. On the outside Internet portion, the proxy server makes a TCP connection of its own to the real Internet IP address of the Web site from its own outside IP interface.

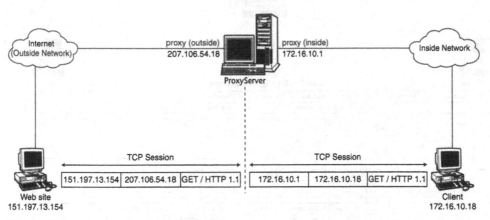

Figure 7-32   Proxy server functionality.

Proxy servers are actually very simple. They intercept TCP sessions and make the request for you (proxy) on the other side of the connection. However, they can be very difficult to troubleshoot when it comes to performance. Since the packet's IP addresses and MAC addresses are different on either side of the proxy server, it is difficult to match up request and response pairs of packets in order to measure the connection latency. Using a dual-port time synched analyzer (Shomiti Explorer in this case), the next section shows how latency can easily be measured.

Measuring Proxy Latency

If you happen to own a dual-port analyzer that has the ability to time-sync both interfaces to a single clock source and interweave the packets from both interfaces, you will be able to easily measure latency on a dual-home proxy server. You simply need to connect either side of your analyzer to both segments of the proxy server.

This connection can be made with either port mirroring or shared minihubs on either end. Once both connections are tapped into, you can take a packet capture while you connect to a Web site. The end result will be a mixed capture of traffic from both sides of the proxy server perfectly interweaved so that the latency is easily seen. Figure 7-33 shows the setup and packet capture.

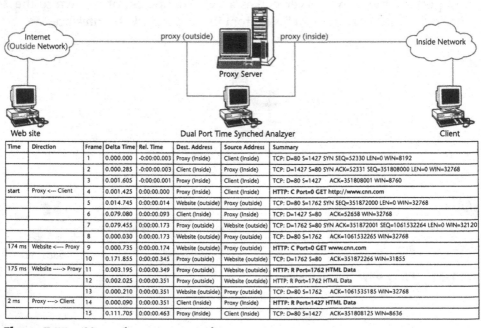

Time	Direction	Frame	Delta Time	Rel. Time	Dest. Address	Source Address	Summary
		1	0.000.000	-0:00:00.003	Proxy (Inside)	Client (Inside)	TCP: D=80 S=1427 SYN SEQ=52330 LEN=0 WIN=8192
		2	0.000.285	-0:00:00.003	Client (Inside)	Proxy (Inside)	TCP: D=1427 S=80 SYN ACK=52331 SEQ=351808000 LEN=0 WIN=32768
		3	0.001.605	-0:00:00.001	Proxy (Inside)	Client (Inside)	TCP: D=80 S=1427 ACK=351808001 WIN=8760
start	Proxy <--- Client	4	0.001.425	0:00:00.000	Proxy (Inside)	Client (Inside)	HTTP: C Port=0 GET http://www.cnn.com
		5	0.014.745	0:00:00.014	Website (outside)	Proxy (outside)	TCP: D=80 S=1762 SYN SEQ=351872000 LEN=0 WIN=32768
		6	0.079.080	0:00:00.093	Client (Inside)	Proxy (Inside)	TCP: D=1427 S=80 ACK=52658 WIN=32768
		7	0.079.455	0:00:00.173	Proxy (outside)	Website (outside)	TCP: D=1762 S=80 SYN ACK=351872001 SEQ=1061532264 LEN=0 WIN=32120
		8	0.000.030	0:00:00.173	Website (outside)	Proxy (outside)	TCP: D=80 S=1762 ACK=1061532265 WIN=32768
174 ms	Website <---- Proxy	9	0.000.735	0:00:00.174	Website (outside)	Proxy (outside)	HTTP: C Port=0 GET www.cnn.com
		10	0.171.855	0:00:00.345	Proxy (outside)	Website (outside)	TCP: D=1762 S=80 ACK=351872266 WIN=31855
175 ms	Website -----> Proxy	11	0.003.195	0:00:00.349	Proxy (outside)	Website (outside)	HTTP: R Port=1762 HTML Data
		12	0.002.025	0:00:00.351	Proxy (outside)	Website (outside)	HTTP: R Port=1762 HTML Data
		13	0.000.210	0:00:00.351	Website (outside)	Proxy (outside)	TCP: D=80 S=1762 ACK=1061535185 WIN=32768
2 ms	Proxy ----> Client	14	0.000.090	0:00:00.351	Client (Inside)	Proxy (Inside)	HTTP: R Port=1427 HTML Data
		15	0.111.705	0:00:00.463	Proxy (Inside)	Client (Inside)	TCP: D=80 S=1427 ACK=351808125 WIN=8636

Figure 7-33   Measuring proxy server latency.

In order to match up the same packets on both sides of the connection, you have to use the application layer to identify the packets. The application layer, HTTP in this case, gives you a clearly visible identifier to use—the GET request.

1. In Frame 4, you can see the initial GET request from the client to the proxy server.

2. Then in Frame 9, you see the same GET request being forwarded out of the proxy server onto the outside connection to the Internet.

3. Next, in Frame 11, you see the first HTTP response frame coming back from the Web site (www.cnn.com in this instance) to the proxy server.

4. Last, in Frame 14, you see the HTTP response being sent back to the client on the inside network.

Using the relative time feature in your analyzer, you can see that after the proxy server received the HTTP GET request that it took 174 milliseconds until it made its own request out to the Internet. Is 174 milliseconds unreasonable?

Continue looking at the trace, and you can decide. In Frame 11, you see the response from the Web site to the proxy server's request, sent in Frame 9. It took 175 milliseconds to receive a response. This includes the amount of time it took the request to travel to and from the Web site. Strangely enough, the initial client request sat inside of the proxy server for a total of 174 milliseconds. Considering the speed of the internal PCI bus architecture and the high-speed processing power of a large Unix host (which the proxy server was), 174 milliseconds is an abysmal amount of time for the processing of a single HTTP request.

Notice, however, that from Frame 11 to Frame 14 it took the proxy server only 2 milliseconds to relay the Web site response back to the client. If the proxy server could relay responses from the outside to inside interfaces in 2 milliseconds, what was happening to cause the extra 172 milliseconds of delay going the other direction? What I found out was that the proxy server was configured to track and log all outbound connection requests. Once I disabled this feature, the delays disappeared.

Analyzing Advanced Web Architectures

Web sites have become very complex. Take, for example, the National Football League's Web site (www.nfl.com), which contains thousands of statistics, up to the minute score updates, and even live streaming audio of games in action. Today, complex Web sites do not exist as single servers but as multiple multi-tiered systems comprised of back-end databases, application servers, and application-aware load-balancing switches. These complex systems require special analysis needs and techniques in order to troubleshoot and analyze.

My first example is an architecture that utilizes the Secure Sockets Layer or SSL. SSL is a protocol that allows application traffic between a user and a Web server to be encrypted. Most financial sites, such as banks or e-commerce sites, usually provide some sort of encryption in order to protect their customer's credit card information as it travels over the public Internet. Unfortunately, encryption is not something Web servers do very well. When a Web server starts performing encryption and deencryption for several hundred users, it tends to start slowing down. The solution to this problem is to offload the encryption process to a separate device that specializes in fast encryption at the hardware level. Figure 7-34 illustrates architecture of this type.

The challenges in troubleshooting an architecture of this type are the multiple points of analysis. In architecture such as this, it is almost better to dedicate a multiple NIC analyzer specifically for its support.

Figure 7-35 shows another complex architecture that may exist in combination with the one shown in Figure 7-34. The architecture in Figure 7-35 is what's known as a three-tier application architecture. The three tiers are composed of the three servers that make up the entire client/server process. It's easy to see how an architecture of this type poses the same problems as the previous one. Analyzing performance problems is very challenging because, once again, there are multiple analysis points that must be taken into consideration to view the entire client/server process.

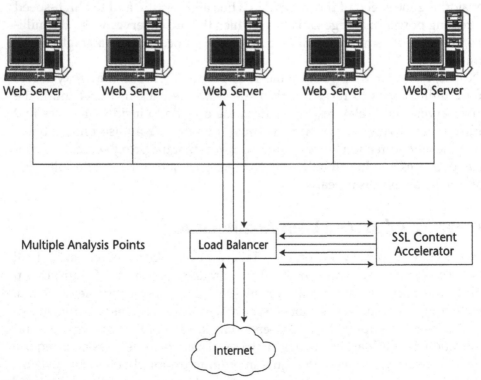

Figure 7-34   Hardware load-balancing Web architecture.

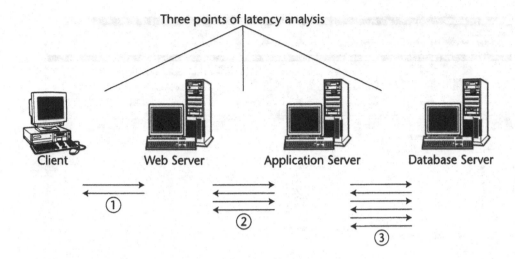

① — Client makes HTTP request of Web Server.
② — Web Server forwards data to Application Server.
③ — Application Server makes database calls to fulfill client request.

Figure 7-35   Three-tier application architecture.

Unless you own an analyzer that allows you to time-sync two or more ports to the same clock source, you are going to need to use three separate analyzers on three separate segments to analyze performance problems in a three-tiered architecture. Try to start capturing on each analyzer at roughly the same time. If all servers are on the same back-end segment, use a packet such as PING to set the relative time on each analyzer after you are done capturing. This technique will let you time-sync each analyzer within microseconds of each other because they all will have seen the PING packet at roughly the same time.

Case Study: Web Site Failure

When analyzing a failure in an application protocol or program, I cannot stress enough the need to analyze and troubleshoot all layers. Many times, an apparent application failure is actually being caused by a problem residing in another layer. Take Figure 7-36, for instance.

A problem with one of my favorite news sites (www.msnbc.com) actually had nothing to do with the Web server or the site itself. The problem was with DNS resolution. Here a DNS name server problem was inhibiting access to the site because the IP address was not able to be resolved. In Frames 2, 4, 6, and 8, you can see my DNS server responding with `Query Status=Server Failure` messages, indicating a failure of the DNS lookup.

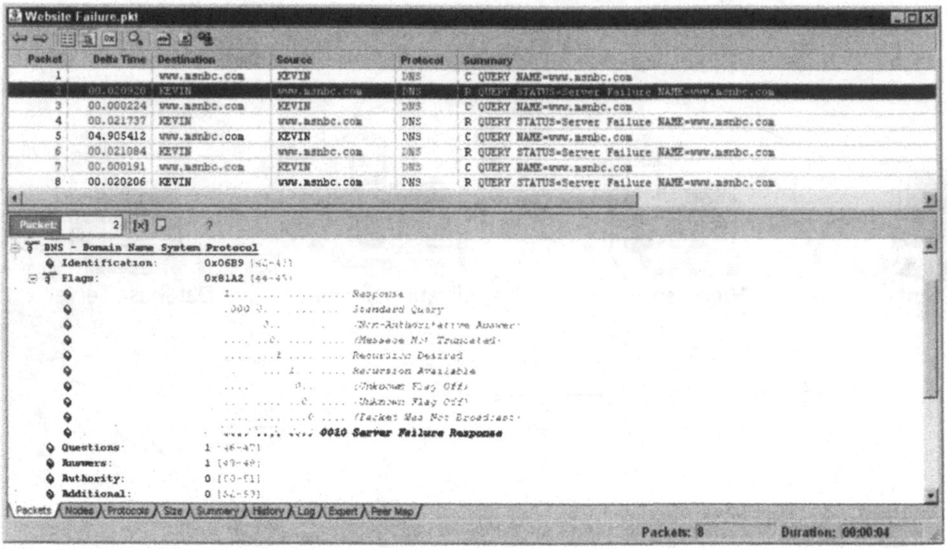

Figure 7-36　Web site failure.

NOTE If you have noticed that I have sometimes mixed case studies involving different protocols under different sections (such as this discussion of a DNS problem in the section of the chapter on HTTP), I have. This mixture of case studies is to stress that not all problems exist in one layer. As an analyst, you must always take into consideration the dependent layers of an application. A user analyzing just the HTTP protocol in this case would never have seen that the real problem is with the session layer or DNS.

Simple Mail Transport Protocol

The second protocol most responsible for Internet growth has to be the Simple Mail Transport Protocol (SMTP). Email has allowed millions of people around the world to communicate. It has broken down geographical boundaries over countries, distance, and sometimes even language. For all it does, it is actually a very simple protocol not much different from FTP. It operates with the same NVT ASCII character set, using simple commands and responses to transfer email messages back and forth. SMTP specifies the use of the commands listed in Table 7-9.

Table 7-9 SMTP Commands

COMMAND	DESCRIPTION
HELO	Used to identify the sender-SMTP to the receiver-SMTP. Actually short for HELLO but all the commands are shortened to a four-character standard
MAIL	Used to initiate a mail transaction in which the mail data is delivered to one or more mailboxes
RCPT	Used to identify an individual recipient of the mail data
DATA	Causes the mail data from this command to be appended to the mail data buffer
SEND	Used to initiate a mail transaction in which the mail data is delivered to one or more terminals
SOML	Used to initiate a mail transaction in which the mail data is delivered to one or more terminals or mailboxes
SAML	Used to initiate a mail transaction in which the mail data is delivered to one or more terminals and mailboxes
RSET	Specifies that the current mail transaction is to be aborted
VRFY	Asks the receiver to confirm that the argument identifies a user
EXPN	Asks the receiver to confirm that the argument identifies a mailing list, and if so, to return the membership of that list
HELP	Causes the receiver to send helpful information to the sender of the HELP command
NOOP	Specifies no action other than that the receiver send an OK reply
QUIT	Specifies that the receiver must send an OK reply, and then close the transmission channel
TURN	Specifies that the receiver must either send an OK reply and then take on the role of the sender-SMTP or send a refusal reply and retain the role of the receiver-SMTP

To send an email using SMTP, only five of the commands in the table are used. I illustrate these five commands in the trace file in Figure 7-37.

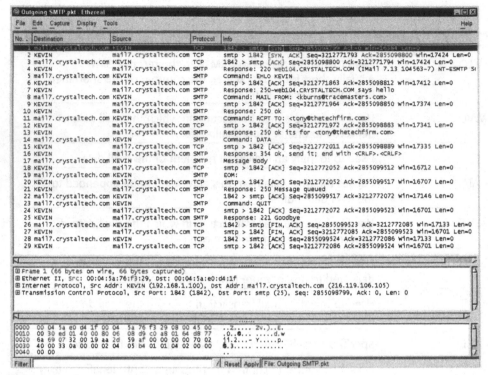

Figure 7-37   SMTP decode of email transmission.

1. In Frame 5, instead of the HELO command, the client sends an EHLO command. The EHLO command lets the remote mailer know that the client supports SMTP mail extensions. EHLO messages can be treated as HELO messages.

2. The remote mail server responds in Frame 7 with a status 250 OK message.

3. In Frame 8, my email address is sent with the MAIL command, which is responded by the mail server with a status 250 OK message.

4. The RCPT command in Frame 11 tells the remote mailer who the email destination is (in this case, tony@thetechfirm). The mail server replies with a 250 OK message.

5. In Frame 14, I send the DATA message, which tells the remote mail server that the next message I send will contain the mail message itself.

6. The mail server responds in Frame 16 with a 354 OK send message, telling us that it's okay to start sending.

7. Frames 17 and 19 contain the actual email data.

8. In Frame 21, you can see that the server responds with a message indicating that the email has been queued for transfer.

9. Upon receiving this message, I send the QUIT command (Frame 23), whereby the remote mail server replies with the GOODBYE message.

As you can see, the process of sending an email message is very simple. If all packets are being transferred back and forth properly, then most likely any problems with the mail transfer will be indicated in an SMTP status message sent by the mail server. A list of SMTP response codes is listed in Table 7-10.

Table 7-10 SMTP Status Codes

CATEGORY	CODE	DESCRIPTION
2xx		Command accepted and processed
	211	System status, or system help reply
	214	Help message
	220	<domain> Service ready
	221	<domain> Service closing transmission channel
	251	User not local; will forward to <forward-path>
3xx		General flow control
	354	Start mail input; end with <CRLF>.<CRLF>
4xx		Critical system or transfer failure
	421	<domain> Service not available,closing transmission channel
	450	Requested mail action not taken: mailbox unavailable
	451	Requested action aborted: local error in processing
	452	Requested action not taken: insufficient system storage
5xx		Errors with the SMTP command
	500	Syntax error, command unrecognized
	501	Syntax error in parameters or arguments

(continued)

Table 7-10   *(continued)*

CATEGORY	CODE	DESCRIPTION
	502	Command not implemented
	503	Bad sequence of commands
	504	Command parameter not implemented
	550	Requested action not taken: mailbox unavailable
	551	User not local; please try <forward-path>
	552	Requested mail action aborted: exceeded storage allocation
	553	Requested action not taken: mailbox name not allowed
	554	Transaction failed

Summary

Upper-layer protocols, although more complex than some of the lower-layer protocols, offer rich command and reply codes that enable you to easily determine problems that are occurring at the application layer. When you analyze an upper-layer protocol, it is critical to understand the sequence of events that makes the protocol work. For example, FTP opens up a control channel, then a data channel; DNS looks up an MX record. When DNS receives a canonical name, it then looks up the address record for that name. All upper-layer protocols have a specific dependent sequence of events that must take place. Once you understand those events, it is easy to determine where the process breaks down.

And as always, never assume that a problem exists only in one layer. Troubleshoot all layers from the bottom up.

CHAPTER 8

Microsoft-Related Protocols

The proliferation of networked Microsoft operating systems has created the need for the understanding of an entirely new set of protocols. Although these protocols are not necessarily specific to Microsoft, their use at such a deep level warrants their inclusion here as relating to Microsoft and its systems. I have included the protocols DHCP, NetBIOS, and SMB in this chapter because they make up the core upper-layer protocols used in Microsoft environments. A good understanding of their operation gives analysts another level of depth in their ability to troubleshoot Microsoft-specific problems.

Dynamic Host Configuration Protocol

The Dynamic Host Configuration Protocol (DHCP) provides dynamic configuration information to hosts running the Internet Protocol. DHCP is based on a client/server model whereby a client requests and receives configuration information from a server, which allows it to operate properly over the IP network. DHCP is specified in RFC 2131, as well as several other RFCs that detail certain options and extensions for the DHCP protocol. By providing dynamic configuration of IP addresses and other parameters, DHCP reduces the time it would normally take an administrator to manually configure a host with this information. With DHCP, workstations can be simply kickstarted on an IP network by selecting the DHCP option in a workstation's IP configuration. DHCP also has the ability to provide optional configuration parameters such as DNS servers or NetBIOS name servers. I discuss these options later in this chapter.

DHCP is the successor to the BOOTP protocol, but the two are still basically the same protocol with several minor exceptions. BOOTP was originally designed for diskless workstations that needed to run the IP protocol. They would boot up, obtain an IP address, and then often download a boot file to specify their startup configuration. DHCP, on the other hand, came about to reduce the management headache of manually assigning an IP address, subnet mask, gateway, and other parameters to each individual workstation. Although DHCP is not exclusively a Microsoft protocol, it was Microsoft, through its development and expansion of the desktop operating system, that popularized the use and furthered the development of standards for DHCP.

DHCP Header

Figure 8-1 shows the DHCP header.

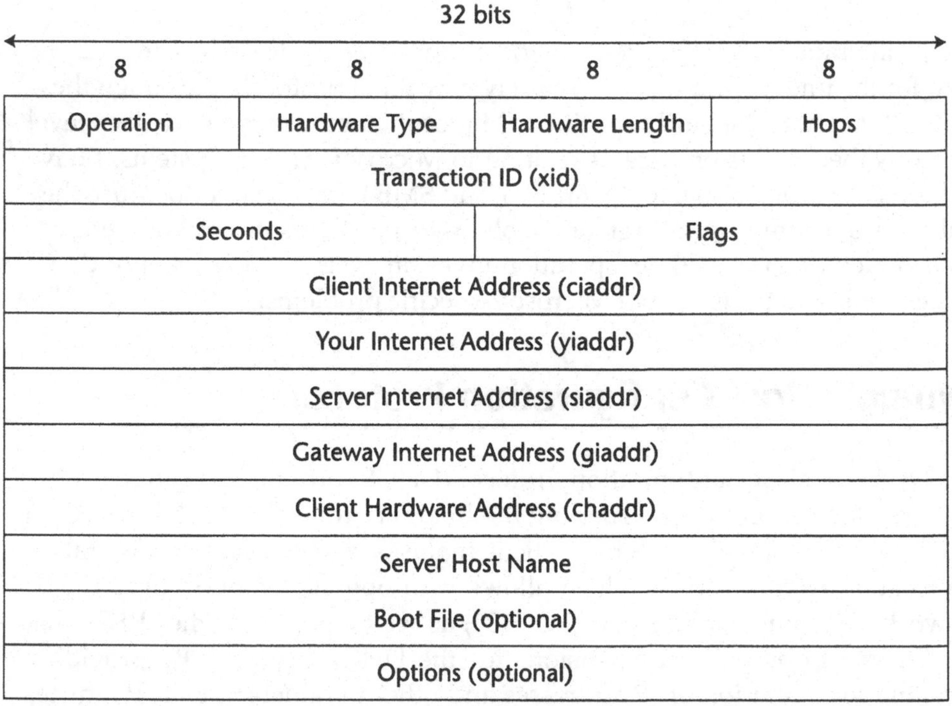

32 bits

8	8	8	8
Operation	Hardware Type	Hardware Length	Hops
Transaction ID (xid)			
Seconds		Flags	
Client Internet Address (ciaddr)			
Your Internet Address (yiaddr)			
Server Internet Address (siaddr)			
Gateway Internet Address (giaddr)			
Client Hardware Address (chaddr)			
Server Host Name			
Boot File (optional)			
Options (optional)			

Figure 8-1 The DHCP header.

The fields in the header are as follows:

- **Operation.** Message operation code (1 = BootRequest, 2 = BootReply).
- **Hardware Type.** Hardware address type (Ethernet, Token-Ring, and so on).
- **Hardware Length.** Hardware address length (for example, 6 bytes for Ethernet).
- **Hops.** Client sets this to zero. This is used optionally by relay agents.
- **Transaction ID (XID).** Random number chosen by the client to associate messages and responses sent between a client and server.
- **Seconds.** Seconds elapsed since client began address acquisition or renewal process.
- **Flags.** Set to indicate if a client can receive unicast frames (0 = Can accept unicast, 1 = Can accept only broadcasts).
- **Client Internet Address.** Filled in if client is in the BOUND, RENEW, or REBINDING state.
- **Your Client Internet Address.** IP address of client.
- **Server Internet Address.** IP address of DHCP server.
- **Gateway Internet Address.** Relay Agent IP Address (usually a router).
- **Client Hardware Address.** Hardware (MAC) address of client.
- **Server Host Name.** Optional hostname of DHCP server.
- **Boot File.** Optional name of boot file (if requested by client).
- **Options.** Optional parameters field.

Figure 8-1 shows the basic format of the DHCP header. Most of the fields are exactly the same as the BOOTP protocol, which, as I previously said, was the precursor to the current DHCP protocol. Both protocols actually use the same UDP port numbers. DHCP clients use UDP port 68, while DHCP servers use UDP port 67.

The basic format of the header is actually of little use without the many optional parameter fields that DHCP provides. The DHCP option fields always begin with the magic cookie field. The magic cookie field contains a default fixed hexadecimal byte value of 63 82 53 63 unless a special vendor magic cookie value is being used. The magic cookie field helps the DHCP server determine the type of vendor options that are being used. The option fields detail the types of options that a DHCP client is requesting from a DHCP server. The following shows a packet decode of the options field:

```
Magic cookie: (OK)
Option 53: DHCP Message Type = DHCP Discover
Unknown Option Code: 251 (1 bytes)
Option 61: Client identifier
```

```
      Hardware type: Ethernet
      Client hardware address: 00:04:5a:76:f3:29
Option 50: Requested IP Address = 192.168.1.100
Option 12: Host Name = "KEVIN"
Option 60: Vendor class identifier = "MSFT 5.0"
Option 55: Parameter Request List
    1 = Subnet Mask
    15 = Domain Name
    3 = Router
    6 = Domain Name Server
    44 = NetBIOS over TCP/IP Name Server
    46 = NetBIOS over TCP/IP Node Type
    47 = NetBIOS over TCP/IP Scope
    31 = Perform Router Discover
    33 = Static Route
    43 = Vendor-Specific Information
End Option
```

In this example, you can see that the client is requesting options 53, 61, 50, 12, 60, and 55. I will further discuss the option fields later in this section.

DHCP Process

The DHCP process contains four packets, each detailing four separate states of the DHCP process. The four states are DISCOVER, OFFER, REQUEST, and ACK.

1. The DISCOVER packet is the first packet a DHCP client sends out. DISCOVER packets are sent to the data link layer broadcast address of FF-FF-FF-FF-FF-FF and contain the source hardware address of the DHCP client. The DISCOVER packet is sent to the IP broadcast address of 255.255.255.255 and uses a source IP address of 0.0.0.0. The 0.0.0.0 address is used because the host has not yet obtained an IP address from the DHCP server.

2. Next, the DHCP server responds with an OFFER packet containing an offer of an IP address and several optional parameter values that either the client requested or were configured to be given out from the DHCP server.

3. If the DHCP client is in agreement with the IP address and associated parameters, it sends back a REQUEST packet indicating that it would like to reserve that IP address and offered options. The DHCP client also sends along other options for which it would like the DHCP server to process.

4. Finally, the DHCP server responds with an ACK packet. This tells the DHCP client that all requested options have been fulfilled and it may start using the IP address and other values immediately.

In Figure 8-2, I show the four packet DHCP processes with the associated option fields for each packet.

No.	Destination	Source	Protocol	Info
1	255.255.255.255	0.0.0.0	DHCP	DHCP Discover - Transaction ID 0x36041a31
2	255.255.255.255	192.168.1.15	DHCP	DHCP Offer - Transaction ID 0x36041a31
3	255.255.255.255	0.0.0.0	DHCP	DHCP Request- Transaction ID 0x36041a31
4	255.255.255.255	192.168.1.15	DHCP	DHCP ACK- Transaction ID 0x36041a31

Frame 1

Option 53: DHCP Message Type = DHCP Discover
Unknown Option Code: 251 (1 byte)
Option 61: Client identifier
Hardware type: Ethernet
Client hardware address: 00:04:5a:76:f3:29
Option 12: Host Name = "KEVIN"
Option 60: Vendor class identifier = "MSFT 5.0"
Option 55: Parameter Request List
1 = Subnet Mask
15 = Domain Name
3 = Router
6 = Domain Name Server
44 = NetBIOS over TCP/IP Name Server
46 = NetBIOS over TCP/IP Node Type
47 = NetBIOS over TCP/IP Scope
31 = Perform Router Discover
33 = Static Route
43 = Vendor-Specific Information
End Option

Frame 2

Option 53: DHCP Message Type = DHCP Offer
Option 1: Subnet Mask = 255.255.255.0
Option 3: Router = 192.168.1.1
Option 6: Domain Name Server
IP Address: 151.197.0.39
IP Address: 151.197.0.38
Option 51: IP Address Lease Time = 1 day
Option 54: Server Identifier = 192.168.1.15
End Option

Frame 3

Option 53: DHCP Message Type = DHCP Request
Option 61: Client identifier
Hardware type: Ethernet
Client hardware address: 00:04:5a:76:f3:29
Option 50: Requested IP Address = 192.168.1.15
Option 54: Server Identifier = 192.168.1.1
Option 12: Host Name = "KEVIN"
Option 81: Client Fully Qualified Domain Name (9 bytes)
Option 60: Vendor class identifier = "MSFT 5.0"
Option 55: Parameter Request List
1 = Subnet Mask
15 = Domain Name
3 = Router
6 = Domain Name Server
44 = NetBIOS over TCP/IP Name Server
46 = NetBIOS over TCP/IP Node Type
47 = NetBIOS over TCP/IP Scope
31 = Perform Router Discover
33 = Static Route
43 = Vendor-Specific Information

Frame 4

Option 53: DHCP Message Type = DHCP ACK
Option 54: Server Identifier = 192.168.1.15
Option 51: IP Address Lease Time = 2 hours
Option 1: Subnet Mask = 255.255.255.0
Option 15: Domain Name = "test.tracemasters.com"
Option 3: Router = 167.26.7.129
Option 6: Domain Name Server
IP Address: 167.26.5.15
IP Address: 167.26.24.28
Option 44: NetBIOS over TCP/IP Name Server
IP Address: 192.168.1.50
IP Address: 192.168.1.55
Option 46: NetBIOS over TCP/IP Node Type = H-node
Option 31: Perform Router Discover = Enabled
Option 81: Client Fully Qualified Domain Name (37 bytes)
End Option

Figure 8-2 DHCP address lease process.

DHCP relies on data link layer broadcasts in order to obtain IP parameters from DHCP servers. During the entire DHCP four-packet process, all frames are sent to the data link broadcast address of FF-FF-FF-FF-FF-FF. Assuming that there are other clients on the same local LAN using DHCP, how is each host able to distinguish which DHCP messages are for it? In Chapter 3, I discuss how every host must process all frames sent to the data link broadcast address. When hosts receive DHCP packets, they look at the value in the Transaction ID field. The value of the Transaction ID field is chosen by the DHCP client and remains the same throughout the entire DHCP process. When the client sees the same value, it knows the DHCP packets are destined for its own local DHCP process.

The fact that DHCP uses data link layer broadcasting as its addressing method presents an interesting problem. You know that routers will not forward Layer 2 broadcast traffic, so how then will DHCP servers on other subnets receive DHCP DISCOVER frames? Do you need to have a DHCP server on every subnet? Actually, no. There is a very simple method of handling DHCP broadcasts in a routed environment. This is done through what is called a DHCP relay agent. DHCP relay agents listen for DHCP broadcasts and forward them as unicasts to the correct DHCP servers. Relay agents are typically configured on routers, allowing them to handle DHCP broadcasts. When a router receives a DHCP broadcast, it forwards the broadcast to a DHCP server as a unicast IP address. Figure 8-3 illustrates the process. In Frame 1, the DHCP client transmits a DHCP Discover packet to both the MAC and IP network layer broadcast address. The DHCP relay agent (enabled on the router) sees the broadcasted Discover packet and forwards it as a unicast IP packet to the DHCP server. When the DHCP server receives the Discover packet, it leases an address to the client and responds with that address in the Offer packet (Frame 2). The Offer packet is also sent as a MAC and IP network-layer broadcast on the client's network. Frame 3 is the Request packet sent by the client to request the offered address from the server. It is also sent as a Layer 2 and 3 broadcast because the client does not yet have an IP address. Frame 4 is the acknowledgment from the server that tells the client it's allowed to use the address it has requested. From this point on, the client is able to "speak" using its own leased IP address. What I haven't yet discussed though about this process is how the DHCP server determines what subnet it should allocate the address from. DHCP servers have the ability to service multiple subnets, so there must be a way for the server to determine on what subnets the clients are located. This requirement is met by functionality in the DHCP relay agent.

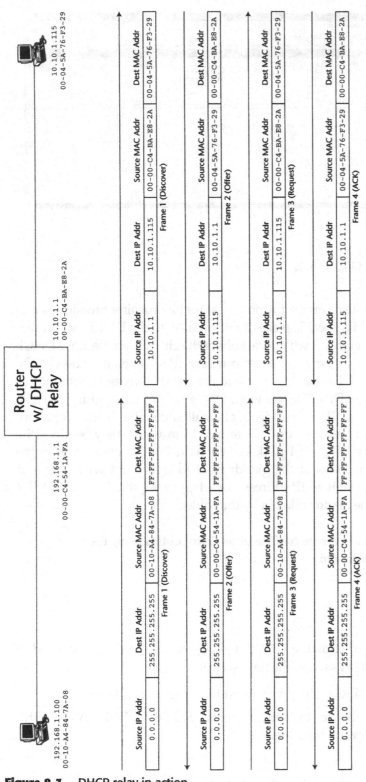

Figure 8-3   DHCP relay in action.

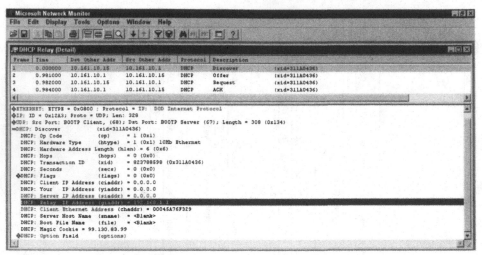

Figure 8-4   Decode of GIADDR field.

DHCP relay agents also serve a purpose besides just turning broadcasts into unicasts. They also add a specific piece of information to the DHCP packet that allows the DHCP server to tell what local subnet the client is on. Because DHCP servers normally service many clients on different IP subnets, they need to be able to figure out from what address scope to hand out addresses. Without this piece of information, the DHCP server would have no idea what address to give the client. In the Gateway IP address field, also called the giaddr field for short, routers will place the IP address of the interface from which they received the DHCP DISCOVER and REQUEST packets. When the DHCP server receives the DISCOVER packets, it looks at the giaddr field to figure out what scope of addresses to lease the client an IP address from. Figure 8-4 shows a DISCOVER packet decode with the giaddr filled in by the router.

TIP DHCP relay agents can be configured on Cisco routers using the IP Helper Address **command.**

DHCP Messages

RFC 2131 specifies the following DHCP message types. They are included in Option 53 (which is discussed in the next section):

- **DHCPDISCOVER.**   Client broadcast to locate available servers

- **DHCPOFFER.**   Server to client in response to DHCPDISCOVER with offer of configuration parameters

- **DHCPREQUEST.** Client message to servers, doing one of the following:

  - Requesting offered parameters from one server and implicitly declining offers from all others

  - Confirming correctness of previously allocated address after, for example, a system reboot

  - Extending the lease on a particular network address

- **DHCPACK.** Server to client with configuration parameters, including a committed network address

- **DHCPNAK.** Server to client indicating client's notion of network address is incorrect (for example, client has moved to new subnet) or client's lease has expired

- **DHCPDECLINE.** Client to server, indicating that a network address is already in use

- **DHCPRELEASE.** Client to server, relinquishing network address and canceling the remaining lease

- **DHCPINFORM.** Client to server, asking only for local configuration parameters; client already has externally configured network address

The first four messages make up the standard DHCP four-packet process, as discussed in the previous section. A server uses DHCP negative acknowledgment messages (NACK) to inform a client that the IP address it is requesting is incorrect. Figure 8-5 shows how the NACK message functions.

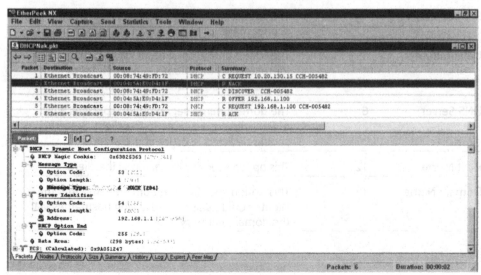

Figure 8-5 DHCP negative acknowledgment (NACK).

In the example, a laptop previously on subnet 10.20.130.0 has been moved to a new subnet of 192.168.1.0. When the laptop boots up, it doesn't know yet that it is on a new subnet and attempts to reacquire its old IP address using the Requested IP Address option. You can see in Frame 1 that the host attempts to request IP address 10.20.130.15. In Frame 2, the DHCP server sends the host a NACK message telling it that this requested address is unacceptable. In Frame 3, the host restarts the DHCP DISCOVER process without requesting an IP address. The process then continues, and the host is handed a proper address of 192.168.1.100 from the server.

DHCP Options

DHCP servers provide information to DHCP clients by the use of the DHCP option fields. At current count the number of DHCP options available totals nearly 100. Luckily, there are only a few that are commonly used. I have included explanations of these options in Table 8-1. All DHCP options are discussed in detail in RFC 2132.

> **TIP** All RFCs can be found at www.ietf.org/rfc.html. Another excellent site, www.zvon.org, provides all RFCs in an easy-to-read format created using XML.

Table 8-1 DHCP Options

OPTION NAME	OPTION NUMBER	EXPLANATION
Subnet Mask	1	The subnet mask option specifies the client's subnet mask.
Default Router	3	The router option specifies a list of IP addresses for routers on the client's subnet. Routers should be listed in order of preference.
DNS Server	6	The domain name server option specifies a list of DNS servers available to the client. Servers should be listed in order of preference.
Host Name	12	This option specifies the name of the client.
Domain Name	15	This option specifies the domain name that the client should use when resolving hostnames via the domain name system.

Table 8-1 *(continued)*

OPTION NAME	OPTION NUMBER	EXPLANATION
Perform Router Discovery	31	This option specifies whether or not the client should solicit routers using the Router Discovery mechanism defined in RFC 1256.
NetBIOS over TCP/IP Name Server Option	44	The NetBIOS name server (NBNS) option specifies a list of RFC 1001/1002 [19] [20] NBNS name servers listed in order of preference.
NetBIOS over TCP/IP Node Type	46	The NetBIOS node type option enables NetBIOS over TCP/IP clients that are configurable to be configured as described in RFC 1001/1002. The value is specified as a single octet that identifies the client type as follows:

		Value	Node Type
		0x1	B-node
		0x2	P-node
		0x4	M-node
		0x8	H-node

OPTION NAME	OPTION NUMBER	EXPLANATION
Requested IP Address	50	This option is used in a client request (DHCPDISCOVER) to enable the client to request that a particular IP address be assigned.
IP Address Lease Time	51	This option is used in a client request (DHCPDISCOVER or DHCPREQUEST) to enable the client to request a lease time for the IP address. In a server reply (DHCPOFFER), a DHCP server uses this option to specify the lease time it is willing to offer.
DHCP Message Type	53	This option is used to convey the type of the DHCP message. The code for this option is 53, and its length is 1. Legal values for this option are as follows:

	Value	Message Type
	1	DHCPDISCOVER
	2	DHCPOFFER
	3	DHCPREQUEST
	4	DHCPDECLINE
	5	DHCPACK
	6	DHCPNAK
	7	DHCPRELEASE

(continued)

Table 8-1 *(continued)*

OPTION NAME	OPTION NUMBER	EXPLANATION
Server Identifier	54	This option is used in DHCPOFFER and DHCPREQUEST messages and might optionally be included in the DHCPACK and DHCPNAK messages. DHCP servers include this option in the DHCPOFFER to allow the client to distinguish between lease offers. DHCP clients indicate which of several lease offers is being accepted by including this option in a DHCPREQUEST message.
Parameter Request List	55	This option is used by a DHCP client to request values for specified configuration parameters. The list of requested parameters is specified as *n* octets, where each octet is a valid DHCP option code as defined in this document.
Vendor Class Identifier	60	This option is used by DHCP clients to optionally identify the type and configuration of a DHCP client. The information is a string of *n* octets, interpreted by servers. Vendors and sites might choose to define specific class identifiers to convey particular configuration or other identification information about a client.
Client Identifier	61	This option is used by DHCP clients to specify their unique identifier. DHCP servers use this value to index their database of address bindings.
Client Fully Qualified Domain Name	81	This option is used to enable the client to convey its FQDN to the server so that the DHCP knows the FQDN for the lease mapping of the clients address.

NOTE During the writing of this section, I noticed another option consistently showing up in my DHCP traces. It was option 251, which strangely enough appears in the private range of DHCP options. RFC 2132 states that the range from 128–254 is reserved for site-specific use. Microsoft apparently is using a DHCP option value out of the private range. Vendors wishing to use a new public DHCP option should refer to RFC 2939, *Procedures and IANA Guidelines for Definition of New DHCP Options and Message Types*. Microsoft apparently chose to implement a new DHCP option type without publishing it.

DHCP Leases

When a DHCP server hands out an IP address to a client, it performs what is called a *lease reservation*. IP addresses contained centrally in the scope definitions of a DHCP are leased out for temporary use by clients. Depending on the size of your network or specific configuration needs, you may use very long or very short DHCP lease times. It is always good to configure your lease times at least for several days in the event that your DHCP server becomes unavailable due to hardware or other failures on the network. Clients will continue to use their addresses until their DHCP leases are up.

Determining how long you have been leased an IP address is easy on a Windows-based computer. Typing **ipconfig /all** shows you your DHCP information as seen in the following example:

```
C:\>ipconfig /all
Windows 2000 IP Configuration
        Host Name . . . . . . . . . . . . . : KEVIN
        Primary DNS Suffix  . . . . . . . :
        Node Type . . . . . . . . . . . . : Broadcast
        IP Routing Enabled. . . . . . . . : Yes
        WINS Proxy Enabled. . . . . . . . : No
Ethernet adapter Local Area Connection:
Connection-specific DNS Suffix  . :
        Description . . . . . . . . . . . : Linksys LNE100TX(v5) Fast
Ethernet Adapter
        Physical Address. . . . . . . . . : 00-04-5A-76-F3-29
        DHCP Enabled. . . . . . . . . . . : Yes
        Autoconfiguration Enabled . . . . : Yes
        IP Address. . . . . . . . . . . . : 192.168.1.103
        Subnet Mask . . . . . . . . . . . : 255.255.255.0
        Default Gateway . . . . . . . . . : 192.168.1.1
        DHCP Server . . . . . . . . . . . : 192.168.1.1
        DNS Servers . . . . . . . . . . . : 151.197.0.39  151.197.0.38
        Lease Obtained. . . . . . . . . . : Saturday, January 11, 2003
8:18:13 PM
        Lease Expires . . . . . . . . . . : Sunday, January 12, 2003
8:18:13 PM
```

In this example it's easy to see that the DHCP server has been configured to lease addresses for one day. Microsoft Windows clients will attempt to renew their DHCP addresses when 50 percent of the lease time has expired. If 87.5 percent of the lease time has expired and the client is unable to renew its address from the original DHCP server, it will attempt to contact any DHCP server to obtain a new address.

NOTE DHCP lease information for Windows 2000 is contained in the registry at

\\HKEY_LOCAL_MACHINE\SYSTEM\CurrentControlSet\Services\Tcpip\
Parameters\Interfaces\<adapter guid>.

Because without an IP address no other protocols can even function, it is critical to ensure that DHCP is working properly. By understanding the processes that occur between DHCP clients, DHCP relay agents, and DHCP servers, you are able to quickly diagnose any issues that arise.

NetBIOS over TCP/IP

I briefly introduced the NetBEUI form of NetBIOS in Chapter 3. NetBEUI ran directly over the data link layer using the services of Logical Link Control type 2. As I discussed in Chapter 3, NetBIOS does not scale very well in large networks due to its flat namespace and problems with excessive broadcasting for name services. NetBIOS over TCP/IP is the next generation of NetBIOS services, allowing NetBIOS to scale on very large networks. NetBIOS uses the transport-layer services of UDP and TCP to provide clients and servers with various session-layer services such as name resolution, name registration, and resource location.

NOTE NetBIOS over TCP/IP concepts and methods are discussed in RFC 1001, while its implementation specifications are discussed in RFC 1002.

The NetBIOS over TCP/IP standards are designed to preserve the functionality of NetBIOS services over a TCP/IP network. NetBIOS over TCP/IP provides three types of services: a session service, a datagram service, and a name service. These three services operate essentially the same over TCP/IP as they do in NetBEUI. It is the flexibility of using a Layer 3 transport protocol to encapsulate NetBIOS frames that allows it to scale to thousands of nodes.

NetBIOS Names

In Microsoft networks using NetBIOS, each host is assigned a specific NetBIOS name called the Computer Name. Whereas a host can have multiple IP addresses on multiple NIC cards, the Computer Name is a unique identifier of the host. NetBIOS names are 16 bytes long.

Microsoft's implementation of NetBIOS, naming reserves the 16th byte of the NetBIOS name for something called the NetBIOS suffix. The NetBIOS suffix is used by Microsoft networking clients and servers to identify specific functionality available on a host. For example, the Windows Workstation service running on host KEVIN would have a NetBIOS name of KEVIN<00>. The following is a list of common NetBIOS suffixes on Microsoft networks.

```
Name                 Suffix(h)  Type  Usage
--------------------------------------------------------------------------
<computername>          00       U    Workstation Service
<computername>          01       U    Messenger Service
```

<\\--__MSBROWSE__>	01	G	Master Browser
<computername>	03	U	Messenger Service
<computername>	06	U	RAS Server Service
<computername>	1F	U	NetDDE Service
<computername>	20	U	File Server Service
<computername>	21	U	RAS Client Service
<computername>	22	U	Microsoft Exchange Interchange(MSMailConnector)
<computername>	23	U	Microsoft Exchange Store
<computername>	24	U	Microsoft Exchange Directory
<computername>	30	U	Modem Sharing Server Service
<computername>	31	U	Modem Sharing Client Service
<computername>	43	U	SMS Clients Remote Control
<computername>	44	U	SMS Administrators Remote Control Tool
<computername>	45	U	SMS Clients Remote Chat
<computername>	46	U	SMS Clients Remote Transfer
<computername>	4C	U	DEC Pathworks TCPIP service on Windows NT
<computername>	42	U	mccaffee anti-virus
<computername>	52	U	DEC Pathworks TCPIP service on Windows NT
<computername>	87	U	Microsoft Exchange MTA
<computername>	6A	U	Microsoft Exchange IMC
<computername>	BE	U	Network Monitor Agent
<computername>	BF	U	Network Monitor Application
<username>	03	U	Messenger Service
<domain>	00	G	Domain Name
<domain>	1B	U	Domain Master Browser
<domain>	1C	G	Domain Controllers
<domain>	1D	U	Master Browser
<domain>	1E	G	Browser Service Elections
<INet~Services>	1C	G	IIS
<IS~computer name>	00	U	IIS
<computername>	[2B]	U	Lotus Notes Server Service
IRISMULTICAST	[2F]	G	Lotus Notes
IRISNAMESERVER	[33]	G	Lotus Notes
Forte_$ND800ZA	[20]	U	DCA IrmaLan Gateway Server Service

There are five types of NetBIOS names.

- **Unique (U).**   The name may have only one IP address assigned to it. On a network device, multiple occurrences of a single name may appear to be registered. The suffix may be the only unique character in the name.

- **Group (G).**   A normal group; the single name may exist with many IP addresses. WINS (Windows Internet Naming Service) responds to a name query on a group name with the limited broadcast address (255.255.255.255). Because routers block the transmission of these addresses, the Internet Group NetBIOS name was designed to service communications between subnets.

- **Multihomed (M).**   The name is unique, but because there are multiple network interfaces on the same computer, this configuration is necessary to permit the registration. The maximum number of addresses is 25.

- **Internet Group (I).**   This is a special configuration of the group name used to manage Windows NT Domain names.

- **Domain Name (D).**   Refers to a Windows NT domain.

NetBIOS names are similar to DNS names in that they are useless to the network layer. For two computers using NetBIOS over TCP/IP to communicate, they must resolve the NetBIOS name to an IP address. Microsoft's method of NetBIOS name resolution is called the Windows Internet Naming Service, or WINS. I talk more about WINS in the section on NetBIOS operations. For now, you just need to know that all NetBIOS names must be resolved to an IP address. After a NetBIOS name is resolved, it is stored in the NetBIOS remote name cache. There are two types of NetBIOS name caches.

- The local cache holds NetBIOS name information specific to the local host.

- The remote cache holds NetBIOS name information that has been resolved for other hosts.

Using the Windows command-line utility called NBTSTAT (see the "NBTSTAT" sidebar), you can query local and remote NetBIOS hosts for the contents of their name cache.

Unlike DNS names, NetBIOS names have no hierarchy. NetBIOS names exist in a single flat namespace very similar to a single DNS domain. Unique NetBIOS names identify a single NetBIOS client, while Group NetBIOS names identify users who share the use of a larger group NetBIOS name or resource. I take a look at how these names interact in the "NetBIOS Operations" section later in this chapter.

NBTSTAT

NBTSTAT is a command-line utiliy available on all Microsoft Windows platforms that allows an administrator to display protocol statistics and NetBIOS over TCP/IP connections. NBTSTAT options are listed below.

```
NBTSTAT [ [-a RemoteName] [-A IP address] [-c] [-n]
         [-r] [-R] [-RR] [-s] [-S] [interval] ]
```

-a (adapter status).   Lists the remote machine's name table given its name

-A (Adapter status).   Lists the remote machine's name table given its IP address

> **-c (cache).** Lists NBT's cache of remote [machine] names and their IP addresses
>
> **-n (names).** Lists local NetBIOS names
>
> **-r (resolved).** Lists names resolved by broadcast and via WINS
>
> **-R (Reload).** Purges and reloads the remote cache name table
>
> **-S (Sessions).** Lists sessions table with the destination IP addresses
>
> **-s (sessions).** Lists sessions table converting destination IP addresses to computer NetBIOS names
>
> **-RR (ReleaseRefresh).** Sends Name Release packets to WINS and then starts Refresh

For example, to view the current NetBIOS services available on the local host, you would type the following:

```
NBTSTAT -n
```

The following is the output from the `nbtstat -n` **command on host KEVIN:**

```
C:\>nbtstat -n

\Device\NetBT_Tcpip_{753BF746-9CBA-4374-AE33-B60DE08CF48A}:
Node IpAddress: [0.0.0.0] Scope Id: []

    No names in cache

Local Area Connection:
Node IpAddress: [192.168.1.103] Scope Id: []

            NetBIOS Local Name Table

    Name               Type         Status
    ---------------------------------------------
    INet~Services  <1C>  GROUP     Registered
    IS~KEVIN.......<00>  UNIQUE    Registered
    KEVIN          <00>  UNIQUE    Registered
    WORKGROUP      <00>  GROUP     Registered
    WORKGROUP      <1E>  GROUP     Registered
    KEVIN          <20>  UNIQUE    Registered
    WORKGROUP      <1D>  UNIQUE    Registered
    .._MSBROWSE__.<01>  GROUP     Registered
```

NetBIOS Services

NetBIOS provides three types of services to upper-layer protocols and applications.

32 bits

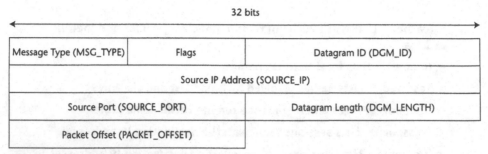

Figure 8-6   NetBIOS datagram header.

- The datagram service is an unreliable service running over UDP. It was designed for use primarily in one-way broadcast-based applications.

- The session service was designed to support end-to-end session services over a reliable transport protocol such as TCP.

- Finally, the name service supports NetBIOS name-to-IP address name resolution. Name services run over UDP.

Datagram Service

The NetBIOS datagram service provides packet transmissions over UDP port 138. Figure 8-6 shows the NetBIOS Datagram Header format.
The Header field definitions are as follows:

- **Message Type (MSG_TYPE).**   Indicates the NetBIOS message type. The following types of messages are specified:
  - 10—DIRECT_UNIQUE DATAGRAM
  - 11—DIRECT_GROUP DATAGRAM
  - 12—BROADCAST DATAGRAM
  - 13—DATAGRAM ERROR
  - 14—DATAGRAM QUERY REQUEST
  - 15—DATAGRAM POSITIVE QUERY RESPONSE
  - 16—DATAGRAM NEGATIVE QUERY RESPONSE
- **Flags.**   Used to specify the NetBIOS node type.
  - 0–3—Reserved
  - 4–5—Node type
    - 00 = B node
    - 01 = P node

> 10 = M node
>
> 11 = NBDD

- 6—FIRST packet flag
- 7—MORE flag

- **Datagram ID (DGM_ID).** Unique identifier of datagram
- **Source IP Address (SOURCE_IP).** IP address of host sending datagram
- **Source Port (SOURCE_PORT).** Source UDP port of host sending datagram
- **Datagram Length (DGM_LENGTH).** Length of datagram
- **Packet Offset (PACKET_OFFSET).** Used to specify data offset in consecutive packets. Usually set to zero.

The decode that follows shows the NetBIOS datagram service being used in the sending of a MSBrowse Host Announcement.

```
NetBIOS Datagram Service - Network Basic Input/Output System
    Packet Type:           0x11  Direct Group Datagram
    Flags:                 0x02  First Fragment  No More Fragments  B-Node
    Datagram ID:           0x8047
    Source IP Address:     10.29.4.109
    Source Port Number:    138  netbios-dgm
    Datagram Length:       187
    Packet Offset:         0
    Source Name:           TANYA <20>  Server Service
    Destination Name:      MOIRAVE <1D>  Master Browser Backup
```

Notice that the packet type is a Direct Group Datagram, indicating that the packet's data is destined for more than one person. The first fragment indicator shows that this is the only data being sent. If a host were sending more data than could fit into a single packet, it would indicate that more fragments are present. Also, notice that the sender's IP address is present in the datagram packet along with the source and destination NetBIOS names with their suffixes. Microsoft utilizes the NetBIOS datagram service for unreliable operations, such as the one-way broadcasting of host announcements.

Session Service

The NetBIOS session service provides packet transmissions over TCP port 139. Figure 8-7 shows the NetBIOS session header format.

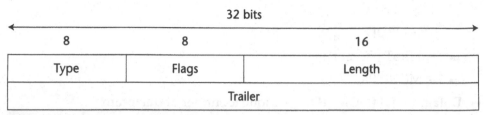

Figure 8-7   NetBIOS session header.

The Header field definitions are as follows:

- **Type.**   Identifies the type of session packet.
  - 00—SESSION MESSAGE
  - 81—SESSION REQUEST
  - 82—POSITIVE SESSION RESPONSE
  - 83—NEGATIVE SESSION RESPONSE
  - 84—RETARGET SESSION RESPONSE
  - 85—SESSION KEEP ALIVE
- **Flags.**   Used to indicate a longer length header.
  - 0–6—Reserved (must be zero)
  - 7—Length extension bit
- **Length.**   Length of the session packet after the length field.
- **Trailer.**   Dependent on session message type.

The NetBIOS session service is used strictly for communication between two NetBIOS hosts. Microsoft's implementation of the session service is over TCP. When two hosts are using NetBIOS over TCP/IP to transfer data, the data is referred to as NetBIOS data. The reason behind this is that the application, such as Server Message Block (SMB), hands down large chunks of data to the NetBIOS layer. It is then the job of NetBIOS to hand down smaller maximum-segment-sized (MSS) chunks to the TCP layer for transmission. The first packet of a large data transmission always indicates the data is NetBIOS data, as shown in the following trace:

```
NetBIOS Session Service - Network Basic Input/Output System
    Packet Type:         0x00  Session Message  [54]
    Flags:               0x00  Length Extension Off  [55]
    Length:              2916
```

If you look at the Length field, it is immediately obvious that 2,916 bytes of data isn't going to fit into a single Ethernet packet. This is the entire amount of NetBIOS data to be transferred to the destination host, so the first 1,460 bytes of data will be sent in one packet, while the remaining 1,456 bytes will be sent in the next packet.

32 bits

Transaction ID (16)		OP-Code (5)	Flags (7)	Response Code (4)
Question Count (16)		Answer Count (16)		
Authority Records Count (16)		Additional Records Count (16)		

Figure 8-8   NetBIOS name service header.

Name Service

NetBIOS name services are known in the Microsoft arena as the Windows Internet Naming Service (WINS). WINS is a method of providing name resolution services for NetBIOS by the implementation of a centralized NetBIOS name server. NetBIOS name services run on UDP port 137. The header format is shown in Figure 8-8.

NOTE WINS is just another name for the NetBIOS name service.

The header fields are defined as follows:

- **Transaction ID (NAME_TRN_ID).**   Transaction ID for Name Service Transaction.
- **OP-Code (OP_CODE).**   Packet type code.
  - Bit 0
    - 0 = Request
    - 1 = Response
  - Bit 1–4
    - 0 = Query
    - 5 = Registration
    - 6 = Release
    - 7 = WACK
    - 8 = Refresh
- **Flags (NM_FLAGS).**   Operation flags.
  - Bit 0—Authority Answer Flag
  - Bit 1—Truncation Flag
  - Bit 2—Recursion Desired Flag
  - Bit 3—Recursion Available Flag

- Bit 4

    0 = Unicast

    1 = Broadcast/Multicast

- **Response Code (RCODE).**   Response code of the request.

    - FMT_ERR: 0x1 = Format error. (Invalid Request Format.)

    - SRV_ERR: 0x2 = Server failure. (Name server cannot process name.)

    - NAM_ERR: 0x3 = Name error. (Name requested does not exist.)

    - IMP_ERR: 0x4 = Unsupported request error.

    - RFS_ERR: 0x5 = Refused Error. (Cannot register or release name due to policy reasons.)

    - ACT_ERR: 0x6 = Active error. (Name owned by another node.)

    - CFT_ERR: 0x7 = Name in conflict error. (Unique name owned by more than one node.)

- **Question Count (QDCOUNT).**   Number of entries in the question section of the name service packet.

- **Answer Count (ANCOUNT).**   Number of resource records in the answer section of the name service packet.

- **Authority Records Count (NSCOUNT).**   Number of authoritative resource records in the authority section of the name service packet.

- **Additional Records Count (ARCOUNT).**   Number of additional resource records in the additional records section of the name service packet.

As mentioned previously, the NetBIOS name service and WINS are the same thing. WINS functions almost identically to DNS with just a few additions to the header fields to incorporate NetBIOS. In fact, early decodes of WINS actually showed it as DNS. The same concepts referring to the functioning to DNS can be applied to WINS. The only difference is that WINS is a flat namespace. It has no hierarchy like DNS does.

NetBIOS Operations

Now, that I have discussed the three types of NetBIOS services, I am going to examine their operations in real-life Microsoft networks. I will discuss the NetBIOS operations in order of dependence.

1. First, I discuss the name service operations because the other two services cannot even operate without proper NetBIOS-to-IP-address name resolution.

2. Next, I discuss the NetBIOS session services and how sessions are used between hosts to transfer data.

3. Last, I discuss what uses the NetBIOS datagram service has and how Microsoft uses it.

Name Service Operations

NetBIOS name services provide a mapping between NetBIOS Computer Names and IP addresses. Depending on the network configuration, NetBIOS name services operate in either unicast or broadcast mode. There are five types of name service operations:

- Registration
- Query
- Release
- Wait Acknowledgment (WACK)
- Refresh

Each name service operation uses a slightly different header format, discussed in the following respective operations sections.

Name Registration

NetBIOS Name Registration services guarantee that a host is using a unique NetBIOS name. In a broadcast NetBIOS environment, Microsoft nodes, on bootup, send out name registration requests to the data link broadcast address. The broadcasts are not really requests per say, but simply notifications to other hosts that a station wishes to use a specific NetBIOS name. Figure 8-9 shows a host sending three Name Registration frames.

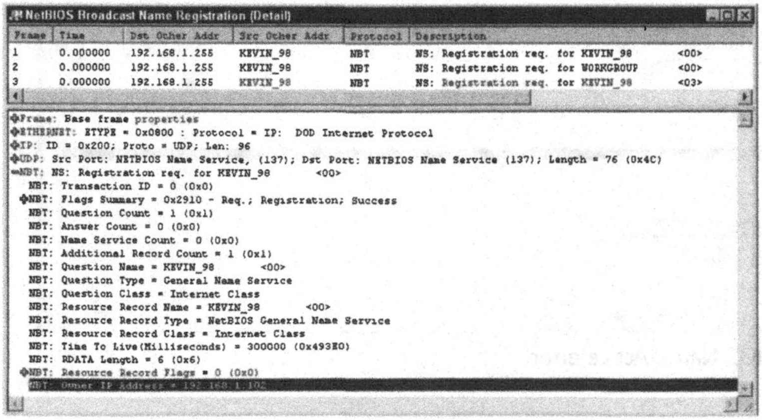

Figure 8-9   NetBIOS Name Registration trace.

Although you can't see the detail of all three packets, the host KEVIN_98 is actually registering three separate NetBIOS names. The first name, KEVIN_98<00>, is for the Workstation service, the second one is for a workgroup simply called WORKGROUP, and the third one is KEVIN_98<03>, for the Microsoft Messenger service. All Microsoft clients will register each individual NetBIOS service they have running locally. In the case of this example though, the registrations are really just notifications to other hosts that the client is using the services.

Figure 8-10 shows what happens when a Microsoft Windows client attempts to use a Computer Name that is already being used by another host. When a host with IP address 192.168.1.102 attempts to register the NetBIOS name of KEVIN, the host using that name (that is, host Kevin) responds with a Name Active error. This tells the host that another computer is already configured with the NetBIOS name it was trying to use. It is important to make sure that all Computer Names on a Microsoft network are unique.

Name Query

Name queries are used to resolve NetBIOS names to IP addresses. NetBIOS name queries are very similar to DNS queries except that they are resolving NetBIOS names instead of DNS hostnames. Each NetBIOS name query contains the following sections:

Figure 8-10   NetBIOS Name Active error.

- ■ **QUESTION_NAME.** The NETBIOS name queried for resolution.
- ■ **QUESTION_TYPE.** The type of request.
  - ■ **NB (0x0020)**—General Name Service Resource Record.
  - ■ **NBSTAT (0x0021)**—NetBIOS Node Status Resource Record.
- ■ **QUESTION_CLASS.** The class of the request is always IN 0x0001 Internet class.

Figure 8-11 shows a decode trace of a NetBIOS name query.

1. In Frame 1 host HENRY broadcasts a Name Query for the IP address of host KEVIN.

2. Host KEVIN upon receiving the broadcast recognizes its own computer name in the question section.

3. Host KEVIN then ARPs for the MAC address of host HENRY and sends its own IP address in a name response packet (Frame 4).

In this example the name queries are sent to the data link broadcast address and also the IP subnet broadcast address. This is because there is no centralized WINS servers. WINS servers as mentioned previously maintain a centralized database of NetBIOS name to IP resolutions. Name queries, whether they are sent to a WINS server or broadcasted out onto the local LAN, are essentially the same.

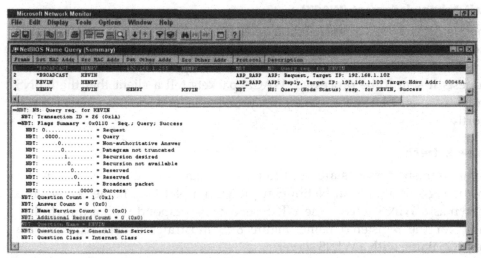

Figure 8-11 NetBIOS name query trace.

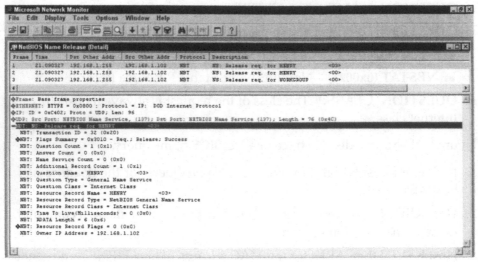

Figure 8-12   NetBIOS Name Release.

Name Release

NetBIOS Name Release messages are used when a host has finished using a NetBIOS name. Release frames notify all hosts that the name is available for use. Figure 8-12 shows host HENRY broadcasting a Name Release packet during its shutdown process.

Wait Acknowledgment (WACK)

The NetBIOS WACK message type is used specifically in environments that use a centralized NetBIOS name server (NBNS). The WACK message is used to tell a client that it needs to wait a longer time period for the name service requests it sent to be processed. WACK packets tell a client that the NBNS server is available but currently busy and will service the name request shortly.

Name Refresh

Name Refresh messages are used to refresh a currently used name. When a host is registering a local NetBIOS name with a NetBIOS name server (also known as a WINS server), the WINS server will respond with a time-to-live value for the registered name. Figure 8-13 illustrates a host registering a NetBIOS name with a WINS server.

In Frame 3, the host receives a positive registration response telling it that it should cache the NetBIOS name for 518400 seconds (6 days, the Windows 2000 default) before sending a Name Refresh message to the WINS server.

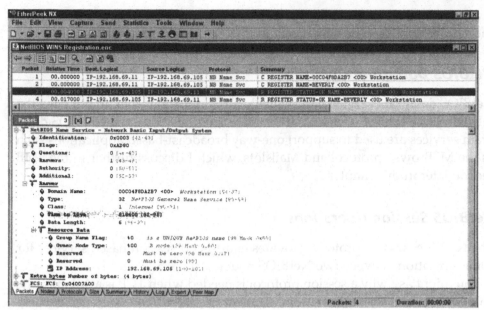

Figure 8-13 WINS registration.

NOTE If you are using Microsoft NetMon, you need to disregard the milliseconds notation next to the Time to Live field in the response packet. NetMon incorrectly reports the field as milliseconds, when it should be reported as seconds.

NetBIOS Node Types

Depending on the name resolution used by a NetBIOS client, the client can be categorized as one of four NetBIOS node types.

- **B-node.** This type of node uses broadcasts only for NetBIOS name resolution.

- **H-node.** First checks the WINS server for NetBIOS names; if the WINS server cannot resolve the name, the host sends a broadcast to try to resolve the NetBIOS name.

- **M-node.** Uses a broadcast first to check for NetBIOS names; if there is no response to the broadcast resolution, the host queries the WINS server.

- **P-node.** Queries only the WINS server for NetBIOS names; does not use broadcasts.

Hosts can be configured for a specific node type by DHCP servers by using the NetBIOS over TCP/IP Node Type Option 46. In Microsoft environments using WINS, the recommended node type is H-node because the client will always attempt to first use the WINS server and then fall back to using broadcasts if the WINS server is unavailable.

NetBIOS Datagram Operations

NetBIOS datagram services are available for applications that do not need the reliability of protocol such as TCP. In Microsoft networks, the NetBIOS datagram services are used to support one-way broadcast-based applications such as the MSBrowse protocol and Mailslots, which I discuss further in the SMB section later in this chapter.

NetBIOS Session Operations

The NetBIOS session protocol provides end-to-end session-based services for communication between two NetBIOS nodes.

You might ask why a session protocol is needed when TCP is available. The answer is it isn't. The main reason Microsoft uses NetBIOS is because of backwards compatibility with older systems. All original Microsoft networking clients, such as LAN Manager and LAN Server, ran over NetBIOS. By running NetBIOS over TCP/IP, Microsoft was able to keep their legacy networking architecture without having to wholly rewrite it for TCP/IP. There are six NetBIOS session packet types.

- Session Request
- Positive Session Response
- Negative Session Response
- Session Message
- Retarget Session Response
- Session Keep Alive

NOTE A Microsoft Active Directory environment in native mode no longer uses NetBIOS; instead it runs directly on top of TCP using port 445.

Session Request

Before any type of reliable data transport can occur between two NetBIOS nodes, a session setup needs to be performed. Figure 8-14 shows the events that take place during a NetBIOS session setup.

After name resolution is complete, the TCP layer must perform its three-way handshake because the NetBIOS session protocol runs over TCP. Once the TCP connection is active, the originating node can send a NetBIOS session request to the destination. Once the destination responds with a positive session response, the host can begin running whatever upper-layer protocol over NetBIOS it needs to.

Positive Session Response

Positive session responses indicate that the NetBIOS session was successfully set up and that the client may proceed with its next action. The following is a positive session response decode from EtherPeek NX.

```
NetBIOS Session Service - Network Basic Input/Output System
    Packet Type:        0x82  Positive Session Response  [54]
    Flags:              0x00  Length Extension Off  [55]
    Length:             0
```

Negative Session Response

Negative session responses are exactly the opposite of positive session responses. They indicate that the NetBIOS session was not set up successfully. NetBIOS session response messages have the following error codes associated with them:

80—Not listening on called name

81—Not listening for calling name

82—Called name not present

83—Called name present, but insufficient resources

8F—Unspecified error

The case study dealing with negative session response, later in this chapter, illustrates the usefulness of this message.

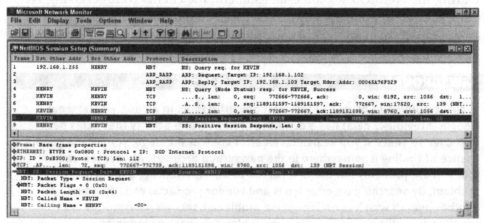

Figure 8-14 NetBIOS session setup.

Session Message

Session messages consist of the data that NetBIOS is carrying. When an upper-layer protocol such as SMB wants to transmit data across the network, it actually hands down large blocks of data to the NetBIOS layer. It then is NetBIOS's responsibility for segmenting that data into blocks to hand down to TCP. In the case of SMB handing down 7,300 bytes of data to NetBIOS, NetBIOS would then hand down five segments of 1,460 bytes each to TCP ($1,460 \times 5 = 7,300$).

Retarget Session Response

Retarget messages are used to redirect (retarget) a user to a different TCP port. This message gives an administrator the flexibility to run NetBIOS over non-standard ports.

Session Keep Alive

NetBIOS session keep alives are useful to keep a NetBIOS session open between two hosts. When a client makes a connection to a shared resource on a server, it will send a session Keep Alive message once an hour in order to keep the session alive.

Case Study: Negative Session Response

During a routine server migration project, it was brought to my attention that users were having problems accessing their mapped drives on a particular Windows 2000 server. Because the servers were located behind network load balancers and a firewall, my initial inclination was that one of the two could have been preventing users from accessing server resources. Not being one for guesswork, I performed a packet capture while one of the administrators attempted to connect to a shared directory on the server. Figure 8-15 illustrates what the packet capture showed.

During the NetBIOS session establishment, the clients were receiving NetBIOS Session Refused messages. You can see in the figure that the expert mode does a nice job of pointing this out for us. Looking into the decode of the

---

NEWSGROUPS

Newsgroups can be one of the most powerful tools in an analyst's arsenal. Google (previously deja) has a database of newsgroup activity that dates back well over 15 years. If you search on an error code or message, you have a good chance of finding it somewhere in the newsgroup archives. Always remember that you are probably not the first person to be experiencing a particular problem. By searching on error types and vendor products, you often find another person who has had the same problem. Users on newsgroups are usually very willing to assist you with problems you are experiencing.

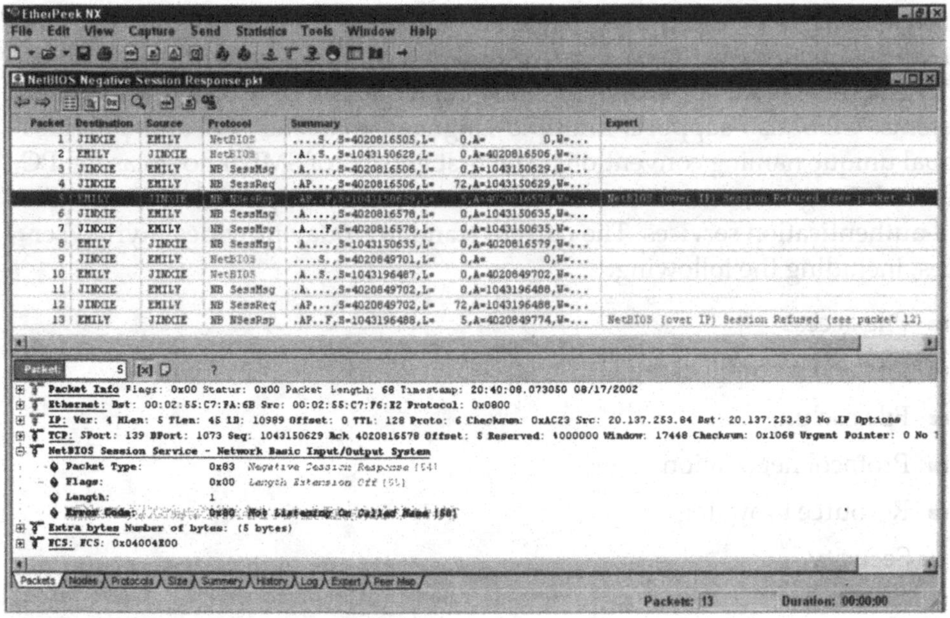

Figure 8-15   Negative session response.

response frame, you can see that the error code is 0x80, Not Listening on
Called Name. What exactly did this mean? Not being an expert on Windows
2000 server administration, I turned to one of the greatest tools at an analyst's
disposal: Google Groups. Google Groups (groups.google.com) contains a
huge database of messages posted on all major newsgroups over the last 10
years. By searching on the error message, I found out that it occurs when file
and print sharing are not enabled on a Windows NT or 2000 server. I checked
with the server administrators, and they confirmed that file and print sharing
had inadvertently been disabled. This example goes to show how powerful a
simple error code can be in the problem-solving process.

Server Message Block

Server Message Block (SMB) is a cross-platform application-layer protocol
used for file, database, and resource access, and authentication. Although
widely popularized by Microsoft, SMB is available on a variety of platforms
such as IBM, Banyan and Vines, and in the Unix flavor SAMBA. Newer versions of SMB are better known as the Common Internet File System (CIFS).
CIFS is simply an updated marketing term for SMB.

NOTE In this text, I refer to the protocol as either SMB or CIFS interchangably.

SMB's many extensions have created a synergistic file-sharing protocol that allows interactions between many different vendors' systems. The goal of CIFS is to enable all applications to open and share files across multivendor systems. CIFS also supports multiple language character sets and provides global unique naming conventions. The first version of SMB, known as the PC Network Program, contained a core set of services that provided simple file and authentication services. The current standard today provides myriad services, including the following:

- File access
- File and record locking
- File caching
- Protocol negotiation
- Resource browsing
- Security

SMB Header

All SMB packets use the same basic header shown in Figure 8-16. The SMB header always starts with the characters SMB in the header.

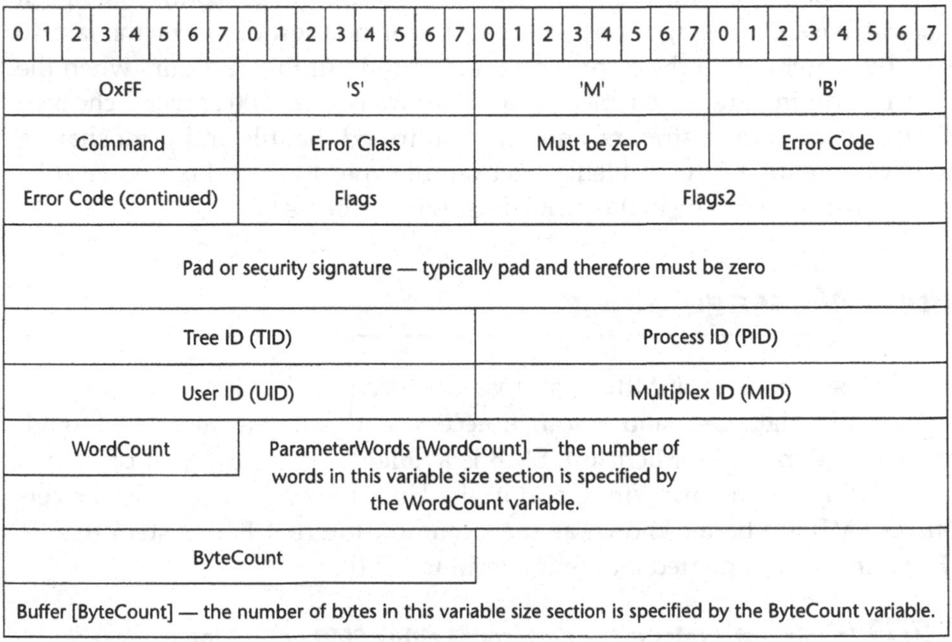

0 1 2 3 4 5 6 7	0 1 2 3 4 5 6 7	0 1 2 3 4 5 6 7	0 1 2 3 4 5 6 7
OxFF	'S'	'M'	'B'
Command	Error Class	Must be zero	Error Code
Error Code (continued)	Flags	Flags2	
Pad or security signature — typically pad and therefore must be zero			
Tree ID (TID)		Process ID (PID)	
User ID (UID)		Multiplex ID (MID)	
WordCount	ParameterWords [WordCount] — the number of words in this variable size section is specified by the WordCount variable.		
ByteCount			
Buffer [ByteCount] — the number of bytes in this variable size section is specified by the ByteCount variable.			

Figure 8-16 The SMB header.

The various fields are as follows:

- **0xFF.** The beginning of every SMB packet contains a 4-byte indicator of 0xFF following the characters "SMB."
- **Command.** One-byte code indicating the SMB packet type.
- **Error Class.** Indicates the class of error. Set to zero if success.
  - **ERRDOS (0x01).** Error is from the core DOS operating system set
  - **ERRSRV (0x02).** Error is generated by the server network file manager
  - **ERRHRD (0x03).** Hardware error
  - **ERRCMD (0xFF).** Command was not in the SMB format
- **Error Code.** Indicates the type of error that has occurred. Set to zero if no error.
- **Error Code.** Used for 32-bit error messages. Status code field.
- **Flags.** Most of the flags are for obsolete LANMAN 1.0 functions with the exception of 3, which is used for indicating case-sensitive path-names, and 7, the Request/Response flag.
  - 0—Reserved for obsolescent requests.
  - 1—Reserved (must be zero).
  - 2—Reserved (must be zero).
  - 3—When on, all pathnames in this SMB must be treated as caseless. When off, the pathnames are case sensitive.
  - 4—Canonical filename indicator (obsolescent).
  - 5—Opportunistic locks request (obsolescent).
  - 6—Modification notification (obsolescent).
  - 7—Request/response flag (Request = 0, Response = 1).
- **Flags2.** More specific options chosen by the host sending the request or response.
  - 0—If set in a request, the server may return long components in pathnames in the response.
  - 1—If set, the client is aware of extended attributes.
  - 11—If set, the client is aware of extended security.
  - 12—If set, any request pathnames in this SMB should be resolved in the Distributed File System.
  - 13—If set, indicates that a read will be permitted if the client does not have read permission, but does have execute permission. This

flag is useful only on a read request.

- 14—If set, specifies that the returned error code is a 32-bit error code in Status.Status. Otherwise the Status.DosError.ErrorClass and Status.DosError.Error fields contain the DOS-style error information. When the use of NT status codes is negotiated, this flag should be set for every SMB.

- 15—If set, any fields of data type STRING in this SMB message are encoded as UNICODE. Otherwise, they are in ASCII.

- **Pad/Security Signature.**   Reserved for use of security signature, otherwise set to all zeros.

- **Tree ID (TID).**   Identifies the resource that this packet is referring to.

- **Process ID (PID).**   Identifies which process is issuing the SMB request on the client.

- **User ID (UID).**   Identifies the user who is issuing SMB requests on the client side.

- **Multiplex ID (MID).**   Used to allow multiple outstanding client requests to exist without confusion.

- **WordCount.**   Indicates length of ParameterWords field.

- **ParameterWords.**   Contains command-specific data.

- **ByteCount.**   Indicates length of Buffer field.

- **Buffer.**   Holds variable amount of command or response data.

The fields in the SMB header are used differently, depending on whether the SMB packet is a request or a response (indicated by the Request/Response flag). The Command field specifies the exact SMB command that is in use (SMB commands are discussed in the next section). The Flags fields notify servers and clients of SMB options specific to the version of SMB running on the host. The TID, PID, UID, and MID fields all work together to identify users and the resources they are accessing. The WordCount, ParameterWords, Byte-Count, and Buffer fields all serve as pointers for any subcommands or data that SMB is carrying. I will discuss the specifics of some of the header fields in the "SMB Operations Analysis" section later in the chapter.

SMB Commands

SMB commands are organized into top-level commands and subcommands. A top-level command will specify the subcommand below it, and the subcommand will specify any subcommands below it. The commands used by SMB depend on the type of operation being performed. For example, opening a file uses the SMB_COM_NT_CREATE_ANDX command, while closing a file will use the SMB_COM_CLOSE command. The type of operation stipulates the command. Table 8-2 shows a complete list of commands in the SMB specification.

Table 8-2 SMB Command Codes

COMMAND	CODE
SMB COMMAND CODES	
SMB_COM_CREATE_DIRECTORY	0x00
SMB_COM_DELETE_DIRECTORY	0x01
SMB_COM_OPEN	0x02
SMB_COM_CREATE	0x03
SMB_COM_CLOSE	0x04
SMB_COM_FLUSH	0x05
SMB_COM_DELETE	0x06
SMB_COM_RENAME	0x07
SMB_COM_QUERY_INFORMATION	0x08
SMB_COM_SET_INFORMATION	0x09
SMB_COM_READ	0x0A
SMB_COM_WRITE	0x0B
SMB_COM_LOCK_BYTE_RANGE	0x0C
SMB_COM_UNLOCK_BYTE_RANGE	0x0D
SMB_COM_CREATE_TEMPORARY	0x0E
SMB_COM_CREATE_NEW	0x0F
SMB_COM_CHECK_DIRECTORY	0x10
SMB_COM_PROCESS_EXIT	0x11
SMB_COM_SEEK	0x12
SMB_COM_LOCK_AND_READ	0x13
SMB_COM_WRITE_AND_UNLOCK	0x14
SMB_COM_READ_RAW	0x1A
SMB_COM_READ_MPX	0x1B
SMB_COM_READ_MPX_SECONDARY	0x1C
SMB_COM_WRITE_RAW	0x1D

(continued)

Table 8-2 *(continued)*

COMMAND	CODE
SMB COMMAND CODES	
SMB_COM_WRITE_MPX	0x1E
SMB_COM_WRITE_COMPLETE	0x20
SMB_COM_SET_INFORMATION2	0x22
SMB_COM_QUERY_INFORMATION2	0x23
SMB_COM_LOCKING_ANDX	0x24
SMB_COM_TRANSACTION	0x25
SMB_COM_TRANSACTION_SECONDARY	0x26
SMB_COM_IOCTL	0x27
SMB_COM_IOCTL_SECONDARY	0x28
SMB_COM_COPY	0x29
SMB_COM_MOVE	0x2A
SMB_COM_ECHO	0x2B
SMB_COM_WRITE_AND_CLOSE	0x2C
SMB_COM_OPEN_ANDX	0x2D
SMB_COM_READ_ANDX	0x2E
SMB_COM_WRITE_ANDX	0x2F
SMB_COM_CLOSE_AND_TREE_DISC	0x31
SMB_COM_TRANSACTION2	0x32
SMB_COM_TRANSACTION2_SECONDARY	0x33
SMB_COM_FIND_CLOSE2	0x34
SMB_COM_FIND_NOTIFY_CLOSE	0x35
SMB_COM_TREE_CONNECT	0x70
SMB_COM_TREE_DISCONNECT	0x71
SMB_COM_NEGOTIATE	0x72
SMB_COM_SESSION_SETUP_ANDX	0x73
SMB_COM_LOGOFF_ANDX	0x74
SMB_COM_TREE_CONNECT_ANDX	0x75
SMB_COM_QUERY_INFORMATION_DISK	0x80
SMB_COM_SEARCH	0x81

Table 8-2   *(continued)*

COMMAND	CODE
SMB COMMAND CODES	
SMB_COM_FIND	0x82
SMB_COM_FIND_UNIQUE	0x83
SMB_COM_NT_TRANSACT	0xA0
SMB_COM_NT_TRANSACT_SECONDARY	0xA1
SMB_COM_NT_CREATE_ANDX	0xA2
SMB_COM_NT_CANCEL	0xA4
SMB_COM_OPEN_PRINT_FILE	0xC0
SMB_COM_WRITE_PRINT_FILE	0xC1
SMB_COM_CLOSE_PRINT_FILE	0xC2
SMB_COM_GET_PRINT_QUEUE	0xC3
SMB_COM_READ_BULK	0xD8
SMB_COM_WRITE_BULK	0xD9
SMB_COM_WRITE_BULK_DATA	0xDA
SMB_COM_TRANSACTION2 SUBCOMMAND CODES	
TRANS2_OPEN2	0x00
TRANS2_FIND_FIRST2	0x01
TRANS2_FIND_NEXT2	0x02
TRANS2_QUERY_FS_INFORMATION	0x03
Reserved	0x04
TRANS2_QUERY_PATH_INFORMATION	0x05
TRANS2_SET_PATH_INFORMATION	0x06
TRANS2_QUERY_FILE_INFORMATION	0x07
TRANS2_SET_FILE_INFORMATION	0x08
TRANS2_FSCTL	0x09
TRANS2_IOCTL2	0x0A
TRANS2_FIND_NOTIFY_FIRST	0x0B
TRANS2_FIND_NOTIFY_NEXT	0x0C
TRANS2_CREATE_DIRECTORY	0x0D

(continued)

Table 8-2   *(continued)*

COMMAND	CODE
SMB_COM_TRANSACTION2 SUBCOMMAND CODES	
TRANS2_SESSION_SETUP	0x0E
TRANS2_GET_DFS_REFERRAL	0x10
TRANS2_REPORT_DFS_INCONSISTENCY	0x11
SMB_COM_NT_TRANSACTION SUBCOMMAND CODES	
NT_TRANSACT_IOCTL	2
NT_TRANSACT_SET_SECURITY_DESC	3
NT_TRANSACT_NOTIFY_CHANGE	4
NT_TRANSACT_RENAME	5
NT_TRANSACT_QUERY_SECURITY_DESC	6

SMB Responses

SMB responses contain specific data, depending on the command. They also contain four classes of error codes that indicate the general success or failure of a command. Figure 8-17 shows the four classes of errors and their respective error codes. Error codes also show up as 32-bit status codes of which there are too many to list in this chapter. I have included a listing of an 32-bit SMB codes in Appendix B.

The following case study concerning directory access illustrates the use of SMB status codes.

Many times when I am unable to access a directory on a network server, I run a protocol trace to find out what the server's response is to my request. In this case, I was able to see a share on an NT server but was unable to access the directories within it. Figure 8-18 shows how easily you can determine the nature of a problem by looking at the SMB status codes.

Take a look at Frame 11. It contains a type of status code called a DOS Error. DOS Error codes were left over from the early days of Microsoft's LANMAN server product and are still sparsely used in NT servers. So in this case, rather than a 32-bit status code, I have received a DOS Error code, which, if you look into the detail of the packet, is Access Denied. No wonder I could not access the directories under the share. Armed with this information I was able to call the help desk and get a quick resolution to my access problem. Understanding these simple status codes, such as the Access Denied message, can save you hours of guesswork when attempting to resolve server communication problems.

SUCCESS Class

Class	Code	Comment
SUCCESS	0	The request was successful.

Error	Code	Description
ERRerror	1	Non-specific error code
ERRbadpw	2	Bad password
ERRaccess	4	The client does not have the necessary access rights
ERRinvtid	5	The Tid specified in a command was invalid.
ERRinvnetname	6	Invalid network name in tree connect.
ERRinvdevice	7	Invalid device
ERRqfull	49	Print queue full
ERRqtoobig	50	Print queue full -- no space.
ERRqeof	51	EOF on print queue dump.
ERRinvpfid	52	Invalid print file FID.
ERRsmbcmd	64	The server did not recognize the command received.
ERRsrverror	65	The server encountered an internal error, e.g., system file unavailable.
ERRbadBID	66	(obsolete)
ERRfilespecs	67	The Fid and pathname parameters contained an invalid combination of values.
ERRbadLink	68	(obsolete)
ERRbadpermits	69	The access permissions specified for a file or directory are not a valid combination.
ERRbadPID	70	
ERRsetattrmode	71	The attribute mode in the Set File Attribute request is invalid.
ERRpaused	81	Server is paused. (Reserved for messaging)
ERRmsgoff	82	Not receiving messages. (Reserved for messaging)
ERRnoroom	83	No room to buffer message.(Reserved for messaging)
ERRrmuns	87	Too many remote user names.(Reserved for messaging)
ERRtimeout	88	Operation timed out.
ERRnoresource	89	No resources currently available for request.
ERRtoomanyuids	90	Too many Uids active on this session.
ERRbaduid	91	The Uid is not known as a valid user identifier on this session.
ERRusempx	250	Temporarily unable to support Raw, use MPX mode.
ERRusestd	251	Temporarily unable to support Raw, use standard read/write.
ERRcontmpx	252	Continue in MPX mode.
ERRbadPassword	254	(obsolete)
ERR_NOTIFY_ENUM_DIR	1024	Too many files have changed since the last time a NT_TRANSACT_NOTIFY_CHANGE was issued
ERRaccountExpired	2239	
ERRbadClient	2240	Cannot access the server from this workstation.
ERRbadLogonTime	2241	Cannot access the server at this time.
ERRpasswordExpired	2242	
ERRnosupport	65535	Function not supported.

ERRDOS Class

Error	Code	Description
ERRbadfunc	1	Invalid function.
ERRbadfile	2	File not found
ERRbadpath	3	Directory invalid
ERRnofids	4	Too many open files
ERRnoaccess	5	Access denied,
ERRbadfid	6	Invalid file handle.
ERRbadmcb	7	Memory control blocks destroyed.
ERRnomem	8	Insufficient server memory to perform the requested function.
ERRbadmem	9	Invalid memory block address.
ERRbadenv	10	Invalid environment.
ERRbadformat	11	Invalid format.
ERRbadaccess	12	Invalid open mode.
ERRbaddata	13	Invalid data
ERRbaddrive	15	Invalid drive specified.
ERRremcd	16	A Delete Directory request attempted to remove the server's current directory.
ERRdiffdevice	17	Not same device (e.g., a cross volume rename was attempted)
ERRnofiles	18	A File Search command can find no more files matching the specified criteria.
ERRbadshare	32	The sharing mode specified for an Open conflicts with existing FIDs on the file.
ERRlock	33	A Lock request conflicted with an existing lock or specified an invalid mode, or an Unlock requested attempted to remove a lock held by another process.
ERRfilexists	80	The file named in the request already exists.
ErrQuota	512	The operation would cause a quota limit to be exceeded.
ErrNotALink	513	A link operation was performed on a pathname that was not a link

Figure 8-17 SMB error codes.

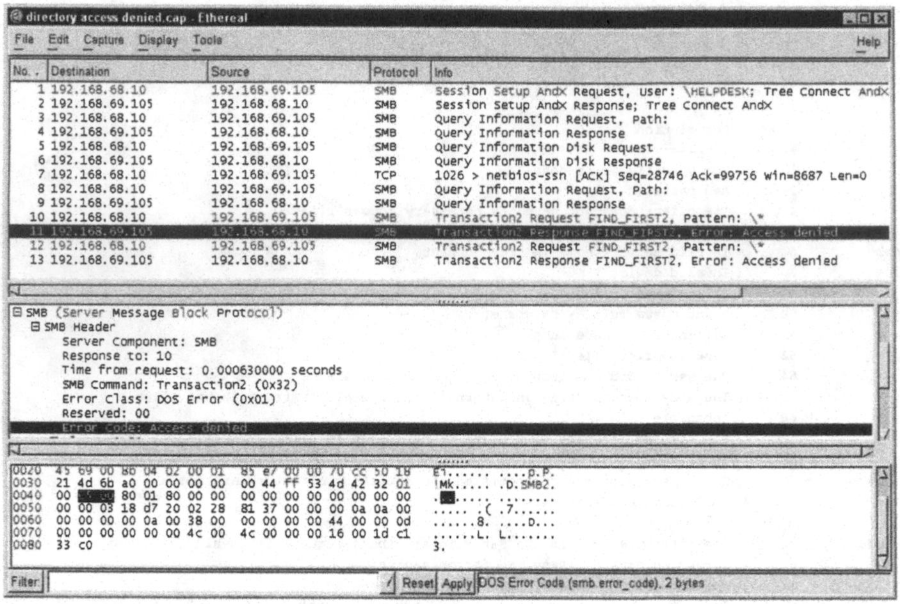

Figure 8-18   SMB status code—Access Denied.

> **NOTE**   Microsoft SMB uses two levels of file security, share level and user level. Share level security applies only to a shared resource, such as a printer or directory. User level rights can override share level rights, which can make troubleshooting difficult because share rights and user level rights can differ.

> **CROSS-REFERENCE**   Please refer to Appendix B for a full listing of SMB status codes.

SMB Operations Analysis

SMB is probably one of the most complex protocols an analyst could wish (or not) to encounter. It would be impossible to cover every SMB command and response used in Microsoft environments, so I have chosen to explore the most common ones used in the majority of network operations. SMB is almost like a multilayered protocol unto itself, as it has multiple layers and command extensions. In the following examples, I examine these layers, which SMB calls subcommands. In my years of analysis, I have discovered few problems with the SMB protocol itself. Microsoft has done a fantastic job of weeding out small bugs and providing quick fixes. In this section, I intend to cover several examples that illustrate the inner workings of SMB.

Initial Connection

SMB is a command/response oriented protocol. In order to send an SMB command to a server, you must first connect with something called the IPC$ share. IPC stands for interprocess communication. It is a resource on all SMB servers that represents the SMB command/response system. When you are sending commands using core SMB commands, such as the SMB Transaction command, you are actually communicating with the IPC$ share.

> **NOTE** IPC$ is referred to with a dollar sign because it is a hidden share. All hidden shares have a dollar sign attached to the end of the share name.

Connecting to the IPC$ share enables interprocess communication. There are several types of interprocess communication, and I will further discuss them in the "Interprocess Communication" section later in this chapter. For now, take a look at Figure 8-19. It illustrates a client connection to the IPC$ of an SMB server.

> **NOTE** It should be noted that when I refer to an SMB server, I am referring to any host that has the ability to provide SMB file services. In Microsoftland, this means just about any host, including Windows 98, NT, 2000, and XP. The versions of SMB on various versions of Windows differ slightly in the commands they use to perform certain tasks.

In Figure 8-19, you can see the following steps taking place:

1. TCP three-way handshake (Frames 1–3)
2. NetBIOS session establishment (Frame 4–5)
3. SMB version negotiation (Frames 6–7)
4. SMB authentication (Frames 8–11)
5. Connection to IPC$ share (Frames 12–13)

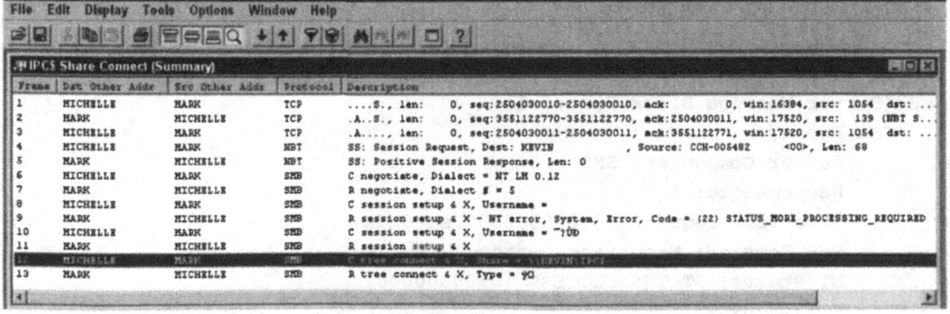

Figure 8-19   Packet analysis of Windows 2000 authentication.

Now, I want to examine the inner workings of Steps 3 through 5—version negotiation, authentication, and the IPC$ connection.

Version Negotiation

Having evolved throughout the years, SMB has many versions. Because these many versions exist, it is necessary for hosts to query SMB servers as to what version of SMB they can support. The following is a decode of Frame 6 from Figure 8-19:

```
Packet #6
SMB (Server Message Block Protocol)
    SMB Header
        Server Component: SMB
        Response in: 7
        SMB Command: Negotiate Protocol (0x72)
        NT Status: STATUS_SUCCESS (0x00000000)
        Flags: 0x18
        Flags2: 0xc853
        Reserved: 00000000000000000000000000
        Tree ID: 0
        Process ID: 65279
        User ID: 0
        Multiplex ID: 0
    Negotiate Protocol Request (0x72)
        Word Count (WCT): 0
        Byte Count (BCC): 98
        Requested Dialects
            Dialect: PC NETWORK PROGRAM 1.0
            Dialect: LANMAN1.0
            Dialect: Windows for Workgroups 3.1a
            Dialect: LM1.2X002
            Dialect: LANMAN2.1
            Dialect: NT LM 0.12
```

In the last lines of this decode example, the client is telling the SMB server which SMB versions (or dialects) it can support using the SMBNegotiate command. In its response, the server will choose the version that it wishes the client to use. As seen in the following example (a decode of Frame 7 in Figure 8-19), the server chooses dialect 5.

```
Packet #7
SMB (Server Message Block Protocol)
    SMB Header
        Server Component: SMB
        Response to: 6
        Time from request: 0.000558000 seconds
        SMB Command: Negotiate Protocol (0x72)
        NT Status: STATUS_SUCCESS (0x00000000)
        Flags: 0x98
        Flags2: 0xc853
```

```
            Reserved: 000000000000000000000000
            Tree ID: 0
            Process ID: 65279
            User ID: 0
            Multiplex ID: 0
        Negotiate Protocol Response (0x72)
            Word Count (WCT): 17
            Dialect Index: 5, greater than LANMAN2.1
            Security Mode: 0x03
            Max Mpx Count: 10
            Max VCs: 1
            Max Buffer Size: 4356
            Max Raw Buffer: 65536
            Session Key: 0x00000000
            Capabilities: 0x8000e3fd
            System Time: Jan 13, 2003 23:22:36.742609024
            Server Time Zone: 300 min from UTC
            Key Length: 0
            Byte Count (BCC): 16
            Server GUID: F8DAD40959CB2A4E99E8331C3FB6B416
```

SMB Authentication

After choosing a version of SMB to use, the client now must perform authentication with the SMB server. This authentication is accomplished by using the NT LanManager Secure Service Provider (abbreviated NTLMSSP). NTLMSSP uses what is known as a *challenge response system*, which enables the client to provide its server password in an encrypted format. The NTLMSSP process is performed using the SMB SessionSetupAndX command.

> **NOTE** From a protocol standpoint, Windows NT and 2000 security features are very complex. Readers wishing to learn more about Microsoft's security implementation can refer to Luke Kenneth Casson Leighton's excellent book *DCE/RPC over SMB: Samba and Windows NT Domain Internals* from Macmillan Technical Publishing.

Referring back to Figure 8-19, Frames 8 through 11 contain the NTLMSSP challenge and response process. Normally, when the guest account is active on a server, the IPC$ is available for connection by any users. For this example, I disabled the guest account. Not having the guest account enabled forces clients to submit a valid username and password for the SMB server. Frame 9 (in the decode that follows) shows the response to the NTLMSSP negotiate command in Frame 8.

```
Packet #9
SMB (Server Message Block Protocol)
    SMB Header
        Server Component: SMB
```

```
            Response to: 8
            Time from request: 0.000440000 seconds
            SMB Command: Session Setup AndX (0x73)
            NT Status: STATUS_MORE_PROCESSING_REQUIRED (0xc0000016)
            Flags: 0x98
            Flags2: 0xc807
            Reserved: 0000000000000000000000000
            Tree ID: 0
            Process ID: 65279
            User ID: 2048
            Multiplex ID: 16
        Session Setup AndX Response (0x73)
            Word Count (WCT): 4
            AndXCommand: No further commands (0xff)
            Reserved: 00
            AndXOffset: 235
            Action: 0x0000
                .... .... .... ...0 = Guest: Not logged in as GUEST
            Security Blob Length: 118
            Byte Count (BCC): 192
            Security Blob: 4E544C4D53535000020000000A000A00...
                NTLMSSP
            Native OS: Windows 5.0
            Native LAN Manager: Windows 2000 LAN Manager
```

It is in this example where you can see your first SMB Status code indicating that more processing is required. You can also see in the `Action` section that the guest account is not enabled. This forces the client to supply a valid login and password using the NTLMSSP challenge/response process.

IPC$ Connection

Once the authentication process is complete and the user is authorized, the client will make a connection to the IPC$ share as shown in the following decode of Frame 12 of Figure 8-19:

```
Packet #12
SMB (Server Message Block Protocol)
    SMB Header
        Server Component: SMB
        Response in: 13
        SMB Command: Tree Connect AndX (0x75)
        NT Status: STATUS_SUCCESS (0x00000000)
        Flags: 0x18
        Flags2: 0xc807
        Reserved: 0000000000000000000000000
        Tree ID: 0
        Process ID: 65279
        User ID: 2048
        Multiplex ID: 48
```

```
Tree Connect AndX Request (0x75)
     Word Count (WCT): 4
     AndXCommand: No further commands
     Reserved: 00
     AndXOffset: 76
     Flags: 0x0008
     Password Length: 1
     Byte Count (BCC): 33
     Password: 00
     Path: \\Michelle\IPC$
     Service: ?????
```

SMB clients use the `TreeConnectAndX` command when making a connection to a resource share. Take particular note in the decode of the `Tree ID` field. It is set to zero. The `Tree ID` is a numerical identifier of a shared resource. It is used so that from this point on the client can refer to a specific share using the `Tree ID` instead of its actual resource name (that is, `//Michelle/DATA`).

Next, in Frame 13 of Figure 8-19, you can see the server response to the IPC$ share connection request.

```
Packet #13
SMB Header
     Server Component: SMB
     Response to: 12
     Time from request: 0.000532000 seconds
     SMB Command: Tree Connect AndX (0x75)
     NT Status: STATUS_SUCCESS (0x00000000)
     Flags: 0x98
     Flags2: 0xc807
     Reserved: 00000000000000000000000000
     Tree ID: 2048
     Process ID: 65279
     User ID: 2048
     Multiplex ID: 48
Tree Connect AndX Response (0x75)
     Word Count (WCT): 7
     AndXCommand: No further commands
     Reserved: 00
     AndXOffset: 56
     Optional Support: 0x0001
     Word parameter: 0x01ff
     Word parameter: 0x0000
     Word parameter: 0x01ff
     Word parameter: 0x0000
     Byte Count (BCC): 7
     Service: IPC
     Extra byte parameters
```

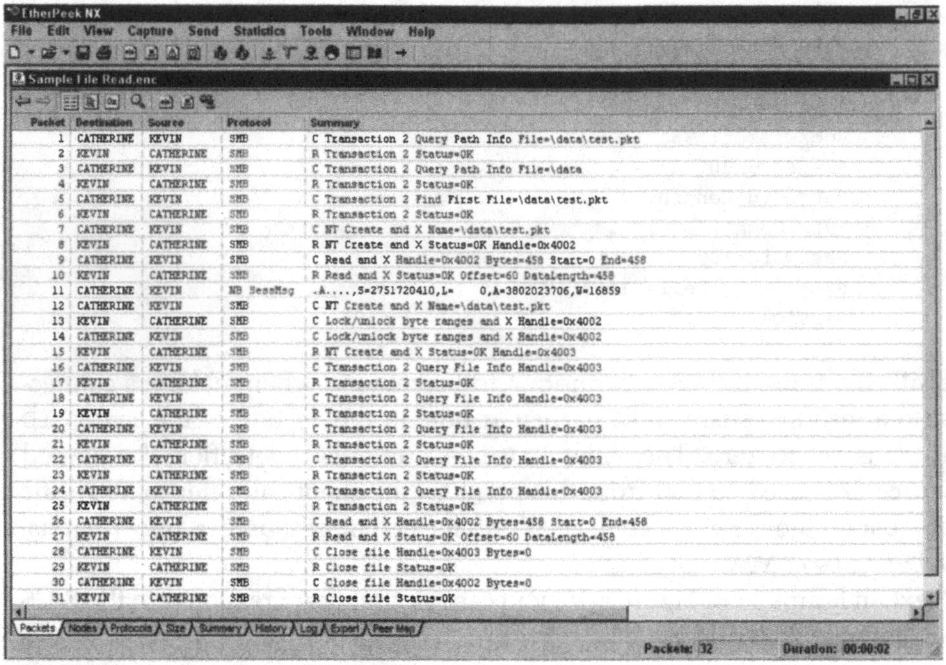

Packet	Destination	Source	Protocol	Summary
1	CATHERINE	KEVIN	SMB	C Transaction 2 Query Path Info File=\data\test.pkt
2	KEVIN	CATHERINE	SMB	R Transaction 2 Status=OK
3	CATHERINE	KEVIN	SMB	C Transaction 2 Query Path Info File=\data
4	KEVIN	CATHERINE	SMB	R Transaction 2 Status=OK
5	CATHERINE	KEVIN	SMB	C Transaction 2 Find First File=\data\test.pkt
6	KEVIN	CATHERINE	SMB	R Transaction 2 Status=OK
7	CATHERINE	KEVIN	SMB	C NT Create and X Name=\data\test.pkt
8	KEVIN	CATHERINE	SMB	R NT Create and X Status=OK Handle=0x4002
9	CATHERINE	KEVIN	SMB	C Read and X Handle=0x4002 Bytes=458 Start=0 End=458
10	KEVIN	CATHERINE	SMB	R Read and X Status=OK Offset=60 DataLength=458
11	CATHERINE	KEVIN	NB SessMsg	.A....,S=2751720410,L= 0,A=3802023706,W=16859
12	CATHERINE	KEVIN	SMB	C NT Create and X Name=\data\test.pkt
13	KEVIN	CATHERINE	SMB	C Lock/unlock byte ranges and X Handle=0x4002
14	CATHERINE	KEVIN	SMB	C Lock/unlock byte ranges and X Handle=0x4002
15	KEVIN	CATHERINE	SMB	R NT Create and X Status=OK Handle=0x4003
16	CATHERINE	KEVIN	SMB	C Transaction 2 Query File Info Handle=0x4003
17	KEVIN	CATHERINE	SMB	R Transaction 2 Status=OK
18	CATHERINE	KEVIN	SMB	C Transaction 2 Query File Info Handle=0x4003
19	KEVIN	CATHERINE	SMB	R Transaction 2 Status=OK
20	CATHERINE	KEVIN	SMB	C Transaction 2 Query File Info Handle=0x4003
21	KEVIN	CATHERINE	SMB	R Transaction 2 Status=OK
22	CATHERINE	KEVIN	SMB	C Transaction 2 Query File Info Handle=0x4003
23	KEVIN	CATHERINE	SMB	R Transaction 2 Status=OK
24	CATHERINE	KEVIN	SMB	C Transaction 2 Query File Info Handle=0x4003
25	KEVIN	CATHERINE	SMB	R Transaction 2 Status=OK
26	CATHERINE	KEVIN	SMB	C Read and X Handle=0x4002 Bytes=458 Start=0 End=458
27	KEVIN	CATHERINE	SMB	R Read and X Status=OK Offset=60 DataLength=458
28	CATHERINE	KEVIN	SMB	C Close file Handle=0x4003 Bytes=0
29	KEVIN	CATHERINE	SMB	R Close file Status=OK
30	CATHERINE	KEVIN	SMB	C Close file Handle=0x4002 Bytes=0
31	KEVIN	CATHERINE	SMB	R Close file Status=OK

Figure 8-20 File open/read operation.

Notice how now the `Tree ID` field contains the share identifier of `2048`. This field will be used throughout the life of the client's connection to the server. You know that the IPC$ connection was successful by the `STATUS_SUCCESS` response code.

After the negotiation, authentication, and IPC$ share connection are completed, the client can start utilizing further SMB commands in order to perform specific operations, such as accessing file services or printing.

File Transfer

File services are at the heart of SMB's functionality. All file activities that occur across a Microsoft-based infrastructure are handled by SMB. In this section, I discuss how SMB handles searches, file openings, closings, and file and directory manipulation. File operations, like much else in SMB, are very complex. Although the definitions of SMB function calls are well defined, the actions of the Microsoft client software are not. In many instances in these and other examples, you will see reoccurring SMB function calls that seem to have no value. Unfortunately, as an analyst, sometimes you can only seek to understand what happens, and not why, especially with such intricate protocols as SMB.

In this example, I use EtherPeek NX to examine an SMB file read operation. Figure 8-20 shows the steps that occur in the SMB protocol to open and read a file's contents. They are as follows:

1. Query for file and directory information (Frames 1–6)

2. Open file for read/write access (Frames 7–8)

3. Read file's contents (Frames 9–11)

4. Open file for read access (Frames 12, 15)

5. Oplock break notification (Frames 13–14)

6. File verification (Frames 16–27)

7. File close operation (Frames 28–31)

The first transaction that SMB will perform when undertaking a file read operation is to validate that the filename is properly formatted and that the file actually exists. SMB performs these functions by using the Transaction 2 (trans2) subcommands QUERY_PATH_INFORMATION and FIND_FIRST2. The following decode allows you to examine the first file query in Frame 1.

```
Packet #1
SMB - Server Message Block
Protocol ID:            SMB
  Command Code:         50  Transaction2 - Function, Byte In/Out
  NT Status:            0x00000000
  Flags:               0x18
  Flags2:              0xC807
  Reserved:
  ............     00 00 00 00 00 00 00 00 00 00 00 00
  Tree ID (TID):       0x0800
  Process ID (PID):    0x0258
  User ID (UID):       0x0800
  Multiplex ID (MID):  0x02B0
SMB Transaction2 - Function, Byte In/Out  Request
  Word count:          15  [90]
  Total Param Bytes:   36  [91-92]
  Total Data Bytes:    0   [93-94]
  Param Bytes To Recv: 2   [95-96]
  Data Bytes To Recv:  40  [97-98]
  Setup Bytes To Recv: 0   [99]
  Reserved:            0x00   [100]
  Flags:               0x0000 [101-102]
  Timeout (millisec.): 0   [103-106]
  Reserved:            0x0000 [107-108]
  Params This Buffer:  36  [109-110]
  Params Bytes Offset: 68  [111-112]
  Data This Buffer:    0   [113-114]
  Data Bytes Offset:   0   [115-116]
  Setup Word Count:    1   [117]
  Reserved:            0x00   [118]
  Setup Words:         0x0500 [119-120]
  Byte Count:          39  [121-122]
  Padding:             0x000000 [123-125]
  Trans2 Query Path Information: Get File Attributes Given Path
```

```
Information Level:     1004  Unknown Command  [126-127]
Reserved               0  Must be zero  [128-131]
Filename:              \data\test.pkt  [132-161]
```

Before examining the detail of this function call, I want to examine how SMB nests its commands. You can see from looking at this example that the `Trans2` command contains the subcommand `Query Path Information`. For the analyzer to be able to figure out what the subcommand is, there needs to be some indicator in the SMB packet of the subcommand code. There is. Look at the frame decode. The `Setup Words` field contains the SMB command code of the `Trans2` subcommand. In the decode, you can see that it is `0x0500`. But wait, didn't I just say that the subcommand specified in the Transaction 2 header was `Query Path Information`? In Table 8-2, the `Query Path Information` subcommand code is `0x05` not `0x0500`. The way 2-byte command codes are sometimes represented in the standard is confusing. Here, the least significant byte of the code is dropped to yield `0x05`.

Under the `Query Path Information` subcommand, you'll see something called the `Information Level`. This is the level of information that is being requested by the client. If you look in the SMB standard, you won't see an `Information Level` code of `1004`, but you will find the code `0104`. In this case, the most significant byte (10 in this example) actually has to be reversed to match up with the information levels specified in the SMB standard. By reversing the nibbles in the decimal 10, you get 01, which when paired with the low order-byte 04, gives you `0x104`.

The response to the request for `Information Level` `0x104` is decoded as follows using Ethereal.

```
Packet #2
QUERY_PATH_INFORMATION Parameters
        EA Error offset: 0
    Padding: 0001
    QUERY_PATH_INFORMATION Data
      Created: Dec  2, 2002 11:09:56.069999694
      Last Access: Jan 13, 2003 00:00:00.000000000
      Last Write: Jan  1, 2003 21:21:22.000000000
      Change: No time specified (0)
      File Attributes: 0x00000020
            .... .... ..1. .... = Archive: This is an ARCHIVE file
            .... .... ...0 .... = Directory: This is NOT a directory
            .... .... .... 0... = Volume ID: This is NOT a volume ID
            .... .... .... .0.. = System: This is NOT a system file
            .... .... .... ..0. = Hidden: This is NOT a hidden file
            .... .... .... ...0 = Read Only: This file is NOT read only
```

This frame gives our client the information it needs to make a proper decision about what is being requested of it. If, for example, the file is read-only, then the client is surely not going to be able to perform a write operation on it.

```
SMB (Server Message Block Protocol)
  SMB Header
  NT Create AndX Request (0xa2)
    Word Count (WCT): 24
    AndXCommand: No further commands (0xff)
    Reserved: 00
    AndXOffset: 57054
    Reserved: 00
    File Name Len: 28
    Create Flags: 0x00000016
      .... .... .... .... .... .... 0... = Create Directory: Target of open can be a file
      .... .... .... .... .... .... .1.. = Batch Oplock: Requesting BATCH OPLOCK
      .... .... .... .... .... .... ..1. = Exclusive Oplock: Requesting OPLOCK
    Root FID: 0x00000000
    Access Mask: 0x00020089
    Allocation Size: 0
    File Attributes: 0x00000080
      0... .... .... .... .... .... .... .... = Write Through: This object does NOT require write through
      ..0. .... .... .... .... .... .... .... = No Buffering: This object can be buffered
      ...0 .... .... .... .... .... .... .... = Random Access: Random access is NOT requested
      .... 0... .... .... .... .... .... .... = Sequential Scan: This object is NOT optimized for sequential scan
      .... .0.. .... .... .... .... .... .... = Delete on Close: This object will not be deleted on close
      .... ..0. .... .... .... .... .... .... = Backup: This object does NOT support backup semantics
      .... ...0 .... .... .... .... .... .... = Posix: This object does NOT support POSIX semantics
      .... .... .... .0.. .... .... .... .... = Encrypted: This is NOT an encrypted file
      .... .... .... ..0. .... .... .... .... = Content Indexed: This file MAY be indexed by the content indexing service
      .... .... .... ...0 .... .... .... .... = Offline: This file is NOT offline
      .... .... .... .... 0... .... .... .... = Compressed: This is NOT a compressed file
      .... .... .... .... .0.. .... .... .... = Reparse Point: This file does NOT have an associated reparse point
      .... .... .... .... ..0. .... .... .... = Sparse: This is NOT a sparse file
      .... .... .... .... ...0 .... .... .... = Temporary: This is NOT a temporary file
      .... .... .... .... .... 1... .... .... = Normal: This file is an ordinary file
      .... .... .... .... .... .0.. .... .... = Device: This is NOT a device
      .... .... .... .... .... ..0. .... .... = Archive: This is NOT an archive file
      .... .... .... .... .... ...0 .... .... = Directory: This is NOT a directory
      .... .... .... .... .... .... 0... .... = Volume ID: This is NOT a volume ID
      .... .... .... .... .... .... .0.. .... = System: This is NOT a system file
      .... .... .... .... .... .... ..0. .... = Hidden: This is NOT a hidden file
      .... .... .... .... .... .... ...0 .... = Read Only: This file is NOT read only
    Share Access: 0x00000003
      .... .... .... .... .... .... .0.. .... = Delete: Object can NOT be shared for delete
      .... .... .... .... .... .... ..1. .... = Write: Object can be shared for WRITE
      .... .... .... .... .... .... ...1 .... = Read: Object can be shared for READ
    Disposition: Open (if file exists open it, else fail) (1)
    Create Options: 0x00000044
    Impersonation: Impersonation (2)
    Security Flags: 0x03
    Byte Count (BCC): 31
    File Name: \data\test.pkt
```

Figure 8-21   CreateAndX decode.

The next four frames request various information from the server to verify that the operation can be performed on the file in question. Once all file and directory information is verified, the client can send the server a file open request using the `CreateAndX Request` shown decoded in Figure 8-21.

NOTE Taking a look at Figure 8-21, you can really see the breadth of capabilities that SMB possesses when it comes to devices and file types. It is truly a remarkable protocol. To understand the details of such a complex protocol, you need days if not months of time to analyze every detail of its operation. It is a task few have tackled. Even though it might be interesting to understand every nuance and detail of a protocol as complicated as SMB, it will rarely come in handy unless you are intricately involved in the protocol's development or a product that uses it. The information I have provided in this chapter is sufficient to troubleshoot most issues arising with applications using the SMB protocol.

The `CreateAndX` command is misleading if you consider its name alone. It is used both to create and open files. In Figure 8-21, you can see in the `Disposition` field an option to open the file. During the file create process, SMB will actually search for the filename that you wish to create, and upon determining it does not exist, will create the file.

In the same figure, you can also see two other important pieces of information :

- The client has opened up the file requesting an `Exclusive Oplock`, which I discuss later in the chapter.

- It has also opened the file for Read and Write access.

After the file open process, you can see in Frame 8 of Figure 8-20 that the server has assigned a file handle to the file. File handles are similar to Tree IDs in that they allow the client to use them as placemarkers when referring to the file in the future. *File handles* are 16-bit identifiers the server places in the File ID field of the SMB CreateAndX response. Clients use the File ID instead of the filename when referring to the opened file. The following is the decode of the CreateAndX response from the server.

```
Frame 8 (197 bytes on wire, 197 bytes captured)
SMB (Server Message Block Protocol)
    SMB Header
    NT Create AndX Response (0xa2)
        Word Count (WCT): 42
        AndXCommand: No further commands
        Reserved: 00
        AndXOffset: 135
        Oplock level: Batch oplock granted (2)
        FID: 0x4002
        Create action: Open (if file exists open it, else fail) (1)
```

```
Created: Dec  2, 2002 11:09:56.069999694
Last Access: Jan 13, 2003 00:00:00.000000000
Last Write: Jan  1, 2003 21:21:22.000000000
Change: Jan  1, 1980 00:00:00.000000000
File Attributes: 0x00000020
Allocation Size: 8192
End Of File: 458
File Type: Disk file or directory (0)
IPC State: 0x0007
Is Directory: This is NOT a directory (0)
Byte Count (BCC): 0
```

Although I don't show it in this example, there is an SMB Success Status code in the header. It is important to always look for the status code in the SMB header to confirm that the operation a client has requested has been performed successfully. Here in the decode of Frame 8, you can see that a Batch Oplock has been granted and the file opened. You can also see several of the file's attributes in the response. One very important piece of information in the response is something called the End of File field. This tells the client how many bytes there are until the end of the file. Clients reading files use this information to know how many bytes to request from the server.

In Frame 9 (Figure 8-20), you can see the read request from the client. Notice that it is using the ReadAndX request command for File ID 4002, which is our file handle. It is also requesting to read 458 bytes from offset 0. The offset in this case is the beginning of the file.

NOTE When they are performing large file read operations, you will see clients specifying different offsets as they move through the file reading chunks of bytes at a time until they are complete.

After reading the file, the client does something interesting in Frame 12. Take a look at the decode for Frame 12.

```
Frame 12 (176 bytes on wire, 176 bytes captured)
SMB (Server Message Block Protocol)
    SMB Header
    NT Create AndX Request (0xa2)
        Word Count (WCT): 24
        AndXCommand: No further commands (0xff)
        Reserved: 00
        AndXOffset: 57054
        Reserved: 00
        File Name Len: 28
        Create Flags: 0x00000016
        Root FID: 0x00000000
        Access Mask: 0x00020089
        Allocation Size: 0
        File Attributes: 0x00000000
```

```
            Share Access: 0x00000001
                .... .... .... .... .... .... .... .0.. = Delete
                .... .... .... .... .... .... .... ..0. = Write
                .... .... .... .... .... .... .... ...1 = Read
            Disposition: Open (if file exists open it, else fail) (1)
            Create Options: 0x00200044
            Impersonation: Impersonation (2)
            Security Flags: 0x03
            Byte Count (BCC): 31
            File Name: \data\test.pkt
```

Now, after reading the file contents, the client is changing the file access mode from read/write to simply read.

This causes something else interesting to happen. In Frame 13, the server sends the client what is known as an Oplock Break request telling the client that because it has the file open for read access it does not need to keep the file opened with a Batch Oplock. Oplocks, which I discuss in the next section of the chapter, are methods of locking out a file or parts of a file so that other users cannot modify them. Batch and exclusive oplocks are used for Write mode access, while something called Level II oplocks are used for read access. Here is the decode for the Oplock Break request from the server.

```
Frame 13 (113 bytes on wire, 113 bytes captured)
SMB (Server Message Block Protocol)
    SMB Header
    Locking AndX Request (0x24)
        Word Count (WCT): 8
        AndXCommand: No further commands (0xff)
        Reserved: 00
        AndXOffset: 0
        FID: 0x4002
        Lock Type: 0x02
            ...0 .... = Large Files: Large file locking format not
requested
            .... 0... = Cancel: Don't cancel outstanding lock request
            .... .0.. = Change: Don't change lock type
            .... ..1. = Oplock Break: This is an oplock break
notification/response
            .... ...0 = Shared: This is an exclusive lock
        Oplock Level: Level 2 oplock currently held by client (1)
        Timeout: Return immediately (0)
        Number of Unlocks: 0
        Number of Locks: 0
        Byte Count (BCC): 0
```

In Frame 14, the client acknowledges the Oplock Break request, and in Frame 15, the server responds to its file open (CreateAndX) request from Frame 12. In the decode of Frame 15 that follows, you can see that the server replied to the client, granting it a Level II oplock, which is a suitable locking type for read access of files. Also, notice that the server has given the client a new file handle to use in the File ID field.

```
Frame 15 (197 bytes on wire, 197 bytes captured)
SMB (Server Message Block Protocol)
    SMB Header
    NT Create AndX Response (0xa2)
        Word Count (WCT): 42
        AndXCommand: No further commands
        Reserved: 00
        AndXOffset: 135
        Oplock level: Level II oplock granted (3)
        FID: 0x4003
        Create action: Open (if file exists open it, else fail) (1)
        Created: Dec  2, 2002 11:09:56.069999694
        Last Access: Jan 13, 2003 00:00:00.000000000
        Last Write: Jan  1, 2003 21:21:22.000000000
        Change: Jan  1, 1980 00:00:00.000000000
        File Attributes: 0x00000020
        Allocation Size: 8192
        End Of File: 458
        File Type: Disk file or directory (0)
        IPC State: 0x0007
        Is Directory: This is NOT a directory (0)
        Byte Count (BCC): 0
```

In the next group of Frames (16–27) in Figure 8-20, the client, having read the contents of the file into its local memory buffers, goes ahead and performs some file verification procedures using the QUERY_FILE_INFORMATION command. Although it appears from the summary viewpoint that the client is simply performing the same task over again, it actually is requesting different levels of file information as it did in the first example using the QUERY_PATH_INFORMATION command. In Frames 26–27, you see the client once again reading the file contents for good measure. Because this file is small (only 458 bytes), the client is able to verify the contents of the entire file. Once the client is finished with verifying the file contents and information, it closes both file handles in Frames 28–31.

File Locking

One of SMB's best features is its file caching. When a client opens up a file from a remote server, it caches the file in local memory. When a user needs to access the file, it can be accessed from local memory instead of performing the file open processes all over again. But what if another user has modified the file on the server? How can the contents of the local cache be guaranteed to be the same?

In SMB, file locks are called opportunistic locks because the protocol allows a client to exclusively lock a file if the opportunity presents itself. There are three types of opportunistic locks, or oplocks.

- **Exclusive oplocks.**   Exclusive oplocks guarantee that a client is the accessor of a file. If the file being accessed was previously opened by any other user, the client would be denied an exclusive oplock. When a client exclusively locks a file, it is able to completely buffer the read contents into its local file cache. This speeds up the file access process considerably. If a client has an exclusive oplock and another client attempts to open the file, the server will notify the first client that it must break its oplock. When the client receives the oplock break request, it must send the server any write data that it has buffered locally. This guarantees that the file on the server contains an up-to-date copy of the file's contents. The first client must also clear its local file buffers because the second client may modify the contents of the file.

- **Batch oplocks.**   Batch oplocks are similar to exclusive oplocks with regard to other clients accessing currently opened files. The difference with batch oplocks is that a client is able to perform multiple read or write requests without constantly opening and closing a file. Normally, a file read or write request will close a file when it has accessed the file's contents. A batch oplock will keep the file open for more read or write requests to be performed.

- **Level II oplocks.**   Level II oplocks are designed for multiple clients to have the same file open for read access but not write access. Servers will notify clients that they should switch to a Level II oplock if they currently have an exclusive oplock and are not writing to the file. You already saw an example of this type of oplock in the previous section. If a group of clients has a Level II oplock on a file and another client opens the file with an exclusive lock, the server will then notify the Level II clients that they are required to break their oplocks and request all file data directly from the server.

Interprocess Communication

The mechanisms provided by Microsoft to enable communications and data sharing between applications are known as interprocess communications (IPC). The most common mechanisms supported by IPC are named pipes, mailslots, and remote procedure calls.

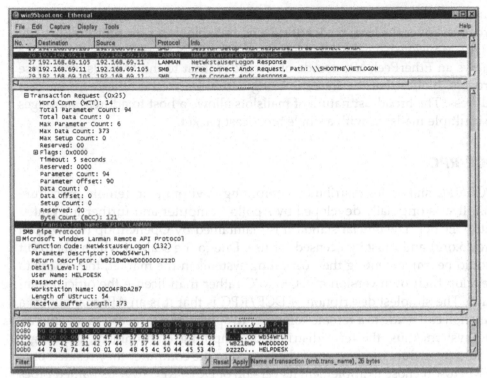

Figure 8-22 Windows 95 workstation logon request.

Named Pipes

Named pipes allow two-way communications to be established between two applications residing on separate hosts over a network. Named pipes act like virtual file systems. Standard SMB read and write commands are used to transfer data between a named pipe connection. Each named pipe has a unique name that distinguishes it from other named pipes. The naming format for named pipes is \\ServerName\pipe\PipeName, where the ServerName is the name of the remote computer where the named pipe is located, and the PipeName is the name of the named pipe. In Figure 8-22, I show a Windows 95 station sending a workstation logon request to the LAN Manager service, which is running over a named pipe. Windows 95 and 98 make heavy use of named pipes, while Windows NT, 2000, and XP make heavy use of RPCs, which I talk about shortly.

Mailslots

Mailslots are interprocess communication mechanisms used for one-way communications. Mailslots act in a similar fashion to real mailboxes. Clients send messages addressed to specific mailslots. Named pipes perform the same function, but mailslots are used for their simplicity. Mailslot messages are broadcast over the local media using a nonreliable transport protocol (usually UDP). Mailslots have the name format of \\mailslot*[path]**name*. Figure 8-23 shows an EtherPeek NX decode of a write request to the \\mailslot\browse process. Notice that the frame is being addressed to the Ethernet broadcast address. The broadcast nature of mailslots allows a host to address messages to multiple mailslots with a single broadcast packet.

DCE/RPC

DCE/RPC stands for distributed computing environment/remote procedure call. It was originally developed by Apollo Computer and further integrated into DECnet. The official standard is maintained by OpenGroup (www.open group.org) and must be licensed for use. Due to the scale at which Microsoft would be implementing their operating systems in the market, they chose to develop their own version of DCE/RPC rather than license the official standard. The simplest description of DCE/RPC is that it is an API that allows a function call made to a remote computer to appear as a local call to the operating system, thus, the term distributed computing environment. No longer would procedures and functions be limited to the computer they resided on.

Microsoft chose to implement its version of DCE/RPC over its named pipes mechanism, the named pipe being particular to a group of functions. Each named pipe is referenced by a universally unique identifier (UUID). Table 8-3 contains a partial listing of UUIDs and the application types they represent.

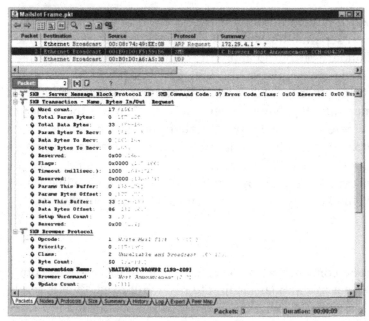

Figure 8-23   Mailslot browse write request.

Table 8-3 Universally Unique Identifiers for Microsoft Services

APPLICATION PROCESS	UUID	DESCRIPTION
NetLogon	12345678-1234-ABCD-EF00-01234567CFFB	Used for logging onto an NT or 2000 domain
winreg	338cd001-2244-31f1-aaaa-900038001003	Used for remotely accessing the Windows Registry
lsarpc	12345778-1234-ABCD-EF00-0123456789AB	Local Security Authority
wkssvc	6BFFD098-A112-3610-9833-46C3F87E345A	Workstation Service
SrvSvc	4B324FC8-1670-01D3-1278-5A47BF6EE188	Server Service
Spoolss	12345678-1234-ABCD-EF00-0123456789AB	Printer Spooling Service
MS Exchange	F5CC5A18-4264-101A-8C59-08002B2F8426	MS Exchange Services
Directory Service	F5CC5A18-4264-101A-8C59-08002B2F8426	Exchange Directory Service
Information Store	A4F1DB00-CA47-1067-B31F-00DD010662DA	Exchange Information Store
Message Transfer Agent	9E8EE830-4459-11CE-979B-00AA005FFEBE	Exchange Message Transfer Agent (MTA)

In order for a client or server to use an RPC function, it must first connect to the named pipe that allows a connection to be opened between the client and the particular RPC function group. Figure 8-24 illustrates this process.

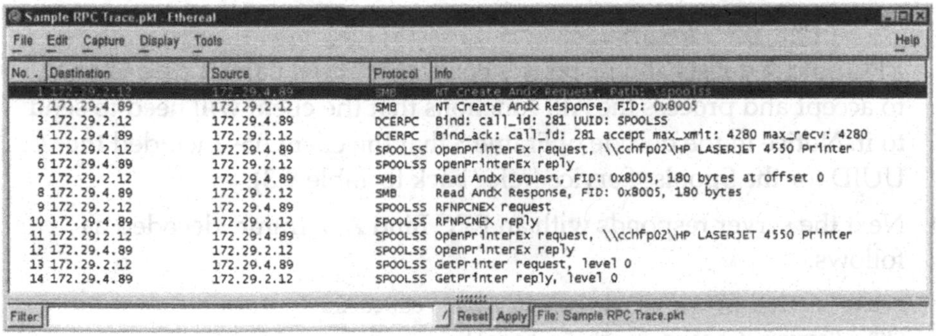

Figure 8-24 RPC communication process.

1. In Frame 1, the client uses the SMB `CreateAndX` command to open a file handle to the named pipe named /spoolss.

2. In Frame 2, the client receives a status response and a `File ID` of 8005. The client will use this File ID from now on when referencing the named pipe.

3. In Frame 3 (decoded as follows) the client sends an RPC Bind request to the server.

```
Frame 3 (218 bytes on wire, 218 bytes captured)
SMB (Server Message Block Protocol)
    SMB Header
    Transaction Request (0x25)
SMB Pipe Protocol
    Function: TransactNmPipe (0x0026)
    FID: 0x8005
DCE RPC
    Version: 5
    Version (minor): 0
    Packet type: Bind (11)
    Packet Flags: 0x03
    Data Representation: 10000000
    Frag Length: 72
    Auth Length: 0
    Call ID: 281
    Max Xmit Frag: 4280
    Max Recv Frag: 4280
    Assoc Group: 0x0000e777
    Num Ctx Items: 1
    Context ID: 0
    Num Trans Items: 1
    Interface UUID: 12345678-1234-abcd-ef00-0123456789ab
    Interface Ver: 1
    Interface Ver Minor: 0
    Transfer Syntax: 8a885d04-1ceb-11c9-9fe8-08002b104860
    Syntax ver: 2
```

RPC bind requests and responses confirm that the named pipe is open to accept and process the API functions that the client will need to send to it. Notice in the decode of Frame 3 that the client has included the UUID for the Spoolss Service (refer back to Table 8-3).

4. Next the server responds with an RPC Bind Ack frame, decoded as follows.

```
Frame 4 (186 bytes on wire, 186 bytes captured)
SMB (Server Message Block Protocol)
    SMB Header
    Transaction Response (0x25)
SMB Pipe Protocol
```

```
         Function: TransactNmPipe (0x0026)
         FID: 0x8005
    DCE RPC
         Version: 5
         Version (minor): 0
         Packet type: Bind_ack (12)
         Packet Flags: 0x03
         Data Representation: 10000000
         Frag Length: 68
         Auth Length: 0
         Call ID: 281
         Max Xmit Frag: 4280
         Max Recv Frag: 4280
         Assoc Group: 0x0000e777
         Scndry Addr len: 14
         Scndry Addr: \pipe\spoolss
         Num results: 1
         Ack result: Acceptance (0)
         Transfer Syntax: 8a885d04-1ceb-11c9-9fe8-08002b104860
         Syntax ver: 2
```

The Bind ack response includes a result code indicating if the Bind request was successful. A failure will indicate that the server's process is not functioning and cannot accept API calls.

In Frames 3 and 4, also note the use of the Call ID field, which is set to 281 in both the Bind Request and Bind Response. The Call ID field is used to match RPC requests to responses and increments as more requests are made.

5. Now that the client has confirmed the named pipe to be opened and functioning, it can send an API call to the server. API calls for each RPC service are identified by their operation number, or opnum. Opnum 69 is the OpenPrinter Extended function. Frame 5's decode shows this function.

```
Frame 5 (384 bytes on wire, 384 bytes captured)
SMB (Server Message Block Protocol)
SMB Pipe Protocol
    Function: TransactNmPipe (0x0026)
    FID: 0x8005
DCE RPC
Microsoft Spool Subsystem
    Operation: OpenPrinterEx (69)
    Reply in frame 6
    Printer name pointer: 0x0101af60
    UNISTR2: \\cchfp02\HP LASERJET 4550 Printer
        Length: 35
```

```
           Offset: 0
           Max length: 35
           Data
     PRINTER_DEFAULT
           Datatype pointer: 0x00000000
           DEVMODE_CTR
               Size: 0
               Devicemode pointer: 0x00000000
           Access required: 0x00000000
               Generic rights: 0x00000000
               Standard rights: 0x00000000
               Specific rights: 0x00000000
     User switch: 1
     USER_LEVEL
         Info level: 1
         User level pointer: 0x01bcff08
         USER_LEVEL_1
```

Here, the client is sending an OpenPrinterEx call to the Microsoft Spool Subsystem, also known as the named pipe /spoolss.

6. Frame 6 contains the return code from the server indicating that the API call was processed without error.

```
Frame 6 (166 bytes on wire, 166 bytes captured)
SMB (Server Message Block Protocol)
    SMB Header
    Transaction Response (0x25)
SMB Pipe Protocol
    Function: TransactNmPipe (0x0026)
    FID: 0x8005
DCE RPC
Microsoft Spool Subsystem
    Operation: OpenPrinterEx (69)
    Request in frame 5
    Policy Handle: \\cchfp02\HP LASERJET 4550 Printer
    Return code: Success (0x00000000)
```

This extended example represents the basics of how Microsoft's DCE/RPC protocol functions. Volumes could be written about the hundreds of API calls available through the various named pipe processes on NT and 2000 servers. There is very little published documentation of Microsoft's DCE/RPC API functions. Besides Leighton's *DCE/RPC over SMB: Samba and Windows NT Domain Internals* book (mentioned previously in the chapter), the best resources for understanding the functionality of DCE/RPC is the Microsoft Developer network and various SAMBA newsgroups and listservs.

When analyzing a problem with an application using DCE/RPC, it is important to understand the layering affect of the protocols.

1. First, a connection to a named pipe is made by standard SMB commands such as CreateAndX or OpenAndX.

2. Next, the Bind Request/Bind Ack process is completed. This confirms that the named pipe is fully available for API function requests.

3. Finally, the actual API calls are sent over the wire to the server, and responses are sent back, indicating a success or failure.

Along with understanding those three parts of the process, you need to familiarize yourself with how an application functions using DCE/RPC. The only way to do this is to capture the applications in action over the network. Look at the process, try to understand it, and research the operation codes and API calls. You may never fully understand the in-depth processes that take place (only the developers do), but you will be able to familiarize yourself with what happens during a normal error-free application transaction. When a failure occurs, you need only compare the good with the bad to determine the cause.

Microsoft Applications

Nearly all Microsoft applications use some form of named pipes, mailslots, or DCE/RPC. After getting a basic understanding of the three interprocess communication mechanisms, analyzing the individual applications will be much easier. In this section, I am going to discuss two Microsoft-specific applications and how they use the three types of interprocess communications I have discussed in the chapter.

NetLogon

The NetLogon service is used by Windows clients to locate available Microsoft NT domain controllers. The discussion of Microsoft's Domain architecture is beyond the scope of this book, but I will touch on it in order to provide non-Microsoft savvy readers with some background into how the Netlogon service relates to the Domain architecture.

Microsoft authentication services are handled by domain controllers. A domain represents a single security database that is located on something called a Primary Domain Controller. To provide redundancy, the database is distributed over other domain controllers called Backup Domain Controllers. When a Windows 95/98, NT, 2000, or XP client attempts to locate domain servers on its local subnet, it sends a message to a mailslot called //MAIL-SLOT/TEMP/NETLOGON. The message is sent as a broadcast, and any server on the local subnet running the NetLogon service will respond to the broadcast. In Frames 10–12 of Figure 8-25, you can see that two servers have responded to the broadcast mailslot message.

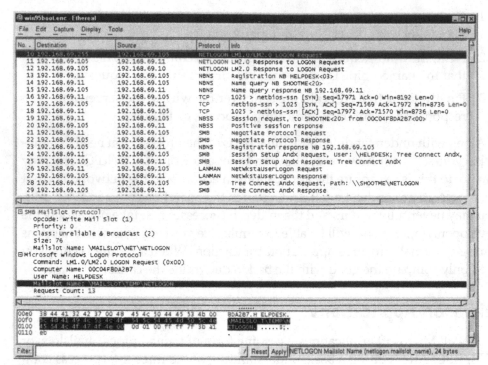

Figure 8-25   Netlogon trace.

This response tells the client that these two servers are able to accept a Net-Logon request. The client will then choose one of the servers that responded and send it a TreeConnectAndX request to connect to that server's NetLogon share (shown in Figure 8-26).

NT servers actually track user logins by looking at who has a connection to the NetLogon share.

The NetLogon mailslot also serves another purpose, allowing a client to query a domain controller about which domain controller is the Primary Domain Controller. The following is a decode of the API call over the NetLo-gon mailslot. In this case, you can see the client sending a Query for PDC request over the NetLogon mailslot. Notice how the Query for PDC request is also being sent to its own specific mailslot of \MAILSLOT\NET\GETDC000. This is the nature of how mailslots work, very similar to the real mail system where you send a letter to someone overnight inside of another shipping package (Federal Express, UPS, and so on).

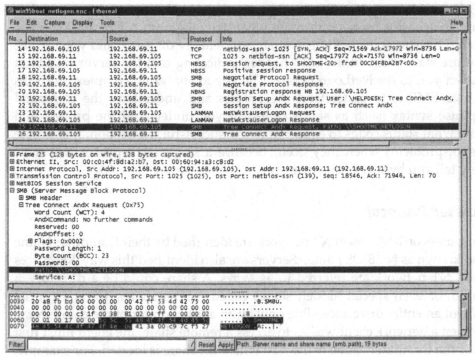

Figure 8-26 Netlogon share connection.

```
SMB MailSlot Protocol
    Opcode: Write Mail Slot (1)
    Priority: 0
    Class: Unreliable & Broadcast (2)
    Size: 63
    Mailslot Name: \MAILSLOT\NET\NETLOGON
Microsoft Windows Logon Protocol
    Command: Query for PDC (0x07)
    Computer Name: 00C04F8DA2B7
    Mailslot Name: \MAILSLOT\NET\GETDC000
    LM10 Token: 0xfffe (WFW Networking)
```

A domain controller receiving this request responds with the NetBIOS name of the Primary Domain Controller, as seen in the following:

```
SMB MailSlot Protocol
    Opcode: Write Mail Slot (1)
    Priority: 1
    Class: Unreliable & Broadcast (2)
    Size: 33
    Mailslot Name: \MAILSLOT\NET\GETDC000
Microsoft Windows Logon Protocol
    Command: Response from PDC (0x0c)
    PDC Name: SHOOTME
```

By understanding how the NetLogon process works, you are able to understand the process users go through when they log onto NT or 2000 servers. Often, I have seen the NetLogon share accidentally disabled, and you can see a failure status code in the SMB header, indicating that the server could not connect you to the NetLogon share. The key to analyzing complex protocols such as SMB is to understand the process and understand the command response syntax (such as status codes). If you understand the process and know what status codes to expect during a successful transaction, it is simple to spot problems when they occur because a single SMB packet will most likely tell you by way of an error code.

Browser Protocol

Computers on a Microsoft NT network are identified by their Computer Name (also known as NetBIOS name). Servers are also identified this way. Resources on an NT network are referred to as *shares*. A share could be a directory, a printer, or even special hidden shares called Admin shares. C$ is a special share of an entire drive accessible only by an administrator of the computer.

When a network client wishes to access a remote share, the client must first know the Computer Name of the host where the share is located. For example, if I would like to access a shared called DATA located on a server with a computer name of SCHARFDEV, I would type the command **net use G: \\SCHARFDEV\DATA**, which would map drive G: to the DATA share on the remote computer. Of course, this assumes that I have rights on the computer to do so.

However, without knowing the Computer Name of every workstation and server, it would be impossible to find shared resources on the network. Microsoft's SMB protocol allows any host to potentially be an SMB server, because all you need to do is enable file sharing and you can accept TreeConnectAndX requests from other clients. The mechanism created by Microsoft to easily locate shared resources on an NT network is called *Browsing*. It is not the same kind of browsing done by a Web browser, but a separate specific protocol enabling the ability of clients to find resource information quickly.

The Browser protocol defines different types of Browser computers that all participate in the Browser protocol. The following types of Browsers are defined:

- **Domain Master Browser.** The Domain Master Browser is always the Primary Domain Controller for the domain. It will register itself with a WINS server using the domain <1B> suffix. Local Master Browsers will query a WINS server for the Domain Name <1B> suffix to find out who the Domain Master Browser is.

- **Local Master Browser.** Local Master Browsers exist on every IP subnet in an enterprise. The Domain Master Browser will assume the role of the Local Master Browser for the subnet it is located on. Local Master Browsers are also called Segment Master Browsers because they store browse information for their local IP segment. Local Master Browsers exchange browse information with Domain Master Browsers. Local Masters will register themselves with a WINS server using the domain <1D> suffix.

- **Backup Browser.** Backup Browsers enable redundancy for Local Master Browsers. There will be one Backup Browser on each segment for each 32 hosts on the segment. Backup Browsers exchange browse information with Local Master Browsers.

- **Browser Client.** Browser Clients are clients that do not assist in maintaining and distributing browse information across the network. Browser Clients will use the Browser protocol to advertise themselves on the network.

- **Potential Browser.** Potential Browsers are any browser clients that could be called on by a Local Master Browser to become Backup Browsers. As the number of hosts increases in increments of 32 hosts, Local Master Browsers request Potential Browsers to become extra Backup Browsers.

Browser Processes

Information about resources on a network are kept by browsers in what are called *Browse Lists*. These lists are simply databases of the resources that the Browser knows about. The process of exchanging and retrieving browse lists is called *enumeration*.

There are six steps that take place in order to establish which hosts on a subnet will become browsers and to perform the process of synchronizing the browse lists between those browsers.

1. **Domain Master Browser WINS registration.** This allows Local Master Browsers to find out who is the Domain Master Browser by performing a WINS Name Query for the name domain <1B>. The following is an example decode of a Primary Domain Controller performing a registration of itself as the Domain Master Browser.

```
NetBIOS Name Service
    Transaction ID: 0x8022
    Flags: 0x2910 (Registration)
    Questions: 1
    Answer RRs: 0
    Authority RRs: 0
    Additional RRs: 1
    Queries
    Additional records
```

```
BEVERLY<1b>: type NB, class inet
    Name: BEVERLY<1b> (Domain Master Browser)
    Type: NB
    Class: inet
    Time to live: 3 days, 11 hours, 20 minutes
    Data length: 6
    Flags: 0x6000 (H-node, unique)
        0... .... .... .... = Unique name
        .11. .... .... .... = H-node
    Addr: 192.168.69.11
```

2. **Election of Local Master Browsers on each subnet.** In order to establish a single Local Master Browser for each subnet, an election process is used. Elections are performed by having each Potential Browser broadcast an election datagram. Each election datagram contains criteria that all listening Potential Browsers use to determine if they should continue in the election process. Table 8-4 shows the election criteria.

Based on the election criteria, a Windows 2000 Professional workstation would have a better criteria than Windows 95 or 98. The election criteria also specifies that a higher election version will win out over a lower election version, high criteria will win over lower criteria, and a host that has been up longer than another host will win over that host. If all else fails, the computer with the lexically lowest name will win.

Table 8-4   Browser Election Criteria

OPERATING SYSTEM TYPE	WINDOWS ELECTION FIELD
Windows for Workgroups and Windows 95 and Windows 98	0x01000000
Windows 2000 Professional and Windows NT Workstation	0x10000000
Windows 2000 Server and Windows NT Server	0x20000000
Election Version	0x00FFFF00
Per Version Criteria	0x000000FF
PDC	0x00000080
WINS System	0x00000020
Preferred Master	0x00000008
Running Master	0x00000004
MaintainServerList	0x00000002
Running backup browser	0x00000001

Elections are caused when a station does not hear a Master Browser Announcement upon booting up. Master Browsers will also initiate an election when they are shut down. This is to guarantee that another Master Browser takes over its role. The decode of an election packet is shown below. Notice that the Browser protocol uses the mailslot name \MAILSLOT\BROWSE.

```
SMB MailSlot Protocol
    Opcode: Write Mail Slot (1)
    Priority: 1
    Class: Unreliable & Broadcast (2)
    Size: 39
    Mailslot Name: \MAILSLOT\BROWSE
Microsoft Windows Browser Protocol
    Command: Browser Election Request (0x08)
    Election Version: 1
    Election Criteria: 0x20010fae
        Election Desire: 0xae
        Browser Protocol Major Version: 15
        Browser Protocol Minor Version: 1
        Election OS: 0x20
            .... ...0 = WfW: Not Windows for Workgroups
            ...0 .... = NT Workstation: Not Windows NT Workstation
            ..1. .... = NT Server: Windows NT Server
    Uptime: 1 minute, 4.093 seconds
    Server Name: SHOOTME
```

3. **Local Master WINS Query for Domain Master Browser.**   After an election, a Local Master Browser will query the WINS server to find out who the Domain Master Browser is. It will do so using the NetBIOS name domain <1D>.

4. **Share enumeration between Domain Master and Local Masters.** Once the Domain Master Browser knows about all of the Local Masters and the Local Masters know about the Domain Master, they perform what is called *share enumeration*. Share enumeration is the exchange of share information between the two servers. Domain Masters and Local Masters will perform share enumeration every 15 minutes. Below I show the NetShareEnum Request that would be sent by either the Domain Master or the Local Master.

```
SMB (Server Message Block Protocol)
SMB Pipe Protocol
Microsoft Windows Lanman Remote API Protocol
    Function Code: NetShareEnum (0)
    Parameter Descriptor: WrLeh
    Return Descriptor: B13BWz
```

```
        Detail Level: 1
        Receive Buffer Length: 4096
```

The following is the response you could see from the server that
received the NetShareEnum request.

```
SMB (Server Message Block Protocol)
SMB Pipe Protocol
Microsoft Windows Lanman Remote API Protocol
    Function Code: NetShareEnum (0)
    Status: Success (0)
    Convert: 49013
    Entry Count: 5
    Available Entries: 5
    Available Shares
        Share PRINTER$
        Share DESKJET610C
        Share DATA
        Share C
        Share IPC$
```

You can see that the server responded with a list of five shared
resources. The requested browser then updates its own browse list with
these entries.

5. **Selection of Backup Browsers by Local Masters.**   Now that Local
   Masters and Domain Masters have synchronized themselves, it's time
   for the Browser protocol to implement some redundancy on its local
   segments. It does so by having the Local Master request Potential
   Browsers to become Backup Browsers. The Backup Browsers will handle share enumeration for the browser clients, leaving the Local Master
   to simply make sure that it is synchronized with the Domain Master
   and the Backup Browser servers.

   When a browser client boots up, it will send a broadcast out with a Get
   Backup List Request message over \MAILSLOT\BROWSE. When the
   Local Master hears this broadcast, it will respond to the browser client
   with a list of Backup Browsers on the subnet. Figure 8-27 illustrates this
   process. Frame 3 is the Get Backup List Request; Frame 8 is the
   response.

   Then, a browser client will choose three Backup Browsers among the
   list (if there are three available). It will then randomly choose one
   Backup Browser to use in share enumeration requests.

6. **Share enumeration between Local Master Browsers and Backup
   Browsers.**   The share enumeration process between Local Masters and
   Backup Browsers is exactly the same as between Domain Masters and
   Local Masters.

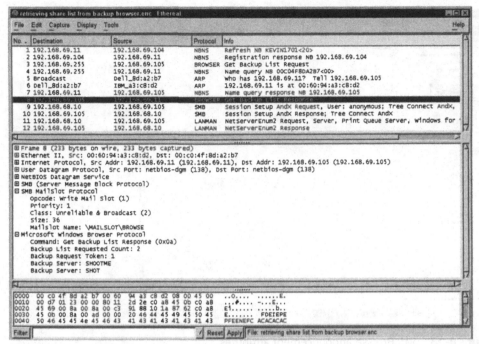

Figure 8-27 Get Backup Browser List request.

Browser Announcements

All hosts will send browser announcements depending on their role. Browser clients send announcements identifying themselves as potential browsers. Host announcements identify the type of operating system and its role in the browsing protocol, whether it is a nonbrowser, Local Master, Backup Browser, or a Domain Master Browser. Figure 8-28 illustrates the multiple attributes inside of the host announcement frame.

Hosts send browse announcements when they boot up every minute and then roughly double their announcement period from 1 to 2 to 4 to 8 minutes, until finally reaching an interval of advertising themselves every 12 minutes. Backup Browsers delete a host from the Browse List if it hasn't heard a host announcement for three advertisement intervals. This equates to 36 minutes before a Backup Browser deletes a host from its browse list. If a Domain Master has just finished updating its Browse List before the 36 minutes has expired, it takes another share enumeration interval for the Domain Master to find out that an entry in the Browse List has been deleted. This is why sometimes you see listings in a network neighborhood that you are unable to connect to; they are no longer active on the network, but the Backup Browsers still

Figure 8-28   MS Browse announcement attributes.

have them in their Browse List. Microsoft's Browsing protocol works very well without any administrator interaction, but because of the protocol's ignorance of the types of machines that Microsoft OS might be running on, it is important to verify that, for example, a Master Browser for a domain isn't running on a machine with low hardware. By understanding the Browser protocol, you can easily identify machines participating as Master Browsers. When users complain about slowness opening their Network Neighborhood, the first place to start is how the Browser protocol is working.

Summary

This chapter has only briefly touched on the many complexities that exist in protocols used on Microsoft networks. Fortunately, the information I provide gives you an excellent base of knowledge from which to start when analyzing problems in the upper layers. I recommend getting a copy of the current CIFS standard to use as a reference when learning and troubleshooting the protocol interactions you see on a Microsoft network. I have included a copy on the companion Web site for this book. Microsoft does an excellent job of documenting its protocols. And as I have discussed throughout the book, taking advantage of such information is the key to furthering your analysis knowledge and skill.

What's on the Web Site

This appendix provides you with information about the contents of the companion Web site that accompanies this book. This Web site can be found by pointing your browser to www.wiley.com/compbooks/burns. Here is what you can find in this appendix:

- System requirements
- What's on the Web site
- Using what's on the Web site with Windows, Linux, and Macintosh
- Troubleshooting

NOTE If you would prefer the contents of the Web site be sent to you on CD, please see the coupon provided at the back of this book for details on ordering.

System Requirements

Make sure that your computer meets the minimum system requirements listed in this section. If your computer doesn't match up to most of these requirements, you may have a problem using the contents of the Web site.

For Windows 9*x*, Windows 2000, Windows NT4 (with SP 4 or later), Windows Me, or Windows XP:

- PC with a Pentium processor running at 120 MHz or faster

- At least 32MB of total RAM installed on your computer; for best performance, we recommend at least 64MB

- Ethernet network interface card (NIC) or modem with a speed of at least 28,800 bps

For Linux:

- PC with a Pentium processor running at 90 MHz or faster

- At least 32MB of total RAM installed on your computer; for best performance, we recommend at least 64MB

- Ethernet network interface card (NIC) or modem with a speed of at least 28,800 bps

For Macintosh:

- Mac OS computer with a 68040 or faster processor running OS 7.6 or later

- At least 32MB of total RAM installed on your computer; for best performance, we recommend at least 64MB

What's on the Web Site

The following sections provide a summary of the materials you'll find on the Web site.

Standards and RFCs

The Web site contains vendor and Internet standards pertaining to the protocols discussed in the book. The Internet standards are in the form of Request for Comments (RFC) documents from the Internet Engineering Task Force (IETF), whose responsibility it is to maintain the RFC databases. The Web site also contains vendor-specific standards, such as Microsoft's implementation of Server Message Block and Browsing protocol. Answers to any questions you might have about a specific protocol mentioned in the book can be found in the standards on the Web site.

Author-Created Materials

You will find the following author-created material on the Web site:

- **Actual tracefiles from the book's examples.** Due to confidentiality reasons, I am not able to put all of the tracefiles from the book on the site, but I attempt to put the most important ones there.

- **Video files where I narrate over the examples in the book.** These video files are in Macromedia Flash format that requires a Flash plug-in for the specific browser being used.

Applications

On the Web site, you will also find links to the following applications elsewhere on the Web:

- **Ethereal Protocol Analyzer (free):** www.ethereal.com
- **Microsoft Port Query Application (free):**
  http://download.microsoft.com/download/win2000adserv
  /Utility/1.0/NT5/EN-US/portqry.exe
- **WildPackets EtherPeek NX (purchase):** www.wildpackets.com
- **DNS Expert (purchase):** www.menandmice.com
- **Microsoft Network Monitor (comes with purchase of Systems Management Server):** www.microsoft.com

Using the Flash Video Examples

Viewing the video examples on the Web site requires a browser plug-in for Macromedia Flash (*.swf) files.

If you do not currently have the plug-in for Flash files, your browser should redirect you to a site where you can download it. If not, the Macromedia Flash Player can be downloaded here: http://sdc.shockwave.com/go /getflash.

After downloading, run the install and select the browser you want to use to view the online Flash files. Your system will require a reboot to complete the installation.

TIP For best results viewing the video examples, set your screen area to 1024x768 and set your color to High (16-bit).

Troubleshooting

If you have difficulty using any of the materials on the companion Web site, first make sure that you have the Macromedia Flash Player installed.

If you still have trouble with the Web site, please call the Customer Care phone number: (800) 762-2974. Outside the United States, call 1 (317) 572-3994. They will provide technical support only for installation and other general quality control items; for technical support on the applications themselves, consult the program's vendor or author.

SMB Status Codes

This appendix contains a listing (Table B-1) of Server Message Block (SMB) status codes. The status codes are found in SMB response packets and indicate the status of a request made to an SMB server. Chapter 8 discusses in more detail using SMB status codes to diagnose problems between a client and server over a Microsoft network.

Table B-1 SMB Status Codes

STATUS CODE	DESCRIPTION
00000000	STATUS_SUCCESS
00000000	STATUS_WAIT_0
00000001	STATUS_WAIT_1
00000002	STATUS_WAIT_2
00000003	STATUS_WAIT_3
0000003F	STATUS_WAIT_63
00000080	STATUS_ABANDONED
00000080	STATUS_ABANDONED_WAIT_0

(continued)

Table B-1   *(continued)*

STATUS CODE	DESCRIPTION
000000BF	STATUS_ABANDONED_WAIT_63
000000C0	STATUS_USER_APC
00000100	STATUS_KERNEL_APC
00000101	STATUS_ALERTED
00000102	STATUS_TIMEOUT
00000103	STATUS_PENDING
00000104	STATUS_REPARSE
00000105	STATUS_MORE_ENTRIES
00000106	STATUS_NOT_ALL_ASSIGNED
00000107	STATUS_SOME_NOT_MAPPED
00000108	STATUS_OPLOCK_BREAK_IN_PROGRESS
00000109	STATUS_VOLUME_MOUNTED
0000010A	STATUS_RXACT_COMMITTED
0000010B	STATUS_NOTIFY_CLEANUP
0000010C	STATUS_NOTIFY_ENUM_DIR
0000010D	STATUS_NO_QUOTAS_FOR_ACCOUNT
0000010E	STATUS_PRIMARY_TRANSPORT_CONNECT_FAILED
00000110	STATUS_PAGE_FAULT_TRANSITION
00000111	STATUS_PAGE_FAULT_DEMAND_ZERO
00000112	STATUS_PAGE_FAULT_COPY_ON_WRITE
00000113	STATUS_PAGE_FAULT_GUARD_PAGE
00000114	STATUS_PAGE_FAULT_PAGING_FILE
00000115	STATUS_CACHE_PAGE_LOCKED
00000116	STATUS_CRASH_DUMP
00000117	STATUS_BUFFER_ALL_ZEROS
00000118	STATUS_REPARSE_OBJECT
40000000	STATUS_OBJECT_NAME_EXISTS
40000001	STATUS_THREAD_WAS_SUSPENDED
40000002	STATUS_WORKING_SET_LIMIT_RANGE

Table B-1 (continued)

STATUS CODE	DESCRIPTION
40000003	STATUS_IMAGE_NOT_AT_BASE
40000004	STATUS_RXACT_STATE_CREATED
40000005	STATUS_SEGMENT_NOTIFICATION
40000006	STATUS_LOCAL_USER_SESSION_KEY
40000007	STATUS_BAD_CURRENT_DIRECTORY
40000008	STATUS_SERIAL_MORE_WRITES
40000009	STATUS_REGISTRY_RECOVERED
4000000A	STATUS_FT_READ_RECOVERY_FROM_BACKUP
4000000B	STATUS_FT_WRITE_RECOVERY
4000000C	STATUS_SERIAL_COUNTER_TIMEOUT
4000000D	STATUS_NULL_LM_PASSWORD
4000000E	STATUS_IMAGE_MACHINE_TYPE_MISMATCH
4000000F	STATUS_RECEIVE_PARTIAL
40000010	STATUS_RECEIVE_EXPEDITED
40000011	STATUS_RECEIVE_PARTIAL_EXPEDITED
40000012	STATUS_EVENT_DONE
40000013	STATUS_EVENT_PENDING
40000014	STATUS_CHECKING_FILE_SYSTEM
40000015	STATUS_FATAL_APP_EXIT
40000016	STATUS_PREDEFINED_HANDLE
40000017	STATUS_WAS_UNLOCKED
40000018	STATUS_SERVICE_NOTIFICATION
40000019	STATUS_WAS_LOCKED
4000001A	STATUS_LOG_HARD_ERROR
4000001B	STATUS_ALREADY_WIN32
4000001C	STATUS_WX86_UNSIMULATE
4000001D	STATUS_WX86_CONTINUE
4000001E	STATUS_WX86_SINGLE_STEP

(continued)

Table B-1   *(continued)*

STATUS CODE	DESCRIPTION
4000001F	STATUS_WX86_BREAKPOINT
40000020	STATUS_WX86_EXCEPTION_CONTINUE
40000021	STATUS_WX86_EXCEPTION_LASTCHANCE
40000022	STATUS_WX86_EXCEPTION_CHAIN
40000023	STATUS_IMAGE_MACHINE_TYPE_MISMATCH_EXE
40000024	STATUS_NO_YIELD_PERFORMED
40000025	STATUS_TIMER_RESUME_IGNORED
80000001	STATUS_GUARD_PAGE_VIOLATION
80000002	STATUS_DATATYPE_MISALIGNMENT
80000003	STATUS_BREAKPOINT
80000004	STATUS_SINGLE_STEP
80000005	STATUS_BUFFER_OVERFLOW
80000006	STATUS_NO_MORE_FILES
80000007	STATUS_WAKE_SYSTEM_DEBUGGER
8000000A	STATUS_HANDLES_CLOSED
8000000B	STATUS_NO_INHERITANCE
8000000C	STATUS_GUID_SUBSTITUTION_MADE
8000000D	STATUS_PARTIAL_COPY
8000000E	STATUS_DEVICE_PAPER_EMPTY
8000000F	STATUS_DEVICE_POWERED_OFF
80000010	STATUS_DEVICE_OFF_LINE
80000011	STATUS_DEVICE_BUSY
80000012	STATUS_NO_MORE_EAS
80000013	STATUS_INVALID_EA_NAME
80000014	STATUS_EA_LIST_INCONSISTENT
80000015	STATUS_INVALID_EA_FLAG
80000016	STATUS_VERIFY_REQUIRED
80000017	STATUS_EXTRANEOUS_INFORMATION
80000018	STATUS_RXACT_COMMIT_NECESSARY

Table B-1   *(continued)*

STATUS CODE	DESCRIPTION
8000001A	STATUS_NO_MORE_ENTRIES
8000001B	STATUS_FILEMARK_DETECTED
8000001C	STATUS_MEDIA_CHANGED
8000001D	STATUS_BUS_RESET
8000001E	STATUS_END_OF_MEDIA
8000001F	STATUS_BEGINNING_OF_MEDIA
80000020	STATUS_MEDIA_CHECK
80000021	STATUS_SETMARK_DETECTED
80000022	STATUS_NO_DATA_DETECTED
80000023	STATUS_REDIRECTOR_HAS_OPEN_HANDLES
80000024	STATUS_SERVER_HAS_OPEN_HANDLES
80000025	STATUS_ALREADY_DISCONNECTED
80000026	STATUS_LONGJUMP
C0000001	STATUS_UNSUCCESSFUL
C0000002	STATUS_NOT_IMPLEMENTED
C0000003	STATUS_INVALID_INFO_CLASS
C0000004	STATUS_INFO_LENGTH_MISMATCH
C0000005	STATUS_ACCESS_VIOLATION
C0000006	STATUS_IN_PAGE_ERROR
C0000007	STATUS_PAGEFILE_QUOTA
C0000008	STATUS_INVALID_HANDLE
C0000009	STATUS_BAD_INITIAL_STACK
C000000A	STATUS_BAD_INITIAL_PC
C000000B	STATUS_INVALID_CID
C000000C	STATUS_TIMER_NOT_CANCELED
C000000D	STATUS_INVALID_PARAMETER
C000000E	STATUS_NO_SUCH_DEVICE
C000000F	STATUS_NO_SUCH_FILE

(continued)

Table B-1   *(continued)*

STATUS CODE	DESCRIPTION
C0000010	STATUS_INVALID_DEVICE_REQUEST
C0000011	STATUS_END_OF_FILE
C0000012	STATUS_WRONG_VOLUME
C0000013	STATUS_NO_MEDIA_IN_DEVICE
C0000014	STATUS_UNRECOGNIZED_MEDIA
C0000015	STATUS_NONEXISTENT_SECTOR
C0000016	STATUS_MORE_PROCESSING_REQUIRED
C0000017	STATUS_NO_MEMORY
C0000018	STATUS_CONFLICTING_ADDRESSES
C0000019	STATUS_NOT_MAPPED_VIEW
C000001A	STATUS_UNABLE_TO_FREE_VM
C000001B	STATUS_UNABLE_TO_DELETE_SECTION
C000001C	STATUS_INVALID_SYSTEM_SERVICE
C000001D	STATUS_ILLEGAL_INSTRUCTION
C000001E	STATUS_INVALID_LOCK_SEQUENCE
C000001F	STATUS_INVALID_VIEW_SIZE
C0000020	STATUS_INVALID_FILE_FOR_SECTION
C0000021	STATUS_ALREADY_COMMITTED
C0000022	STATUS_ACCESS_DENIED
C0000023	STATUS_BUFFER_TOO_SMALL
C0000024	STATUS_OBJECT_TYPE_MISMATCH
C0000025	STATUS_NONCONTINUABLE_EXCEPTION
C0000026	STATUS_INVALID_DISPOSITION
C0000027	STATUS_UNWIND
C0000028	STATUS_BAD_STACK
C0000029	STATUS_INVALID_UNWIND_TARGET
C000002A	STATUS_NOT_LOCKED
C000002B	STATUS_PARITY_ERROR
C000002C	STATUS_UNABLE_TO_DECOMMIT_VM

Table B-1 *(continued)*

STATUS CODE	DESCRIPTION
C000002D	STATUS_NOT_COMMITTED
C000002E	STATUS_INVALID_PORT_ATTRIBUTES
C000002F	STATUS_PORT_MESSAGE_TOO_LONG
C0000030	STATUS_INVALID_PARAMETER_MIX
C0000031	STATUS_INVALID_QUOTA_LOWER
C0000032	STATUS_DISK_CORRUPT_ERROR
C0000033	STATUS_OBJECT_NAME_INVALID
C0000034	STATUS_OBJECT_NAME_NOT_FOUND
C0000035	STATUS_OBJECT_NAME_COLLISION
C0000037	STATUS_PORT_DISCONNECTED
C0000038	STATUS_DEVICE_ALREADY_ATTACHED
C0000039	STATUS_OBJECT_PATH_INVALID
C000003A	STATUS_OBJECT_PATH_NOT_FOUND
C000003B	STATUS_OBJECT_PATH_SYNTAX_BAD
C000003C	STATUS_DATA_OVERRUN
C000003D	STATUS_DATA_LATE_ERROR
C000003E	STATUS_DATA_ERROR
C000003F	STATUS_CRC_ERROR
C0000040	STATUS_SECTION_TOO_BIG
C0000041	STATUS_PORT_CONNECTION_REFUSED
C0000042	STATUS_INVALID_PORT_HANDLE
C0000043	STATUS_SHARING_VIOLATION
C0000044	STATUS_QUOTA_EXCEEDED
C0000045	STATUS_INVALID_PAGE_PROTECTION
C0000046	STATUS_MUTANT_NOT_OWNED
C0000047	STATUS_SEMAPHORE_LIMIT_EXCEEDED
C0000048	STATUS_PORT_ALREADY_SET
C0000049	STATUS_SECTION_NOT_IMAGE

(continued)

Table B-1 *(continued)*

STATUS CODE	DESCRIPTION
C000004A	STATUS_SUSPEND_COUNT_EXCEEDED
C000004B	STATUS_THREAD_IS_TERMINATING
C000004C	STATUS_BAD_WORKING_SET_LIMIT
C000004D	STATUS_INCOMPATIBLE_FILE_MAP
C000004E	STATUS_SECTION_PROTECTION
C000004F	STATUS_EAS_NOT_SUPPORTED
C0000050	STATUS_EA_TOO_LARGE
C0000051	STATUS_NONEXISTENT_EA_ENTRY
C0000052	STATUS_NO_EAS_ON_FILE
C0000053	STATUS_EA_CORRUPT_ERROR
C0000054	STATUS_FILE_LOCK_CONFLICT
C0000055	STATUS_LOCK_NOT_GRANTED
C0000056	STATUS_DELETE_PENDING
C0000057	STATUS_CTL_FILE_NOT_SUPPORTED
C0000058	STATUS_UNKNOWN_REVISION
C0000059	STATUS_REVISION_MISMATCH
C000005A	STATUS_INVALID_OWNER
C000005B	STATUS_INVALID_PRIMARY_GROUP
C000005C	STATUS_NO_IMPERSONATION_TOKEN
C000005D	STATUS_CANT_DISABLE_MANDATORY
C000005E	STATUS_NO_LOGON_SERVERS
C000005F	STATUS_NO_SUCH_LOGON_SESSION
C0000060	STATUS_NO_SUCH_PRIVILEGE
C0000061	STATUS_PRIVILEGE_NOT_HELD
C0000062	STATUS_INVALID_ACCOUNT_NAME
C0000063	STATUS_USER_EXISTS
C0000064	STATUS_NO_SUCH_USER
C0000065	STATUS_GROUP_EXISTS
C0000066	STATUS_NO_SUCH_GROUP

Table B-1 *(continued)*

STATUS CODE	DESCRIPTION
C0000067	STATUS_MEMBER_IN_GROUP
C0000068	STATUS_MEMBER_NOT_IN_GROUP
C0000069	STATUS_LAST_ADMIN
C000006A	STATUS_WRONG_PASSWORD
C000006B	STATUS_ILL_FORMED_PASSWORD
C000006C	STATUS_PASSWORD_RESTRICTION
C000006D	STATUS_LOGON_FAILURE
C000006E	STATUS_ACCOUNT_RESTRICTION
C000006F	STATUS_INVALID_LOGON_HOURS
C0000070	STATUS_INVALID_WORKSTATION
C0000071	STATUS_PASSWORD_EXPIRED
C0000072	STATUS_ACCOUNT_DISABLED
C0000073	STATUS_NONE_MAPPED
C0000074	STATUS_TOO_MANY_LUIDS_REQUESTED
C0000075	STATUS_LUIDS_EXHAUSTED
C0000076	STATUS_INVALID_SUB_AUTHORITY
C0000077	STATUS_INVALID_ACL
C0000078	STATUS_INVALID_SID
C0000079	STATUS_INVALID_SECURITY_DESCR
C000007A	STATUS_PROCEDURE_NOT_FOUND
C000007B	STATUS_INVALID_IMAGE_FORMAT
C000007C	STATUS_NO_TOKEN
C000007D	STATUS_BAD_INHERITANCE_ACL
C000007E	STATUS_RANGE_NOT_LOCKED
C000007F	STATUS_DISK_FULL
C0000080	STATUS_SERVER_DISABLED
C0000081	STATUS_SERVER_NOT_DISABLED
C0000082	STATUS_TOO_MANY_GUIDS_REQUESTED

(continued)

Table B-1 *(continued)*

STATUS CODE	DESCRIPTION
C0000083	STATUS_GUIDS_EXHAUSTED
C0000084	STATUS_INVALID_ID_AUTHORITY
C0000085	STATUS_AGENTS_EXHAUSTED
C0000086	STATUS_INVALID_VOLUME_LABEL
C0000087	STATUS_SECTION_NOT_EXTENDED
C0000088	STATUS_NOT_MAPPED_DATA
C0000089	STATUS_RESOURCE_DATA_NOT_FOUND
C000008A	STATUS_RESOURCE_TYPE_NOT_FOUND
C000008B	STATUS_RESOURCE_NAME_NOT_FOUND
C000008C	STATUS_ARRAY_BOUNDS_EXCEEDED
C000008D	STATUS_FLOAT_DENORMAL_OPERAND
C000008E	STATUS_FLOAT_DIVIDE_BY_ZERO
C000008F	STATUS_FLOAT_INEXACT_RESULT
C0000090	STATUS_FLOAT_INVALID_OPERATION
C0000091	STATUS_FLOAT_OVERFLOW
C0000092	STATUS_FLOAT_STACK_CHECK
C0000093	STATUS_FLOAT_UNDERFLOW
C0000094	STATUS_INTEGER_DIVIDE_BY_ZERO
C0000095	STATUS_INTEGER_OVERFLOW
C0000096	STATUS_PRIVILEGED_INSTRUCTION
C0000097	STATUS_TOO_MANY_PAGING_FILES
C0000098	STATUS_FILE_INVALID
C0000099	STATUS_ALLOTTED_SPACE_EXCEEDED
C000009A	STATUS_INSUFFICIENT_RESOURCES
C000009B	STATUS_DFS_EXIT_PATH_FOUND
C000009C	STATUS_DEVICE_DATA_ERROR
C000009D	STATUS_DEVICE_NOT_CONNECTED
C000009E	STATUS_DEVICE_POWER_FAILURE
C000009F	STATUS_FREE_VM_NOT_AT_BASE

Table B-1 *(continued)*

STATUS CODE	DESCRIPTION
C00000A0	STATUS_MEMORY_NOT_ALLOCATED
C00000A1	STATUS_WORKING_SET_QUOTA
C00000A2	STATUS_MEDIA_WRITE_PROTECTED
C00000A3	STATUS_DEVICE_NOT_READY
C00000A4	STATUS_INVALID_GROUP_ATTRIBUTES
C00000A5	STATUS_BAD_IMPERSONATION_LEVEL
C00000A6	STATUS_CANT_OPEN_ANONYMOUS
C00000A7	STATUS_BAD_VALIDATION_CLASS
C00000A8	STATUS_BAD_TOKEN_TYPE
C00000A9	STATUS_BAD_MASTER_BOOT_RECORD
C00000AA	STATUS_INSTRUCTION_MISALIGNMENT
C00000AB	STATUS_INSTANCE_NOT_AVAILABLE
C00000AC	STATUS_PIPE_NOT_AVAILABLE
C00000AD	STATUS_INVALID_PIPE_STATE
C00000AE	STATUS_PIPE_BUSY
C00000AF	STATUS_ILLEGAL_FUNCTION
C00000B0	STATUS_PIPE_DISCONNECTED
C00000B1	STATUS_PIPE_CLOSING
C00000B2	STATUS_PIPE_CONNECTED
C00000B3	STATUS_PIPE_LISTENING
C00000B4	STATUS_INVALID_READ_MODE
C00000B5	STATUS_IO_TIMEOUT
C00000B6	STATUS_FILE_FORCED_CLOSED
C00000B7	STATUS_PROFILING_NOT_STARTED
C00000B8	STATUS_PROFILING_NOT_STOPPED
C00000B9	STATUS_COULD_NOT_INTERPRET
C00000BA	STATUS_FILE_IS_A_DIRECTORY
C00000BB	STATUS_NOT_SUPPORTED

(continued)

Table B-1 *(continued)*

STATUS CODE	DESCRIPTION
C00000BC	STATUS_REMOTE_NOT_LISTENING
C00000BD	STATUS_DUPLICATE_NAME
C00000BE	STATUS_BAD_NETWORK_PATH
C00000BF	STATUS_NETWORK_BUSY
C00000C0	STATUS_DEVICE_DOES_NOT_EXIST
C00000C1	STATUS_TOO_MANY_COMMANDS
C00000C2	STATUS_ADAPTER_HARDWARE_ERROR
C00000C3	STATUS_INVALID_NETWORK_RESPONSE
C00000C4	STATUS_UNEXPECTED_NETWORK_ERROR
C00000C5	STATUS_BAD_REMOTE_ADAPTER
C00000C6	STATUS_PRINT_QUEUE_FULL
C00000C7	STATUS_NO_SPOOL_SPACE
C00000C8	STATUS_PRINT_CANCELLED
C00000C9	STATUS_NETWORK_NAME_DELETED
C00000CA	STATUS_NETWORK_ACCESS_DENIED
C00000CB	STATUS_BAD_DEVICE_TYPE
C00000CC	STATUS_BAD_NETWORK_NAME
C00000CD	STATUS_TOO_MANY_NAMES
C00000CE	STATUS_TOO_MANY_SESSIONS
C00000CF	STATUS_SHARING_PAUSED
C00000D0	STATUS_REQUEST_NOT_ACCEPTED
C00000D1	STATUS_REDIRECTOR_PAUSED
C00000D2	STATUS_NET_WRITE_FAULT
C00000D3	STATUS_PROFILING_AT_LIMIT
C00000D4	STATUS_NOT_SAME_DEVICE
C00000D5	STATUS_FILE_RENAMED
C00000D6	STATUS_VIRTUAL_CIRCUIT_CLOSED
C00000D7	STATUS_NO_SECURITY_ON_OBJECT
C00000D8	STATUS_CANT_WAIT

Table B-1 *(continued)*

STATUS CODE	DESCRIPTION
C00000D9	STATUS_PIPE_EMPTY
C00000DA	STATUS_CANT_ACCESS_DOMAIN_INFO
C00000DB	STATUS_CANT_TERMINATE_SELF
C00000DC	STATUS_INVALID_SERVER_STATE
C00000DD	STATUS_INVALID_DOMAIN_STATE
C00000DE	STATUS_INVALID_DOMAIN_ROLE
C00000DF	STATUS_NO_SUCH_DOMAIN
C00000E0	STATUS_DOMAIN_EXISTS
C00000E1	STATUS_DOMAIN_LIMIT_EXCEEDED
C00000E2	STATUS_OPLOCK_NOT_GRANTED
C00000E3	STATUS_INVALID_OPLOCK_PROTOCOL
C00000E4	STATUS_INTERNAL_DB_CORRUPTION
C00000E5	STATUS_INTERNAL_ERROR
C00000E6	STATUS_GENERIC_NOT_MAPPED
C00000E7	STATUS_BAD_DESCRIPTOR_FORMAT
C00000E8	STATUS_INVALID_USER_BUFFER
C00000E9	STATUS_UNEXPECTED_IO_ERROR
C00000EA	STATUS_UNEXPECTED_MM_CREATE_ERR
C00000EB	STATUS_UNEXPECTED_MM_MAP_ERROR
C00000EC	STATUS_UNEXPECTED_MM_EXTEND_ERR
C00000ED	STATUS_NOT_LOGON_PROCESS
C00000EE	STATUS_LOGON_SESSION_EXISTS
C00000EF	STATUS_INVALID_PARAMETER_1
C00000F0	STATUS_INVALID_PARAMETER_2
C00000F1	STATUS_INVALID_PARAMETER_3
C00000F2	STATUS_INVALID_PARAMETER_4
C00000F3	STATUS_INVALID_PARAMETER_5
C00000F4	STATUS_INVALID_PARAMETER_6

(continued)

Table B-1 *(continued)*

STATUS CODE	DESCRIPTION
C00000F5	STATUS_INVALID_PARAMETER_7
C00000F6	STATUS_INVALID_PARAMETER_8
C00000F7	STATUS_INVALID_PARAMETER_9
C00000F8	STATUS_INVALID_PARAMETER_10
C00000F9	STATUS_INVALID_PARAMETER_11
C00000FA	STATUS_INVALID_PARAMETER_12
C00000FB	STATUS_REDIRECTOR_NOT_STARTED
C00000FC	STATUS_REDIRECTOR_STARTED
C00000FD	STATUS_STACK_OVERFLOW
C00000FE	STATUS_NO_SUCH_PACKAGE
C00000FF	STATUS_BAD_FUNCTION_TABLE
C0000100	STATUS_VARIABLE_NOT_FOUND
C0000101	STATUS_DIRECTORY_NOT_EMPTY
C0000102	STATUS_FILE_CORRUPT_ERROR
C0000103	STATUS_NOT_A_DIRECTORY
C0000104	STATUS_BAD_LOGON_SESSION_STATE
C0000105	STATUS_LOGON_SESSION_COLLISION
C0000106	STATUS_NAME_TOO_LONG
C0000107	STATUS_FILES_OPEN
C0000108	STATUS_CONNECTION_IN_USE
C0000109	STATUS_MESSAGE_NOT_FOUND
C000010A	STATUS_PROCESS_IS_TERMINATING
C000010B	STATUS_INVALID_LOGON_TYPE
C000010C	STATUS_NO_GUID_TRANSLATION
C000010D	STATUS_CANNOT_IMPERSONATE
C000010E	STATUS_IMAGE_ALREADY_LOADED
C000010F	STATUS_ABIOS_NOT_PRESENT
C0000110	STATUS_ABIOS_LID_NOT_EXIST
C0000111	STATUS_ABIOS_LID_ALREADY_OWNED

Table B-1   *(continued)*

STATUS CODE	DESCRIPTION
C0000112	STATUS_ABIOS_NOT_LID_OWNER
C0000113	STATUS_ABIOS_INVALID_COMMAND
C0000114	STATUS_ABIOS_INVALID_LID
C0000115	STATUS_ABIOS_SELECTOR_NOT_AVAILABLE
C0000116	STATUS_ABIOS_INVALID_SELECTOR
C0000117	STATUS_NO_LDT
C0000118	STATUS_INVALID_LDT_SIZE
C0000119	STATUS_INVALID_LDT_OFFSET
C000011A	STATUS_INVALID_LDT_DESCRIPTOR
C000011B	STATUS_INVALID_IMAGE_NE_FORMAT
C000011C	STATUS_RXACT_INVALID_STATE
C000011D	STATUS_RXACT_COMMIT_FAILURE
C000011E	STATUS_MAPPED_FILE_SIZE_ZERO
C000011F	STATUS_TOO_MANY_OPENED_FILES
C0000120	STATUS_CANCELLED
C0000121	STATUS_CANNOT_DELETE
C0000122	STATUS_INVALID_COMPUTER_NAME
C0000123	STATUS_FILE_DELETED
C0000124	STATUS_SPECIAL_ACCOUNT
C0000125	STATUS_SPECIAL_GROUP
C0000126	STATUS_SPECIAL_USER
C0000127	STATUS_MEMBERS_PRIMARY_GROUP
C0000128	STATUS_FILE_CLOSED
C0000129	STATUS_TOO_MANY_THREADS
C000012A	STATUS_THREAD_NOT_IN_PROCESS
C000012B	STATUS_TOKEN_ALREADY_IN_USE
C000012C	STATUS_PAGEFILE_QUOTA_EXCEEDED
C000012D	STATUS_COMMITMENT_LIMIT

(continued)

Table B-1 *(continued)*

STATUS CODE	DESCRIPTION
C000012E	STATUS_INVALID_IMAGE_LE_FORMAT
C000012F	STATUS_INVALID_IMAGE_NOT_MZ
C0000130	STATUS_INVALID_IMAGE_PROTECT
C0000131	STATUS_INVALID_IMAGE_WIN_16
C0000132	STATUS_LOGON_SERVER_CONFLICT
C0000133	STATUS_TIME_DIFFERENCE_AT_DC
C0000134	STATUS_SYNCHRONIZATION_REQUIRED
C0000135	STATUS_DLL_NOT_FOUND
C0000136	STATUS_OPEN_FAILED
C0000137	STATUS_IO_PRIVILEGE_FAILED
C0000138	STATUS_ORDINAL_NOT_FOUND
C0000139	STATUS_ENTRYPOINT_NOT_FOUND
C000013A	STATUS_CONTROL_C_EXIT
C000013B	STATUS_LOCAL_DISCONNECT
C000013C	STATUS_REMOTE_DISCONNECT
C000013D	STATUS_REMOTE_RESOURCES
C000013E	STATUS_LINK_FAILED
C000013F	STATUS_LINK_TIMEOUT
C0000140	STATUS_INVALID_CONNECTION
C0000141	STATUS_INVALID_ADDRESS
C0000142	STATUS_DLL_INIT_FAILED
C0000143	STATUS_MISSING_SYSTEMFILE
C0000144	STATUS_UNHANDLED_EXCEPTION
C0000145	STATUS_APP_INIT_FAILURE
C0000146	STATUS_PAGEFILE_CREATE_FAILED
C0000147	STATUS_NO_PAGEFILE
C0000148	STATUS_INVALID_LEVEL
C0000149	STATUS_WRONG_PASSWORD_CORE
C000014A	STATUS_ILLEGAL_FLOAT_CONTEXT

Table B-1 *(continued)*

STATUS CODE	DESCRIPTION
C000014B	STATUS_PIPE_BROKEN
C000014C	STATUS_REGISTRY_CORRUPT
C000014D	STATUS_REGISTRY_IO_FAILED
C000014E	STATUS_NO_EVENT_PAIR
C000014F	STATUS_UNRECOGNIZED_VOLUME
C0000150	STATUS_SERIAL_NO_DEVICE_INITED
C0000151	STATUS_NO_SUCH_ALIAS
C0000152	STATUS_MEMBER_NOT_IN_ALIAS
C0000153	STATUS_MEMBER_IN_ALIAS
C0000154	STATUS_ALIAS_EXISTS
C0000155	STATUS_LOGON_NOT_GRANTED
C0000156	STATUS_TOO_MANY_SECRETS
C0000157	STATUS_SECRET_TOO_LONG
C0000158	STATUS_INTERNAL_DB_ERROR
C0000159	STATUS_FULLSCREEN_MODE
C000015A	STATUS_TOO_MANY_CONTEXT_IDS
C000015B	STATUS_LOGON_TYPE_NOT_GRANTED
C000015C	STATUS_NOT_REGISTRY_FILE
C000015D	STATUS_NT_CROSS_ENCRYPTION_REQUIRED
C000015E	STATUS_DOMAIN_CTRLR_CONFIG_ERROR
C000015F	STATUS_FT_MISSING_MEMBER
C0000160	STATUS_ILL_FORMED_SERVICE_ENTRY
C0000161	STATUS_ILLEGAL_CHARACTER
C0000162	STATUS_UNMAPPABLE_CHARACTER
C0000163	STATUS_UNDEFINED_CHARACTER
C0000164	STATUS_FLOPPY_VOLUME
C0000165	STATUS_FLOPPY_ID_MARK_NOT_FOUND
C0000166	STATUS_FLOPPY_WRONG_CYLINDER

(continued)

Table B-1 *(continued)*

STATUS CODE	DESCRIPTION
C0000167	STATUS_FLOPPY_UNKNOWN_ERROR
C0000168	STATUS_FLOPPY_BAD_REGISTERS
C0000169	STATUS_DISK_RECALIBRATE_FAILED
C000016A	STATUS_DISK_OPERATION_FAILED
C000016B	STATUS_DISK_RESET_FAILED
C000016C	STATUS_SHARED_IRQ_BUSY
C000016D	STATUS_FT_ORPHANING
C000016E	STATUS_BIOS_FAILED_TO_CONNECT_INTERRUPT
C0000172	STATUS_PARTITION_FAILURE
C0000173	STATUS_INVALID_BLOCK_LENGTH
C0000174	STATUS_DEVICE_NOT_PARTITIONED
C0000175	STATUS_UNABLE_TO_LOCK_MEDIA
C0000176	STATUS_UNABLE_TO_UNLOAD_MEDIA
C0000177	STATUS_EOM_OVERFLOW
C0000178	STATUS_NO_MEDIA
C000017A	STATUS_NO_SUCH_MEMBER
C000017B	STATUS_INVALID_MEMBER
C000017C	STATUS_KEY_DELETED
C000017D	STATUS_NO_LOG_SPACE
C000017E	STATUS_TOO_MANY_SIDS
C000017F	STATUS_LM_CROSS_ENCRYPTION_REQUIRED
C0000180	STATUS_KEY_HAS_CHILDREN
C0000181	STATUS_CHILD_MUST_BE_VOLATILE
C0000182	STATUS_DEVICE_CONFIGURATION_ERROR
C0000183	STATUS_DRIVER_INTERNAL_ERROR
C0000184	STATUS_INVALID_DEVICE_STATE
C0000185	STATUS_IO_DEVICE_ERROR
C0000186	STATUS_DEVICE_PROTOCOL_ERROR
C0000187	STATUS_BACKUP_CONTROLLER

Table B-1 (continued)

STATUS CODE	DESCRIPTION
C0000188	STATUS_LOG_FILE_FULL
C0000189	STATUS_TOO_LATE
C000018A	STATUS_NO_TRUST_LSA_SECRET
C000018B	STATUS_NO_TRUST_SAM_ACCOUNT
C000018C	STATUS_TRUSTED_DOMAIN_FAILURE
C000018D	STATUS_TRUSTED_RELATIONSHIP_FAILURE
C000018E	STATUS_EVENTLOG_FILE_CORRUPT
C000018F	STATUS_EVENTLOG_CANT_START
C0000190	STATUS_TRUST_FAILURE
C0000191	STATUS_MUTANT_LIMIT_EXCEEDED
C0000192	STATUS_NETLOGON_NOT_STARTED
C0000193	STATUS_ACCOUNT_EXPIRED
C0000194	STATUS_POSSIBLE_DEADLOCK
C0000195	STATUS_NETWORK_CREDENTIAL_CONFLICT
C0000196	STATUS_REMOTE_SESSION_LIMIT
C0000197	STATUS_EVENTLOG_FILE_CHANGED
C0000198	STATUS_NOLOGON_INTERDOMAIN_TRUST_ACCOUNT
C0000199	STATUS_NOLOGON_WORKSTATION_TRUST_ACCOUNT
C000019A	STATUS_NOLOGON_SERVER_TRUST_ACCOUNT
C000019B	STATUS_DOMAIN_TRUST_INCONSISTENT
C000019C	STATUS_FS_DRIVER_REQUIRED
C0000202	STATUS_NO_USER_SESSION_KEY
C0000203	STATUS_USER_SESSION_DELETED
C0000204	STATUS_RESOURCE_LANG_NOT_FOUND
C0000205	STATUS_INSUFF_SERVER_RESOURCES
C0000206	STATUS_INVALID_BUFFER_SIZE
C0000207	STATUS_INVALID_ADDRESS_COMPONENT
C0000208	STATUS_INVALID_ADDRESS_WILDCARD

(continued)

Table B-1 *(continued)*

STATUS CODE	DESCRIPTION
C0000209	STATUS_TOO_MANY_ADDRESSES
C000020A	STATUS_ADDRESS_ALREADY_EXISTS
C000020B	STATUS_ADDRESS_CLOSED
C000020C	STATUS_CONNECTION_DISCONNECTED
C000020D	STATUS_CONNECTION_RESET
C000020E	STATUS_TOO_MANY_NODES
C000020F	STATUS_TRANSACTION_ABORTED
C0000210	STATUS_TRANSACTION_TIMED_OUT
C0000211	STATUS_TRANSACTION_NO_RELEASE
C0000212	STATUS_TRANSACTION_NO_MATCH
C0000213	STATUS_TRANSACTION_RESPONDED
C0000214	STATUS_TRANSACTION_INVALID_ID
C0000215	STATUS_TRANSACTION_INVALID_TYPE
C0000216	STATUS_NOT_SERVER_SESSION
C0000217	STATUS_NOT_CLIENT_SESSION
C0000218	STATUS_CANNOT_LOAD_REGISTRY_FILE
C0000219	STATUS_DEBUG_ATTACH_FAILED
C000021A	STATUS_SYSTEM_PROCESS_TERMINATED
C000021B	STATUS_DATA_NOT_ACCEPTED
C000021C	STATUS_NO_BROWSER_SERVERS_FOUND
C000021D	STATUS_VDM_HARD_ERROR
C000021E	STATUS_DRIVER_CANCEL_TIMEOUT
C000021F	STATUS_REPLY_MESSAGE_MISMATCH
C0000220	STATUS_MAPPED_ALIGNMENT
C0000221	STATUS_IMAGE_CHECKSUM_MISMATCH
C0000222	STATUS_LOST_WRITEBEHIND_DATA
C0000223	STATUS_CLIENT_SERVER_PARAMETERS_INVALID
C0000224	STATUS_PASSWORD_MUST_CHANGE
C0000225	STATUS_NOT_FOUND

Table B-1 (continued)

STATUS CODE	DESCRIPTION
C0000226	STATUS_NOT_TINY_STREAM
C0000227	STATUS_RECOVERY_FAILURE
C0000228	STATUS_STACK_OVERFLOW_READ
C0000229	STATUS_FAIL_CHECK
C000022A	STATUS_DUPLICATE_OBJECTID
C000022B	STATUS_OBJECTID_EXISTS
C000022C	STATUS_CONVERT_TO_LARGE
C000022D	STATUS_RETRY
C000022E	STATUS_FOUND_OUT_OF_SCOPE
C000022F	STATUS_ALLOCATE_BUCKET
C0000230	STATUS_PROPSET_NOT_FOUND
C0000231	STATUS_MARSHALL_OVERFLOW
C0000232	STATUS_INVALID_VARIANT
C0000233	STATUS_DOMAIN_CONTROLLER_NOT_FOUND
C0000234	STATUS_ACCOUNT_LOCKED_OUT
C0000235	STATUS_HANDLE_NOT_CLOSABLE
C0000236	STATUS_CONNECTION_REFUSED
C0000237	STATUS_GRACEFUL_DISCONNECT
C0000238	STATUS_ADDRESS_ALREADY_ASSOCIATED
C0000239	STATUS_ADDRESS_NOT_ASSOCIATED
C000023A	STATUS_CONNECTION_INVALID
C000023B	STATUS_CONNECTION_ACTIVE
C000023C	STATUS_NETWORK_UNREACHABLE
C000023D	STATUS_HOST_UNREACHABLE
C000023E	STATUS_PROTOCOL_UNREACHABLE
C000023F	STATUS_PORT_UNREACHABLE
C0000240	STATUS_REQUEST_ABORTED
C0000241	STATUS_CONNECTION_ABORTED

(continued)

Table B-1 *(continued)*

STATUS CODE	DESCRIPTION
C0000242	STATUS_BAD_COMPRESSION_BUFFER
C0000243	STATUS_USER_MAPPED_FILE
C0000244	STATUS_AUDIT_FAILED
C0000245	STATUS_TIMER_RESOLUTION_NOT_SET
C0000246	STATUS_CONNECTION_COUNT_LIMIT
C0000247	STATUS_LOGIN_TIME_RESTRICTION
C0000248	STATUS_LOGIN_WKSTA_RESTRICTION
C0000249	STATUS_IMAGE_MP_UP_MISMATCH
C0000250	STATUS_INSUFFICIENT_LOGON_INFO
C0000251	STATUS_BAD_DLL_ENTRYPOINT
C0000252	STATUS_BAD_SERVICE_ENTRYPOINT
C0000253	STATUS_LPC_REPLY_LOST
C0000254	STATUS_IP_ADDRESS_CONFLICT1
C0000255	STATUS_IP_ADDRESS_CONFLICT2
C0000256	STATUS_REGISTRY_QUOTA_LIMIT
C0000257	STATUS_PATH_NOT_COVERED
C0000258	STATUS_NO_CALLBACK_ACTIVE
C0000259	STATUS_LICENSE_QUOTA_EXCEEDED
C000025A	STATUS_PWD_TOO_SHORT
C000025B	STATUS_PWD_TOO_RECENT
C000025C	STATUS_PWD_HISTORY_CONFLICT
C000025E	STATUS_PLUGPLAY_NO_DEVICE
C000025F	STATUS_UNSUPPORTED_COMPRESSION
C0000260	STATUS_INVALID_HW_PROFILE
C0000261	STATUS_INVALID_PLUGPLAY_DEVICE_PATH
C0000262	STATUS_DRIVER_ORDINAL_NOT_FOUND
C0000263	STATUS_DRIVER_ENTRYPOINT_NOT_FOUND
C0000264	STATUS_RESOURCE_NOT_OWNED
C0000265	STATUS_TOO_MANY_LINKS

Table B-1 (continued)

STATUS CODE	DESCRIPTION
C0000266	STATUS_QUOTA_LIST_INCONSISTENT
C0000267	STATUS_FILE_IS_OFFLINE
C0000268	STATUS_EVALUATION_EXPIRATION
C0000269	STATUS_ILLEGAL_DLL_RELOCATION
C000026A	STATUS_LICENSE_VIOLATION
C000026B	STATUS_DLL_INIT_FAILED_LOGOFF
C000026C	STATUS_DRIVER_UNABLE_TO_LOAD
C000026D	STATUS_DFS_UNAVAILABLE
C000026E	STATUS_VOLUME_DISMOUNTED
C000026F	STATUS_WX86_INTERNAL_ERROR
C0000270	STATUS_WX86_FLOAT_STACK_CHECK
C0009898	STATUS_WOW_ASSERTION
C0020001	RPC_NT_INVALID_STRING_BINDING
C0020002	RPC_NT_WRONG_KIND_OF_BINDING
C0020003	RPC_NT_INVALID_BINDING
C0020004	RPC_NT_PROTSEQ_NOT_SUPPORTED
C0020005	RPC_NT_INVALID_RPC_PROTSEQ
C0020006	RPC_NT_INVALID_STRING_UUID
C0020007	RPC_NT_INVALID_ENDPOINT_FORMAT
C0020008	RPC_NT_INVALID_NET_ADDR
C0020009	RPC_NT_NO_ENDPOINT_FOUND
C002000A	RPC_NT_INVALID_TIMEOUT
C002000B	RPC_NT_OBJECT_NOT_FOUND
C002000C	RPC_NT_ALREADY_REGISTERED
C002000D	RPC_NT_TYPE_ALREADY_REGISTERED
C002000E	RPC_NT_ALREADY_LISTENING
C002000F	RPC_NT_NO_PROTSEQS_REGISTERED
C0020010	RPC_NT_NOT_LISTENING

(continued)

Table B-1 *(continued)*

STATUS CODE	DESCRIPTION
C0020011	RPC_NT_UNKNOWN_MGR_TYPE
C0020012	RPC_NT_UNKNOWN_IF
C0020013	RPC_NT_NO_BINDINGS
C0020014	RPC_NT_NO_PROTSEQS
C0020015	RPC_NT_CANT_CREATE_ENDPOINT
C0020016	RPC_NT_OUT_OF_RESOURCES
C0020017	RPC_NT_SERVER_UNAVAILABLE
C0020018	RPC_NT_SERVER_TOO_BUSY
C0020019	RPC_NT_INVALID_NETWORK_OPTIONS
C002001A	RPC_NT_NO_CALL_ACTIVE
C002001B	RPC_NT_CALL_FAILED
C002001C	RPC_NT_CALL_FAILED_DNE
C002001D	RPC_NT_PROTOCOL_ERROR
C002001F	RPC_NT_UNSUPPORTED_TRANS_SYN
C0020021	RPC_NT_UNSUPPORTED_TYPE
C0020022	RPC_NT_INVALID_TAG
C0020023	RPC_NT_INVALID_BOUND
C0020024	RPC_NT_NO_ENTRY_NAME
C0020025	RPC_NT_INVALID_NAME_SYNTAX
C0020026	RPC_NT_UNSUPPORTED_NAME_SYNTAX
C0020028	RPC_NT_UUID_NO_ADDRESS
C0020029	RPC_NT_DUPLICATE_ENDPOINT
C002002A	RPC_NT_UNKNOWN_AUTHN_TYPE
C002002B	RPC_NT_MAX_CALLS_TOO_SMALL
C002002C	RPC_NT_STRING_TOO_LONG
C002002D	RPC_NT_PROTSEQ_NOT_FOUND
C002002E	RPC_NT_PROCNUM_OUT_OF_RANGE
C002002F	RPC_NT_BINDING_HAS_NO_AUTH
C0020030	RPC_NT_UNKNOWN_AUTHN_SERVICE

Table B-1 *(continued)*

STATUS CODE	DESCRIPTION
C0020031	RPC_NT_UNKNOWN_AUTHN_LEVEL
C0020032	RPC_NT_INVALID_AUTH_IDENTITY
C0020033	RPC_NT_UNKNOWN_AUTHZ_SERVICE
C0020034	EPT_NT_INVALID_ENTRY
C0020035	EPT_NT_CANT_PERFORM_OP
C0020036	EPT_NT_NOT_REGISTERED
C0020037	RPC_NT_NOTHING_TO_EXPORT
C0020038	RPC_NT_INCOMPLETE_NAME
C0020039	RPC_NT_INVALID_VERS_OPTION
C002003A	RPC_NT_NO_MORE_MEMBERS
C002003B	RPC_NT_NOT_ALL_OBJS_UNEXPORTED
C002003C	RPC_NT_INTERFACE_NOT_FOUND
C002003D	RPC_NT_ENTRY_ALREADY_EXISTS
C002003E	RPC_NT_ENTRY_NOT_FOUND
C002003F	RPC_NT_NAME_SERVICE_UNAVAILABLE
C0020040	RPC_NT_INVALID_NAF_ID
C0020041	RPC_NT_CANNOT_SUPPORT
C0020042	RPC_NT_NO_CONTEXT_AVAILABLE
C0020043	RPC_NT_INTERNAL_ERROR
C0020044	RPC_NT_ZERO_DIVIDE
C0020045	RPC_NT_ADDRESS_ERROR
C0020046	RPC_NT_FP_DIV_ZERO
C0020047	RPC_NT_FP_UNDERFLOW
C0020048	RPC_NT_FP_OVERFLOW
C0030001	RPC_NT_NO_MORE_ENTRIES
C0030002	RPC_NT_SS_CHAR_TRANS_OPEN_FAIL
C0030003	RPC_NT_SS_CHAR_TRANS_SHORT_FILE
C0030004	RPC_NT_SS_IN_NULL_CONTEXT

(continued)

Table B-1 *(continued)*

STATUS CODE	DESCRIPTION
C0030005	RPC_NT_SS_CONTEXT_MISMATCH
C0030006	RPC_NT_SS_CONTEXT_DAMAGED
C0030007	RPC_NT_SS_HANDLES_MISMATCH
C0030008	RPC_NT_SS_CANNOT_GET_CALL_HANDLE
C0030009	RPC_NT_NULL_REF_POINTER
C003000A	RPC_NT_ENUM_VALUE_OUT_OF_RANGE
C003000B	RPC_NT_BYTE_COUNT_TOO_SMALL
C003000C	RPC_NT_BAD_STUB_DATA
C0020049	RPC_NT_CALL_IN_PROGRESS
C002004A	RPC_NT_NO_MORE_BINDINGS
C002004B	RPC_NT_GROUP_MEMBER_NOT_FOUND
C002004C	EPT_NT_CANT_CREATE
C002004D	RPC_NT_INVALID_OBJECT
C002004F	RPC_NT_NO_INTERFACES
C0020050	RPC_NT_CALL_CANCELLED
C0020051	RPC_NT_BINDING_INCOMPLETE
C0020052	RPC_NT_COMM_FAILURE
C0020053	RPC_NT_UNSUPPORTED_AUTHN_LEVEL
C0020054	RPC_NT_NO_PRINC_NAME
C0020055	RPC_NT_NOT_RPC_ERROR
40020056	RPC_NT_UUID_LOCAL_ONLY
C0020057	RPC_NT_SEC_PKG_ERROR
C0020058	RPC_NT_NOT_CANCELLED
C0030059	RPC_NT_INVALID_ES_ACTION
C003005A	RPC_NT_WRONG_ES_VERSION
C003005B	RPC_NT_WRONG_STUB_VERSION
C003005C	RPC_NT_INVALID_PIPE_OBJECT
C003005D	RPC_NT_INVALID_PIPE_OPERATION
C003005E	RPC_NT_WRONG_PIPE_VERSION
400200AF	RPC_NT_SEND_INCOMPLETE

Index

Wiley Publishing
Mail-In Coupon

If you would like the files from this book's Web site without downloading them, we are offering the file on CD. If you'd like the files sent to you, please:

1. Complete the coupon.
2. Include a check or money order for $5.00 (U.S. funds) for orders shipping within the U.S. or $10.00 (U.S. funds) for orders outside the U.S.
3. Send it to us at the address listed at the bottom of the coupon.

Place where book was purchased _____

Name _____

Company_____

Address _____

City _____**State** _____ **Postal Code** _____

Country _____

❏ Check here to find out what we're up to by joining our email list – a convenient way to receive news about our products and events as well as about special discount offers.

Return this coupon with the appropriate US funds to:

TCP/IP Analysis and Troubleshooting Toolkit 0471429759
Fulfillment
Media Development
Wiley Publishing, Inc.
10475 Crosspoint Blvd.
Indianapolis, IN 46256

Terms: Void where prohibited or restricted by law. Allow 2-6 weeks for delivery. Wiley is not responsible for lost, stolen, late, or illegible orders. For questions regarding this fulfillment offer, please e-mail us at MediaDev@wiley.com.

E-mail _____ Telephone _____